Legislative Delegation

Bogdan Iancu

Legislative Delegation

The Erosion of Normative Limits in Modern Constitutionalism

Springer

Dr. Bogdan Iancu
University of Bucharest
Faculty of Political Science
Str. Sf. Stefan Nr. 24
023997 Bucharest
Romania
bogdan.iancu@fspub.unibuc.ro

ISBN 978-3-642-22329-7 ISBN 978-3-642-22330-3 (eBook)
DOI 10.1007/978-3-642-22330-3
Springer Heidelberg New York Dordrecht London

Library of Congress Control Number: 2012932277

Printed with the financial support of the Alexander von Humboldt Foundation

Printed on acid-free paper

Springer is part of Springer Science+Business Media (www.springer.com)

Auch heute lebe ich der Ueberzeugung, dass unsere Rechtswissenschaft und unser Rechtsleben nur gedeihen können, wenn der Positivismus es versteht dem Rechtsgedanken die ihm vom Naturrecht erkämpfte Ursprünglichkeit und Selbstständigkeit zu wahren. Jeden Versuch einer Wiederkehrung des Naturrechts zu einem leiblichen Dasein, das nur ein Scheinleben sein kann, halte ich für verfehlt. Aber seine unsterbliche Seele lässt sich nicht tödten. Wird ihr der Einzug in den Körper des positiven Rechts versagt, so flattert sie gespenstisch durch die Räume und droht, sich in einen Vampyr zu verwandeln, der dem Rechtskörper das Blut aussagt. Es gilt, die äussere Erfahrung, dass alles geltende Recht positiv ist, und die innere Erfahrung, dass die lebendige Kraft des Rechtes aus der mit dem Menschen gebornen Rechtsidee stammt, zu einer einheitlichen Grundauffassung zum Wesen des Rechts zu verbinden.[1]

Otto von Gierke, Johannes Althusius und die Entwicklung der naturrechtlichen Staatstheorien (1880 (Zusätze vom Jahre 1902))

Freiheit, die immer relativ ist, ist nur innerhalb der Gegebenheiten einer festen Ordnung konkretisierbar und der Gewährleistung fähig. Innerhalb dynamischer Prozesse (...) wird Freiheit notwendig zum bloßen Glücksfall.[2]

Ernst Forsthoff, Der Staat der Industriegesellschaft – Dargestellt am Beispiel der Bundesrepublik Deutschland (1971).

[1] I am still convinced that our legal science and practice can thrive only if positivism understands to protect the source and integrity bequeathed by natural law to the idea of law. Any attempt at reviving natural law to its former glory would be certainly amiss. But its soul will not die so easily. If its access to the house of positive legal rules is blocked, natural law will haunt the corridors like a troubled spirit, threatening to turn into a vampire and drain the legal body of its blood. It is thus imperative to merge the external experience that all valid law is a positive enactment with the inner knowledge that the living force of the law is the innate human idea of justice, into a coherent, unitary, foundational conception of law. (Unless otherwise indicated, the translations are mine.)

[2] Freedom, which is always a relative, can only be guaranteed in the actuality of a clearly determined, concrete ordering. Within dynamic processes, freedom becomes necessarily as contingent as a pure stroke of luck.

Preface and Acknowledgements

This manuscript has been underway for the past 11 years. The original text was a doctoral dissertation defended in 2006. Most of it has been rewritten in the meanwhile; the analytical structure and the argument as such are different.

Much of the credit (and, of course, none of the blame) for writing and rewriting it up to this form goes to the people I was fortunate to encounter. Over a decade is a long time in one's life and thus provides ample opportunities to travel academically and meet people. That being said, I was particularly lucky in this respect, to have encountered that rare and ever scarcer breed: genuine scholars, for whom ideas are neither dead and dull nor something trifling to merely toy with.

I owe my former dissertation advisor, Professor András Sajó of the Central European University, a good deal of gratitude for grudgingly pointing me to the right books at the right time. It was also auspicious that András Sajó momentarily broke with his Socratic methodological predispositions at an early stage. He mentioned, namely, that, in an early draft chapter rightly deemed worth discarding, only three words, *self-subverting rationality*, had to do with my topic. The borrowed strength of that early insight awakened and later confirmed my own intuitions. During my doctoral studies, in 2000–2001, I spent a full academic year away from Budapest, doing research at the University of Toronto and the Yale Law School. I am grateful to Professors David Dyzenhaus of Toronto and Jerry L. Mashaw of Yale for their readiness to welcome my work and me. During the 2 years (2002–2004) spent researching and teaching in Montreal, as a Boulton Fellow at McGill University's Faculty of Law, I had interesting conversations with Professors Fabien Gélinas, Roderick Macdonald, Desmond Manderson, Armand de Mestral, and Stephen Scott. They all have my unalloyed appreciation.

When the initial dissertation was written I could not read German and was therefore at the mercy of translations. I will always be in the debt of the Alexander von Humboldt Foundation for awarding me a 4-month language fellowship to study German and a 2-year research fellowship to read and think about this book at leisure. Each new language learnt is another shell for one's intellectual personality but German has revealed a thinking world I had no idea existed. Without immediate access to it my thinking and writing would have been much impoverished. My host at the Humboldt University of Berlin, Professor Dieter Grimm, has read the final drafts of the first two parts and commented on them. His writings on the conceptual reliance of constitutionalism on "positivized" natural law categories and on the practical dependence of constitutional law on clear foundational distinctions have influenced my work considerably. Thanks are due to him also for our many talks in Berlin and for his untiring and impeccable courtesy.

Bucharest Bogdan Iancu

Contents

Chapter 1
Introduction

1.1 Delegation: Doctrinal, Metaphorical, and Constitutional-Philosophical Implications

Delegation and its conceptual concomitants (mandate, agency, representation, proxy, etc.) are constitutive of the legal mind. It is the typical trade of the lawyer to inquire into and question the authority by virtue of which a certain power is asserted, whether the title is valid, to what purpose it was conveyed, and how far it extends. This conceptual lens is all the more relevant to modern constitutionalism, whose theoretical justifications presuppose regarding government as a concatenation of confined lines of attribution, and whose practices reside in a systematic probing of the title, purpose, scope, and outer legal limits of each exercise of power. These concerns apply with even more force to the constitutional limitations on legislation. If constitutionalism is the theory and practice of limited government by delegation, then the foremost public power, that of legislating, is limited and derived (i.e., delegated) law-making under the fundamental law.

As the theoretical notion has positive law correspondents, we do not have to remain for long in the realm of purely abstract musings and speculations. With few exceptions, most conspicuously the English constitution, whose descriptive, essentially medieval structure resists normative limitations on the legislature, modern constitutional systems have dealt with this matter expressly. The various relevant provisions either allow the delegation of legislative power under restrictive terms (Germany under the Basic Law), allow delegation by way of exception and within a confined normative domain (the current French and Romanian constitutions, for instance) or even forbid it altogether in express terms (the constitution of the Fourth French Republic). It is indicative for the relevance of this constraint that in the constitutional law of the US, even though a specific limitation was not provided for in the text, the theoretical requirement that the law-making power cannot be delegated became judicially enforceable constitutional law indirectly. At a very early stage, the Supreme Court derived nondelegation as a necessary doctrinal

B. Iancu, *Legislative Delegation*,
DOI 10.1007/978-3-642-22330-3_1, © Springer-Verlag Berlin Heidelberg 2012

corollary from both the economy of the text and the assumptions of limited government behind the textual provisions.[1]

In order to identify the existence of the limitation as a matter of positive fundamental law and thus restrict our object of inquiry, it is of lesser relevance how the legal rule is precisely phrased and whether, for instance, a certain system prohibits "the delegation of legislative power" (the US) or allows it, provided it is sufficiently constrained by a legislative specification of the "content, purpose, and scope" of the delegation (Germany). Where and how the stress falls is, of course, not irrelevant but, for comparative legal purposes and prima facie, it is important only to determine that a constitutional restriction on parliamentary enactments is found in a given system and that the limitation is of a substantive nature or, rather, it is not purely formal.[2] Purely procedural constitutional arrangements, by virtue of which any grant of authority based on a statute, no matter how broad in its terms, is not considered a questionable delegation, are of little practical consequence as constitutional limitations (and will therefore be of no direct interest to this argument). This reservation applies with like force to practically irrelevant principles to the effect, for instance, that parliament can "delegate" but not expressly "abdicate" its power.[3] Furthermore and related to these two observations, the delegation as such by parliaments of the power to make subordinate rules of legislative force and the procedures and checks which apply to it (i.e., the merely technical problematic of delegated legislation) is highly relevant but analytically secondary and incidental to the primary constitutional concern. To restate the issue, a normative limitation on how much law-making the parliament can leave to the decision of other organs or branches of government is a prohibition on or restriction of legislative delegation. Based on such a limitation, judicial review will be expected to curb parliamentary practices exceeding the boundaries of constitutionally permissible statutory authorization.

Consequently, one can now surmise that academic commentary (including the current endeavor) can proceed as a matter of course to the more or less routine task of analyzing, classifying, and comparing terms of validity, tests, and standards of review within and across jurisdictions. This is however the point where the flow of self-evidence must end abruptly. As will be later shown, delegation-related judicial decisions, across constitutional systems, are notoriously hard to reconcile, inconsistent, and erratic. More nebulous yet are the relevant theoretical debates.

[1] *The Cargo of the Brig Aurora, Burn Side, Claimant, v. The United States*, 11 U.S. (7 Cranch) 382 (1813).

[2] *See*, for instance, *Whitman v. American Trucking Assns.*, 531 U.S. 457 (2001), Stevens (Concurring), arguing that, insofar as safeguards and limitations are provided, the power devolved upon a Congressional agent should be recognized as legislative in nature. This lexical change (from "no delegation permissible" to "some delegation acceptable"), however, will be in itself of little legal import. The stress will simply move from the inquiry into what is not legislative power proper and thus not delegation to an attempt to devise tests distinguishing "good" from "bad delegation." In substance, the difference is minimal to non-existent.

[3] *In Re Gray*, 57 S.C.R. 150 [1918].

Beginning at the semantic level, one encounters, often with respect to the pertinent literature within the same constitutional jurisdiction, a bewildering terminological diversity. For instance, albeit referring to the same rules, practices, phenomena, and conceptual frameworks, various authors employ indifferently and sometimes interchangeably the terms nondelegation of the legislative "power(s)", "function(s)" or "authority."[4] These words ("power", "function", "authority"), even when used with respect to the same referent, are not fully synonymous, and neither is the plural or singular form of the nouns semantically inconsequential. Since the words we use and the ways in which we use them structure and reveal our thought, this lexical laxity may reflect, already at first sight, a degree of analytical imprecision and epistemological uncertainty. And things appear yet more intractable in strictly substantive terms. Thus, the Danish legal realist scholar Alf Ross observed in a 1958 comparative survey of the extensive literature on the topic that, even though this had been "a subject that has greatly exercised many minds and kept both law and political science occupied," the analytical cacophony was by then already so confusing that one was inclined to think of delegation as a "mystical" and "magical", rather than legal, notion. Ross proposed a thorough advance pruning of the metaphysical–mystical offshoots, in order to give the notion of delegation a workable, narrowing definition, confined by clear, discernable jurisprudential criteria, so that it could be rendered practically serviceable as a legal–technical concept and enforceable rule of public law.[5] Closer to us in time, two American jurists have gone even further in this vein, to argue that the polysemy of delegation reaches the point of conceptual vacuity. Once the metaphysical, rhetorical, and historical layers are peeled off it and progressively discarded as inapposite, redundant, or inconsequential, what remains would be mere "metaphor." Since empty stylistic flamboyance has no practical use in constitutional adjudication and confounds sound theoretical analysis, Eric Posner and Adrian Vermeule have suggested simply discarding the "delegation metaphor" altogether.[6]

One can certainly dismiss most foundational concepts of constitutional theory and law (separation of powers, representation, the rule of law, state neutrality, etc.) in this pragmatic–commonsensical way. Looked at from a "realist" standpoint or read in a dogmatic positivistic key, such concepts may seem ambivalent and ambiguous, surrounded and obfuscated by baroque historical context and philosophical glosses. From a "no-nonsense," "matter-of-fact" perspective, these notions

[4] Providing specific examples would be unnecessary. A text search performed on 02.09.2010 in HeinOnline, restricted to the "Law Journal Library" database, yielded hundreds of relevant hits for each of the mentioned variants (for instance, 164 matches for "delegation of legislative functions"); a LexisNexis or Westlaw search including caselaw would result in additional matches. The uses refer to the same legal issue, the US "nondelegation doctrine" (also referred to as the "delegation doctrine").

[5] Alf Ross, "Delegation of Power-Meaning and Validity of the maxim *delegata potestas non potest delegari*" 7 *Am. J. Comp. L.* 1 (1958).

[6] Eric A. Posner and Adrian Vermeule, "Interring the Nondelegation Doctrine," 69 *U. Chi. L. Rev.* 1721 (2002).

could be therefore regarded to be not properly "legal" and duly done away with. If pushed too far, such clarity would be most likely purchased at a taxing price, trading simplicity of viewpoint and reference order for a simplistic view of the legal world. Nonetheless and caveat aside, this line of critique contains a kernel of highly pertinent truth and its insight applies with particular strength to our topic. Legislative delegation has an inevitably irreducible conceptual structure, insofar as the term can only be explained by means of related constitutional presuppositions and notions attaching to legislation and law-making, whose meanings are assumed and anticipated by the word "delegation." In this respect, the metaphorical connotations are undeniable and inextricable. The term 'carries' or transfers understandings from germane legal concepts, which have to be clarified and whose premises have to be in turn correspondingly stated, before an informed discussion of delegation can occur. Unless one untangles the presuppositional threads, a debate regarding delegation is bound to be carried out at cross purposes. An introductory taxonomical exercise will be useful at this point.

First, the argument that the power to legislate should not be delegated anticipates a rule of law-derived limitation. In this sense, an impermissible delegation is the formal law that, due to its vagueness, gives the individual no or little anticipation with respect to the conduct actually required of him. A vague law deflects the actual normative decision as to the requisite conduct and projects it to the level of enforcement, so that those subject to it are in effect exposed to unfettered executive, administrative, or judicial discretion. What is delegated is discretionary power over people. The concern animating the nondelegation argument, namely the possibility of abuse in the absence of a clear posited rule, resonates with a long line of commentary in political and legal philosophy, ranging from Aristotle to Fuller, about the demands and prerequisites of "a government of laws and not of men." However, the argument for antecedent rules is qualified by the account, of equally venerable lineage, regarding the inflexibility of general rules and the need for equity as a countervailing component of justice. Second, a legislature could be said, from a separation of powers standpoint, to be delegating the power to make laws when and since the vacuity of the legislative prescription aggrandizes the power of another branch. In this context, the concern informing the notion of delegation and delegation-related debates is with the resulting imbalance in the power structure. In a more purist, analytically-oriented form of the separation of powers-related argument, the legislature could be said to be divesting itself of its constitutionally assigned function. This latter formulation of the separation of powers-related delegation argument requires substantive distinctions among the core functions deemed constitutionally proper to the respective branches (legislation, executive action, administration, adjudication). What is being delegated in the logic of this line of arguments is a branch-specific constitutional function; but how the legislative duty is defined in relation to the various provinces of other branches will depend on the particular separation of powers theory one embraces, which will further rest on other assumptions, such as the professed vision of law and of the state.[7] Third and last, the democratic strain in delegation debates starts from the premise that we elect representatives (as the Lockean phrase goes) "only to make laws, and not to make legislators," that is, they are elected to take the actual decisions that govern our lives. By not making the controlling choice on a given matter at the level of parliamentary enactments, the legislature shoulders off its representative burdens, at the same time eluding or deflecting responsibility and thus electoral accountability. In this sense, the decision as such is said to be delegated, a decision that, by virtue of its constitutionally validated democratic mandate, the parliament would have to take alone. This latter strain of delegation arguments is also not devoid of tensions, resulting from the way in which one defines representative democracy, accountability, legitimacy, and the proper balance of these concerns within a given constitutional order.[8] As can by now be noticed, taxonomy explains to a certain degree the terminological variety, namely, the presuppositions packed, sometimes unselfconsciously, into the various phrasings (authority, power, function) of nondelegation arguments.

At the same time this brief discussion makes apparent the fact that, although distinct as analytical ideal types, the various delegation-related arguments also overlap, as, for instance, separation of powers theories intersect with representative democracy or rule-of-law related accounts. It could surely be opined that the nondelegation doctrine or constitutional provisions restricting delegation are simply legal devices that functionally serve these various constitutional values (rule of law, separation of powers, and representative democracy-related concerns regarding the legitimacy and accountability of legislative enactments). But such an argument would have things in the wrong order. How specific or general, abstract or concrete, rule-, standard-, or presumption-like a particular legislative provision has to be cannot be determined solely on the basis of the notion of delegation or on the wording of a nondelegation proviso. Obversely, the normative cast of a parliamentary enactment and thus the determination regarding its constitutional permissibility cannot be decided without specifying in advance a relevant concern or informing value. But the requirements deriving from various relevant concerns and values are not fully and not always coextensive, since the definitions of legislation deriving from them cannot be perfectly juxtaposed. Rule of law considerations, to give just one example, do not apply with equal degree of persuasiveness to the specificity level of criminal law and to risk- and technology-

[7] *See* Ernst-Wolfgang Böckenförde, *Gesetz und gesetzgebende Gewalt: von den Anfängen der deutschen Staatsrechtslehre bis zur Höhe des staatrechtlichen Positivismus* (Berlin: Duncker & Humbolt, 1958).

[8] On the tensions between and embedded in the concepts of representation and democracy, *see* Ernst-Wolfgang Böckenförde, "Mittelbare/repräsentative Demokratie als eigentliche Form der Demokratie-Bemerkungen zu Begriff und Verwirklichungsproblemen der Demokratie als Staats- und Regierungsform," in Georg Müller et al. (Eds.), *Staatsorganisation und Staatsfunktionen im Wandel-Festschrift für Kurt Eichenberger zum 60. Geburtstag* (Basel/Frankfurt am Main: Helbing & Lichtenhahn, 1982), pp. 301–328.

intensive fields of regulation (environmental legislation, health and safety rules, and the like).

All the assumptions relating to the notion of delegation do converge analytically in the presupposition of a constitutional ideal of legislation; a coherent and consistent constitutional theory of legislation will result in an intelligible theory of delegation. Nonetheless, pursuing further the introductory dissection of the various definitional lines of inquiry (legislation as normative yardstick of conduct, legislation as will, legislation as collective deliberation, legislation as institutional function, legislation as participative act, etc.) would be duplicative at this point, therefore redundant and tediously counterproductive. The exercise above was useful in outlining the conceptual challenges at hand. But it was also of use in laying out the outer explanatory limits of its own pattern: at a certain point in the course of our logical pursuit we seem to be left with a number of notions that, in the abstract, turn to partly diverge and partly feed presuppositions circuitously into each other's definitions. There is no a priori reason to reduce the notion of delegation to any of its major assumptions and no way in which the vicious circle can be rationally broken. One can certainly stipulate a definition of legislation and many theoretical possibilities spring to mind. Knowledge-wise, the gains (coherence and consistency, analytical elegance of the conceptual framework) of this solution would come at the usual price of all closed abstract systems, i.e., that of unduly cramming both reality and conceptual order into a procrustean theoretical bed.

Besides and related, one does not have to fully embrace Holmes's tart dichotomy that the life of law has been experience not logic, in order to agree that constitutional law is also a living, evolving reality. This leads to the observation that further guidance on the matter can derive from looking at the facts themselves. Even assuming a relatively high measure of functional institutional homogeneity across liberal legal systems—as of necessity a comparatist must[9]—and, consequently, a certain degree of synchronicity among exemplary Western legal orders, constitutionally-presupposed understandings and dominant theories of legislation are historically contingent. Discrete constitutional landscapes will produce specific sets of arguments regarding legislation and the advisability of delegating it. Moreover, and more pertinent to our introductory foray, the adoption of specific constitutional provisions often responds directly to particular changes in context. It can therefore be fully understood only by way of coming to grips with the phenomenon.

---

[9] *But cf.* Mark Tushnet, "The Possibilities of Comparative Constitutional Law," 108 *Yale Law Journal* 1225 (1999), (arguing that the primary use of comparative constitutional law is not a general and objectively epistemological but a reflexive subjective one, namely a means by which we can understand our own system better) and *also cf.* Susanne Baer, "Verfassungsvergleichung und reflexive Methode: Interkulturelle und intersubjektive Kompetenz," 64 *ZaöRV* 735–758 (2004), arguing that the main use of comparative constitutional law is that of helping students find global corporate village jobs. The study of comparative constitutional law instills "intercultural, inter-subjective competence," namely contemplative aptitudes and particularized knowledge of "the other"; in our globalized economy, this competence is a vital "key qualification" on the market, instrumental in the pursuit of an international legal career.

1.2 Delegation as Phenomenon, Slogan, and Constitutional Reaction

Delegation became for the first time a common topic of academic and public debate in all Western political systems as a direct response to the twentieth century crises of the state. As the general story is well-known and many of its strands will be revisited in due detail at a later point, only the contours need to be sketched here.

Starting with the late nineteenth and continuing into the early decades of the twentieth century, the technological, social, and economic pressures of advanced capitalism, together with the increasingly more frequent and urgent demands of concentrating state power in response to emergencies (war, demobilization, economic depression), determined an unprecedented acceleration in the need for government action. This need was met to a large degree by the legal means of formal parliamentary enactments either conferring upon the executive and the administration wider powers of intervention in previously unregulated fields or validating ex post preemptive executive measures. Unsurprisingly, the new governmental reality was from the onset met with hostility by a legal theory largely articulated along different constitutional representations.

As early as 1915, Albert Venn Dicey, the Victorian dean of English constitutional law, became worried by the growing powers of government departments and related statutory discretion. He remarked that such changes would imperil the rule of law and that the public law of England had already begun to evince certain features of the French *droit administratif*.[10] In 1929, the Chief Justice of England himself, Lord Hewart of Bury, published an influential tract in which the new practices were castigated as a bureaucratic cabal, a covert ploy by which the civil service undermined the authority of Parliament and the liberty of the subject. He warned against the tendency of this "new despotism" "to subordinate Parliament, to evade the courts, and to render the will, or the caprice, of the Executive unfettered and supreme."[11] But the Donoughmore Committee, appointed by the Lord Chancellor in the wake of the controversy stirred by the book, to inquire into the merits of Hewart's anti-bureaucratic jeremiad, did not validate his findings. The final report of its investigation concluded with the somewhat offhanded observation that the practice of delegation as such was inevitable: "The truth is that if Parliament were not willing to delegate law-making power, Parliament would be unable to pass the kind and quantity of legislation which modern public opinion requires."[12] Delegated legislation needed only, like all public powers and, indeed, all things human, to be kept in check and under ongoing scrutiny.

[10] Albert V. Dicey, "The Development of Administrative Law in England", 31 *Law Quarterly Review* 148 (1915).

[11] Lord Hewart of Bury, *The New Despotism* (London: Ernest Benn, Ltd., 1929), p. 17.

[12] *Committee on Ministers' Powers Report*, H.M.S.O. (Cmd. 4060) (1932), at p. 23.

And yet further continental events seemed to confirm and vindicate those early warnings, as parliamentary government fell into disrepute and disarray across Europe. Indeed, Hitler would come to full power precisely by the legal means of executive legislation and parliamentary blanket mandates. Weimar Germany was largely ruled through delegations and Art. 48 emergency decrees, before it finally succumbed to one of the most sweeping, certainly the most ominous examples of enabling legislation. According to the controlling provision of the March 1933 *Ermächtigungsgesetz* (Enabling Law): "Federal legislation (*Reichsgesetze*) can be also adopted by the Government, by way of exception from the common procedures set forth by the Constitution."[13] In 1936, reviewing in a short comparative study the developments up to that date, Carl Schmitt identified three general causes of the phenomenon (planning, emergency, and "the collectivization of international life") and pointed out, with characteristically fine sense of legal tension and theatrical momentum, that such delegations, insofar as they were constitutional, were "always legal bridges; but these bridges can both lead back to an earlier constitutional legality, as well as forth to a completely new constitutional reality. The practice of enabling laws is therefore a litmus test for the entire constitutional development, and it is fully understandable that the constitutionality of enabling legislation has become in recent years a primary topic of all constitutional conflicts."[14] Schmitt concluded tersely, with an equally characteristic sense of personal opportunity, that the failure of Western constitutional systems to rein in delegations presaged the end of liberal notions of law-making framed by nineteenth century conceptions of separated powers. This, he reckoned, would inevitably lead back to an "Aristotelian-Thomistic understanding of law as practical reason," and namely "not that of just any given individual but specifically the practical reason of he who leads and governs the community"[15] The study was to be soon republished in French translation, in a 1938 Festschrift for the famous comparatist Edouard Lambert.[16] It served as a timely omen of the French republican demise. The governments of the French Third Republic had been, particularly after WWI, ever more often mandated to legislate through *décrets-lois*. French liberal democracy fell prey, in July 1940, to the legal means of a *"décret-constituant,"* enabling Marshall Pétain to change the constitution at will.

In the United States alone, the Supreme Court struck down on nondelegation grounds, in a couple of famous 1935 cases, a part of President Roosevelt's New Deal reforms. But this could hardly be seen in retrospect as a triumph of classical constitutionalism. On the one hand, those cases predated the 1937 retraction of the

[13] Gesetz zur Behebung der Not von Volk und Reich (Ermächtigungsgesetz) vom 23.3.1933, Reichsgesetzblatt T. I. (1933), Nr. 25, S. 141.

[14] Carl Schmitt, "Vergleichender Überblick über die neueste Entwicklung des Problems der gesetzgeberischen Ermächtigungen (Legislative Delegationen)", 6 *ZaöRV* 252, at 253 (1936).

[15] *Id*, at 267–268.

[16] "L'évolution récente du problème des délégations législatives" in *Introduction à l'etude du droit comparé-Recueil d'Études en l'honneur d'Édouard Lambert* (Paris: Sirey, 1938), pp. 200–210.

Supreme Court from its prior systematic interferences with social and economic legislation and the accompanying post-New Deal constitutional transformations. Even though the two rulings were decided by overwhelming majorities (one was rendered unanimously), a certain ambivalence inevitably surrounded the subsequent constitutional relevance of the delegation cases. Times of constitutional upheaval (especially before legal revolutions begin to crystallize into new status quos) breed suspect constitutional adjudication. On the other hand, the impugned practices went ahead unabated, as the needs of military mobilization, war, and demobilization, extended the power of government to an unprecedented sweep. Towards the end of the war, Friedrich von Hayek's best-seller, *The Road to Serfdom,* warned that, given the sway of governmental regulation and administrative discretion and the way in which more recent emergencies reinforced pre-war tendencies, the difference between Western democracies and the totalitarianism of Nazi Germany threatened to become one of degree rather than kind.

All these developments and the fears engendered by them influenced post-war Western constitutionalism to various degrees. In the United Kingdom and (to a lesser extent) in other Westminster systems, after the initial bout of attention and debate occasioned by the fracture between Victorian constitutional understandings and modern style cabinet government, "delegation" remained, from a positive legal standpoint, a mere ideological reaction. The doctrine of parliamentary sovereignty precludes any vision of law or past reality of legislative practices from gaining entrenched constitutional status. Practices as such were realigned to accommodate pragmatic needs of coordination and rule of law requirements (parliamentary control, public debate and transparency, publicity, and so on).[17] But since, in the logic of the Westminster system, practices alone dictate the constitutional concept of legislation, the new arrangements did not impact the constitutional duty of parliament. On the Continent, steps were taken along the post-war realignment of constitutionalism to remedy what was perceived as a major pre-war structural constitutional failure. The constitutional reaction was, as expected, strongest where the past appeared to caution it the most: the first post-war French constitution forbade delegated law-making categorically, whereas the German Basic Law rationalized parliamentarism, barring in explicit terms future resort to open-ended enabling legislation. Paradoxically, in the United States, where the nondelegation doctrine pre-dated by long the emergence of the modern state and where the Supreme Court enforced it vigorously at the peak of the New Deal, no other judicial decision invalidated federal legislation on nondelegation grounds. The doctrine did however become a leading topic of legal debate. It has in fact proven, over time, unmitigated theoretical resilience in spite of judicial neglect. In effect, the radicalism of the Vermeule-Posner realist critique and the impatience of numerous other less pugnacious commentators can be attributed to sheer irritation. A measure of discontent appears legitimate: why would theorists split hairs endlessly discussing

[17] *See, generally,* Hermann Pünder, "Democratic Legitimation of Delegated Legislation—A Comparative View on the American, British and German Law," 58 *ICLQ* 353 (2009).

an antiquated doctrine that was judicially acknowledged in 1813, only occasionally mentioned afterwards, suddenly enforced in 1935, and then forgotten anew by the Court and never again used to invalidate one federal statute ever since? Surely, there must be more urgent practical matters to busy oneself with.

This historical incursion, far from bringing forth any clarifications or answers, raises only additional lines of questions. How can the temporal discontinuities between US and European constitutionalism be explained? Were the two New Deal decisions an accident? If so, what could explain the ongoing and intense subsequent theoretical debate on a legal topic with no practical stakes? And what accounts for the prior, long-lasting recognition of delegation as a valid but unenforced doctrine under the US constitution? Was the European inclusion of nondelegation limitations a belated, perhaps misguided constitutional reaction to a new reality or was it a conscious and well-directed attempt to grapple with a genuine contemporary problem? What purpose do these limitations serve nowadays and what is their place in the structure of contemporary constitutionalism? If content-based constraints on legislation are constitutionally useful, what are the optimal levels of judicial enforcement applicable? Obversely, what constitutional story does the lack of enforcement tell? Is there any purpose to a constitutional rule, if courts cannot seem to give it substance? Does a theoretical concept whose positive legal avatar is neglected by practice fulfill any useful role, hermeneutical or otherwise?

In sum, what is the present explanatory and constitutional-legal value of the delegation concept and rule?

1.3 Problem and Method

This work seeks the answers by means of an inquiry into the conceptual, historical, and legal genealogy of legislative delegation limitations. The book will locate the intellectual conditions of the possibility of the delegation concept in constitutionalism and the historical intersection of these justifications with constitutional law, before approaching the contemporary use of delegation-related constitutional law rules.

Thus, it is argued that "purely legal" (where "legally pure" equals strictly judicially enforceable positive law) discussions about these matters would yield scant conclusions at the cost of significant reductions in epistemological value. To wit, whether a purely positivist approach is at all possible in constitutional law is a larger question, worth posing in its own right. In this particular case, the answer must be trenchantly negative; there are, as we have seen, simply too many presuppositions and implications entwined around the legal rules regarding delegation. Furthermore, if unilateral methodological benchmarks are to be avoided for reasons that have to do with the essentials of legal knowledge, the instrumentalism of limited perspectives is to be averted for less foundational but equally sound epistemological and prudential considerations. Namely, most usually, arguments "against" delegation based on a specific assumption risk reducing the notion unduly to one of its facets and thus fall prey to its reductive metaphorical traps. Obversely, arguments "for" delegation are constantly exposed to the risk of reproducing endlessly supposedly pragmatic stereotypes about modernity, the speed of life in technological advanced societies, the limited time of parliament, the fall of the diletanti and the social need for experts who run things well and smoothly. Consequently, lest we run into the same perils, we will seek to understand first what place did and does this notion and its patterns of conceptual affinities occupy in the architecture of constitutionalism (what does delegation mean), prior to asking whether it would be good for us today to have a nondelegation doctrine or provision more vigorously applied by constitutional judges and what implications would be entailed by that judicial posture.

The first chapter traces the historical evolution of constitutional concepts of legislation. A particular historical timeframe will be inevitably accompanied by a dominant, coherent, and consistent ideal of law and law-making. The assertion is not meant in a vulgar deterministic sense. The argument is made, rather, that legal practices characteristic of a particular historic period are fused at the hip with an archetypal idea of law and legislation that at the same time explains and justifies the phenomena. True, there is always a distance between justificatory ideals of law and the justified actuality of legal practice. When, however, the distance and dissonance become unbridgeable, when the normative structures of justification are too remote from phenomena, the time of both concepts and institutions is close at hand; we are then in the presence of an emerging shift of paradigm (new legal concepts, mirroring new realities). This morphing of conceptual paradigms in relative lockstep with practices is a constantly evolving, indeed an ongoing process. One can observe for instance in contemporary literature how patterns of institutional change unaccounted for by the extant vocabulary strive for new words to express their distinctiveness. The ever-increasing recurrence of the "governance" concept is an apposite example, inasmuch as its users seek to showcase a growing detachment or emancipation of administrative and regulatory structures from the reign of politics and traditional lines of accountability. The frequent use of the term "societal constitutionalism" is another such currently ubiquitous conceptual newcomer, which competes with and seeks to partly displace the classical, hierarchical understanding of politics and law.[18] This is certainly a two-way road. New patterns of justification can be adopted for primarily ideological and polemical reasons, in which case, often enough, the mark may be overstated. By the same token, strong theoretical undercurrents are often halcyons of new emerging practices, albeit their grasp on new legal facts will be properly assessed only in retrospect. Be that as it may, the concept of legislative delegation becomes comprehensible if located in its proper intellectual environment. It is germane, as we will see, to a particular

[18] Dieter Grimm, "Gesellschaftlicher Konstitutionalismus-Eine Kompensation für den Bedeutungsschwund der Staatsverfassung?" in *Festschrift für Roman Herzog zum 75. Geburtstag* (München: C.H. Beck, 2009), pp. 68–81.

juncture of Enlightenment-derived models of legal rationality and pertains to specific structures of legal and political authority. The notion expresses a limited understanding of legislation, which presupposed, in turn, a set of clear delineations between the state and the individual and among distinct fields of state action and specific exercises of state power. Such divisions rested upon clear delineations between the relative domains of politics and law, and therefore also between distinct kinds of rationality. This particular cluster of justifications and justified practices vied for supremacy, successfully insofar as constitutionalism struck roots in the Western legal world, with other Enlightenment-derived legal ideals.

This leads us to the intersection of normative account and constitutional phenomenon. The second chapter will follow the metamorphosis of legislative practices from the beginnings of normative constitutionalism till the beginning of the twentieth century major transformations of the law and state.[19] It is argued that modern constitutionalism incorporated the particular set of presuppositions and justifications and the ideal-typical concept of legislation showcased by the delegation notion. The story supporting this argument builds on a series of historical patterns of development deemed representative of the Western legal tradition. While occasional reference to British and Canadian law and parliamentary history will also be made, constitutional evolutions within three legal systems considered paradigmatic (the US, Germany, and France) will be subjected to more thorough scrutiny. The history of US federal constitutional law receives disproportionate attention throughout the book and a justification for this preferential treatment must be advanced. For our analytical needs, American transformations offer a perfectly controlled constitutional environment, since: (1) the country adopted a constitution in the wake of the "century of the Enlightenment" and consciously built its constitutional law on the fundament of a thorough understanding of natural law dictates; (2) the constitutional limitations were, from very early on, considered valid positive law, subject to enforcement by way of judicial review; (3) the Supreme Court readily recognized the validity of a nondelegation limitation, as implicit in text and structure and subject to judicial enforcement against a trespassing legislature. Thus, what can be observed elsewhere only piece-meal and occurring fragmentarily, in patchworks of justifications unequally met by practices or legislative and judicial practices unsupported by constitutional imperatives, constitutes in America a clear, uninterrupted continuum of the three parallel narrative threads running through our delegation tale: normative account, historical changeover, and contemporary constitutional law.

Positive, contemporary constitutional (and to a certain extent administrative) law forms the exclusive object of the third, and last, chapter of this book. This

---

[19] *See*, for an elaboration on the distinction between modern "normative" and pre-modern "descriptive" constitutionalism, the discussion in the introduction to Dieter Grimm, *Deutsche Verfassungsgeschichte 1776–1866: Vom Beginn des modernen Verfassungsstaats bis zur Auflösung des Deutschen Bundes* (Frankfurt a.M.: Suhrkamp, 1988), pp 10–42.

sequence has an argumentative purpose, related to the choice of jurisdictions. Even though academic lawyers are predisposed, by virtue of an intellectual occupational hazard of sorts, to overstate the efficiency and effectiveness of legal rules, few would push such propensities to the point of denying the relevance of context to the emergence and application of law. It should be stressed again that the countries under scrutiny trod partly dissimilar social, political, and legal-constitutional paths. The United States constitutes the paragon of constitutional stability and modernity: its constitutional structure rested from the very onset upon auspicious social circumstances, most notably a relatively free and homogenous social system and a modern private law system (i.e., to a large degree unencumbered by feudal restrictions).[20] The 1787 document is still in force, in textually unaltered form, and the quasi-sacralization of its original legal form testifies to its centrality in constituting the political and social life of the country. France, whose initial constitutional emancipation was achieved at roughly the same time, had to simultaneously secure a measure of social and legal modernization which in America could be more or less taken for granted, namely, the social preconditions of political freedom and the private law preconditions of autonomy.[21] The syncopated French constitutional evolution, evidenced by the plethora of constitutions and *lois constitutionnelles* which kept replacing each other with great frequency since 1791, reflects the difficulties of achieving these mutually reinforcing goals at different paces. Germany, until late "the most medieval state of the continent,"[22] is the stereotypical modernization laggard. Indeed, for a good stretch into the course of our future story, one cannot actually speak of "Germany" as a political unit in the modern sense. Its state evolved fragmentarily from the Holy Roman Empire of German Nation into a hybrid and partly pre-modern type of federal constitutionalism towards the end of the nineteenth century, then proceeded to undergo breakneck speed, short-lived, and unequal constitutional modernization during the Weimar Republic. German constitutional evolution was truly completed only after WWII, under the Basic Law. The significance of these evolutionary differences accounts for the place of contemporary legal issues in the general economy of the book: it is of relevance if different roads reach the same destination in the end. Hence, if, in spite of the distinct historical conditions and irrespective of how the delegation-relevant constitutional provisions are formulated, the judicial treatment of delegation-related provisions can be shown to be very similar

[20] James Willard Hurst, *Law and the Conditions of Freedom in the Nineteenth-Century United States* (Madison, *etc.*: The University of Wisconsin Press, 1967), *passim*. Albeit feudal tenures were only abolished in New York in 1846, *Id.*, at p. 13.

[21] Hanna Arendt, *On Revolution* (New York: Viking Press, 1965).

[22] Karl Bosl, cited by Hans Maier, *Die ältere deutsche Staats- und Verwaltungslehre (Polizeiwissenschaft) – Ein Beitrag zur Geschichte der politischen Wissenschaft in Deutschland* (Neuwied am Rhein und Berlin: Luchterhand, 1966), at p. 56.

nowadays across jurisdictions (in terms of both causes and effects), the finding will reflect tellingly on the current state of Western constitutionalism as such.

The methodology, informed by the conviction that normative accounts, historical transformations, and positive law cannot be separated, at least not without losing sight of the full scope of law, can be ascribed to the school of "integrative jurisprudence."[23] This belief that the virtues of all these dimensions of law (legal philosophy, legal history, legal practice) and of the three major schools of legal thought (natural law theory, positivism, the historical school) can be welded into a more complex, single theory, is a profession of legal-scientific faith at the same time combative and bold in its quest. It is daring inasmuch as narrow methodological specialization passes for properly scientific nowadays. It is combative, insofar as it rejects outright such one-sided perspectives as misguided and impoverished. Namely, the juridical study of positive constitutional limitations that neglects their philosophical underpinnings and their historically situated and changing meanings makes a false promise of legal objectivity and fulfills it by delivering most usually stale verbiage, words about words. Philosophical presuppositions, if they are immediately applied to actual legal problems without being anchored in and filtered through history, run the usual risk of counterfactuals or dystopic/utopian imagination. Constitutional history, if it purports to extract from the past no sense of the (dis)continuity of concepts and institutions and thus no answers to our current queries, is a dry collection of data and insofar a pointless antiquarian exercise; the world is full to the brim with facts, a receding infinity of them. Otto von Gierke once defined legal concepts as "living historical-intellectual structures" (*lebendige geschichtliche Geistesgebilde*) and his insight is particularly apposite in the case of constitutionalism. [24] We can only understand fundamental legal practices (and also changes in them) if attention remains focused both on the normative stakes implicated by such practices and on the way in which normativity responds to phenomenal transformations. Consequently, constitutional law will be treated here as "a process, in which rules and values and facts—all three—coalesce and are actualized."[25]

Since the *dramatis personae* and the plot have now been outlined, it is proper form to give out the crux of the argument to follow. It will be contended that the concept of delegation is a legal-philosophical corollary, which rests on substantive, systemic implications about law and law-making. It was constitutionalized in early American constitutional practice as a necessary incident of those systemic assumptions. By the same token, the legal limitation was not actually enforced, because its claims are metaphysically too taxing, too incommensurable for judges to give them legal effect and due to the fact that, while the underlying premises held

[23] Harold J. Berman, "Toward an Integrative Jurisprudence: Politics, Morality, History," 76 *Cal. L. Rev.* 779 (1988).

[24] Otto von Gierke, "Labands Staatsrecht und die deutsche Rechtswissenschaft," 7 *Schmollers Jahrbuch* 1097 (1883), at p. 1111.

[25] Jerome Hall, cited by Berman, at p. 782.

out, there was no need for such a judicial corrective. As the underpinnings on which the concept rested changed, the use of delegation provisions appeared as a reaction to those changes, in the attempt to find a purely positive law remedy to the problem of dissolving normative foundations. But, since legal reasoning cannot function in the absence of concrete reference points, positive legal limitations alone could not offer a suitable substitute for systemic changes of such magnitude. The constitutional control of delegation, as a legal rule, is therefore a symptom and an epiphenomenal, instinctive legal reaction to a deeper problem: the erosion of normative limits in constitutional law.

Chapter 2
The Genealogy of the Concept of Delegation: Constitutional Presuppositions

The concept of legislative delegation is subordinated to the notion of legislation but, as the notion of legislation raises a congeries of parallel conceptual implications, this subordination is not a very strict one. To wit, in Henry Sumner Maine's analysis of the development of law, legislation appears as the last stage of legal evolution. Lon Fuller, commenting on Maine, identifies the defining feature of legislation as the "recognition of the simple fact that law can be brought into existence by explicit declarations of intent, incorporated in the words of legal enactments."[1] The emphasis is therefore on the intentionality, explicitness, and rationality of positive, self-consciously human-made law. To Jeremy Waldron, the contemporary theoretical champion of law-making by assembly, the definition of legislation is more properly associated with a "constitutional instinct (...) that if there is explicit law-making or law reform to be done in society, it should be done in or under the authority of a large representative assembly."[2] For him, the stress falls on deliberation, participation, and institutional setting.

This goes to show that the term is multifarious and any of its aspects and nuances can be privileged by an analytical definition, stressing either the desired qualities of the process (will or reason, deliberation or participation, ideal institutional setting, etc.) or of its product (e.g., intentionality, rationality, normativity). In what follows, it is assumed that, in order to have a clear understanding of the concept of delegation, an incursion into the theoretical history of legislative paradigms is inevitable. All public law notions develop in a polemical evolution, inextricably related to other concepts. Concrete mutations and theoretical accounts of major legal concepts do not exist free-floating in a temporal vacuum, but rather proceed—to paraphrase a Burkean metaphor—by "insensible degrees" of differentiation, which an a-historical analysis cannot understand and properly disentangle.

[1] Lon L. Fuller, *Anatomy of the Law* (Westport, CT: Greenwood Press, 1976 (1968)), pp. 49–54, at p. 54.

[2] Jeremy Waldron, "Speech: Legislation by Assembly," 46 *Loyola Law Review* 507 (2000), at p. 510.

B. Iancu, *Legislative Delegation*,
DOI 10.1007/978-3-642-22330-3_2, © Springer-Verlag Berlin Heidelberg 2012

But in order to be useful to our conceptual quest, this inquiry into the historical evolution of legislation concepts has to have a constitutional dimension.

2.1 A Constitutional History of Legislation Concepts

Before we proceed with our actual historical account, it should first be explained what it means for practices to be underpinned by historically situated conceptual justifications and in what sense do conceptual justifications have a constitutional dimension.

Both differences as such between norms of different reach and subject-matter relevance and normative constraints on public rules go back to the Antiquity. For instance, in fourth-century Athens, the distinction between law and decree and the relative supremacy of the former were entrenched as a matter of practice and were safeguarded by a number of procedural and substantive checks. After the codification of 403/402 BC, an organic law was passed to define what would in the future count as legislation: "Law: magistrates must under no circumstances use unwritten law. No decree passed by the Council or the people may have higher validity than a law. No law may be passed that applies only to a single person. The same law shall apply to all Athenians, unless otherwise decided [in a meeting of the Assembly] with a quorum of 6000, by secret ballot."[3] *Nomoi* (laws, statutes) were thus limited to enactments of a more general and permanent nature, whereas through *psephismata* (decrees and resolutions) were taken individual decisions or adopted general norms of a more transient character.[4] The Assembly of the People (*ekklesia*) could only pass decrees, and a proposal to amend or abrogate an old

[3] Andokides, "On the Mysteries," in Mogens Herman Hansen, *The Athenian Democracy in the Age of Demosthenes*, J. A. Cook transl. (Oxford UK & Cambridge USA: Blackwell, 1991), p. 170.

[4] Mogens Herman Hansen, at 162: "*Nomos* meant a general norm without limit of duration, whereas *psephisma* meant an individual norm which, once carried out, was emptied of its content." *See*, same, for a chart, statistics, and discussion, pp. 170–175. An example of a *nomos* is provided at p. 171: "*Nomos eisangeltikos* against anyone who attempts to overthrow the democracy or to betray the Athenian armed forces or to speak to the people after taking bribes." [permanent and general nature] A decree (*psephisma*), conferring the title of *proxenos* and benefactor of Athens, for himself and all his descendants [permanent and individual nature] to a certain Macedonian who interceded with king Philip on behalf of Athens is reproduced in full at p. 148. A certain ambivalence should be pointed out, nonetheless. *See*, for instance, J. M. Kelly, *A Short History of Western Legal Theory* (Oxford: Clarendon Press, 1992), p. 11: "A further source of confusion was the unclear relationship of *psēphismata* (resolutions, decrees) to *nomoi*, statutes more strictly so called; the most that can be said is that *nomoi* were envisaged as permanent general dispositions, while *psēphismata* were *ad hoc* or supplementary or effectuating mesaures; though Aristotle uses the word in the sense of something which modifies a general law to meet the equity of a particular case, and *psēphismata* are occasionally themselves included in the category of *nomoi*."

law or make a new one would be passed on to a different body, the *Nomothetai*.[5] A new law would trump prior decrees. Furthermore, should a decree inconsistent with the body of legislation be carried through the Assembly, any citizen could initiate in the People's Court an invalidation procedure, *graphe paranomon* ("public prosecution for unconstitutional proposal of a decree")[6] and, if an incompatibility were found, have the initiator convicted and punished and the decree nullified and expunged from the public records.

The word "legislation" derives etymologically from Latin. *Lex* itself referred at first to codification of custom (*Lex Duodecim Tabularum,* the Law of XII Tables, about 451–449 BC), then to law-making proper. *Legis-latio* was the formal procedure by which the magistrate moved a law, after it had already been drafted, for approval before *comitiae* (*curiata, centuriata, tributa*)[7] and, following *Lex Hortensia de plebiscitis* (probably 287 BC), before the assembly of the plebs (*concilium plebis*). A magistrate who possessed *ius agendi cum populo/plebe* presented the bill and posed the question, to which the assemblies were expected to respond by clear-cut negation or affirmation. *Legis-latio* was taken, at least in the early usage of the term, to signify something clearly distinct from its antonym, *legis-datio*, which referred to the imposition of norms upon a *municipium* or new *coloniae*. According to Walter Ullmann, this procedure related therefore to an "ascending" conception or thesis of government.[8] One should however be cautious of anachronistic projections of similes. The crux of the issue in the procedure of

[5] These were bodies convened *ad-hoc* (when the need to make a new law or change or repeal an old one arose) and composed of citizens who had taken the Heliastic Oath (needed to be a juror, *dikastai*, in the People's Courts and administered on a yearly basis). The procedure was almost judicial in its nature, with parties arguing for or against a particular piece of legislation (or for/against the new/old law), and the *nomothetai* cast their votes for one or the other legislative "party."

[6] Mogens Herman Hansen, at p. 166, 174.

[7] *Curia* used to be an old religious, administrative, and military unit, roughly synonymous to 'clan,' which gradually lost importance during the Republic; laws submitted to the *curiae* were adopted almost exclusively in the domains of family and religion (for instance, adoptions, inheritance). Laws regarding political matters were submitted to the people assembled by *centuriae* (military and fiscal divisions). The *Comitia Tributa* (people assembled by tribes, territorial divisions) had essentially the same character as the *Concilium Plebis* (Assembly of the Plebs), except that from the latter patricians were excluded. After *Lex Hortensia* in 287 B.C., laws moved by the plebeian magistrates, the tribunes of the plebs, to the Plebeian Assembly, were made binding on the whole Roman People and *plebiscita* gained the same force as *leges*. *See* Bernard Manin, *The Principles of Representative Government* (Cambridge: Cambridge University Press, 1997), pp. 44–51.

[8] Walter Ullmann, *Principles of Government and Politics in the Middle Ages* (Frome and London: Butler & Tanner Ltd., 2nd ed., 1966). Mommsen describes however the whole evolution of the Roman state as a continuous struggle between the democratic and aristocratic elements, plebs and patricians, or –in his wording- the "Optimates" and the Populares" 'parties,' *see* Theodor Mommsen, *The History of Rome, An Account of Events and Persons from Carthage to the End of the Republic*, Dero Saunders and John A. Collins (Eds.) (Clinton, Mass.: Meridian Books, Inc., c1958).

rogatio was not deliberation by the citizenry, not even finding out what the people wanted but rather whether they approved of already arrived at rules. Therefore, the scope of participation was limited, taking into account the extent to which a popular assembly was conditioned by the limited reach of its task—giving or denying consent—and by the particular manner in which the magistrate chose to pose the question.

Moreover, legislation proper did certainly have a privileged place in the overall structure of the Roman legal order. A dictator could for instance dispense with most usual limitations (magisterial collegiality, intercession by the tribunes, the right of a citizen to appeal to the people in case of a death sentence) and could adopt decrees with legislative force on any subject but he could not initiate legislation proper.[9] This was however not a place analogous to modern understandings regarding systemic hierarchy and consistency of legal sources. *Leges* were used sparsely throughout the Republic; the edicts of the magistrates (*ius honorarium*) and the "advisory opinions" (*senatus consulta*) of the Senate were also original sources of law, an exemplification of the Roman constitution's "mixed nature."[10] Part of the answer for this clear procedural delimitation of functions and for the place of democratically validated law in the Roman legal framework can be found in the pragmatic Roman understanding of law.[11] Along with the Empire came a blurring of the distinctions and of the taxonomy, an increase in the pace of positive law as the main source of law, the necessity of uniform interpretation, and a growing need for codification. Ulpian's famous *dicta*, incorporated in Justinian's *Digest*, condense the new ("descending") thesis of government: "Princeps legibus solutus est."[12] and "Quod principi placuit, legis habet vigorem."[13] At that time, nonetheless, the

[9] Clinton Rossiter, *Constitutional Dictatorship-Crisis Government in the Modern Democracies* (Princeton: Princeton University Press, 1948), pp. 15–28, at 25.

[10] Polybius describes the Roman republic as a mixed constitution, an auspicious admixture of democratic (popular assemblies), aristocratic (Senate), and monarchic (consuls) elements (Polybius, *History*, Book VI, 11–18, et seq.).

[11] Hannah Arendt, *On Revolution* (New York: Viking Press, 1965), at p. 188: "Unlike the Greek νόμος, the Roman *lex* was not coeval with the foundation of the city and Roman legislation was not a pre-political activity. The original meaning of the word *lex* is 'intimate connection' or relationship, namely something which connects two things or two partners whom external circumstances have brought together." This pragmatic standpoint should not be understood as ignorance of substantive constraints on positive law. *Lex Duodecim Tabularum* contained a rule prohibiting the passing of laws aimed against specific individuals (in modern terms, a bill of attainder).

[12] Ulp. D. I, 3, 31. "The emperor is not subject to law." This sentence, extracted from the context of a commentary by Ulpian on *Lex Iulia et Papia*, was later interpreted to mean that the emperor (the king) was unrestricted by statutory law.

[13] "What pleases the emperor has the force of law." The entire paragraph from which the *dictum* is taken runs thus: Ulp. D. I. 4. I. (Inst. I, 2, 6) "Quod principi placuit legis habet vigorem: utpote cum lege regia, quae de imperio eius lata est, populus ei et in eum omne suum imperium et potestatem conferat." Taken later to mean that the emperor (in the Middle Ages, also the king) had absolute legislative power, by virtue of the fact that he had been *delegated* this power by the Roman people,

maxims never meant a full-fledged legal rubberstamp on naked imperial absolutism. Late imperial codifications were depicted as *ratio scripta*, literally written reason. Imperial power, legislation included, was supposed to be exercised for the public good, the emperor was in principle elected, whereas the Senate remained the repository of *auctoritas* and an independent check on imperial power. The formal procedure of *rogatio*, submission of bills to the people, was never specifically abolished. It rather fell into obsolescence towards the end of the Republic and the beginning of the Empire, whereas, as a legal fiction, the notion that indirect popular assent and legitimacy was conferred through the *lex de imperio* on the imperial decrees was maintained.[14]

Also to the Antiquity date back justifications of law and law-making that anticipate analytically most relevant modern discussions. The philosophical lineage of subordinating human law to a remedial project of virtue can be traced back to Plato's description of law as an ideal derived from moral verities, to which the human legislator should constantly strive. Plato's law-maker must target this ideal beyond the practicalities of particular arrangements and instrumental considerations, aiming always higher, "like an archer": "Where law is subject to some other authority and has none of its own, the collapse of the state is not far off; but if law is the master of the government and the government is its slave, then the situation is full of promise

which, through the *lex regia* (later *lex de imperio*), divested itself of its original *potestas* and *imperium*, bestowing them upon the emperor. In fact, the people never had any *imperium* to transfer since, in Roman public law, the notion of *imperium* pertained strictly to the magistrates and their sphere of jurisdiction. Throughout the Middle Ages, whereas the Church and the Empire used the maxim to legitimize claims of absolute power (on the argument that the delegation had in fact been an *irreversible abdication* of power in favor of the emperor), their opponents could point to the notion of *delegation* (which might imply the necessity of popular legitimization of secular power, an implicit proviso of exercise for the common good, or even Escheat or Reversion to the original delegator). *See*, for a discussion of Medieval theories related to the interpretation of the *lex regia*, Otto von Gierke, *Political Theories of the Middle Ages*, translated by Frederic William Maitland (Cambridge: Cambridge University Press, 1987 (1900)). Only Justinian and – much later- during the age of Absolutism, Frederick II, would advance the thesis that the *lex regia* bestowed on the ruler a legally unfettered power to make and change laws. Throughout the Middle Ages, the maxim was usually interpreted and understood in a more limited sense. Bracton cites it in a modified form and interprets it to mean that the king would be limited by the consent of the Council and the laws of the kingdom, thus limiting its reach to a meaning far remote from unfettered legislative authority. For a discussion of the relevant passage in Bracton and a presentation of a wealth of interpretations of Bracton's rendition of the maxim, *see* Ewart Lewis, "King Above Law? 'Quod Principi Placuit' in Bracton" 39 (2) *Speculum* 240 (April, 1964).

[14] Wolfgang Kunkel, *Roman Legal and Constitutional History*, J. M. Kelly transl. (Oxford: Oxford University Press, 1996), p. 119. *Lex regia* (*lex de imperio principis*) is sometimes considered apocryphal. A part of such a law, conferring additional powers, including the power to depart from old and make new law, on Vespasian (*lex de imperio Vespasiani, 69/70 A.D.*) was in fact preserved to our days and the bronze slab can still be seen at the Capitoline Museum. *See*, more generally, P.A. Brunt, "Lex de Imperio Vespasiani," 67 *The Journal of Roman Studies* 95 (1977).

and men enjoy all the blessings that the gods shower on a state." [15] A good state, it is argued, should actively foster virtuous living, since the aim of law and of the political community is moral perfection.[16]

The parallel philosophical tradition, of law viewed as a project of practical reason, goes back to Aristotelian arguments, in which the conceptual implications of most major distinctions that dominate contemporary debates are already laid out. The essential defense of participation in law-making can be found in the famous allegory of the banquet. A feast to which many guests contribute their due is said to be better than one catered by a single man. Likewise, a multitude is less corruptible ("like the greater quantity of water, which is less easily corruptible than a little") and wiser in its deliberations than a single sage: "Now any member of the assembly, taken separately, is certainly inferior to the wise man. But the state is made up of many individuals. And as a feast to which all the guests contribute is better than a banquet furnished by a single man, so a multitude is better judge of many things than any individual."[17] Parallel reasons prompt caution with respect to the role of "expertise" in public affairs. The multitude is the best judge in electing and calling to account administrators, not only because of the beneficial effects of pooling knowledge but, more importantly, since the authoritative judge of expertise is, in most cases, the user thereof. I am always more qualified than the cook or the builder to appreciate if the food is fine and the house is well built.[18]

Modern rule of law arguments, in their essential conceptual breakdown, are also foreshadowed in the *Politics*, since the epistemological and egalitarian arguments mentioned above are neither an unqualified endorsement of majority rule nor a proto-positivistic argument. That the many are better qualified than the few to pass judgment on public issues does not mean, by inference, that whatever judgment they pass can, simply by virtue of its being made by "the multitude," be dignified with the name of law, since "[r]ightly constituted laws should be the final sovereign; and personal rule, whenever it be exercised by a single person or a body of persons, should be sovereign only in those matters on which law is unable, owing to the difficulty of framing general rules for all contingencies, to make an exact pronouncement."[19] This disjunction between the general or universal (laws) and the particular (individual measures, decrees, and judgments according to law or equity)

---

[15] Plato, *The Laws*, (Trevor Saunders transl.) (Penguin Books edition), at p. 715.

[16] *Id.*, 707: "We do not hold the common view that a man's highest view is to survive and continue to exist. His highest good is to become as virtuous as possible and to continue to exist in that state as long as life lasts." More significantly, at 713–714: "...we should run our private and public life, our home and our cities, in obedience to what little spark of immortality lies in us, and dignify these edicts of reason with the name of 'law.'"

[17] *Politics*, Ernest Barker transl. (Oxford: Clarendon Press, 1948) III, 15, 1286a.

[18] III, 11, 1282a.

[19] III, 11, 1282b. (Barker) Translations differ slightly. The generality of law part of the argument in 1282b and 1269a appears, for instance, as "laws, *which must be universal*" in the 1986 Apostle-Gerson annotated edition (Grinnell, Iowa: The Peripatetic Press).

will resurface in natural law theory and in classical liberal accounts of the rule of law; it can be traced in different expositions to a vast array of sources, ranging from the Monarchomachs to Kant. Laws should be written and promulgated, general, and relatively stable since publicity, generality, and stability give the citizen what we nowadays call a "fair warning" and protect against arbitrariness.[20] Generality should be tempered by equity since a general rule, of necessity, cannot either foresee or accommodate in its procrustean command the richness of contingencies which arise in its actual application; excessive rigidity would do violence to *ex post*, contextual needs for justice in actual cases. Likewise, stability should be tempered by amendment, when change is dictated by necessity. To use a slightly anachronistic terminology, the supremacy of law is guaranteed by making structural provision for stability (laws should be difficult to change or amend)[21] and by rendering laws formally superior to concrete decrees or executive measures in the hierarchy of norms.

In Aristotle can also be found, albeit in inchoate form, the main strands of modern separation of powers arguments (the balance and mutual check of countervailing power centers and the distribution among these of distinct public functions). His "best" form of government, the polity[22] is not an unalloyed model but a mixture of two political forms, aristocracy and democracy, which partakes of the advantages and alleviates the peculiar downfalls of both: "The more perfect the admixture of political elements, the more lasting will be the constitution."[23] In practice, the law is sovereign when there is no sovereign in the sense of unfettered, absolute, despotic power. Consequently, care should be taken to mix political forms in the actual allocation of governmental functions.[24] Functionally, each government

[20] "The essence of a State is that men should live by known rules, which will enable them to recognize in advance the results of their action: the very savage clothes himself in the garb of custom." Sir Ernest Barker, *The Political Thought of Plato and Aristotle* (New York: Russell & Russell, 1959), p. 453.

[21] *See* the whole discussion at 1269a, of which I will reproduce a particularly relevant part: "It is evident from these facts, then, that at certain times some laws must be changed. On the other hand, if the situation is examined from a different point of view, one might think that great caution must be taken. For whenever the benefit is small, getting into the habit of changing laws readily is an evil."

[22] "Best" in pragmatic as opposed to ideal terms.

[23] IV, 12, 1297a (Jowett translation). This particular passage refers to the stabilizing importance of the middle class in a mixed polity. The middle class would serve as an arbitrator and counterpoising mean between extreme democracy (political domination by the poor) and oligarchy (domination by the wealthy, patrician classes in the city).

[24] This is probably the earliest separation and balance of powers argument (in the sense of mixed government or mixed constitution). In this respect, it matters but little that, for Aristotle, emphasis lay on achieving unity of the state through a union of classes rather than a limitation of the state through a balance and distribution of power among distinct power centers (a 'synthesis' and not an 'antithesis'). *See*, for a very interesting analysis and comparison, Barker 1959, "The Mixed Constitution," pp. 471–486, at p. 484 (*note* 4): "One may say that Aristotle desires a union of classes for the sake of equity; Polybius a union of constitutions for the sake of stability; and Montesquieu a division of powers for the sake of liberty."

comprises three essential elements (a deliberative part, magistracies, and a judicial part) and a wise legislator[25] will take into account divergences of political form in the attribution of magistracies and in the exercise of the "deliberative part" of government, for instance by mixing election (which favors merit, an aristocratic principle) and selection by lot (which corresponds perfectly to the notion of equality of the free-born, an essentially democratic concept).[26]

This introductory detour serves to point out that all sophisticated analytical inquiries into the nature of law arrived at atemporally mature conceptual grammars, pertinent to ensuing, indeed to contemporary quests. With respect to the major distinctions that structure thinking about law and law-making (types of equality, generality of norms and individual justice, meanings of justice, the value and appropriate place of deliberation in public affairs, etc.), the subsequent millennia have not brought stupendous improvements to the Aristotelian categories. Even leaving aside their influence on Aquinas, in fact on the entire High Middle Ages, it suffices to note that Hobbes, in his *Leviathan* defense of the newly emerging seventeenth-century concepts of state and sovereignty, still polemicized extensively with Aristotle's definitions of balanced powers and supremacy of law.[27] Nowadays, Jeremy Waldron builds his influential polemical defense of ideal law-making around an Aristotelian allegory (the banquet to which all guests contribute) and concept (*endoxa*, the wisdom of the multitude). At the same time and likewise, any legal order of a certain degree of complexity exhibits a measure of reflexivity

[25] Here the word 'legislator' is used in a pre-political sense. Aristotle uses the term 'legislation' both in the meaning of positive law (which needs to correspond to rule-of-law normative constraints) and in a sense close to the modern word 'constitution' (which needs to be directed towards the attainment of the proper political arrangement). A point which can be clarified-reinforced by the following short excerpt from the *Nicomachean Ethics*, H. Rackham translation (Cambridge, Mass., and London, England: Harvard University Press, 1994), VI. viii: "Of Prudence as regards the state, one kind, as supreme and directive, is called Legislative Science; the other, as dealing with particular occurrences, has the name Political Science, that really belongs to both kinds. The latter is concerned with actions and deliberation (for a parliamentary enactment is a thing to be done, being the last step in a deliberative process), and this is why it is only those persons who deal with particular facts that are spoken of as 'taking part in politics,' because it is only they who perform actions, like workmen in an industry."

[26] "What I mean is that it is regarded as democratic that magistracies should be assigned by lot, as oligarchic that they should be elective, as democratic that they should not depend on a property qualification, and as oligarchic that they should." (IV, 9, 1294b) The distinction is not necessarily archaic or anachronistic and hence not completely irrelevant today. That election (and therefore also modern representative government), as opposed to selection by lot, always includes, *sub rosa*, an aristocratic element, has been more recently pointed out by Bernard Manin in *The Principles of Representative Government* (Cambridge: Cambridge University Press, 1997).

[27] "It is men and arms, not words and promises, which make the power of the laws. And therefore this is another error of Aristotle's *Politics* that in a well-governed commonwealth not men should govern but the laws. What man that hath his natural senses, though he can neither write nor read, does not find himself governed by them he fears, and believes can kill or hurt him when he obeyeth not? Or believes that law can hurt him: that is, words and paper, without the hands and swords of men?" Thomas Hobbes, *Leviathan* (Oxford Edition, 1909 (1651)) Part IV, p. 533.

with respect to law-making and the relationships of different norms to one another, which can be in a loose sense characterized as constitutional. The more sophisticated the legal order, the greater the degree of reflexivity and differentiation among institutions, procedures, functions, and norms. More is however needed, for practices and conceptual orders to have a constitutional dimension, namely historical situation and structural interrelation of concepts and practices. The inquiry into the constitutional dimension of legislation concepts, in the sense relevant for this argument, must proceed at a later stage. We have to start our query at the beginnings of the Western legal tradition to which modern constitutional orders can be traced back. One needs to identify the emergence of systemic distinctions by virtue of which law-making arises as a function separated from other exercises of authority and embedded in an order that can be characterized as constitutional in a sense akin to the modern meaning of this term. This sense of constitution presupposes both (1) a relative systemic closeness, therefore a measure of autonomy and functional differentiation, of the institutions that exercise gradually more distinct kinds of authority; (2) a relative universality and coherence of legally relevant patterns of justifications, normative points of reference, and types of legally-relevant rationality; and (3) a symbiosis and mutual interaction between the two levels (of fundamental legality and legitimacy).

This process of gradually developing autonomy of fundamental legal institutions and relevant normative environments resulted eventually in the modern constitution, an "evolutionary achievement" that claims to control not only the reproduction of the legal system as such, by establishing conditions of validity for the production of subordinate norms (and even for the change of the constitution itself), but also the normative arguments within the system (the constitutionally-relevant legitimacy model).[28] This matter is of the highest relevance to our topic, given that a central implicit question of this book is whether and to what extent the modern normative constitution is in fact capable of fulfilling its "evolutionary" legal-systemic task of "regulating and restricting the delegation possibilities," by establishing to a substantial degree its own legal-rational conditions of the

[28] Niklas Luhmann, "Verfassung als evolutionäre Errungenschaft",9 *Rechtshistorisches Journal* 176 (1990), at p. 187: "Folglich ist die Verfassung diejenige Form, mit der das Rechtssystem auf die eigene Autonomie reagiert. Die Verfassung muß, mit anderen Worten, Außenanlehnungen, wie sie das Naturrecht postuliert hatte, ersetzen. Sie ersetzt sowohl das Naturrecht im älteren kosmologischen Verständnis als auch das Vernunftrecht mit seinen transzendentaltheoretischen Konzentrat der Selbstreferenz in der sich selbst beurteilenden Vernunft. An die Stelle tritt ein teilweise autologischer Text." ("The modern constitution is therefore the form through which the legal system reacts to its own autonomy. The constitution must, in other words, replace external references, as they had been postulated by natural law. The constitution replaces not only older natural right but also the rational natural law tradition with its transcendental self-referentiality anchored in the application of reason unto its operations. On their place appears a partly autological text.")

possibility.[29] A closely related, equally important inquiry, bears on whether the model of rationality on which the modern constitution relies is a purely procedural-formal one or requires a meta-textual, substantive dimension regarding the constitutionally presupposed concept of law and legislation.

Throughout the remainder of the chapter, this process of increasing rationalization and abstractization of the fundamental law is traced by identifying the succession of changes that lead to the legal and intellectual presuppositions of the modern normative constitution. These presuppositions, it shall be argued, shed light on the concept of delegation, explaining at the same time its legal and conceptual limitations. Paradigm shifts, in the sense in which they are under scrutiny here, represent "structural couplings"[30] incorporating the dominant practices with respect to law-making and the dominant model of justification against which the legitimacy of the practices was (at any particular time) legally assessed. Needless to say, this kind of exercise, like all ideal-typical reductions and all incursions into the parallel histories of ideas and institutions, takes upon itself a hefty burden of persuasion. In doing so, it exposes itself to a wide array of possible reservations. Given the historical time-span and the philosophical breadth of the matters at stake, the number of events unaccounted and authors not included may initially appear, to the historian and philosopher alike, legion. The customary leave should be therefore expressly requested in advance, that the relevance of the events and ideas incorporated in this theoretical-historical account should be judged against justificatory needs of the argument alone.

2.2 *God Himself as Law*: Law Between Faith and Tradition

> You are also aware, dear son, that while you are permitted honorably to rule over human kind, yet in things divine you bow your head humbly before the leaders of the clergy and await from their hands the means of your salvation.
>
> (Letter of Pope Gelasius to Emperor Anastasius, 494 AD)

> Ego sum Caesar, ego Imperator.[31]
>
> Pope Boniface VIII (1294–1303)

> We be informed by our Judges, that we at no time stand so highly in our estate Royal as in the time of Parliament; wherein we as Head, and you as Members, are conjoyned and knit together into one body politick.
>
> Henry VIII, 1525 Speech in Parliament, in relation to the case of Ferrers

[29] *Id.*, at p. 190. For evidence that Luhmann's argument regarding the closeness of the constitution has a substantive, normative component, *see* discussion at pp. 205–208.

[30] This Luhmannian expression is borrowed without the whole social-scientific baggage of its theoretical context.

[31] "I am the king, I am the Emperor." In Ernst H. Kantorowicz, *Kaiser Friedrich der Zweite* (Stuttgart: Klett-Cotta, 1998), p. 36.

St. Augustine characterizes true nature as an antithesis to the reality of things directly accessible to our senses; the latter are, in a nowadays strikingly counter-intuitive portrayal, corrupted and hence not natural at all. True nature is extra-sensorial, discernible only by grace, revelation, and theological inquiry, and can be found only by an insight of faith, in the perfect state before the Fall. In the same way, positive law is innately devoid of justice,[32] law which is not just is not law, states without justice are nothing but great bands of robbers: *Remota justitia quid sunt regna nisi magna latrocinia*.[33] Earthly dominion (the *civitas terrena*) is possibly corrupt in itself, uninteresting as such for the true believer, thus relegated to the minimal role of maintaining peace and order. Meanwhile, as the argument runs further, true justice exists in the City of God, in the heavens. The secular ruler, emperor or king, is seen preeminently as an instrument, a tool, which cannot bring earthly felicity, yet should, and this is its preordained purview, punish the evil. The prince, as St. Paul had pointed out "beareth not the sword in vain."[34] Yet the City of God is represented on Earth by the community of the faithful, which in turn Augustine has a strong bent on identifying with the visible Church.[35] Two relevant issues can already be derived from this summation.

First, the Middle Ages knew, up until the Reformation, a unity of law in a higher, metaphysical sense, apparent in St. Augustine. Since the whole Christian realm was perceived in a sense as a *Respublica Christiana*, sharing in a super-imposed universal religion (and thus morality), the secular powers could not be the primary locus of legislation. Although the existence as such of the state in the Middle Ages still is under a fair amount of controversy, Meinecke was certainly right to assert in principle that "[t]he new universal religion set up at the same time a universal command, which even the State must obey, and turned the eyes of individual men on other-worldly values; thus all secular values, including heroism as the herald of power politics and *raison d'état*, were caused to give ground... The State certainly

[32] *See*, on St. Augustine's "legal" thinking, Carl J. Friedrich, *The Philosophy of Law in Historical Perspective*, 2nd ed. (Chicago and London: University of Chicago Press, 1968).

[33] "Without justice what are states but great bands of robbers." *City of God*, IV, 4.

[34] KJB, Romans 13: 3–4: "For rulers are not a terror to good works, but to the evil. (...) for he beareth not the sword in vain: for he is the minister of God, a revenger to execute wrath upon him that doeth evil."

[35] This identification and the *correct* interpretation of Saint Augustine (in the sense of what he actually meant) are, of course, open to debate. *See*, for instance, for a number of different readings, Frederick William Loetscher, "Saint Augustine's Conception of the State," 4 (1) *Church History* 16 (Mar., 1935), Rex Martin, "The Two Cities in Augustine's Political Philosophy," 33 (2) *Journal of the History of Ideas* 195 (Apr.-Jun. 1972), and Anton-Hermann Chroust, "The Philosophy of Law of Saint Augustine," 53 (2) *The Philosophical Review* 195 (Mar., 1944). This brief exposition is a plausible one and, much more importantly for our present purposes, it is the one that relates to medieval debates about law and legislation.

existed in the Middle Ages, but it did not rank supreme. Law was set above it; it was a means for enforcing the law."[36]

Law therefore and also thinking about the law acquired an unselfconscious quality, an almost prelapsarian innocence. This continuous orientation toward a higher law (according to the *Sachsenspiegel* "Law is dear to God, as God himself is law.") had meant that law-making could not be perceived and approached in an explicit and intentional key. The exemplary way of law-making was therefore law-finding, a judgment that would seek in past wisdom the just decision for an individual case.[37] True it is that, occasionally, more assertive rulers would clothe their claims in the stylistic garb of the Byzantine Emperors, asserting unfettered law-making power and the status of *lex animata* (living law). At the Diet of Roncaglia in 1158, the bishop of Milan addressed Friedrich Barbarossa thus, in portentous phrases redolent of the imperial principles in the *Digest*: "Know, that the entire law-making power of the people was transferred to you! Your will is law, as it stands written: What pleases the Prince, has the power of law, since the people have granted him such dominion and power. Whatever the Emperor establishes, decides, decrees, has the force of law!"[38] But behind the rhetorical flourishes, the reality of things was rather modest. In order to "make" new law, an Emperor or Prince needed to go through the usual judicialized procedure or secure unanimity; in the Imperial

[36] Friedrich Meinecke, *Machiavellism – The Doctrine of Raison d'Etat and Its Place in Modern History*, Douglas Scott transl. (New Haven: Yale University Press, 1957), p. 27. *Also* in von Gierke, *Political Theories*, at pp. 74–75: "The thought that State and Law exist by, for and under each other was foreign to the Middle Age. . ..however many disputes there might be touching the origin of Natural Law and the ground of its obligatory force, all were agreed that there was Natural Law, which, on the one hand, radiated from a principle transcending earthly power an, on the other hand, was true and perfectly binding Law."

[37] "Legislation was in fact part of the judicial procedure. Law was seen as the embodiment of the law of God in the custom of the community, and the actions of the King in his Council making formal statements of the law were seen as clarificatory acts. There could, therefore, be only one "function" of government- the judicial function; all acts of government were in some way justified as aspects of the application and interpretation of the law" M. J. C. Vile, *Constitutionalism and the Separation of Powers* (Oxford: Clarendon Press, 1967). A classical exposition and analysis of the shift of paradigm from the Medieval notion of law-declaring or law-finding to the modern conception of law-making can be found in Charles Howard McIlwain, *The High Court of Parliament and Its Supremacy – An Historical Essay of the Boundaries between Legislation and Adjudication in England* (New Haven: Yale University Press, 1910). According to McIlwain, the notion that Parliament is a law-making machine emerged in an incipient form with the Tudors and became an accepted idea only during the Civil War, with the Long Parliament: "England had seen practically for the first time a legislative assembly of the modern type,- no longer a mere law-declaring, but a law-making machine. . ..The great phases of the English Parliament have been its history as a court, then as a legislature, and finally as a government-making organ. Parliament definitely passed out the first of these stages at the first session of the Long Parliament." (at 93) *See also* Heinz Mohnhaupt, "Potestas legislatoria und Gesetzesbegriff im Ancien Régime" IV *Ius Commune* 188–239 (1972).

[38] In Wilhelm Ebel, *Geschichte der Gesetzgebung in Deutschland*, 2, erweiterte Auflage (Göttingen: Otto Schwartz & Co., 1958), at p. 43.

Diet, up until the end of the Holy Roman Empire, all decisions were taken unanimously.[39] Even the great imperial legislation meant to secure the peace of the land (*Landfrieden, contitutio pacis*) rested on consensus (acquiring in effect the character of a contract) and had limited duration. Unwritten trumped written law. Wilhelm Ebel mentions the interesting gloss on an article of the Norwegian twelfth century code *Gulathingslag*, to the effect that "if the written law should be unjust, one should go back to the rules, as they had been before, as the law-bearer Atle had recited them once before the people in Gule."[40] General yielded to particular and local norms. In this respect, the influence of the Middle Ages endured until relatively recent times. Paradoxically, a modern codification imbued with the rationalistic-contractarian spirit of the Enlightenment century, the 1794 *Allgemeines Landrecht für die preußischen Staaten*, still had in practice subsidiary character and stood therefore under a belated medieval spell.[41]

Second, the Augustinian imagery explains both the very important role of the papacy in maintaining this unity and, in turn, the place of faith in justifying its authority. Papal law is the epitome of the "descending" thesis of government in the Middle Ages and some of its self-portrayal runs along the otherworldly Augustinian argument. If earthly dominion is by nature corrupt and built on sin, then it is by self-evident consequence inferior to the Church and relegated to the execution of the Pope's commands. As an extreme but therefore all the more revealing example, to Pope Gregory VII kingship was quite simply "the invention of those who in ignorance of God, and by instigation of the Devil, have presumed to tyrannize over their equals." [42] By the same token, however, papal legislation rested its *raison d'être* and justification for intervening in mundane relationships on the building block of a very juristic argument.

I shall try to briefly explain why. First and foremost, the existence of a medieval man was not severed into the various independent domains in whose splintered, fractured partiality, we moderns perceive our selves and ascribe our memberships. Contrariwise, it was a claim of totality, since all actions of a Christian were meant to be directed at the attainment of eternal life. The Church itself was seen as a corporation of the faithful, *congregatio fidelium*, in which membership came from and through the act of baptism. The pope, head of this corporation, who admits of no equal and cannot be judged, derives his vicarious power from Saint Peter, who in turn received it from Christ.[43] Any pope is a continuation of the legal personality of Peter, acquiring title deed by means of inheritance, like in Roman *ab*

---

[39] *Id.*, at p. 45.

[40] *Id.*, at p. 19.

[41] Hermann Conrad, *Die geistigen Grundlagen des Allgemeinen Landrechts für die preußischen Staaten* (Köln und Opladen, Westdeutscher Verlag, 1958).

[42] (Epp., viii., 21) *In* William E. Brytenson, "Roman Law and Legislation in the Middle Ages," 41 (3) *Speculum* 420)). *Also see* von Gierke, *Political Theories*, at p. 10, note 10.

[43] "Christus ascende in coelum unum reliquit in terris vicarius, sic necesse est, ut ei omnium, qui Christiani esse cupiunt, subdantur capita populorum." (Pope Gregory IX).

intestat inheritance.[44] He can therefore bind and loose everything on earth, with effects in the afterlife. Binding, in turn, is *ligare*, a word with clear legal connotations (the word *lex,* law, was perceived to have derived from it). Since attainment of eternal life is the ultimate end of all actions and given that faith outside the monastic cell is not a matter to be pursued by the solitary individual, guidance needed to be given uniformly. Therefore, those who have *scientia* and *auctoritas*, the church and the pope, regulated punctually, even minutely, through emphatically legal instruments (decretals, encyclical letters, bulls, mandates, deposition and excommunication orders), denying constantly that a separation of the temporal and the spiritual can be maintained and consequently interfering in a myriad issues, from feudal relations to the application of Roman law in the British Isles. All this is a beautifully crafted, objection-proof, essentially juristic argument. There is nothing mystical about it, except perhaps the fact that the whole edifice rests on faith, and the entire argument stands or collapses with unquestioned belief in its validity. If we were to reason in familiarly post-Enlightenment categories, it is a rational legal argument backed by the irrational element of faith. The rational-legal aspect, and the practical attempts at securing a certain level of conformity of conduct and uniformity of interpretation entailed as an immediate effect positive law, a certain degree of codification, archival records of written documents, church bureaucracy and domination through knowledge, all of which Max Weber appositely characterized as "the bureaucratic rationalization of the church."[45] It is not coincidental that both the Medieval Catholic Church and the Holy Roman Empire made good use of legists trained in Roman law at the University of Bologna.

Transforming the Church into rationalized administration put a huge strain on religion and had perhaps, over time, a detrimental effect on faith. Be that as it may, it is important to point out that the future state mimetically learned some of its patterns of law-making and justification from church organization, to the same extent and in the same manner that the church itself borrowed the system and coherence of secular, Roman legal institutions: "The church borrowed secular ideas just as the state borrowed ecclesiastical ones; *the church had to become half a state before the state could become half a church*."[46] Institutional and procedural changes led inevitably to substantive rationalization of canon law; the most revealing example in this respect is the 1215 Fourth Lateran Council, forbidding priests to

[44] The basic principle, bestowal upon Peter of a general power to bind and loose authoritatively on earth with direct effects in the afterlife, is based upon the famous section in Matthew 16:18–19. Transmission of the Petrine commission by St. Peter to successive popes is ascribed to a letter by St. Clement I to St. James in Jerusalem, dating roughly in the end of the second century A.D. (*see*, more generally, Ullmann 1966, at pp. 32–114).

[45] Max Weber, *Economy and Society: An Outline of Interpretive Sociology*, Guenther Roth and Claus Wittich, Eds. (Berkeley and Los Angeles: University of California Press, 1978), at p. 1172.

[46] Emphasis supplied. Brian Tierney, *Religion, Law, and the Growth of Constitutional Thought* (Cambridge: Cambridge University Press, 1982), at p. 12. *See also* von Gierke, *Political Theories*, at p. 36: "It was within the Church that the idea of Monarchical Omnicompetence first began to appear. It appeared in the shape of a *plenitudo potestatis* attributed to the Pope."

take part in ordeals. In time, it is precisely the formalization and rationalization of Church law throughout the High Middle Ages that would have a ratchet effect on secular law. Indeed, the category as such of secular law appears as a remote result of this process: the formation in the eleventh century of canon law as internally rational and consistent body of rules, reproducible according to its own internal logic and with a claim on universal validity, will in the end result in the creation of parallel interacting legal "systems" (of urban, feudal, mercantile, manorial, and royal law).[47] Once Pope Gregory VII asserted explicitly in his 1075 *Dictatus papae* exclusive power to legislate, make new laws ("condere novas leges"), other counterclaims would inevitably follow suit.[48]

A number of germane processes of rationalization evolve towards the eleventh and twelfth and eventually coagulate until the late thirteenth century. Joseph Strayer's thesis that already by the end of the thirteenth century many German and Italian princes and the French and English kings had powers approximating the modern understanding of sovereign prerogatives and—save for the inexistence of the concept as such—even thought of themselves in modern sovereign terms, can be considered too daring.[49] But the processes of building a central administration and increasing bureaucratization are unmistakable. They will prepare and eventually ease the later transition to sovereign statehood. The great treatises of English law by Glanvill and Bracton are written in the late twelfth and thirteenth century, whereas the procedure of common law courts begins to mature at roughly the same time. At the turn of the fourteenth century, the English central courts were already staffed with judges "as highly trained in the English common law as any professor at Bologna was trained in Roman law."[50]

Tendencies towards rationalization at the level of practices had conceptual counterparts, most evident in the revival of classical philosophy and particularly in the rediscovery of Aristotle. The corpus of Aristotelian writings, whose use at the University of Paris still stood partly under papal censorship in 1215, was already translated by 1225 and was widely available until the end of the century. Around 1260, William of Moerbeke turned the *Politics* into Latin, at the behest of St. Thomas Aquinas. The reevaluation of Aristotle by Aquinas is a Christian one but its secular implications and consequences can hardly be overemphasized:

---

[47] Harold J. Berman, *Law and Revolution: The Formation of the Western Legal Tradition* (Cambridge, Mass. *Etc.*: Harvard University Press, 1983).

[48] *Id.*, at p. 535 and *passim. Also see*, Ernst-Wolfgang Böckenförde, "Die Entstehung des Staates als Vorgang der Säkularisation", in *Säkularisation und Utopie: Erbacher Studien. Ernst Forsthoff zum 65. Geburtstag* 75 (Stuttgart u.a.: Kohlhammer, 1967).

[49] Joseph R. Strayer, *On the Medieval Origins of the Modern State* (Princeton: Princeton University Press, 1970); "The Laicization of French and English Society in the Thirteenth Century," 15 *Speculum* 76 (January1940). *But cf.* Dieter Grimm, *Souveränität – Herkunft und Zukunft eines Schlüsselbegriffs* (Berlin: Berlin University Press, 2009), arguing that "sovereignty" in its medieval acception was relative not (as moderns perceive the concept) absolute, *see* criticism of Strayer, pp. 17–20.

[50] Strayer, *Medieval Origins*, p. 33.

"Thus entered the cognitive man (*erkennende Mensch*) into the picture, to displace the speculative individual, directed solely towards the contemplation of God and the inner experience of his own wisdom."[51] All but antithesis to both Augustinian idealism and to the unity of hierocratic domination by the papacy, Aristotelian-Thomistic thinking renders a more empirical, concrete order-oriented vision of law, most apparent in the concept of *duplex ordo* (demarcation between the knowledge of natural and supra-natural spheres), associated with an intense practical interest in secular government. The fact that Aquinas embodies a new tradition in Christian thinking is apparent if one considers his vision of the exception and the stark contrast and departure from Augustinianism that it represents: "[N]ecessity is not subject to law." [52] Even the inconsistencies of Saint Thomas's writings evidence this shift and clash of paradigms. *De Regno,* his unsent letter to the king of Cyprus, dwells on the perfectly orthodox statement that the ruler must be one, and the king is subject to the sole authority of the Holy Church. Yet the tone of the writing contradicts this foundation and the more general argument is replete with secular Aristotelian references, indefatigably advocating that living in common is ordained by the independent reason divinely planted in nature and mankind, that man is a political animal, an intelligent agent, and hence rationally acting in view of an end, by deliberation as to means: "Yet it is natural for man, more than for any other animal, to be a social and political animal, to live in a group."[53] For Aquinas, there is already reason and order in nature, divine grace only perfects them, and a political association is an "artificial thing," which should follow the dictates of the divinely-created nature, since "whatever is in accord with nature is best, for nature always does what is best."[54] Not unexpectedly, the revival of Aristotle had a direct and immediate impact on "populist" writers. Marsilian doctrine, the closest medieval argument to our modern understandings of legislation as the epitome of law and of legal validity as deriving from popular acquiescence is largely a variation on and extension of Aristotelian-Thomistic themes. Marsilius (Marsiglio) of Padua derives from reasoned human will a right of participation in making the law extended to all citizens since, for him, the imperial or royal imprimatur has already been reduced to

[51] Ernst Forsthoff, *Deutsche Verfassungsgeschichte der Neuzeit. Ein Abriss.* (Stutgart: Kohlhammer, 1961), p. 7.

[52] "Necessitas non habet legem." *Summa Theologica*, II, I, 96, 6 (end of *respondeo*).

[53] St. Thomas Aquinas, *On Kingship-To the King of Cyprus* (*De Regno-Ad Regem Cypri*), translated into English by Gerald E. Phelan (Under the Title *On the Governance of Rulers*), revised with an introduction and notes by I. Th. Eschmann, O. P. (Toronto, Canada: The Pontifical Institute of Medieval Studies, 1949), p. 4.

[54] *Id.*, p. 12. In this sense, one could surmise that Aquinas's use of Aristotle anticipates what Gierke refers to as the "new antic-modern thought" for, when it is advanced that God has implanted independent reason in nature and an independent "political nature" in mankind, the eventual inference and consequence will be that: "however certain men might be that the Will of God was the ultimate cause of Politic Society, still this cause fell back into the position of a *causa remota* working through human agency….More and more decisively was expressed the opinion that the very union of men in a political bond was an act of rational, human Will." (at p. 89).

a mere formality.[55] Marsilius deprives law of all metaphysical underpinnings; law is for him primarily recognizable by its enforceability, *praeceptum coactivum*,[56] thus "a-moralized" and "humanized." It pertains to the purview of *auctoritas humana*, it is—in one revealing metaphor—an "eye formed of many eyes. . .the considered comprehension of many comprehenders": *oculus ex multis oculis*.[57]

Aristotelian-Thomistic thinking had a counterpart in the actual, in pre-Renaissance political reality; powerful and influential ideas appear sometimes when circumstances are propitious. Throughout the thirteenth century, numerous corporations (*corpus, universitas, collegium, societas*) had already risen and now were beginning to be recognized the right to control their memberships and to adopt rules and regulations to that effect. By an analogy to the private Roman law on agency, they were also granted the right to be represented (as fictitious entities, as legal persons as we would say nowadays) in legal proceedings *ad agendum et respondendum*, by a *syndicus* or *procurator*. Pope Innocent III, at the very turn of the century, summons some of the chartered cities to appear before his *Curia* by representation. In 1245, for the first time, a papal bull addresses the four faculties of Paris as *universitas*.[58] Among chartered corporations, Italian cities by and large governed themselves, having already arrived at a rather high degree of autonomy from both the emperor and the pope. The emperor was theoretically supposed to have been their ultimate temporal sovereign, *dominus mundi*, and—as it stood written in the *Corpus iuris civilis*—the only proper source of written law. In practice, however, especially after 1250, the death of Frederick II, the last Hohenstaufen emperor exercising effective dominion in the peninsula, the primary sources of law in Florence, Venice, Siena, Lucca, Peruggia, were custom (*consuetudo*) and locally adopted statutes. The latter fitted squarely into the notion of legislation as positive law. The problem was how to overcome this apparent inconsistency and maintain the fiction of imperial sovereignty, while rendering

---

[55] This generous view of participation in law-making can be later found in Nicolaus Cusanus (Niklaus or Nicholas of Cues), who revives the notion that: "'quod omnes tangit, ab omnibus approbari debet' (that which affects everybody should be approved by everybody); the making of law ("legis latio") should be done by all those whom the law is to bind, or by the greatest part of them." Kelly 1992, at p. 173.

[56] Ullmann quips appropriately that Marsilian theory is the Middle Ages equivalent of Kelsen's *Reine Rechtslehre*.

[57] Marsilius of Padua, *The Defender of Peace* (vol. II: *The "Defensor Pacis"*), translated with an introduction by Alan Gewirth (New York: Columbia University Press, 1956), Chapter XI: "On the Necessity of Making Laws (Taken in Their Most Proper Sense); And That No Ruler, However Virtuous or Just, Should Rule Without Laws)," XI:9, at 40: "Since then the law is *an eye composed of many eyes, that is, the considered comprehension of many comprehenders* for avoiding error in civil judgment and for judging rightly, it is safer that these judgments be made according to law than according to the discretion of the judge." [emphasis supplied] A condensed, arguably more enjoyable rendition of Marsilian political and legal theory is offered by the main character in Umberto Eco's *The Name of the Rose*, the Franciscan friar William of Baskerville.

[58] *See*, more generally, Gaines Post, *Studies in Medieval Legal Thought – Public Law and the State, 1100–1322* (Princeton, New Jersey: Princeton University Press, 1964), pp. 27–60.

a legally sound and factually accurate description of autonomous law-making in the Italian cities. How can the theoretically inferior exercise in practice what is theoretically the superior's prerogative, nay, monopoly? Early interpretations of Roman law, notably Accursian glosses, had dealt tersely with the issue, by qualifying local statutes as written custom (*consuetudo scripta*) and maintaining that they were in force precisely because the emperor acquiesced either expressly or tacitly. The Postglossator Bartolus of Sassoferrato, arrived by purely legal interpretation at an account of participative law-making much akin to that of Marsilius. Bartolus works his argument from custom, which was considered an acceptable legal source in the imperial codifications, arising unsystematically over time, from practice validated by unattached tacit consent. Yet statutes as well, he observes, are produced by consent, namely a form of it that is direct, express, and recognizable. Since the nature of both sources of law is consent, Bartolus set the poles together by equating the two types: *Tacitus et expressus consensus equiparantur et sunt paris potentiae*. Therefore, he reasoned, statute law does not need the approval of a superior. Logically, the demonstration is flawed, since it need not be true that tacit and express consent are one and the same thing as a matter of public law.[59] A precedent for self-government through written law was nonetheless set, and, shortly thereafter, Baldus of Ubaldis had to push his teacher's argument only a little further in order to derive a general duty of the emperor to act in view of the common good and a corresponding right to resistance of the cities in case he would be in dereliction of his obligations.[60]

Consent was also entailed by and embedded in lord-vassal relations, since the emperor (and by extension the king, *imperator in regno suo*),[61] even when trying to assert a purely theocratic, God-given authority, was also an overlord, bound by his feudal duties. But, while it must be stressed again that law in general and therefore even written legislation were generally perceived as something to be found rather than made, positive law was possible in emergencies for the defense of the realm. As a concern of the whole *universitas regni*, exceptional taxation, raising armies, legislation and adjudication for this purpose, touched all and therefore needed to be assented to by all (*quod omnes tangit ab omnibus approbari debet*).[62] It is in

[59] Bartolus, one of the most prominent Romanists of his time, was probably aware of the fact that only private Roman law, solely in its latter stages, when the level of formality had been already reduced, started to reason from express (the privileged form) to tacit consent: *Qui tacit consentire videtur*.

[60] Joseph Canning, *The Political Thought of Baldus de Ubaldis* (Cambridge: Cambridge University Press, 1987). *See, also*, Quentin Skinner, *The Foundations of Modern Political Thought*, Vol. I-*The Renaissance* (Cambridge: Cambridge University Press, 1978), pp. 3–12.

[61] The recognition in "law" (of what had already become true in fact) that the king of France admits of no temporal superior (is not subordinated to the Emperor of the Western/Holy Roman Empire, even though the Emperor could and did claim a moral pre-eminence), dates back to Innocent III's decree *Per venerabilem* of 1202.

[62] The principle can be traced to the *Codex Justiniani*, C.5, 59, 5: "ut quod omnes similiter tangit, ab omnibus comprobetur." *See*, on the relevance of the maxim in Medieval representation, Gaines

thirteenth-century England, by the accident of an auspicious course of events, that the notion of consent from the governed gains additional impetus, in the aftermath of John the Lackland's acceptance of *Magna Carta*. To be sure, *Magna Carta* was a *stabilimentum*; the idea of consent by the *communitas regni* encompassed initially only the magnates (barons) and high prelates, as tenants-in-chief of the king.[63] Moreover, this sort of consent had little to do with modern law-making or fiduciary participation: its primary role was to solidify and entrench the customary, feudal *status quo*. For instance, when Charles I sought in 1267 to impose a new tax in his newly acquired kingdom of Sicily, Pope Clement IV immediately reprimanded him: he had to summon first his barons, the clergy, and the town and discuss the circumstances and lawfulness of such endeavors.[64] Nonetheless, events gather over time new interpretations and trigger unintended consequences. The Charter of 1215 prompted from that moment onwards a steady growth of representation into constitutionalism and parliamentarism or—to echo Bracton—into a *Constitutio Libertatis*. To wit, the 1322 Statute of York already includes the knights of the shires and the burgesses—for purposes of taxation alone—into the *status regni, lestat du roialme*.[65]

At the end of the thirteenth century, therefore, one can already notice a number of clear, partly divergent but mutually reinforcing tendencies (hierocratic bureaucratization and "rationalization" of knowledge, centralization of secular power and fragmentation, and respectively demands for participation in it) towards the rationalization of thinking about the law and the individualization of law and law-making as autonomous practices. And yet all these evolutions could not be yet perceived as clear steps towards modern concepts of legislation and legislative practices. Pre-Reformation Europe could not envisage law as synonymous with explicit declarations of intent, not only due to the fact that the dominating model in legal thought and practice was that of finding the law. Moreover, given the diversity of overlapping concrete legal orders, statuses, and acquired rights, and the multiplicity of their sources, a uniform, intentional, and systematized manner of securing

---

Post, "A Roman Legal Theory of Consent, *Quod Omnes Tangit*, In Medieval Representation" 1950 *Wisconsin Law Review* 66 (1950).

[63] *Carta Baronum* conceded by John the Lackland at Runnymede in 1215, was designated *Magna* to differentiate it from a *Parva Carta* or *Carta Foresta* of 1217, *also* a *stabilimentum*, dealing with hunting privileges. The word *libertatum* seems to be a later, more recent, addition.

[64] Strayer 1970, p. 61, *note* 56. *Also*, *ibid*., "Existing usages, guaranteed by law, were a form of property. They could not be changed without due process, any more than property could be seized without due process.

[65] *See* Post 1964, Chapter VI, "Status Regni: Lestat du Roialme in the Statute of York, 1322" pp. 310–322, and Heinrich Mitteis, *The State in the Middle Ages-A Comparative Constitutional History of Feudal Europe*, translated by H. F. Orton (Amsterdam, Oxford: North-Holland Publishing Company, c1975), pp. 298–306.

compliance and coordinating action could not either exist in practice or be theoretically conceived. Throughout the Middle Ages, arguments present themselves in hybrid, composite forms, where theological theories meet feudal law and re-interpretations of Roman legislation are sometimes fused at the hip with organic conceptions of the political community. All claims to superior power are met by a multiplicity of equally plausible counter-claims.[66] Marsilian doctrine or the fleeting and eerily modernistic administrative reforms of the Norman kings of Sicily stand out as anachronistic oddities precisely because they evince a rational, unadulterated clarity and are built on the secularized foundation of a plenitude of power concentrated in one single point and unfettered by any legal limitations. But nothing was yet more foreign to the Middle Ages than, to use Gierke's apt and memorable words "a theoretical concentration of right and power in the highest and widest group on the one hand and the individual man on the other, at the cost of all intermediate groups."[67]

2.3 Legislation Between Will and Tradition

> Mais si l'on demande, si le Roy peut faire et publier tous ces changemens de Loix et d'Ordonnances, de sa seule auhorité, sans l'aduis de son Conseil, ny de ses Cours souveraines. A quoi l'on respond, que cela ne reçoit point de doute, pource que le Roy est seul Souverain dans son Royaume; et que la souveraineté n'est non plus divisible, que le poinct en la geometrie.
>
> Cardin Le Bret, *De la souverainete du Roy*, livre I, chapitre LX (1632)[68]

> Reason is too large. Find me a precedent and I will accept it.
>
> James I

2.3.1 Like the Point in Geometry*: Legislation and the Question of Sovereignty*

> The content of this plenitude needed no explanation, its substance was inalienable, impartible and proof against prescription, and all subordinate power was a mere delegation from it.
>
> Otto von Gierke, *Political Theories of the Middle Age*

---

[66] This overlapping normative entanglement caused Weber to remark that the Middle Ages were also a form of *Rechtsstaat,* in the sense that they comprised of a "bundle of subjective rights."

[67] Meinecke 1957, at p. 87.

[68] "But if one should ask whether the king could make and publish all these changes of laws and ordinances, by his own authority, without asking for the opinion of his courts or Council, the answer is: undoubtedly yes. And that is so since the king is sovereign in his kingdom; and sovereignty is no more divisible than the point in geometry." In Mohnhaupt 1972, at p. 201.

Machiavelli already anticipates the logic of the modern state, by way of his technical manner of thinking about politics and the law: "the new scientific method."[69] His Prince is cautioned to act primarily in terms of empirical necessity and, while we are told that there are two ways of maintaining the subjects in obedience, one with laws, the other with force, one proper to humans, the other to beasts, they are equally inviting in case the state requires it.[70] Since people are innately bad, acquisitive, and selfish beasts, virtuous only by necessity (they "forget more easily the death of their fathers than the loss of their goods"), it seems to be the case that force and cruelty properly wielded, rather than laws, would be commonly needed. [71] A prince should lean on the *populo*, just because it is safer to do so, and then play it, with *astuzia fortunata*, against the *grandi*. Whereas, admittedly, his prince was not intended to be "Machiavellian" in the ominous sense this word was to acquire later on, the utilitarian manner of perceiving the state and people, and the "heathen" nature of the concepts around which his reasoning revolves were major breaks from all Medieval thinking. The conceptual age of Absolutism presupposes however more than just this technical-instrumental bent on perceiving the proper use of power. It needs the very idea of the State, which will appear in the wake of Reformation, together with the notion that the State alone is the only locus of law. With the disappearance of common presuppositions regarding content, locating legitimacy solely in the source of law seemed to be the readily apparent and only solution.[72]

[69] Meinecke 1957, at *supra* note 36, p. 39. *See also*, Carl Schmitt, *La Dictature* (*Die Dikatur*), transl. Mira Köller & Dominique Séglard (Paris: Éditions du Seuil, 2000), p. 29: "Du rationalisme de cette technicité dérive d'abord le fait que l'artiste constructeur d'État considère la masse des homes, qu'il faut organiser en État, comme un objet à mettre en forme, c'est à dire comme un matériau." *Also see*, at p. 31: "La convérgence de ces trois éléments-rationalisme, téchnicité et pouvoir exécutif-, en direction de la dictature (le terme dictature est ici employé au sens d'une sorte de commandement qui, par principe, est indépendent du consentement ou de la compréhension du destinataire et n'attend pas son approbation) marque les débuts de l'État moderne." *Also see* Gierke, *Political Theories*, at p. 86: "During the Middle Age we can hardly detect even the beginnings of that opinion which would free the Sovereign (whenever he is acting in the interest of the public weal) from the bonds of the Moral Law in general, and therefore from the bonds of the Law of Nature. Therefore when Machiavelli based his lesson for Princes upon this freedom from restraint, this seemed to the men of his time an unheard of innovation and also a monstrous crime."

[70] Niccolò Machiavelli, *Il Principe* (*E Pagine Dei "Discorsi" E Delle "Istorie"*) A Cura Di Luigi Russo, Tredicesima Edizione (Firenze: G.C. Sansoni, Editore., 1973), Cap. XVIII: 2. "Dovete adunque sapere come sono dua generazioni di combattere: l'uno con le leggi, l'altro con la forza; quel primo è proprio dello uomo, quell secondo è delle bestie; ma, perché il primo molte volte non basta, convienne ricorrere al secondo."

[71] When he advises the prince not to touch property, Machiavelli adds the reason, "perché uomini sdimenticano piú presto la morte del padre che la perdita del patrimonio." Cap. XVII: 3, 45–50.

[72] "Thus, it has sometimes been argued that legal positivism first emerged as a strategy for stabilizing the ship of state in the tumult of religious wars. This can certainly be said of Bodin's attempt to locate legitimacy in the easily identifiable source, rather than the infinitely disputable content, of law." Stephen Holmes, *Passions and Constraint – On the Theory of Liberal*

What arises is an idea of law that can be spelled out as a series of identifications. Law is located in the state, equals positive law, which in turn is equated with a command, that is, with the will of the absolute sovereign. Jean Bodin, who famously defined sovereignty as "the absolute and perpetual power of a Republic," is usually credited with the inauguration of this simple and clear equation.[73] In contradiction with the characteristically medieval idea of law-finding, the first mark of sovereignty is in his rendition precisely legislative power. Custom exists only "by sufferance," universal principles of jurisprudence based on Roman law, the obsolete rules of a dead society, are absurd, legislative power as exercised by the prince does not need to secure any consent from the governed, the idea of a right to resistance or appeal from *loi* to *droit* is unthinkable. It would be a crime of leze majesty to oppose Roman law to the "ordinance of your king."[74] And the "ordonnance de son prince" is the law itself, since: "law implies command: law is nothing else but the command of the sovereign in the exercise of his power."[75] Yet Bodin still thinks within a medieval template, and thus in a somewhat contradictory manner, limitations are placed on the prince's legislative power (the divine and natural laws, property, the laws of the kingdom).[76] His "republic" is thought of in an organic and naturalist Aristotelian fashion, as an assemblage of many households, "plusieurs ménages."[77] Bodin cannot conceive of a contract between the prince and his *franc sujets*, since the contractually grounded right to resistance of the Monarchomachs is what he seeks to rule out. Meanwhile, however, he shares with the latter a common resentment towards Machiavelli's "poisonous" and "erroneous" doctrine.[78]

Democracy (Chicago: The University of Chicago Press, 1995), p. 106. *See*, relevant, the chapters on Hobbes and Bodin.

[73] "la puissance absolue et perpetuelle d'une République, que les Romains appellaient *majestas*" *Six Livres de la République*, I, 8, p. 122.

[74] *See* Friedrich 1968b, at p. 72: "In consequence, the citizen, called by Bodin *le franc sujet*, is bound to absolute obedience, except for a very limited religious sphere. In this connection, Bodin develops a sharp distinction between the *droit* and the *loi*, and insists that the citizen must not appeal from the *loi* to the *droit*, from the positive law to the law of nature."

[75] "La loi emporte commandement: car la loi n'est autre que le commandement du souverain usant sa puissance." *Six Livres de la République*, I, 8, p.155.

[76] The inconsistency or contradiction can be explained by the fact that, for Bodin, these normative limitations are considered internal rather than–as was the case for the Monarchomachs—external.

[77] *Six Livres de la République*, I, 2, p. 10. For the opinion that this reading of Aristotle came with the later interpretation by St. Thomas Aquinas, which blurred the original Aristotelian distinction between realm of the household and the realm of the political, *oikos* and *polis*, *see* Hannah Arendt, *The Human Condition* (Chicago: University of Chicago Press, 1958), *esp.* pp. 22–28.

[78] Bodin wrote at the peak of the Huguenot rebellion, and the book is intended to be both anti-Machiavelli and a reasoned defense of strong kingship, which could avert and keep in check both the Catholic League and the Huguenots. *See generally*, Quentin Skinner, *The Foundations of Modern Political Thought* (Vol. II-"The Age of Reformation") (Cambridge: Cambridge University Press, 1978), Chapter 8-"The Context of the Huguenot Revolution."

When, in 1632, Cardin Le Bret, the jurisprudent of Cardinal Richelieu, defines sovereignty as "no more divisible than the point of geometry,"[79] he synthesizes an absolutist logic come to ripeness. Conceptually, this presupposes a truly abstract reasoning, steeped in a paradigm dominated by voluntarism, rationalism, and a technical spirit, a cast of mind that finds its theoretical defense in Hobbes. The *Leviathan* can be seen as a point of ascription in a conceptual evolution of legislation. Hobbes sought, just like Bodin had attempted almost a century before him, to give a meaningful foundation for political and legal authority in the wake of the religious civil wars. His law is clearly a command and not "counsel," since "Auctoritas non Veritas, facit Legem." Reason could not possibly offer a solid mooring because any man has a different one, and Hobbes scoffs, in anticipation of Bentham's "nonsense upon stilts," at the notion of "Lawes of Nature" as unwritten law, "whereof wee see so many volumes published, and in them so many contradictions of one another, and of themselves."[80] Since law is command, all substantive limitations on legislation (the Rule of Law qualitative constraints which lie at the heart of constitutionalism, most notably generality) are dismissed cavalierly: "[e]very man seeth, that some lawes are addressed to all the subjects in general, some to particular Provinces, some to particular Vocations, and some to particular Men."[81] For Hobbes, if and when a statute is general, it presents this form by natural necessity or purely instrumental utility, when addressed to classes of persons, directing them to perform or refrain from performing kinds of actions.

Legal command is grounded in will. Will, a subjective state of mind, needs by inference to be undivided; it rejects a priori all normative limitations deriving from reason or truth, deliberation and considered consent. Custom only exists, just like in Bodin's account, because the sovereign permits it to continue, by tacit acquiescence. Hobbes is particularly explicit in exemplifying what he means with precision, so that no shade of doubt could subsist: "COMMAND is where a man saith, *Doe this*, or *Doe not this*, without expecting other reason than the Will of him that sayes it."[82] Law is positive law and the Legislator, "one Man" or "one Assembly of men" is "only the Soveraign. . .he that maketh the Law."[83] Himself, he would prefer

[79] In Mohnhaupt 1972, at p. 201.

[80] Thomas Hobbes, *Leviathan* (Everyman's Library edition, New York: E. P. Dutton and Company, Inc, London: J. M. Dent and Sons, Limited, 1950), Chap. XXVI, Of CIVILL LAWES, p. 147. In this sense, Gerald J. Postema, "Law as Command: The Model of Command in Modern Jurisprudence," 35 *Noûs* 470 (October 2001), at 471: "It is especially noteworthy that Hobbes made a special point of conceding that the Laws of Nature he defended (for example in Leviathan, chs. 14 and 15) are not *proper laws*, but 'only Conclusions, or Theoremes concerning what conduceth to the conservation and defence of [men].' They can be regarded properly as laws, he argued, only 'if we consider the same Theoremes, as delivered in the word of God, that by right commanded all things'" [emphasis in original] For Hobbes, even Divine Commands are only resting, ultimately, on God's "irresistible power." [*De Cive*, 15:5].

[81] *Id.*, Chap. XXVI, Of CIVILL LAWES.

[82] *Ibid.*, Chap. XXV, Of COUNSELL, p 134.

[83] *Ibid.*, Chap. XXVI, Of CIVILL LAWES, pp. 140–141.

"one Man," since deliberation in making the law is not a positive occurrence in the least. It brings 'Inconstancy from the Number' and while "...a Monarch cannot disagree with himselfe, out of envy, or interest; [but] an Assembly may; and that to such a height, as may produce a Civill Warre."[84] But once there is no difference in principle between the sovereign and government, even though Hobbes was partial towards monarchy, it ultimately mattered very little, in the logic and future development of the argument, which the sovereign was.

Hobbes is the first to neatly and consistently divorce the state and law from a divine will or divine reason grounding and the first that could have truly stated what Grotius or Leibniz later entertained merely as a figure of style or purely theoretical hypothesis. His consistent system of thought can assess and justify law even if God did not exist.[85] God and theology become ancillary to the general argument or simple metaphors. They appear at most in the nature of remote causes of a man-made order that stands above all other orders, grounded in the absolute will of the sovereign and justified by the absolute survival interest of the individual. The commonwealth becomes thus an *animal artifficiale*, an *automaton* or a *machina machinarum,* the machine of all machines, animated by the sovereign-representative. In this sense, Hobbes is an unwilling forerunner of a modern rationalism that assumes the State "to be a mechanical contrivance, which may be taken to pieces and manufactured afresh by every Abbé Siéyès who arises."[86] Given the embryo of individualism and utilitarianism in the *Leviathan* (reason itself is, we are reminded, *Ratio*, *Addition* and *Subtraction*, mathematical calculation), he is also a forerunner of one type of modern rationalism that implies the future steps from his "mechanically contrived state of advantage and expediency" to the moment where the citizen becomes a consumer of the modern state.[87] His thought makes it easier to see from hindsight how law came to be regarded as representing either the product-command of an absolute will or, conversely, a rational tool, explicitly made, which can be intentionally used to effect discrete changes into the world.

Hobbes's account was undoubtedly influenced by the historical realization, during the struggle for supremacy between Charles I and the forces behind the Long Parliament, that laws are made by the sovereign and not found by a court.

[84] Chapter XIX, Of the severall Kinds of Common-wealth by Institution, and of Succession to the Soveraigne Power, p. 99.

[85] *See* Leo Strauss, *The Political Philosophy of Hobbes-Its Basis and Genesis*, transl. by Elsa M. Sinclair (Chicago and London: The University of Chicago Press, 1963), p. 129 ff.

[86] John Neville Figgis, *The Divine Right of Kings* (Gloucester, Mass.: Peter Smith, 1970), at p. 259.

[87] *See* Meinecke 1957, *supra* note 36, Chapter 8, "A Glance at Grotius, Hobbes and Spinoza," pp. 207–223.

Then, for the first time, the notion of legislative sovereignty struck men "with all the force of a discovery."[88] Legislation, as in fact all exercise of state power began to appear as a delegation-commission derived from this legally unfettered power. Yet the pure argument from sovereignty, namely that a normative limitation on positive law is logically absurd because a legal limitation on sovereignty is logically impossible, outstretched the confines of its historical context. Just a few decades before the Civil War, James I, that most "absolutist" of the Stuarts, was claiming in Parliament that the king could "cry up and downe" his loyal subjects, just "like men at the Chesse,"[89] and was admonishing the Courts not to question his prerogative by meddling with "the mysterie of the Kings power."[90] But, even as he strayed dangerously away from the characteristically medieval notions of kingship as office and king as the preeminent member of the body politic, he rested his authority solely on Divine Right and his own interpretation of tradition. Likewise, even after the Stuart Restoration, in 1660, the royalists summoned arguments similar to those later expounded in Sir Robert Filmer's *Patriarcha*, where kingship is presented as being paternal in nature and resting ultimately on divine ordinance. They regarded with just suspicion, and even hostility, a theory that legitimizes absolute, legally unfettered power solely on the basis of political abstractions. For the purpose of a better and more grounded understanding of this latter remark, pause should be briefly taken to illustrate with one example of actual public law history the transition we have been discussing thus far in point of theoretical developments.

---

[88] Figgis 1970, at p. 232.

[89] "Kings are justly called Gods, for they exercise a manner of resemblance of Diuine power upon earth: For if you consider the Attributes to God, you shall *see* how they agree in the person of a King. God hath power to create, or destroy, make, or unmake at his pleasure, to give life, or send death, to judge all, and to be judged nor accomptable no none, and to make things high low at his pleasure, and to God are both soule and body due. And the like power haue Kings. . . .They haue power to exalt low things, and abase high things, and make of their subjects like men at the Chesse: A pawne to take a bishop or a Knight, and to cry up or downe any of their subjects, as they do their money." "A Speach to the Lords and Commons of the Parliament at White-Hall, March 21, 1609," Works of James in Charles Howard McIlwain (ed.) *The Political Works of James I: Reprinted from the Edition of 1616* (Cambridge: Cambridge University Press, 1918), p. 529.

[90] "If there fall out a question that concernes my Prerogative or mysterie of State, deale not with it, till you consult with the King or his Counciell, or both: for they are transcendent matters. . . .That which concernes the mysterie of the Kings power, is not lawful to be disputed; for that is to wade into the weakness of Princes, and to take away the mysticall reverence, that belongs unto them that sit into the Throne of God." "A Speach in the Starre Chamber, The XX of June. Anno 1616," in McIlwain, *The Political Works of James I, supra* at pp. 332–333.

2.3.2 Rocher de Bronze: *A Historical Illustration*

> . . .ich komme zu meinen Zweg und stabiliere die Suverenitet und setze die Krone fest wie ein Rocher von Bronse und lasse die herren Junker den windt von Landt dahge.[91]
> Friedrich Wilhelm I

In France, the unitary, centralized administration gradually swept aside and rendered irrelevant all "intermediary powers," so that by the eve of the Revolution there was almost no institutional mediation between the subject and the irresistible power of the State. In contradistinction, some of the German principalities associated in the moribund Holy Roman Empire of German Nation preserved traces of legal medievalism as late as the beginning of the nineteenth century.[92]

The relationship between the territorial ruler of a given principality and his subjects was modeled on a medieval template by virtue of which the prince possessed, as a person,[93] the bundle of rights of superiority whose totality marked or constituted his territorial superiority (*Landeshoheit*).[94] All these rights and prerogatives extended until or were countered and limited by the validity of the legal just title presented in support of a given claim or pretension and the corresponding and opposed acquired rights (*jura quaesita, droits acquis*) of the subjects, just like in civil law the extension of a right finds its validity in the legal title presented to support it and the limit in the corresponding obligation and opposed right of another.[95] Even the prescription of rules of prospective applicability, legislation, was a prerogative of the given territorial ruler, limited in principle,

[91] "I will achieve my purpose and stabilize sovereignty and establish the crown as solid as a rock of bronze and will leave the gentlemen Junkers only the wind of the Landtag." In Heinrich Otto Meisner, "Staats- und Regierungsformen in Deutschland seit dem 16. Jahrhundert", 77 (2/3) *AöR* 225, at p. 229 (note 9) (1951/1952).

[92] *See* Carl Schmitt, *Théorie de la Constitution,* "Naissance de la constitution," pp. 177–193 and the chapter on Wallenstein and the problem of sovereignty in the Holy Roman Empire in *La dictature*.

[93] In the sense that he exercises rights of territorial preeminence in his own name and not as the embodiment or representative of the State.

[94] Otto Mayer, *Le droit administratif allemand,* Édition française par l'auteur (Paris: V. Giard & E. Brière, 1903), Vol. I, pp. 26–27: "Ce n'est pas l'Etat qui se trouve en présence des sujets; cette notion abstraite ne fera son apparition que plus tard, pour produire alors tout de suite un effet puissant. . .. Ces droits ne sont pas les manifestations d'une plénitude de puissance dans le sens des droits de l'Etat, tel que nous les comprendrons aujourd'hui; ils sont acquis chacun séparément, l'un après l'autre, à des titres différents, aquis d'un côté vis-à-vis de l'Empire, comme démembrements de la puissance originaire de l'Empereur, acquis d'un autre côté vis-à-vis des *sujets, qui, en principe, sont reputes francs et libres de toute charge et ne sont soumis au prince qu'en tant qu'il peut produire contre eux un titre juridique.*" [emphasis added].

[95] Acquired rights are not perceived as derivations from an originally unlimited natural liberty of the individual but as legal rights derived from special title: "non infringere liceat jus quaesitum, i.e., nifallor, quod speciali titulo acquiritur, non ex solo libertate naturaliter obtinet." (In Mayer, *supra*, FN 13, p. 32).

just like any other exercises of power.[96] In case of a conflict, after the exhaustion of internal remedies, one could appeal for a judicial decision on a given conflict to the two Imperial tribunals, constituted in 1495 and 1501, the *Reichskammergericht* and the *Reichshofrat*.[97]

In the late absolutist transition to the police state (whose well-known epitome is Prussia), the legal paradigm appears surrounded by a changed theoretical justification and attended by dissimilar practical consequences. The king is seen now more often as only the representative or the embodiment of a State that admits of no legal limitation.[98] As the final judge of the public interest or public utility, the king can, in principle and in theory, intervene in any domain by a direct exercise of an act of sovereignty: "C'est au prince qu'appartient en propre la tâche immense de poursuivre le but de l'Etat. Si la nature humaine le permettrait, seul il ferait tout. . . .Vis-à-vis des sujets, son pouvoir n'a pas de limites de droit; ce qu'il veut est obligatoire."[99] Even the existence of an autonomous private law appears, again at least in principle, as a self-imposed limitation from which derogations are possible at any time.[100] In what goes outside the purview of strictly private relationships between individuals and concerns directly the public relationship between State and citizen (e.g., taxation, military affairs, police regulations), there are, in Otto Mayer's concise description, public laws but there is no public law: "il n'y a pas de droit public."[101] A police ordinance was for all respects and purposes issued as an order. It was made public for purely instrumental reasons and not for considerations of justice and was only general since an order, when addressed and meant to be obeyed by a larger group of individuals, needs of natural necessity to embrace a general form. Since there is no legal limitation or remedy, public law appears in the form of a commission limited only internally (from the point of view of the administrative mechanism of enforcement) and unlimited

[96] *Id.*, at p. 33, note 15: "Le droit acquis est une barrière pour la législation du prince aussi bien que pour ses actes individuels; la législation n'est pas, comme aujourd'hui, une manifestation spécialement caracterisé de la volonté souveraine; c'est l'exercise d'une prerogative comme les autres."

[97] *See Ibid.*, pp. 15–42, for a number of qualifications to this account and an interesting list of excerpts from the jurisprudence of the *Reichskammergericht*. For instance, at p. 32, note 13, the example is given of a refusal by the government of Hanover to grant a residence permit, quashed for lack of reasons.

[98] *Ibid*, at p. 43: "L'idée de l'Etat apparaît au premier plan. Ce n'est pas pour soi-même ni en vertu d'une prerogative qui lui appartient, que le prince prétend à tout cela; c'est au nom de la personne idéale dont il est représentant."

[99] *Ibid*, at p. 44.

[100] In time, strictly financial disputes in which the State is a party will be incorporated into private law and submitted to the jurisdiction of the civil courts, by the means of a fiction, the "doctrine of the Fisc." In virtue of this doctrine, the State, in purely financial litigations, dealing with the mine and thine characteristic of the private law, becomes a different moral person, the Fisc, subordinated to and commanded by the State-as-Sovereign ("the political association, the moral person of public law") to submit to private litigation as a private person. (*see* Mayer, at pp. 55–63).

[101] Mayer, at p. 53.

externally (from the point of the view of the subjects, who, in this regard, appear purely as the objects of an exercise of public power).

And yet, justifications of paramount power need to be perceived in and cut down to their proper context. This is not just a matter of the technical possibilities of realization, related to the still sparing means by which power could in fact be exercised. Central bureaucratic organs certainly existed but the absolute state was still highly dependent, for the implementation of its decrees, on intermediary, non-state powers. For instance, in German principalities, the mandates, edicts, orders of the prince were publicized by means of having the local preachers read them from the pulpit, up until the 1800s.[102] It is primarily, and more importantly, an issue of conceptual context. The rationalism implicit in the newly emergent ideas of sovereignty and state was dampened until the late eighteenth and beginning of the nineteenth century by the lagging organicist way of perceiving law and the state. The primary meaning of police was until the late eighteenth century that of good order, meaning in most cases not externally imposed but the past, "natural" order or course of things. Many police orders duplicated in fact the status quo, by decreeing for instance the proper behavior during church attendance or the address of an apprentice toward the master, regulating the wearing of luxury clothing in order to maintain proper distinctions between the various estates, or curtailing the importation of such goods: "The new [administrative and police] state detached in time the individual from his local and social power structures; but it still thought in terms of closed social spheres. It replaced the bilateral process of law-creation [characteristic of the Middle Ages], in which law appears as a result of a struggle between partners, by the unilateral order of the prince. But it did not yet achieve the modern form of clearly dividing private and public law, in which the demands of the state and of the individual are settled so to speak against each other. It rather remained trapped within the dualisms of the older social structure (claim and power, right and duty)...in which a concrete status-oriented way of thinking subsisted."[103]

In other words: in order to change the world by legislative and administrative means, one has to be able to see, to imagine the law and administration as mechanisms, as rational tools fully exterior to their environment, rather than embedded in it. Such an external viewpoint was not proper to the age. The beginnings of a detachment and replacement of the old eudaemonistic primary meaning of police (promotion of good harmony and public welfare) by the fully modern one of prevention of future harms can be traced back in both practice and theories to 1770.[104] But "Police Science" (*Policeywissenschaft*) remained a science of "good policy" lodged in a practical philosophy partly indebted to medieval-

---

[102] Maier 1966, at p. 187 *note* 244 and associated text.

[103] *Id.*, at p. 94. *Also see* Franz-Ludwig Knemeyer, "Polizeibegriffe in Gesetzen des 15. bis 18. Jahrhunderts – Kritische Bemerkungen zur Literatur über die Entwicklung des Polizeibegriffs," 92 (2) *AöR* 153 (1967).

[104] *Ibid.*, at p. 198.

Aristotelian categories and incorporating in an amalgamated, indistinct form, philosophy, public law, administration proper, economy, and political science until much later. This conceptual syncretism subsisted up until the mid-nineteenth century, when it started to clash head-on with those now "value-free rationalized" and thus scientifically individualized new academic disciplines. Late echoes of this struggle can still be found in 1832, when Robert von Mohl expresses evident discomfort with the equation or reduction of police science (*Polizeiwissenschaft*) and police law (*Polizeirecht*): "Who would like to live in a state that only exercises justice but provides no police help?"[105]

This last remark is already anticipating too much the substance of later discussions. Suffice it to point out in the closing of this one, as exemplary for the way in which the power of facts lagged behind rational representations of power, the tense, ambivalent relation between the advancing Age of Reason and absolutism. On the one hand, an absolute monarch seemed to be the ideal executor of the dictates of reason: "Rationalization of the state and modernization on the one hand and the enlightenment optimistic ideology of progress on the other went together for a very long stretch."[106] But there was no guarantee that he would not intervene again in a newly created, "enlightened" order of affairs. This unease was not just an expression of the eternal constitutional problem (constituant-constituted power) but also a necessarily deepening rift between ontologically different kinds of rationality and perceptions of authority. When Frederick the Great, in spite of the solemn assurances in his *Political Testament* "never again to trouble the course of procedure" intervened swiftly with a *Machtspruch* in favor of the miller Arnold and quashed a judicial decision, the ensuing outcry and commotion among the finer classes of society was caused much more by the clashing orders of reason and essential representations of justice than by the actual merits of Friedrich's decision.[107]

2.4 Reason Unbound: Two Faces of the Enlightenment

> La condition meme de ces écrivains les préparait à goûter les theories générales et abstraites en matière de gouvernement et à s'y confier aveuglément. Dans l'éloignement presque infini où ils vivaient de la pratique, aucune expérience ne venaint tempérer les ardeurs de leur naturel...
>
> Alexis de Tocqueville, *L'Ancien Régime et la Révolution*

[105] *Ibid.* pp. 247–248.

[106] Barbara Stollberg-Rillinger, *Europa im Jahrhundert der Aufklärung* (Stuttgart: Reclam, 2000), p. 206.

[107] "je me suis résolu à ne jamais troubler le cours de la procedure: c'est dans les tribunaux où les lois doivent parler et où le souverain doit se taire." (in Schmitt, *La Dictature*, at p. 303, note 43). *See*, on the events surrounding the miller Arnold case, David M. Luebke, "Frederick the Great and the Celebrated Case of the Millers Arnold (1770–1779)-A Reappraisal," 32 (4) *Central European History* 379 (1999).

> I have become entangled in my own data, and my conclusions directly contradict my original premises. I started out with the idea of unrestricted freedom and I have arrived at unrestricted despotism. I must add, however, that any solution of the social problem other than mine is logically impossible.
>
> Shigalyov[108]

The Enlightenment is, to be sure, a very abused word, perhaps the biggest simultaneous synecdoche and metonymy of all times. One can refer to it in order to praise or scold almost everything under the sun since the germ of everything that is conspicuously modern, in thought and experience, can be found in that age; the dictatorship of absolute values in Leibniz as well as the empathetic fascination for the local particularity and the exotic at Bougainville; the fanatically optimistic visions of progress through science in Condorcet's *Historical Sketch* and the outlandish naturalism of progress-pessimism in Rousseau's *Discourse on Inequality*; the beginnings of a militant atheism as well as of purist versions of faith, radically averse to the Age of Reason; the adoration of science and of the lights of intellect (*les Lumières*) as well as the fetishizing of the secretive, esoteric, and occult. Sometimes one can note irreconcilable tensions within the work of the one and same author. Montesquieu exemplifies ideally this ambivalence, with his fine but fragile balance between the extraction of universals, of essences ("the spirit of laws") pertaining to a certain regime, on the one hand, and the constant about-faces toward the sociological determinations influencing a given order, on the other.

A careful account should therefore be given for the general reference and the selection to follow. The Enlightenment is a crucial crossroads in the history of legislation concepts, since only in that age did it become possible to think of law and legal systems in a purely abstract, deductive fashion, in a "mathematical" or "geometrical" way. The idea comes to full fruition, namely, that "what concerns law and justice *in themselves* cannot be derived from the experience."[109] More importantly, it becomes now possible to "manufacture" rationally the premises from which the line of deductions starts. This is primarily, but not only, due to the infinite uses to which the Enlightenment-specific concept of "nature" lent itself. What was "natural" for Hobbes (survival and the desire to preserve one's life by trading for social safety the natural freedom to live a "solitary, poor, nasty, brutish, and short" life in the wild, i.e., obedience in exchange for protection) still had an empirical kind of commonsensical anthropological concreteness, an almost palpably natural dimension attached to it. A century later, the state that is "natural" becomes a purely discretionary material by means of which the designer can

---

[108] One of the characters in Dostoyevsky's *The Possessed* (New York: Signet Classics, 1962 ed.), pp. 384–385.

[109] Emphasis supplied. Ernst Cassirer, *Die Philosophie der Aufklärung* (Hamburg: Felix Meiner, 2007), p. 248. *See also*, on law and "geometrical" thinking, M. H. Hoeflich, "Law & Geometry: Legal Science from Leibniz to Langdell," 30 (2) *The American Journal of Legal History* 95 (Apr., 1986).

build an entire legal and political system, like a demiurge. Thus, splinters of rationality grow from nothingness into complete rational worlds, against the mirror image of which the fundamental legal reality as such can already in imagination be created and recreated anew. Rousseau and Bentham illustrate this metamorphosis as conceptual epitomes. They hypostasize the two relevant extremes of reason unbound: the elated utopian redemption project in Rousseau and the detailed and obsessive dystopian outlook of social engineering in Bentham. These are only at a first and superficial glance distinct. In essence, nonetheless, the exaltation of lost virtues by Rousseau and the nitty-gritty Benthamite tendency towards regulating life into its furthest nooks and crannies are very much alike, Janus-faced examples of self-subverting rationality.

In France, the Absolutist state had, by the eighteenth century, reduced government to a highly effective royal administration, centralized in Paris and functioning through subordinated levels of jurisdiction (*Conseil du Roi*, *intendants*, *subdélégués*). Deliberation regarding public affairs, whose practical role in state administration had shrunk progressively, had by necessity been moved into the space of purely intellectual discussion, in the realm of the *République des Lettres*. By then, Medieval orders and in fact all intermediary orders had become almost devoid of any self-government functions and autonomous mediating influence, reduced to mere ceremonial and ornamental roles. Even the sphere of competence of the courts of law, the *parlements,* had come to be increasingly encroached upon by the administrative jurisdiction of the *Conseil* in Paris. For instance, by the 1720s, at the time when Montesquieu was a senior judge, one of the *Présidents à Mortier* of the Bordeaux Parliament, the few attempts made to exercise, through the procedure of the *remonstrance*, the control of the legality of royal ordinances, were motivated by narrow caste interests.[110] By the dawn of the French Revolution, the Estates-General had not been summoned for the better part of two centuries.[111]

All these factors resulted in a total lack of any practical sense of self-government, merged however with a deep belief in the independent task-solving capacity

[110] The *parlements*, sovereign medieval courts (by the seventeenth century, offices could be transmitted by inheritance or even sold; Montesquieu, for instances, inherited his judgeship from his great-uncle in 1716 and sold it in 1728) administered justice according to custom and positive law, i. e., properly registered royal ordinances (*ordonnances*). Registration was however not a mere formality and every now and again a *parlement* would exercise control of legality (*remonstrance*) and refuse to register an ordinance. Sometimes the issue would be submitted to the king, who would decide with finality on the matter (the procedure was called *lit de justice*) and sometimes—very often—their judgments were simply ignored by the *intendants* or the parliament's *exequendus* would be prevented from enforcing a court order by the royal officers. The issue went back and forth, yet with fewer and fewer attempts to assert the *droit de remonstrance* during the seventeenth and eighteenth century. Louis XIV, in the edict of Saint-Germain (1641) and then again in 1661 expressly forbade the Parliaments to touch on any matters "qui peuvent concerner l'Etat, administration et gouvernement d'icelui." *See* Mayer, at pp. 67–68. *See, also*, on pre-Revolutionary control of administration, François Bourdeau, *Histoire du droit administratif (de la Révolution au début des années 1970)* (Paris: Presses Universitaires de France, 1995), pp. 29–40.

[111] Since 1614, to be precise. Grimm, *Souveränität*, at p. 27.

of the State. In the telling phrase of one Physiocrat, Bodeau: "The state makes of people what it wishes."[112] Coupled with the adoration of the *Lumières* for capitalized Reason, this led to an unfathomable desire in Enlightenment thought to harness this might and efficiency of the State, and thereafter uses it vicariously through—how else?—"Enlightened" legislation. Power would need to be united and, since the "Gothic" architecture of the Medieval orders could only hamper effectiveness, past hindrances like tradition and intermediary orders (the *parlements,* for instance) needed to be eradicated with a clean sweep. In Tocqueville's words: "the diversity as such is hideous to them: they loved liberty into servitude. Everything that embarrasses their designs must be smashed. Contractes inspire little respect, private right none, but solely a public usefulness."[113] This way, the task of restoring lost virtue by recreating and perfecting the people would be easily fulfilled, through positive legislation enacted rationally according to one single plan, enforced dictatorially by the absolute state, now to be converted and made subservient to absolute reason: "There is no question about destroying this absolute power, it must only be converted. 'The state should govern according to the rules of the essential order,' says Mercier de la Rivière', 'and when it does so, then it must be omnipotent.'"[114] The problem of government is thus reduced to the matter of replacing the hideous tyrant, his *despotisme arbitraire*, with an enlightened despotism of the positive law, *le despotisme légal.*[115] In order to be effective in translating into reality eccentric schemes of custodial legislation, power needs to remain undivided. The issue is not legislation reflecting the people's interests, not political freedom and guaranteeing equal, active shares in the government, but educational redemption of the people from the corrupted state in which they were allegedly steeped. There is a huge cleavage of perception between a Montesquieu interested in the English art of safeguarding political liberty through pragmatic institutional arrangements of dividing power and his roughly contemporary compatriot Voltaire, who travels to England as well, admires Scottish empiricism, marvels at the London Chamber of Commerce, yet manages to write in his diary no word at all about the English Parliament.

This abstract-literary politics, the *politique abstraite et littéraire* that Tocqueville so insightfully describes and rightly abhors in his *Old Regime and the Revolution*

[112] "L'Etat fait des hommes tout ce qu'il veut." In Alexis de Tocqueville, *Oeuvres complètes*, Tome II, *L'Ancien Régime et la Révolution* (Paris: Librairie Gallimard, 1952), p. 212.

[113] ". . .la diversité même leur est odieuse: ils adoreraient l'égalité jusque dans la servitude. Ce qui les gêne dans leurs desseins n'est bon qu'à briser. Les contrats leur inspirent peu de respect; les droits privés, nuls égards; ou plutôt il n'y a déjà plus à leurs yeux, à bien parler, des droits privés, mais seulement une utilité publique." *Id.*, p. 210. Public utility or the public interest is taken as something self-evident, an axiomatic value.

[114] "Il ne s'agit donc pas de détruire ce pouvoir absolu, mais de le convertir. 'Il faut que l'Etat gouverne suivant les règles de l'ordre essentiel', dit Mercier de la Rivière, 'et quand il en est ainsi, il faut qu'il soit tout-puissant.'" *Id.*, p 212.

[115] Schmitt 2000, at p. 114, on Le Mercier de la Rivière: "*La théorie des contre-forces est une chimère*. Dicter des loi positives, c'est commander, et la force publique, sans laquelle toute législation est impuissante, est comprise dans cet acte." [emphasis supplied].

finds an extreme exemplification in Rousseau's vision of legislation. The *Social Contract* fuses at the hip all the Enlightenment idiosyncrasies with an irrationalism of absolute will already implicit in Hobbes.[116] Just like the absolute sovereign of Thomas Hobbes needed only recognition through a social contract of subjection, Rousseau's *general will* is solely grounded in a *contrat d'association.*[117] Liberal constitutionalism presupposes two merged contracts, one of association, by which society is created, another of subjection, by which the state is separated from society and limited in its scope. This type of argument is explicit in Locke, and its direct and logical consequence is a further limitation of state by some form of functional separation of powers. The artifice of obscuring the dual nature of the social contract and conflating it into the powerful yet fallacious fiction of one single form allows Rousseau (and Hobbes) to define sovereignty and its expression, legislation, on the template of one, undivided will. By way of consequence, Rousseau derides attempts to limit and break sovereign power both in principle and in object. In a telling paragraph, by means of a rather strange allegory, he compares theoretical endeavors to reconcile sovereignty with the separation of powers with the tricks of the "swindlers of Japan" who would allegedly cut a child into pieces, throw it in the air and then have it fall back on the ground "reassembled" again.[118]

In the writing of this romantic deist, just like the God of deism is omnipotent yet never actually intervenes, Rousseau's beloved people, apparently the main actor in his play, is turned into an abstraction that populates the whole book in a confusing and disquieting form of cloak-and-dagger drama, yet never materializes or is substantiated in any way. "The people" expresses itself by means of legislation, expression of the general will. Since this will, a subjective, unattached, fluctuating yet undivided state of mind, is by no means an aggregation of interests lodged in the individuals, Rousseau rules out the possibility of translating it through legislation enacted by representative assemblies. In a book otherwise replete with ambiguities and contradictions, the prohibition against representative government is explicitly spelled out. The English think they are free but their freedom is only real on Election Day, afterwards they are mere slaves, they become nothing.[119]

[116] Leo Strauss is certainly right when pointing out that: "The holder of the sovereign power is not the 'head', that is, the capacity to deliberate and plan, but the 'soul' that is, the capacity to command, in the State. There is only a step from this to Rousseau's theory that the origin and seat of sovereignty is *la volonté générale*. Rousseau made completely clear the break with rationalism which Hobbes had instituted." Strauss 1963, at 160.

[117] Jean-Jacques Rousseau, *Du Contrat Social ou Principes du Droit Politique*, in *Oeuvres Choisies* (Paris: Éditions Garnier Frères, 1962), Chap. XVI, at 304: "Il n'y a qu'un contrat dans l'État, c'est celui de l'association: celui-là seul en exclut tout autre. On ne sauroit imaginer aucun contrat public qui ne fût une violation du premier."

[118] *Id.*, Chap. II, at 251.

[119] "Les députés du people ne sont que ses commissaires; ils ne peuvent rien conclure définitivement. Toute loi que le peuple en personne n'a pas ratifiée est nulle; ce n'est point une loi. Le peuple anglois pense être libre, il se trompe fort; il ne l'est que durant l'éléction des membres du parlement: sitôt qu'ils sont élus, il est esclave, il n'est rien." *Ibid.*, Chap. XV, at p. 302.

Perceiving Rousseau's *Social Contract* as a project of virtue rather than democracy dispels some of the confusion.[120] He identifies his model of legislation with Sparta, not Athens, and explicitly states that Corsica, a country less tainted by modern civilization, with simple morals, somewhat isolated from the continent, etc., would be the ideal place for concretizing the social contract. This virtue-oriented penchant also explains the peculiar choice for a Legislator, who poses the legislation that will redeem the people, transforming the pre-contractual human, "a stupid and limited animal," into "an intelligent being and a man."[121] In this reading, legislation becomes a rigid moral code, which would foster and preserve virtue, slowing down what Rousseau believed to have been an otherwise continuous process of moral degeneration. But in this way, Rousseau's democracy and legislation are turned perversely into justificatory abstractions, to be used by proxy and turned into the will and project of whoever can ably claim to concretize them and identify his particular model of intentionality and/or virtue with the people's general will. Little wonder that the book served, on the one hand, as the "Bible of the Jacobins" during the Terror and, on the other hand, gave Napoleon a reason to picture himself as the mythical Legislator.

If Rousseau turns the Hobbesian sovereign willfulness into the irrationality of a "mask of virtue," Bentham represents the twin face of distorted Enlightenment. He takes two intimations entertained by Hobbes and reverts their logic. If will was preeminent in Hobbes, because reason is detrimental, leaving too much place for dissimilar conceptions of the good, in Bentham reason is sublimated, reduced to extreme rationalism, utilitarian rational thinking, so that will becomes just a means to enforce it. Bentham fuses thus the model of law as command lodged in the will with the germ of calculative, instrumental rationality implicit albeit only latent and dimly visible in the *Leviathan*.[122] The result is another account of legislation that epitomizes and streamlines law-making into the "Procrustean form of individual intentionality."[123]

Benthamite studies do not exhibit the eerie penchant of the French *philosophes-economistes* (or Rousseau's) to discuss law and legislation in totally abstract, ungrounded terms. Contrariwise, he is very interested in the instrumentalities, in coherent drafting, promulgation, interpretation, spells out deficiencies in actual statutes, points to detail, makes minutely detailed proposals *de lege ferenda*. On more than one occasion, he actually takes statutes of the Hanoverian Parliaments

---

[120] Arendt, On Revolution, pp. 68–94, and Stephen Holmes, *Benjamin Constant and the Making of Modern Liberalism* (New Haven and London: Yale University Press, 1984), *esp.* chapter three, "Rousseau and the Masks of Virtue," pp. 79–103.

[121] *Ibid.*, Chap. VIII, at 247.

[122] Henry Sumner Maine, *Lectures on the Early History of Institutions* (Whitefish, Mont.: Kessinger, 2004), p. 201: "No geniuses of an equally high order so completely divorced themselves from history as Hobbes and Bentham, or appear, to me at all events, so completely under the impression that the world has always been more or less as they saw it."

[123] Jeremy Waldron, *Law and Disagreement* (Oxford: Oxford University Press, 1999), at p. 43.

and sedulously shows how the ideally well-drafted legislation should look like. He is more than happy to have his reader see how a law on stealing sheep, for instance, can be cut down, logically, so that at the end, after he has weeded out redundant verbosity, one is left with forty-some articles out of the initial number of over 300. This meticulous, but somewhat exasperating, interest in legislative drafting and more generally in detail is probably what prompted Marx's contempt to 'the metaphysics of an English shopkeeper.' [124]Yet, while Marx's scorn is in form undeservedly harsh, if we try to see past the detailed legal-technical aspects, Jeremy Bentham's account of legislation is in fact primarily metaphysics. He exhibits the Enlightenment strand of thought antipodean to utopian exaltation, namely geometric thinking according to one unified rational plan. Instrumental rationalism is reason in the Hobbesian understanding, *Ratio*, mathematical calculation, *Addition/Subtraction*. Bentham grafts it onto the principle of utility.

He has built only on the foundation of utility, Bentham writes to Voltaire in 1776. This implies "setting out, in all the operations of the judgment, from the calculation or comparison of pains and pleasures, and in not allowing the interference of any other idea."[125] Legislation needs to be drafted starting from a point of ascription, the principle of utility, and then broken down into actual command-rules, through the method of "bifurcation." All laws are commands, and therefore, for him, each legal provision contains in itself two laws, one *principal* and *normative*, and, backing the former, explicitly or implicitly, a *punitive* law which sanctions disobedience to the normative command. It is crucial to translate the principle of utility into positive law, into legislation drafted and promulgated according to—and Bentham is relentless in stressing this—one unified plan, so that: "in a map of law executed upon such a plan there are no *terrae incognitae*, no blank spaces: nothing is at least omitted, nothing unprovided for."[126] Once we undertake this task, that is, once parliament understands the principle and legislates accordingly, all uncertainties will be solved. So far mankind has been wading cheerfully through the filth of confusion: badly drafted laws, conflicting, unclear legislation. Once his project is understood properly, salvation is at hand. Unsurprisingly, therefore, what Bentham resented the most was not parliamentary law-making (which as a matter of fact did exhibit in his time most of the evils he

---

[124] In addition to the primary sources, I am largely relying, in my interpretation of Bentham, on Gerald J. Postema, *Bentham and the Common Law Tradition* (Oxford: Clarendon Press, 1986), and David Lieberman, *The Province of Jurisprudence Determined-Legal Theory in Eighteenth-Century Britain* (Cambridge: Cambridge University Press, 1989).

[125] Jeremy Bentham, *Theory of Legislation* (London: Truebner & Co., MDCCCLXXI), at p. 3.

[126] Jeremy Bentham, *Limits of Jurisprudence Defined-Of Laws in General*, edited by H.L.A. Hart (London: University College of London, Athlone Press, 1970), at 246.

tried to eradicate). He was primarily opposed to the common law, because the common law, by its apparently unsystematic existence grounded in the past, is resistant to absolute prediction and evades the equation-like overall structure in which Bentham wanted to fit all law.[127] Common law literally irked him: it is the *irrational* prejudice and power of "Judge and Company," not a science at all. Historical-traditional accounts are more generally found repellent and Bentham is self-admittedly closer to Voltaire and Helvetius than to Coke or Blackstone. His interest lies in having Parliament disciplined and enacting his ideal model of what legislation should be, not in observing how the legislature came about in his own country, or under what conditions humans can adopt good laws for themselves through representative assemblies.

He never considered apparently that, perhaps, utility is not a given, fixed point of reference from which codes can stretch out into punctilious detail, but rather might fluctuate in a directly proportional manner with interests, individual or unattached, and thus it can only be assessed through the intermediary mechanism of representation. Gerald Postema cites an interesting passage in which Bentham, writing about the common law calls it "Dog law": "When your dog does anything you want to break him of, you wait till he does it, and then beat him for it. This is the way you make laws for your dog: and this is the way the judges make law for you and me. They won't tell a man beforehand what is it he *should not do*...they lie by till he has done something which they say he should not *have done*, and then hang him for it."[128] But then the *Pannomion* is as liberating as the *Panopticon*.[129] Bentham's own account of legislation, modeled on rational command, predicated upon the assumption of one enlightened mind, in spiteful neglect of individual volition, boils down to just a different form of (ostensibly milder, scientific, enlightened) "Dog Law."

[127] One could draw an interesting analogy between the Benthamite paradigm and Roscoe Pound's later criticism of the common law in "Common Law and Legislation," Vol. XXI *Harvard Law Review* No. 6 (April, 1908), pp. 383–407.

[128] [emphasis in original] Cited by Postema 1986, at p. 277.

[129] What interested Bentham most, perhaps to the point of absurdity, was rational, coherent, gap-proof systematization of human conduct in positive law, hence his life-time obsession with "a law...meaning one entire but single law" (*Introduction to the Principle of Morals and Legislation,* Chapter XVII, 29), a complete code which he called, suggestively, *Pannomion*: hence his obsession with eliminating all things 'irrational,' most notably the common law. Gerald Postema notes that Bentham differs from other command theorists, to the extent that, in his account, the 'directive role' of positive law is supplemented by the "epistemic role of law in society...Law's fundamental task was to facilitate the coordination of social interaction." (at p. 493) That is true only to the extent that one takes into consideration the basic template of Bentham's narrative. For Bentham, law 'facilitates human interaction' only since and insofar as positive law is the product of a rational science, a directive or dictate of rationality translated into positive law.

2.5 Reason, Within Limits: Legislation in Constitutionalism and the Delegation Concept

> It hath sovereign and uncontrollable authority in the making, confirming, enlarging, restraining, abrogating, repealing, reviving, and expounding of laws, concerning matters of all possible denominations, ecclesiastical or temporal, civil, military, maritime, or criminal: this being the place where that absolute despotic power, which must in all governments reside somewhere, is intrusted by the constitution of these kingdoms.
>
> Sir William Blackstone, *Commentaries on the Laws of England* (Bk. 1, Chapter 2: Of the Parliament)

> There is nothing which so generally strikes the imagination, and engages the affections of mankind, as the right of property; or that sole and despotic dominion which one man claims and exercises over the external things of the world, in total exclusion of the right of any other individual in the universe.
>
> Sir William Blackstone, *Commentaries on the Laws of England* (Bk. 2, Chapter 1: Of Property, in General)

Even though the "constitutionalist" idea of fettering the exercise of power by legal and institutional limitations largely predates the actual emergence of the concept, the term as such began to be used in the course of the nineteenth century, in reference to a new intellectual and practical reality: the modern normative constitution.[130] This late eighteenth century innovation differed from its older, descriptive counterpart, in that it was a legal document laden with considerable rationality requirements and charged with foundational tasks. The constitution had to literally constitute, *i.e.*, to predetermine and integrate, both the political life and the entire legal system underneath it; the modern fundamental law is one of the most daring and in retrospect successful achievements of the Age of Reason.[131] Yet this was from the beginning also a project of limited or bounded rationality, straddling two worlds: the newly found audacity in using the power of human thought to self-consciously shape reality and the older tradition of perceiving fundamental laws as embedded in an order perceived and premised as given, as natural. Both the existence as such of the constitution and the proper functioning of its legal limitations presupposed from the onset a number of clear distinctions deriving from this foundational dichotomy. The notion of legislative delegation is conceptually incidental to those distinctions, whereas constitutional and administrative practices associated with it are epiphenomenal to the existence and preservation of those

---

[130] András Sajó, *Limiting Government-An Introduction to Constitutionalism* (Budapest: Central European University Press, 1999), at p. 9: "At the beginning of the nineteenth century, when people began referring to this concept, constitutionalism was an intellectual trend that could be relatively well-defined; but it is clear that it did not have, nor will it have, an unambiguous schoolbook definition." For a historical study of the tradition of constitutionalism as a limitation on political power, *see* Charles Howard McIlwain's *Constitutionalism, Ancient and Modern* (Ithaca, NY: Cornell University Press, 1940).

[131] *See* Dieter Grimm, "The Constitution in the Process of Denationalization," 12 *Constellations* 447 (2005).

demarcations. And just as the original intellectual environment of the constitution reflects the notion of delegation, the concept of delegation illuminates the conditions of the possibility of post-Enlightenment constitutionalism.

As it was pointed out at the beginning of this book, delegation has a metaphorical character: it takes on different meanings, according to different understandings of legislation that proceed from a number of central constitutional concepts. The argument that, in the original understanding of constitutionalism, these different assumptions, whose delegation-related interpretations nowadays appear to yield a good measure of analytical circularity, had a coherent and consistent intellectual structure was also anticipated throughout this chapter. The theoretical assumptions that inform the notion of "legislative delegation" in constitutional theory must be therefore reiterated, before we proceed with the inquiry into how these merge with each other in relation to constitutional supremacy.

2.5.1 Representation

> The diversity in the faculties of men, from which the rights of property originate, is not less an insuperable obstacle to a uniformity of interests. The protection of these faculties is the first object of government. From the protection of different and unequal faculties of acquiring property, the possession of different degrees and kinds of property immediately results; and from the influence of those on the sentiments and views of the respective proprietors, ensues a division of the society into different interests and parties.
> *The Federalist 10* (James Madison)

Although this nuance has long faded, the designation of magistrates or lawmakers by election was historically seen as an inherently aristocratic method of government (since it favors merit or wealth), in opposition to selection by lot, which was, conversely, regarded as the essence of democracy (since it is the best expression of equality, a democratic principle).[132] As late as 1748, Montesquieu was still able to perceive the ambivalence of representation, when he argued that: "[t]he suffrage by lot is natural to democracy; as that by choice is to aristocracy. The suffrage by lot is a way of selecting that offends no one; but it leaves to each citizen a reasonable expectation of serving his country."[133]

At the beginnings of constitutionalism, the essential question was whether parliamentary representation, which had evolved over centuries in English practice,

[132] Both Plato and Aristotle perceived and theoretically developed this difference. For Aristotle, as we have already seen, the best polity was one in which democracy and aristocracy as political forms (and—respectively—lot and election as methods of political selection) were so well commingled that the ensuing regime partook perfectly of the advantages and overcame best the disadvantages of them both, to the effect that an observer could define it as both democracy and aristocracy...and neither. For a study of representative government that developed most consistently this distinction in theory and practice up to its contemporary consequences *see* Bernard Manin 1997.

[133] *Spirit of Laws,* Book II, Ch. 2., p. 11 (Cosimo Classics 2007 ed.).

without any master plan, could be transplanted elsewhere or whether there was perhaps a constitutionally correct, higher and "essential" understanding of representation that could be extracted and directly implemented. The implementation had, moreover, to reconcile the aristocratic perils implicit in representation with the new dogma of popular sovereignty. This is by no means an analytically easy feat. Thus, enamored with the elated sort of sophistries of which the writings of Rousseau are emblematic and replete, the French revolutionists arrived for instance at the bafflingly hypocritical solution of combining a fairly restrictive electoral system with the arrogation of an unlimited competence for the legislative bodies, as representatives and custodians of the general will.[134]

The best tradition of constitutionalism, by contrast, perceived representation as both a bulwark against democracy and the best (most reasonable under the actual circumstances) modern expression thereof. Benjamin Constant famously countered the Rousseauian concept of people's democracy, showing that the "liberty of the ancients," which derived from active and constant participation in public affairs, is starkly different from the "liberty of the moderns," for whom being left alone to live their private lives unhindered by state meddling is a much more valued state of things. As Constant observed, from the vantage point of one who had lived through the Terror, practical attempts to force political virtue on people ("to force them to be free," in Rousseauian terms), can only degenerate into Jacobin educational dictatorships, by means of which an actual democracy is indefinitely suspended in the name of a true democracy yet to be created.[135] The political liberty of modern man could only be democracy by representation, under and within the limits of a constitution: "The representative system is a proxy given to a certain number of men by the mass of people who wish their interests to be defended and who nevertheless do not have time to defend them themselves (...) [T]he people who, in order to enjoy the liberty which suits them, resort to the representative system, must exercise an active and constant surveillance over their representatives, and reserve for themselves, at times which should not be separated by too lengthy intervals, the right to discard them if they betray their trust, and to revoke the powers which they might have abused."[136] Representation is for Constant a form of

[134] For a study of these tensions in French revolutionary history, *see* Patrice Gueniffey, *Le nombre et la raison-La Révolution française et les élections* (Paris: Éditions de l'École des Hautes Études en Sciences Sociales, 1993).

[135] I am paraphrasing Carl Schmitt, *The Crisis of Parliamentary Democracy* (1926 revised ed.), Ellen Kennedy transl. (Cambridge and London: MIT Press, 1988).

[136] Benjamin Constant, "The Liberty of the Ancients Compared with that of the Moderns," in *Political Writings*, translated and edited by Biancamaria Fontana (Cambridge: Cambridge University Press, 1993 (c1988)), at pp. 325–326. Yet, with the subtlety which characterizes his distinctions, Constant (like Tocqueville) was quick to notice the potential downfalls of "modern liberty": "The danger of modern liberty is that, absorbed in the enjoyment of our private independence, and in the pursuit of our particular interests, we should surrender our right to share in political power too easily." (at p. 326) For a comprehensive analysis of Benjamin Constant's political and constitutional thought, *see* Holmes 1984.

delegation where each elector (the delegator) has the possibility of controlling the delegate, between terms through the intermediary of public opinion and at regular intervals by casting a ballot. The two aspects are interrelated and mutually reinforcing, since public opinion and its pre-requisites (free speech, freedom of assembly, a free and independent press), make an informed election possible.

Such a procedural perception is perhaps inevitable and derives from the constitutional nature of representation. There are of course conceptions of representation that seek to bridge institutionally the gap between democracy and representation.[137] Their best expression are the so-called "descriptive theories," such as John Adams's contention that a representative assembly "should be an exact portrait, in miniature, of the people at large, as it should think, feel, reason and act like them" or James Wilson's assertion that a legislative assembly should be a portrait of the people, whereas "the portrait is excellent in proportion to its being a good likeness."[138] The entire theoretical strain of descriptive representation revolves around a bevy of related metaphors, which resemble the legislature with a mirror, a portrait, a map, a photograph, a "condensation" of the whole, etc. Nonetheless, even in point of pure theory, there are serious pitfalls in this perception, since it is unclear whether there is anything fixed or set in a society that can be "captured" faithfully. And then any society changes rapidly: anything fixed in it, assuming as a cognitive premise that a fixed something existed, quickly varies. A faithful map (or, for that matter, portrait or mirror) would therefore need to include a map of a map of a map, with a legend of a legend of a legend and so on, *ad infinitum*. Moreover, the practical application of this perception is unclear; it would perhaps require either a selection by lot of representatives or a corporatist solution with the possibility of recall, whereby the legislature would be composed of representatives of all classes and interests in society.

Once election is brought in, descriptive representation has to yield and Constant's argument is forcefully brought back in. Liberal constitutionalism does not perceive representation as solely a project of democracy. Actual people are being represented, and their concrete interests and wishes are being substantiated in the process of law-making, through deliberation and decision on concrete measures. The by-product of deliberation equates the public interest to the extent that it constitutes the best aggregation possible, arrived at through a process that streamlines discussion and facilitates decision, while reducing factionalism (the capture of the public will by private interests). Through the intermediary of representation, the people make laws and impose burdens on themselves. Yet in

---

[137] *See* Hanna Fenichel Pitkin, *The Concept of Representation* (Berkeley, Los Angeles, London: University of California Press, 1967), *esp.* "'Standing For': Descriptive Representation", pp. 60–92.

[138] *Id.*, Pitkin traces the notion of descriptive representation as early back as the Monarchomachs: "The idea of a representative assembly should be a condensation of the whole nation is a venerable one, appearing as early as the Monarchomachs, whose ideal legislature was an *epitome regni, regni quasi epitome*." (at p. 73).

what manner a representative assembly should make these laws, in order for it to have fulfilled its constitutional and electoral mandate, cannot be answered in the abstract. Conceptions of representation change over time, in suitable lockstep with transformations of the representative system. At the end of the eighteenth century Burke could think of Parliament as essentially a gentlemen's debating club. If an interest were represented by at least one of the honorable members, then it already found enough parliamentary support, since the viewpoint could be cogently aired in debates. Gentlemen listen to the each other's arguments and opinions with all proper decorum and thoughtful consideration. But only three decades after the Reform Act, Mill could already offer a much more sobering view. The proper tasks of a representative assembly were those of controlling the government and of *enacting* laws which could just as well be drafted by an expert government body. Representation supplied an "element of will" and legitimacy to the "element of intelligence" provided by an expert Commission of Legislation and the true value of Parliament resided not in being primarily a *legislative* body but rather in its constituting "the nation's Committee of Grievances and its Congress of Opinions": "But it is equally true, though only of late and slowly beginning to be acknowledged, that a numerous assembly is as little fitted for the direct business of legislation as for that of administration.... Instead of the function of governing, for which it is radically unfit, the proper office of a representative assembly is to watch and control the government..."[139]

This brings us to the representation/delegation dilemma. On the one hand, it seems to be intuitively the case that, inasmuch as we elect legislatures to make laws and they delegate their law-making function to the executive or the administration, democracy is subverted and this collective mandate is not fulfilled. For, if my representatives do not make clear choices, how can I be expected to bring them to book at the polls? Once the legislature is legally limited in its competence by the text of the constitution, this intuition seems to revert into a constitutional problem. On the other hand, representation is not pure democracy[140] and the representative is not a delegate in the sense of private law. The public law mandate is a free mandate and the democratic check on this mandate is brought in only as a veto, at the moment of choosing the representative or in the "court of public opinion."

[139] John Stuart Mill, *Considerations on Representative Government* (Buffalo, N.Y.: Prometheus Books, 1991), at pp. 109–115.

[140] For a long time representative democracy was perceived to be the exact opposite of direct democracy, to the effect that, in early American state constitutional law, a number of laws whose application was made contingent by the legislature on local option or whose promulgation was made dependent on a state referendum were declared unconstitutional on nondelegation grounds (e.g., Rice v. Foster 4 Harr. 479 (Del. 1847), Barto v. Himrod 8 NY 483 (153)).

2.5.2 Separation of Powers: Balance and Function

This seemeth One Reason, why our Ancestors did so willingly follow the Voyce of *Nature*; in placing the Power *Legislative, Iudiciall, & Executive*, in 3 distinct Estates; (as in *Animals, Aerials, Etherials,* or *Celestials*, 3 regions; and 3 Principles in *Naturals*:) that so, they might be forced to Consult Often and Much, in All they did.

John Sadler, *Rights of the Kingdom; or Customs of Our Ancestors* (London, 1649)

A Commonwealth swerveth not by principle but by institution. A Commonwealth rightly instituted never swerveth.

John Harrington, *The Commonwealth of Oceana* (London, 1656)

Separation of powers is itself a metaphor, referring to wildly diverse ideas and historical contingencies. Two conceptual strands stand apart, one interested in analytical distinctions between functions, the other in the balance and counterpoise of powers or institutions. The balance argument originates in the theory of the mixed constitution. Its classical early account is Polybius's description of the Roman Republic; the Greek historian declared that what made the greatness of republican Rome was a blend of monarchical, aristocratic, and democratic elements, as embodied in the institutions of the consulate, the Senate, and the popular assemblies, respectively, and as evidenced by the coordinate exercise of different attributions of state power (the Senate proposes laws, which the popular assemblies can reject or approve, the consuls have control over the deployment of troops and command in the field, the Senate controls all expenditures, while the people alone decide with finality over war and peace, etc.). The emphasis is on the fragmentation of power by institutional design and mutual checks. At no point is the sum-total of state power fully concentrated and the various exercises thereof never go unchecked.[141]

This argument resurfaces during the struggles for political supremacy in seventeenth century England, where its concrete and contextual nature is evidenced by an intensely polemical use. In 1642, Charles I resorts to "mixed monarchy," in an address to the Long Parliament, to chastize what he perceived to be the latter's extravagant assertions of monolithic power: "There being three kinds of government amongst men, absolute monarchy, aristocracy, and democracy, and all these having their particular conveniences and inconveniences. The experience and wisdom of your ancestors hath so moulded this [government] out of a mixture of these, as to give this kingdom (as far as humane prudence can provide) the

[141] Histories, VI, II: "All the three types of government which I have mentioned before were found together in the Roman Republic. In fact they were so equally and harmoniously balanced, both in the structure of the political system and in the way in which it functioned in everyday practice, that even a native could not have determined definitely whether the state as a whole was an aristocracy, a democracy, or a monarchy. This is indeed quite natural. For if we fix our attention on the power of the consuls the government appears quite monarchic and seems to resemble kingship. If we look upon the power of the Senate, it seems to be aristocratic, and, finally, if one regards the power of the people, it seems clearly a democracy." In Kurt von Fritz, *The Theory of the Mixed Constitution in Antiquity: A Critical Analysis of Polybius' Political Ideas* (New York: Columbia University Press, 1954), Appendix I, Excerpts, p. 367.

convenience of all three, without the inconvenience of any one, as long as the balance hangs even between the three estates, and they run jointly on their proper channel (begetting verdure and fertility in the meadows on both sides) and the overflowing of either on either side raise no deluge or inundation. . . ."[142] The notion of "mixed" government, as antithesis to despotism, "pure," unchecked power could be likewise wielded to counter all assertion of absolutism, be it that of the Stuarts, the Long Parliament, the Lord Protector or the Commons. In the course of the XVIII century, Bolingbroke was to praise the values of "mixed and well-tempered government," writing against the ministerial system and the "corruption" of the House of Commons by Sir Robert Walpole.

The theoretical defense of separation of powers that influenced the most modern constitutionalism can be found in Chapter VI, Book XI ("On the Constitution of England") of Montesquieu's *Spirit of Laws*. Montesquieu departs from the characteristically antic-mediaeval notion of balance of classes (understood as political forms of government) and extracts the modern essence, the main principle. Political liberty is best safeguarded from despotism in "moderate governments," where "by the disposition of things" power is always balanced and checked by countervailing power.[143] The starting point of his analysis is a pragmatic concern with unchecked

---

[142] *See generally*, Michael Mendle, *Dangerous Positions-Mixed Government, the Estates of the Realm, and the Answer to the xix propositions* (Alabama: University of Alabama Press, 1985). A history of the concept, with taxonomies and thorough distinctions is provided in the classical separation of powers studies in the English language, M. J. C. Vile, *Constitutionalism and the Separation of Powers* (Oxford: Clarendon Press, 1967) and W. G. Gwyn, *The Meaning of the Separation of Powers* (New Orleans: Tulane University Press, 1965). The latter work focuses more specifically on English developments and draws more clearly the distinction between the balance and normative/rule of law separation of powers theories.

[143] *See* Schmitt, *La Dictature*, at pp. 107–108: "Pour illustrer sa construction, Montesquieu emploie l'image de la '*balance*', qui était utilisée aux XVIIe et XVIIIe siècles pour n'importe quelle type d'harmonie veritable (dans l'univers, dans la politique intérieure et extérieure, dans la morale et l'économie politique), image qui ne devait pas nécessairement être une abstraction rationnelle. Ce qu'on appelle la théorie de la separation des pouvoirs est incomprehensible tant qu'on s'en tient au terme de 'séparation plutôt qu'à celui de '*balance*.' (. . .) L'image de la balance, en revanche, désigne une unité réalisée par voie de l'équilibre. C'est la raison pour laquelle ce qu'on appelle la séparation des pouvoirs est tout sauf un schème doctrinal. Elle concerne toujours des situations politiques concrètes, et entraîne avec elle le fait que l'usage de l'image s'oppose toujours à celui qui dérange ou qui, par ses prétentions unilatérales au pouvoir, par sa dictature, fait obstacle à l'équilibre resultant d'une entente." [emphases in original]

De Lolme will also describe the essence and virtues of the English constitution in terms of balance: "There might be danger, that if, the Parliament should ever exercise their privilege to its full extent, the prince, reduced to despair might resort to fatal extremities; or that the Constitution, which subsists only by virtue of its equilibrium, might in the end be subverted." J. L. De Lolme, *The Constitution of England or An Account of the English Government In which it is compared, both with the REPUBLICAN form of GOVERNMENT, and the other Monarchies in EUROPE*, The Fourth Edition, Corrected and Enlarged (London: G. Robinson and J. Murray, MDCCLXXXIV), at pp. 78. Blackstone himself would later give a similar description in his *Commentaries*: "But the constitutional government of this island is so admirably tempered and compounded, that nothing can endanger or hurt it, but destroying the equilibrium of power between one branch of the

power and its natural tendency to be abused. The foundational moderate and pragmatic anthropological skepticism ("Who would think it? Virtue itself is in need of limits."), together with the analytical detachment of the notion of balance from its older association with social classes and its application to institutions, rightfully make Montesquieu one of the founders of modern constitutionalism.[144] But Montesquieu never uses the term "separation."[145] In his story, the balance argument and a functionalist account are analytically independent. The tendency of modern commentators to conflate the issues arises to a certain extent from terminology (Montesquieu uses the term "power" to refer both to state functions and to actual state powers) and from the related fact that he treats in the economy of the same chapter both variants of the separation of powers, the rule of law-oriented functionalist and checks and balances version, respectively.

Yet the two maters can be distinguished. At the beginning of the chapter, he enumerates three "powers" and renders a functional-rule-of-law analysis of their interrelations. The three "powers" enumerated at this juncture are: (1) legislative (the expression of the general will of the state), (2) "Executive power over the things depending on the right of nations" ("the executive power of the state"),[146] (3) and "executive power over the things depending on civil right" ("the power of judging"). Here, Montesquieu separates functions analytically, with an eye to the

---

legislature and the rest. For if ever should happen that the independence of any of the branches should be lost, or that it should become subservient to the views of either of the other two, there would soon be an end of our constitution." William Blackstone, *Commentaries on the Laws of England* (New York: W. E. Dean Printer & Publisher, 1845 (1765)), pp. 34–35.

[144] Charles Louis –Secondat, Baron de la Brède et de Montesquieu, *De L'Esprit des Lois* (Esprit des Lois par Montesquieu Avec Les Notes de l'Auteur et un Choix des Observations par De Dupin, Crevier, Voltaire, Mably, La Harpe, Servan, *etc.*, Librairie de Paris, Firmin-Didot et Cie, Imprimeurs-Éditeurs, Paris, 1849), at 128: "La liberté politique ne se trouve que dans les gouvernements modérés. Mais elle n'est pas toujours dans les États modérés: elle n'y est que lorsqu'on n'abuse pas pas du pouvoir; mais c'est une expérience éternelle, que tout homme qui a du pouvoir est porté à en abuser; il va jusqu'à ce qu'il trouve des limites. Qui le dirait! La vertu meme a besoin de limites. Pour qu'on ne puisse abuser du pouvoir, il faut que, par la disposition des choses, le pouvoir arête le pouvoir." It is interesting to note, in passing, that a skeptical approach to the historically proven human tendency to abuse political power needs neither the abstract assumption of an absolute anthropological profession of faith nor a counterfactually constructed premise. This moderate foundational skepticism is shared by the Founding Fathers of the American Constitution: "The supposition of universal venality in human nature is little less an error in political reasoning than the supposition of universal rectitude." *The Federalist*, No. 76 (Alexander Hamilton). Madison wrote that while ". . .there is a degree of depravity in mankind which requires a certain degree of circumspection and distrust, so there are other qualities in human nature, which justify a certain portion of esteem and confidence." *The Federalist*, No. 55 (James Madison).

[145] As this was aptly put by Ernst Cassirer: "His eye for the particular and his love of detail protected him, even in his purely theoretical works, from any one-sided doctrinairism. He always successfully resisted any merely schematic presentation, any reduction of the variety of forms to an absolutely rigid pattern." In Ernst Cassirer, *The Philosophy of the Enlightenment*, Fritz C. A. Koellin and James P. Petergrove transl. (Princeton, N.J.: Princeton University Press, c1951), at p. 215.

[146] Synonymous with Locke's "federative power." Montesquieu assumed it to be "executive" of the laws of nations.

problem of discretion. Among them, the "power of judging" is considered "so terrible among men" and must be "separated," since the judiciary applies the law to particular individuals in particular circumstances and thus poses the biggest dangers of abuse. Later on, in the course of the discussion related to the prevention of tyranny, the powers considered are those that present a political problem (aggrandizement, tendency towards despotism), the legislature and the executive. Here, the essential argument is that mutual checks and institutional divisions will produce balance (a state of "rest or inaction" in his own words). When unity in action will be needed, all branches of power will "move in concert" "by the necessary motion of things." In this part of the argument, the judiciary is not taken into account as a "power." Montesquieu presents the judge now as innocuous, "solely the mouthpiece of the law." The irrelevance of the judiciary at this juncture derives from the fact that it is politically neutral.

The two aspects (balance of powers and separation of functions) cannot be reconciled in a doctrinaire fashion. In post-revolutionary America, state constitutions hastened to embrace the maxim of separation of powers, which was already widely known at the time, primarily through the intermediary of Polybius, Montesquieu, and Blackstone, and would later on become more popular as a result of John Adams's well-known tract on the topic.[147] Since, as a matter of constitutional design, the principle was at the beginning concretized along purely functional lines, and faith in its observance rested with the democratically-elected state legislatures, post-colonial experience quickly delivered the lesson that a democratically elected body could turn out to be just as whimsical or tyrannical as the former royal governors.[148] A related reproof taught by early state constitutional experiences was that precatory functional admonitions in the constitution could not be relied upon to cure the evils of

[147] Six constitutions expressly endorsed the doctrine (Georgia, Maryland, Massachusetts, New Hampshire, North Carolina, and Virginia). Art. XXX of the Massachusetts Bill of Rights of 1780 is probably the most 'enthusiastic' endorsement: "In the government of this commonwealth, the legislative department shall never exercise the executive and judicial powers, or either of them: the executive shall never exercise the legislative and judicial powers, or either of them: the judicial shall never exercise the legislative or executive powers, or either of them: to the end it may be a government of laws and not of men." In *Constitutions That Made History*, Albert P. Blaustein, Jay A. Sigler, Eds. (New York: Paragon House Publishers, 1988), at 48. For purposes of contrast, *see* the moderate and sober instantiation in the text of the New Hampshire Constitution (1784), Art. 37, Bill of Rights: "In the government of this state, the three essential powers thereof, to wit, the legislative, executive, and judicial, ought to be kept as separate from, and independent of, each other, as the nature of a free government will admit, or as is consistent with that chain of connection that binds the whole fabric of the constitution in one indissoluble bond of unity and amity."

[148] The body of literature is enormous. For survey of the various intellectual influences on the American understanding of separation of powers, *see* Malcolm Sharp, "The Classical American Doctrine of 'The Separation of Powers'" 2 *University of Chicago Law Review* 385 (1934–1935). On the influence of colonial and post-colonial experience with legislative abuses *see*, for instance, Wright, "The Origin of the Separation of Powers in America," 13 *Economica* 169 (1933); for an interesting survey of "adjudication" by a pre- revolutionary provincial legislature, "Judicial Action by the Provincial Legislature of Massachusetts," (Note) 15 *Harvard Law Review* 208 (1901).

unchecked power. The best check on political power is always power itself. As a direct result, the debates during the Constitutional Convention in Philadelphia centered on very pragmatic issues pertaining to institutional mechanisms that would best ensure the autonomy and interdependence of the branches. The few interventions regarding supposedly "orthodox" functional delineations were brushed aside without much ceremony.[149] The same pragmatic approach can be later observed in James Madison's rebuffs to Anti-Federalist concerns regarding an allegedly unorthodox application of the theory in the new constitution. Reviewing Montesquieu, the British constitutional system his theory envisaged, and the provisions on separation of powers in several state constitutions, Madison states that political liberty is best safeguarded when a concentration of power in the same department is prevented, rather than when a rigid delineation is ordained between branches exercising functions analytically different in quality: "His meaning, as his own words import, and still more conclusively as illustrated by the example in his eye, can amount to no more than this, that where the *whole* power of one department is exercised by the same hands which possess the *whole* power of another department, the fundamental principles of a free constitution are subverted."[150] (emphasis in original) Even more revelatory is the discussion in *The Federalist*, No. 51, of the "expedient…for maintaining in practice the necessary partition of power among the several departments as laid down in the Constitution."[151] The answer is trenchant and completely pragmatic: what is of the utmost concern is always the proper

---

[149] Surprisingly enough, one such intervention came from Madison, during the session of Friday, June 1st 1787, when he moved to insert in what would become Art. II, a phrase which provided, in pertinent part "that a national Executive ought to be instituted…to execute such other powers (*'not Legislative nor Judiciary in their nature.'*) as may from time to time be delegated by the national Legislature." (emphasis added) This part of Madison's motion was only seconded by one other member (Edmund Randolph) and struck out (partly as a result of Charles Pinkney's commonsensical observation that they were redundant, since implied in "the power to carry into effect the national laws," an early version of the future Take Care Clause). *See* Max Farrand, *The Records of the Federal Convention of 1787* (New Haven, Ct., London, Engl.: Yale University Press, 1974(c1966)), at pp. 66–68.

[150] *The Federalist Papers* (N.Y.: Mentor Books, 1961), Clinton Rossiter, Ed., No. 47 (Madison), at pp. 302–303.

[151] *The Federalist*, No. 51 (Madison), at 320: "The only answer that can be given is that as all these exterior provisions are found to be inadequate the defect must be supplied, by so contriving the interior structure of the government as that its several constituent parts may, by their mutual relations, be the means of keeping each other in their proper places." *See also* the particularly interesting observation, in *The Federalist*, No. 48, on the long-term efficacy of purely *legal* limitations on tyranny (of course, with the proviso that, as is well-known, in light of the above-mentioned post-colonial experiences, legislative rather than executive tyranny was the main concern of the Framers): "Will it be sufficient to mark, with precision, the boundaries of these departments in the constitution of the government, and to trust to these parchment barriers against the encroaching spirit of power? This is the security which appears to have been principally relied on by the compilers of most of the American constitutions. But experience assures us that the efficacy of the provision is has been greatly overrated; and that some more adequate defense is indispensable necessary for the more feeble against the more powerful branches of the government." (Rossiter edition, at pp. 308–309).

arrangement (mode of election, financial independence, mutual checks) for best ensuring that "each department should have a will of its own."[152]

Contrariwise, proceeding upon the unwarrantable constitution-making premise of an indivisible sovereignty, and following the dubious constitution-drafting methodology of logical deductions from an *a priori* principle, the French Constitutional Assembly of 1791 sought consistently to completely distinguish in practice, as in thought, adjudication, legislation, and execution as mutually independent fractions of delegated sovereignty.[153] What resulted was by and large an attempt to reiterate in a practical setting a misunderstanding of Rousseau's abstract aphorisms, with all the deleterious practical consequences inevitably invited by like undertakings. Even though the members of the *Assemblée nationale* were well acquainted with the descriptions of the English constitution in Montesquieu and De Lolme, concrete examples derived from history and contemporary foreign practices were dismissed as parochial peculiarities. These were "English prejudices" which, since of no overarching consequence, should give way to the pure doctrinal "principle."[154] Mounier's intervention during the opening of the debates is particularly indicative of the general tenor of the discussions: "We have to prevent the reunion of powers; the National Assembly must not confuse the legislative and executive powers...we have to pose sacred limits to each of them."[155] As a direct consequence, not only is the executive refused the power to initiate or veto legislation but even an original and residual executive decree-making power (*pouvoir réglementaire*) is considered inadmissible, since, following from this absurdly dogmatic understanding, "only the legislative power has the right to make and interpret laws."[156] In a discourse on the 21st of September 1789, Robespierre would

---

[152] *Id.*, at 321.

[153] "Dominée par l'esprit classique, pasionnée pour les formules générales et abstraites, amoureuse des theories de métaphysque politique, l'Assemblée nationale voit dans la séparation des pouvoirs une division de la souveraineté en divers éléments, souveraineté qui reste qui reste une e indivisible malgré l'existence des divers éléments qui la constituent, chacun de ces éléments étant délégué par représentation à un organe distinct, qui logiquement sera indépendent et souverain dans la sphere de souveraineté qui lui est atribuée par représentation." *Traité de droit constitutionnel*, 3e éd., 5 vols., (Paris: Fontemoing, 1928), vol. 2, at p. 668.

[154] "Et n'avons-nous pas sur l'Angleterre, le précieux avantage de pouvoir ordonner en meme temps toutes les parties de notre Constitution, tandis que la sienne a été faite à différentes époques et à différentes reprises? Les Anglais eux-mêmes ont été obligés de composer avec préjuges, et nous n'avons aujourd'hui que les droits et les intérêts du peuple... Il suit de là que c'est moins les exemples que les principes qu'il faut consulter." Intervention by constitutionnaire Alexandre de Lameth, in *Archives parlementaires*, 1re série, t. VIII, p. 417 (12 août 1789).

[155] [emphasis supplied] In Léon Duguit, "La séparation des pouvoirs et l'Assemblée nationale de 1789," in three parts, *Revue d'Économie Pollitique*, Vol. VII (1893), pp. 99–132, 336–372, and 567–615.

[156] Intervention by Pétion de Villeneuve, *Archives parlementaires*, 1re série, t. IX, p. 219. The debates will result in the final form of Art. 6 (Section I, Chapter IV, Title III) of the 1791 Constitution: "Le pouvoir exécutif ne peut faire aucune loi, même provisoire, mais seulement des proclamations conformes aux lois, pour en ordonner ou en rappeller l'exécution." The principle had already been established by the law of 15–20 October 1789, which forbade the

likewise state, commenting on the veto power, that: "he who claims that an individual has a right to oppose the law says that the will of one is above the will of all. If he adds that such a right belongs to the man exercising the executive power, he says that the man established by the Nation has the right to negative and enchain the will of the nation."[157] Also revealing is the debate on the pardon power of the king. To give the executive the *droit de grâce* would not only be an impressible blending of executive and judicial "powers" but, more importantly, such empowerment would necessarily render a "private will above the general will."[158]

It stands to reason that a measure of functional division of powers should accompany institutional separation (this is after all the essence of the separation-derived delegation argument). But, in the abstract, the balance aspect, with its pragmatic-institutional and descriptive-polemic nature, and functional delineations based on dogmatic definitions of state attributions cannot be reconciled. A normative reconciliation is however necessary and implicit in the idea of a written, enforceable constitution.

2.5.3 Legislation as a Rule of Law: Separation and Delegation

In point of theory, the conceptual solution to this analytical quandary is achieved by Locke's argument in the *Second Treatise*. For Locke, writing on the assumption of a legally bound government, all the limitations on the exercise of state power are normative rather than constitutive and present themselves consistently in adjudicatory form. Since the state appears as a sum of limited competences, his question is always "Who will be the judge?" in case of a trespass or misuse of public power. The key concern is always arbitrariness and not tyranny or despotism writ large or, rather, tyranny as a concrete problem related to the actual possibility of aggrandizement to unlimited power becomes arbitrariness as a systemic, justice-related concern of the discrete individual.[159] Institutionally, what the normative

Conseil du roi to make any original decree ("arrêt de propre mouvement"). (*See* discussion in François Bourdeau, *Histoire du droit administratif (de la Révolution au début des années 1970)* (Paris: Presses Universitaires de France, 1995), pp 42 et sequitur.) The confusion resulting from the very doctrinaire understanding of separation of powers is also perceptible in the curious terminological uncertainty which marks the interchangeable use of "loi" and "décret" during the debates regarding the name which should be given to the acts of the legislative body.

[157] In Michel Troper, *La séparation des pouvoirs et l'histoire constitutionnelle française* (Paris: LGDJ, 1973), at p. 32.

[158] Pétion de Villeneuve and Goupil de Préfeln, *Archives parlementaires*, 1re série, t. XXVI, p. 734 (4 juin 1791). The abolition of the pardon power finally PT found its way in a provision of the Penal Code of 1791, not in the text of the Constitution itself. *See* discussion in Duguit 1893, pp. 596–598.

[159] "Absolute Arbitrary Power" is defined as the "Governing *without settled standing Laws.*" John Locke, *Second Treatise of Civil Government* (Indianapolis: Hackett Publishing, 1980 (1690)) C.B. Macpherson, Ed., Par. 137.

understanding of the separation of powers doctrine presupposes is an impartial (and therefore independent) judiciary.[160] The fact that Locke looks at state functions through this legalistic, analytical, and judicialized prism makes him the father of modern constitutionalism.

Functional distinctions are understood in a normative sense: their interrelation unfolds starting from the premise of a concept of legislation. Four "powers" are thus distinguished. The "legislative" is the power to prescribe "settled standing laws. . .stated rules of right and property."[161] Material limits are crucial since, while Locke's legislature is the "supreme power of the commonwealth. . .sacred and unalterable in the hands where the community have once placed it,"[162] its supremacy is bound by the normative limitations placed on it.[163] A law loses its character once enacted in particularized or constitutive (non-normative) form. The distinction between "established, promulgated, standing laws" and "arbitrary, extemporary dictates and resolutions" is ubiquitously re-stated throughout the entire work.

The executive power appears as the mere subsumption of general rules to particular cases, a "*ministerial* and subordinate power."[164] [emphasis supplied] The distinction is, again, purely analytical: Locke is adamant in stressing throughout the book that "be the thing understood, [he is] indifferent as to the name" of the functions. What is meant by executive is analogous to our contemporary understandings of "non-discretionary administration of the law" and "adjudication," *i.e.*, once the law is a clear, general, non-discretionary rule, its implementation ("execution") will be relatively unproblematic. In "moderate monarchies," he notes in passing, it is necessary that "the legislative power and executive power [be] in distinct hands."[165] But this apportionment of functions among distinct branches or organs is not predicated

[160] *See* Gwyn 1965, more generally, on the rule of law (in his taxonomy, "impartiality") version of the separation of powers. An interesting development of this understanding of the separation of power and its consequences in constitutional law is provided by Paul R. Verkuil in "The American Constitutional Tradition of Shared and Separated Powers: Separation of Powers, the Rule of Law and the Idea of Independence," 30 *William and Mary Law Review* 301 (Winter, 1989). This is the form that the separation of powers finds in British jurisdictions, where the Parliament is legally sovereign (*see*, for instance, W. Jethro Brown, "The Separation of Powers in British Jurisdictions," 31 *Yale Law Journal* 24 (1921–1922)). Historically, the independence of the judiciary was first recognized during Charles I, who accepted in 1642, however reluctantly, to respect the appointment of judges "during good behavior" (*quamdiu se bene gesserint*). During the Glorious Revolution, William and Mary accepted judicial independence as a condition for their accession to the throne (in the Heads of Grievances the issue is itemized as "making judges' commissions quamdiu se bene gesserint, and for ascertaining and establishing their salaries, to be paid out of the public revenue only; and for preventing their being removed and suspended from the execution of their offices, unless by due course of law." These practices are finally raised to statutory-constitutional status, being enacted in the Act of Settlement 12& 13 W. II, c. 2 (1701).

[161] Par. 137.

[162] Par. 137.

[163] Vile 1967, at 63: "The legislative authority is the authority *to act in a particular way*."

[164] Par. 152.

[165] Par. 159.

upon the necessity of fragmenting power institutionally, rather proceeds on the assumption that legislation, given the limited trust that the government is, constitutes *an exceptional activity* and therefore, when the legislature is not in session, there is a need for a "power always in being." Put simply, there is no need for continuous law-making yet the laws, once made, need naturally to be always enforced.[166]

The further functional breakdown is, conceptually, also indebted to and revolves around the normativity-generality version of the rule of law which pervades and dominates the logic of the entire work. The federative and prerogative "powers" are the result of Locke's insightful observation that the exercise of political power will inevitably bear on issues that cannot, *by their very nature,* be predetermined by legal rules (especially once legislative rules have been restricted to a specific object and form). Since the body politic as a whole is still in the state of nature in its relation to other commonwealths, what foreigners do cannot be accurately predicted or effectively regulated and thus "their actions and the variations of designs and interests" cannot be normatively encompassed by a rule of conduct. Therefore, the federative power is functionally distinguished from performance of ministerial or administrative tasks (the executive proper).[167] The power of prerogative is also analytically and functionally dependent on the notion of legislation, qualitatively defined, since prerogative is nothing more than "[the] power to act according to discretion, for the public good, without the prescription of the law, and sometimes even against it."[168]

The first and most specific articulation of the principle that the legislature cannot delegate its law-making function can be found in Locke and is the correlative of all these distinctions. The relevant passage must be quoted at length:

> *Fourthly*, The *Legislative cannot transfer the Power of Making Laws* to any other hands. For it being but a delegated Power from the People, they, who have it, cannot pass it over to

---

[166] Par. 153: "It is not necessary, no, nor so much as convenient, that the legislative should be always in being; but absolutely necessary that the executive power should, because there is not always need of new laws to be made, but always need of execution of the laws that are made."

[167] Pars. 145–148. For our purposes, the following citation from Par. 147 is of particular interest: "And though this federative power in the well or ill management of it be of great moment to the common-wealth, yet it is much less capable to be directed by antecedent, standing, positive laws, than the executive; and so must necessarily be left to the prudence and wisdom of those, whose hands it is in, to be managed for the public good: for the laws that concern subjects one amongst another, being to direct their actions, may well enough precede them. But what is to be done in reference to foreigners, depending much upon their actions, and the variations of designs and interests, must be left in great part to the prudence of those, who have this power committed to them, to be managed by the best of their skill, for the advantage of the commonwealth."

[168] Locke's prerogative is an admixture of emergency powers (sometimes dispatch in the actions of government is needed when the legislative is not in session or the executive must act in respect to "things ... which the law can by no means provide for") and equity (a restatement and the equivalent of the Aristotelian notion of equity: the inflexibility and occasional severity of rules must be mitigated and particularized for considerations of justice in individual cases, a rule, precisely as a consequence of its very generality and impartiality, cannot foresee all future occurrences and thus exceptions and derogations or additions must be made to the law, in favor of the law itself). Chapter XIV-*Of Prerogative*.

> others. The People alone can appoint the Form of the Commonwealth, which is by Constituting the Legislative and appointing in whose hands that shall be. And when the People have said, We will submit to rules and be govern'd by *Laws* made by such Men, and in such Forms, no Body else can say other Men shall make *Laws* for them; nor can the people be bound by any *Laws* but such as are enacted by those whom they have Chosen and Authorized to make *Laws* for them. The power of the *Legislative*, being derived from the people by a positive voluntary Grant and Institution, can be no other than what the positive Grant conveyed, which being only to make *Laws*, and not to make *Legislators*, the *Legislative* can have no power to transfer their Authority of making Laws, and place it in other hands.[169]

If a nondelegation limitation constrains the legislature, this proviso can only be understood as a consequence of the mandate by which the government itself is constrained and as an implication of the fact that there are normative limitations on legislation proper. Nondelegation is not essentially a democratic argument, since Locke's legislature is not just a transmission belt for momentary interests and desires. The people have already decided on the proper purview and the legal limitation on the government, namely through the social contract. The legislature cannot delegate the power to make laws, its legislative function, because it exercises it in trust and is itself legally bound to act in a certain way.[170] The legislature is bound so by virtue of the social contract and the foundational assumption that the only purpose of the government is to secure the natural rights of life, liberty, and property, whose equal use it must regulate but over which it has no right to dispose arbitrarily.

This results on the one hand in an intensely rationalized (meaning, legalized and predictable) field of state action and, on the other, in a number of state attributions that to a certain extent are viewed as "a-rational". These attributions should be exercised "for the public good" and Locke relentlessly stresses this qualification, lest it be understood that not being subject to law means full subjection to the irrationality of whim, to subjective, private caprice. Yet, albeit the "public good" proviso is repeatedly brought to the fore, there is in the analytical logic of argument no rational–legal way of assessing performance of duty in such cases and thus discretionary exercises of state authority are explicitly outside the range of the Lockean legal rationality. The nondelegation limitation is the logical corollary at the intersection of these distinctions.

[169] Par. 141.

[170] To contrast, a nondelegation argument also appears in Rousseau, in a logic whose articulation is partly similar to Locke's (counterintuitive though it may be, the affinity was noted by Rousseau himself, who maintained that he had broached the *Contrat Social* on the same premises and principles, *see Lettres de la Montagne*, Letter VI in C. E. Vaughan (ed.) *The Political Writings of Jean-Jacques Rousseau* (Cambridge, 1915) Vol. II, pp. 205–206). Notwithstanding the similarities between the two accounts, given Rousseau's premise of undivided sovereignty, in the *Social Contract* the relationship between the legislative and the executive powers loses all pragmatic moorings. What in Locke formed a rule-of-law distinction purposes—related to considerations of individual justice—between general rules related to property and liberty (legislative) and their discretion-wise unproblematic enforcement (executive) is reduced in Rousseau to the metaphysical disjunction between *will* and *force*.

Chapter 3
The Constitutional History of Delegation: Rules and Changes

Thus, in the beginning, all the world was America, and more so than that is now...
John Locke, *Second Treatise of Civil Government* (1690)

Liberty and property...c'est le cri anglais...c'est le cri de la nature.[1]
Voltaire (Idées républicaines, 1765)

As it will be argued in this chapter of the book, classical constitutional law incorporated the conceptual assumptions from which the notion of delegation derives. Locke's argument is, in this respect, exemplary of the philosophical presuppositions of classical constitutionalism. It justifies and explains in point of theory premises and distinctions that later reflected themselves in actual legal practices.

This assertion is, of course, not meant to state a causal connection; the Lockean account is simply a conceptual archetype, namely the most accurate philosophical justification of the legal phenomenon. Additional references can be adduced in support of the claim that classical constitutionalism and constitutional law presupposed i. clear-cut conceptual dichotomies, ii. constitutional practices that faithfully instantiated those conceptual distinctions, and iii. almost "geometrically" drawn legal borders by virtue of which the integrity of those divisions was both reflected and protected. A quotation from Benjamin Constant provides sound evidence in this respect: "Government, outside its sphere, must have no power at all; within it, it could not have enough."[2]

Related, the normative constitutionalism of the eighteenth and nineteenth centuries consistently premised man to be a *relatively and relationally* rational being. This presupposition transpired as a counterfactual analytical assumption (as in Locke's argument) or as a pragmatic profession of anthropological faith, derived

[1] Liberty and property...it is the English call...it is the call of nature.

[2] Cited by Wilhelm Röpke, *The Social Crisis of Our Time* (New Brunswick, New Jersey: Transaction Publishers, 2004), p. 193 "Le gouvernement en dehors de sa sphère ne doit avoir aucun pouvoir; dans sa sphère il ne saurait en avoir trop."

B. Iancu, *Legislative Delegation*,
DOI 10.1007/978-3-642-22330-3_3,

from observation and in no need of further defense (as the statement can be found in the *Federalist Papers*). The ultimate fundamental-legal consequence of this foundational premise was the systemic justification and acceptance of limits to legal rationality and therefore also to the manipulation of social and economic relations by means of positive law. Furthermore, this foundational belief in relative human rationality and its "natural" borders, translated conceptually into the natural-law justification of the division between state and society, private and public, right and privilege, internal and external affairs. In terms of fundamental law, it served to constitute systemic arrangements that distinguished between areas or fields of public action more intensely subject to judicial control (therefore intensely rationalized) and, respectively, areas where the intensity of public law judicial interference was minimal. In the latter case, consequently, decisions based on political rationality, i.e., considerations of opportunity or the aggregation of votes prevailed.[3] Legal practices associated with these foundational presuppositions would be, after the demise of classical constitutionalism, characterized as examples of "legal formalism" or of the intrinsic "technicality and formalization" (thus Ernst Forsthoff) of the principal constitutional institutions and structures.[4] Such labels are, nonetheless, only half-true, since they bear the reductionistic imprint of hindsight view. What later appeared formalistic and technical, looked at from the viewpoint of a foundationally "disenchanted" legal world, was, in its original conceptual and legal-phenomenal environment, "natural." The distinctions and limitations for which the concept of delegation served from the onset as a self-evident analytical-legal shorthand were part of a coherent and consistent legal metaphysics.

The remark that US constitutional evolutions offer the best illustration of this interrelation between foundational concepts, phenomena, and positive-legal institutions should be reiterated. By the same token, American constitutional developments provide an ideal vantage point from which the transformation and gradual disentanglement of these three strands can be observed. America adopted European natural law (the universe of justifications derived from classical liberal constitutional theory) with quasi-religious belief in the rightness of its postulates and merged this credo with an intensely religious belief in the evidence of its divine ordinance. Thus, in response to the British assertion of parliamentary sovereignty, James Otis ("The Rights of the British Colonies", 1764) declaimed that: "The supreme power in the state is jus dicere only: -jus dare, strictly speaking, belongs alone to God."[5] Locke in particular was so revered around the revolutionary and

[3] *See generally* the volume contributions in Bogdan Iancu, *The Law/Politics Distinction in Contemporary Public Law Adjudication* (Utrecht & Portland, OR: Eleven International Publishing, 2009).

[4] Ernst Forsthoff, "Begriff und Wesen des sozialen Rechtsstaates", in Ernst Forsthoff (Ed.), *Rechtsstaatlichkeit und Sozialstaatlichkeit-Aufsätze und Essays* (Darmstadt: Wissenschaftliche Buchgesellschaft, 1968), p. 165 ff.

[5] In Dieter Grimm, "Europäisches Naturrecht und Amerikanische Revolution—Die Verwandlung politischer Philosophie in politischer Techne," *Ius Commune* III (1970), 120–151, at p. 146.

constitutional adoption times, that the *Second Treatise* served as "a political gospel" and his theses were ubiquitously put forth "as if he could be relied on to support anything the writers happened to be arguing."[6] The impact of this natural law intellectual foundation on positive fundamental law was enhanced by the vastness of space, remoteness from European convulsions, and the apparent inexhaustibility of resources: the state of nature, as it were. European theorists commonly projected their "state of nature" anthropologies on the remote continent. This was of course a purely imagined rendition and their descriptions differed in direct relation to imagination and the argumentative needs at hand. Thus, Hobbes's Americas are evidence of the warlike and devilish character of human nature in the absence of sovereign power. To Locke, in contrast, the primary inconvenience of the "natural" life in the New World is pre-societal lack of property title, division, and legal security thereof: this is why "an Indian king" is "clad worse than a day labourer in England"[7] But the inhabitants of the new continent also regarded themselves in like fashion and, moreover, they did so with the immediacy and genuineness of direct experience. The Mayflower compacts are the classic example yet the spirit persisted until well into the nineteenth century. James Willard Hurst provides the 1836 example of a newly formed claimants' union in Pike Creek, Wisconsin. They adopted a Claimants' Union Constitution for the purpose of prompting the legal security of their newly occupied lands, a security for the benefit of which, as the preamble stated, they had "encountered the hardships of a perilous journey, advancing into a space beyond the bounds of civilization, and having the many difficulties and obstructions of a state of nature to overcome."[8] All these preconditions offered the singular possibility of turning the eighteenth century theoretical justifications of limited government, writing almost on blank slate, into positive, judicially enforceable constitutional law.

Another earlier remark should now be revisited. It was argued in the introduction that liberal constitutionalism presupposes a certain degree of homogeneity of fundamental constitutional structures and therefore also a measure of constitutional synchronicity. This remark appears at first sight paradoxical, since the legally enforceable constitution and judicial review were, through to the twentieth century, American idiosyncrasies. Enforceable constitutions and the review of constitutionality are in Europe and the rest of the world, at least where they were at all introduced, fairly recent legal phenomena. However, the contradiction is only apparent and superficial. The premise and constitutional preservation of a certain model of legislation and legislative reservation, which in the United States was juridically expressed through the nondelegation doctrine, resulted in other paradigmatic Western legal orders from legal institutions that were functionally analogous in a constitutional sense (meaning, foundational to the legal order). Private law autonomy and structural arrangements partly took over the constitutional function of legal-constitutional

[6] *Id.*, p. 123.

[7] *Second Treatise*, Par. 41.

[8] Willard Hurst 1967, at p. 4.

rules and constitutionally enforceable fundamental rights.[9] In fact, even in the United States, the legislative reservation understood as intrinsic to the Constitution was only expressed through, not enforced by means of the nondelegation doctrine. The major divisions of constitutionalism (state/society, private/public, internal/external, ministerial/discretionary, and—ultimately—politics/law) and the discrete legal arrangements that gave expression to them were not necessarily implemented by means of constitutional law and were certainly not created by fundamental law alone. They were also constitutive of it.

3.1 Delegation of Congressional Legislative Power in American Constitutional History

3.1.1 The Doctrine of Nondelegation and the US Constitution: A Conceptual Framework

In the United States, however, the jurisdiction of the legislature is a judicial question. Here the courts may in a proper case determine whether the popular assembly has stepped outside its circle of power as well as whether the sheriff or the town clerk has exceeded his authority. Thus the courts bring unity into the legal system by keeping all private and governmental persons within the range of their allotted powers.

James Hart, *The Ordinance Making Powers of the President of the United States* (1925)

[L]egislatures have no power to pass a law which is not a law in itself when passed. . ..

Rice v. Foster, 4 Harr. 479 (Del., 1847)

3.1.1.1 Nondelegation as a Doctrine of American Constitutional Law: An Introductory Taxonomy

[E]ven the boundaries between the Executive, Legislative, and Judiciary powers, though in general so strongly marked in themselves, consist in many instances of mere shades of difference.

James Madison, letter to Thomas Jefferson of Oct. 24, 1787

Perhaps there was no argument urged with more success, or more plausibly grounded against the Constitution, under which we are now deliberating, than that founded on the mingling of the Executive and Legislative branches of the Government in one body.

James Madison, House debate in the First Congress, 1789, on the Foreign Affairs Department

Most standard American administrative law casebooks or treatises open with lengthy discussions of the nondelegation doctrine, discussions which regularly

[9] Dieter Grimm, *Recht und Staat der bürgerlichen Gesellschaft* (Frankfurt a. M.: Suhrkamp, 1987), *passim.*

conclude by tersely emphasizing the essentially "ideological" or "philosophical" character of the doctrine and its modern state of legal irrelevance.[10] The delegation doctrine is also one of the most contested topics in modern constitutional law, and rivers of ink are incessantly spilt attacking or defending its constitutional validity and relevance.[11] To wit, the debate on delegation has been proceeding unabated and at the same pace up to now, in spite of the fact that, as critics are usually poised to point out, in only a couple of instances was nondelegation ever used by the Supreme Court as a ground to strike down federal legislation and, furthermore, even those instances pertain to a period of American constitutional history which is nowadays almost unanimously regarded with mixed feelings of hostility and embarrassment.[12] Since 1936, the nondelegation doctrine has been, in an apt characterization, "discussed actively but invoked rarely."[13] It is puzzling at first

[10] For instance, Kenneth Culp Davis opens his *Administrative Law Treatise*, a classic in the field, with long vituperations against the doctrines of the separation of powers, the rule of law, and nondelegation, all labeled dismissively as useless "philosophical thinking": "[p]hilosophical thinking has been a barrier to the developments of administrative law and has contributed little or nothing that is affirmative." (San Diego: K. C. Davis Pub. Co., 1978–1984), Chapter 2-"Philosophical Foundations." *See* for instance at §2: 6, describing the notion of separation of powers as "an empty receptacle for answers that have to be invented" and claiming in essence that... Montesquieu was wrong. *See*, for a more balanced contemporary treatment, Jerry L. Mashaw, Richard A. Merril, Peter M. Shane, *Administrative Law-The American Public Law System: Cases and Materials* (Mashaw et al.) (St. Paul, Minn.: West, c2003), Chapter 2-"The Legislative Connection," *esp*. pp. 59–49.

[11] *See*, for instance, a good and relatively recent breakdown of delegation-related issues and positions in contemporary U.S. constitutional and administrative law, in The Phoenix Rises Again: The Nondelegation Doctrine from Constitutional and Policy Perspectives, Symposium 20 (3) *Cardozo Law Review* (January 1999).

[12] Both *Panama Refining* and *Schechter Poultry* were rendered in 1935. A year later, in 1936, the Bituminous Coal Conservation Act of 1935 (the former Bituminous Coal Code, enacted as federal statute by Congress after the demise of the NIRA) was declared unconstitutional, primarily on Commerce Clause grounds but also because of delegation reasons, in *Carter v. Carter Coal Co.* 298 U.S. 238 (1936). These developments happened before the so-called "shift in time that saved nine" of 1937, that is, before the Supreme Court reversed its 'conservative' pre-New Deal positions (most notably on economic due process and the scope of the Commerce Clause), thus averting FDR's "Court-Packing Plan." Given this inauspicious constitutional context, John Hart Ely notably opined that the post-New Deal demise of the nondelegation doctrine was primarily a matter of "death by association." (John Hart Ely, *Democracy and Distrust: A Theory of Judicial Review* (Cambridge: Harvard University Press, 1980), at p. 133). *See* Douglas Ginsburg, "Delegation Running Riot," (reviewing Schoenbrod, *Power Without Responsibility*) 18 (1) *Regulation* 83 (1995): "So for 60 years the nondelegation doctrine has existed only as a part of the Constitution-in-exile, along with the doctrines of enumerated powers, unconstitutional conditions, and substantive due process, and their textual cousins, the Necessary and Proper, Contracts, Takings, and Commerce Clauses. The memory of these ancient exiles, banished for standing in opposition to unlimited government, is kept alive by a few scholars who labor on in the hope of a restauration, a second coming of the Constitution of liberty-even if perhaps not in their own lifetimes."

[13] Paul Verkuil, "The American Constitutional Tradition of Shared and Separated Powers: Separation of Powers, the Rule of Law and the Idea of Independence," 30 *William and Mary Law Review* 301 (Winter, 1989), at p. 319.

glance why a topic of allegedly so little legal import would be at the foreground of so much academic legal debate and why a doctrine of such apparently inconsequential practical value in contemporary constitutional adjudication would prove to be, non-etheless, so resilient over time. Indeed, in terms of resilience in the face of adversity, in Gary Lawson's vernacular, the nondelegation doctrine has turned out to be the "Energizer Bunny" of US constitutional law.[14]

One could safely opine that the main reason why nondelegation is important to American constitutional and administrative law, as a purely *legal* concept, aside from its general heuristic value in structuring the ongoing legitimacy–accountability, separation of powers, and rule of law debates in constitutional theory, is the very nature of American constitutionalism. Carl Friedrich once claimed that "[i]n America...constitutionalism struck deeper root than almost anywhere on earth...."[15] By this assertion Friedrich meant that, in America, constitutionalism as an umbrella concept of limited government[16] had been, from the very beginning, immediately and very concretely associated with the actual written constitution of the land. The constitution has been in turn, from the onset, primarily perceived as a legal document setting forth clear legal limitations on government, rather than—to juxtapose and contrast with the early European perspective—as a political law and a grant of power.[17] To this extent, the 1787 document and its history constitute the epitomes of 'negative' and 'jurisdictional' constitutionalism.[18] In this vein, it is quite

[14] "No matter how many times it gets broken, beaten, or buried, it just keeps on going and going." Gary Lawson, "Delegation and Original Meaning," 88 *Va. L. Rev.* 327 (April, 2002), at p. 330.

[15] Carl Friedrich, *Constitutional Government and Democracy: Theory and Practice in Europe and America* (Waltham: Blaisdel, c1968) 4th ed., at p. 28.

[16] Encompassing the "set of principles, manners, and institutional arrangements that were used traditionally to limit government," Sajó 1999, at xiv.

[17] Edward Corwin's commentary on the amending provisions of Art. V is very indicative of the American understanding of constitution and constitutionalism: "*The amending, like all other powers organized in the Constitution, is in form a delegated, and hence a limited power*... the one power known to the Constitution which is not limited by it is that which ordains it- in other words, the original, inalienable power of the people of the United States to determine their own political institutions." (emphasis supplied), *The Constitution and What It Means Today* (Princeton: Princeton University Press, 1946), at p. 141. For a good exposition of the American 'constitutional exceptionalism' and an insightful comparison of American and early European constitutionalism, *see* Martin A. Rogoff, "A Comparison of Constitutionalism in France and the United States," 49 *Me. L. Rev.* 21 (1997), pp 31–32: "In America the idea of constitutionalism is intimately attached to, and in fact inseparable from, the actual written constitution of the country. Constitutionalism is not a vague concept calling for the separation and limitation of public power, the rights of the governed, and adherence to certain time-honored procedures, customs, and values. It has rather an immediacy and a tangibility, and an association with a particular document, which is usually lacking even in other constitutional democracies."

[18] "[T]he Constitution is a charter of negative rather than positive liberties. The men who wrote the Bill of Rights were not concerned that government might do too little for the people but that it might do too much for them." Posner, J., *Jackson v. City of Joliet* 715 F.2d 1200, 1203 (1983), certiorari denied 465 U.S. 1049 (1984) (failure by state officers to rescue individuals from a burning car, even if it amounts to reckless negligence, does not amount to a constitutional tort

telling that no less a perceptive observer than Tocqueville himself would early on note in admiring surprise that "[t]here is hardly a political question in the United States which does not sooner or later turn into a judicial one....the spirit of the law, born within schools and courts, spreads little by little beyond them; it infiltrates through society right down to the lowest ranks, till finally the whole people have contracted some of the ways and tastes of a magistrate."[19]

After the early landmark decision in *Marbury v. Madison*[20] "welded judicial review to the political axiom of limited government,"[21] the paramount legal value of the constitution has entailed the consequence that, to the extent that the justiciability requirements are met, the judiciary would effectively harness governmental action and keep it within the four corners of "the supreme law of the land," by enforcing the constitutional limitations on governmental action.

The province of law-making was thus perceived as a matter of legally enforceable jurisdictional limits and the possibility of judicial review has been ever since, correlatively, a principal factor in curbing assertions of unfettered legislative competence.[22] Consequently, in America, a historically situated phenomenon

under the Fourteenth Amendment's Due Process Clause, as a deprivation of life without due process). By 'negative' I understand primarily concerned with limitations, constraining. By 'jurisdictional' I understand that the limitations, primarily those on legislation, are in principle ascertainable in a court of law. In line with the contractualist tradition which informed the Founders, Government as such was arguably perceived as an instrument of limited purposes, limited, that is, by the original compact and the triad of pre-political or 'natural' rights, life, liberty, property (the analogy with Locke's theory is too evident to be restated). The distinction has become eroded as a matter of practices, as we shall *see* in due course, after the New Deal. In terms of political theory, it has come under attack since the Progressive Era, after the Civil War. *See*, for instance, a more recent example of questioning the validity of the distinction between positive and negative constitutionalism and positive and negative rights, Stephen Holmes and Cass Sunstein, *The Cost of Rights: Why Liberty Depends on Taxes* (New York: Norton, 1999), whose title is fairly revealing of the main thesis. As a question of actual constitutional law, the qualification of 'negative constitutionalism' applied to the U.S. Constitution holds true; in this vein, for an elaboration and an illuminating comparison with contemporary German constitutionalism, *see* David P. Currie, "Positive and Negative Constitutional Rights," 53 *U. Chi. L. Rev*. 864 (Summer, 1986), showing that the Supreme Court has consistently refused to recognize third party effects or affirmative state obligations related to the rights guarantees outside active government aggression, unless a 'positive' governmental obligation is directly and inextricably related to the exercise of a negative (defense) right and triggered by intrusive governmental action.

[19] Alexis de Tocqueville, *Democracy in America*, ed. J. P. Mayer, transl. George Lawrence (New York: Harper Perennial, 1988), p. 270.

[20] 5 U.S. 137 (Cranch) (1803). The understanding that the Constitution would need to be a judicially enforceable charter arguably predates the decision; an argument much akin to Justice Marshall's in Marbury can be found in The Federalist, No. 78 (Alexander Hamilton).

[21] Henry P. Monaghan, "*Marbury* and the Administrative State," 83 *Colum. L. Rev*. 1 (January, 1983), at 32.

[22] *Marbury v. Madison*, 5 U.S. 137 (Cranch) (1803), at pp. 176–177 "This original and supreme will organizes the government, and assigns, to different departments, their respective powers. It may either stop here; or establish certain limits not to be transcended by those departments The government of the United States is of the latter description. The powers of the legislature are

which has been posing certain challenges to constitutionalism across Western democracies and irrespective of particular constitutional systems, the peculiarly modern problem of legislative delegations to the executive and the administration, translated simultaneously into an issue of constitutionality and constitutional review. The problem has been that of finding the proper constitutional limit on statutory grants of discretion, i.e., a judicially-enforced, constitutionally-derived jurisdictional limit on the institutional legislature.[23]

The nondelegation doctrine made an early judicial appearance in the case commonly known as *The Brig Aurora*,[24] where the appellant, whose cargo had been condemned pursuant to the revival of the Non-Intercourse Act of 1810 against Britain, argued that Congress had in effect delegated legislative power to the president, by making the revival of the act (against either Britain or France or both) contingent upon a presidential proclamation.[25] The Court, while turning a deaf ear on the nondelegation argument in the specific context at hand, that of contingent legislation in the field of foreign affairs,[26] accepted in principle the general soundness, as a matter of constitutional law, of the argument that Congress cannot delegate legislative power to the executive.[27]

---

defined, and limited; and that those limits may not be mistaken, or forgotten, the constitution is written. To what purpose are powers limited, and to what purpose is that limitation committed to writing, if these limits may, at any time, be passed by those intended to be restrained? The distinction, between a government with limited and unlimited powers, is abolished, if those limits do not confine the persons on whom they are imposed, and if acts prohibited and acts allowed, are of equal obligation. It is a proposition too plain to be contested, that the constitution controls any legislative act repugnant to it. . .."

[23] I am using the phrase "jurisdiction of the legislature," to a certain extent, by way of stylistic licence, even though the use is not totally improper in the context of our discussion. *See*, for instance, Barber 1978, at p. 29: "Why should [the maxim *delegata potestas non potest delegari*] be applicable to delegations of 'jurisdiction' and not to delegations of legislative power? Is not any delegation of rule-making power a delegation of jurisdiction in some sense and to some degree?"

[24] *The Cargo of the Brig Aurora, Burn Side, Claimant, v. The United States*, 11 U.S. (7 Cranch) 382 (1813).

[25] "But Congress could not transfer the legislative power to the President. To make the revival of a law depend upon he President's proclamation, is to give to that proclamation the force of a law." *Id.*, at 386 (argument for the Appellant).

[26] "On the second point, we can *see* no sufficient reason, why the legislature should not exercise its discretion in reviving the act of March 1st, 1809, either expressly or conditionally, as their judgment should direct." *Id.* at 388.

[27] *See*, for instance, the historical overview in David Schoenbrod, *Power Without Responsibility: How Congress Abuses the People through Delegation* (New Haven, CT.: Yale University Press, 1993), pp. 30–31. *But see* Posner and Vermeule 2002, at 1737–1738: "Nothing in *The Brig Aurora* endorses the delegation metaphor; if anything, the Court's terse dismissal of the claim suggests the absence of constitutional limits on statutory grants to the executive." According to the authors, "[t]he nondelegation metaphor, rather, was a legal theory of uncertain provenance that skulked around the edges of nineteenth-century constitutionalism, and wasn't adopted by the Court until 1892." (At 1737.) Nonetheless, considering the actual wording of the decision, where the delegation argument is engaged and not dismissed out

The constitutional value of the rule or doctrine of nondelegation was also expounded and extolled, in succinct and categorical language, in one of the standard early authorities, Cooley's *Constitutional Limitations*[28]; the most relevant passage is worth citing at some length:

> One of the settled maxims in constitutional law is, that the power conferred upon the legislature to make laws cannot be delegated by that department to any other body or authority. Where the sovereign power of the State has located the authority, there it must remain; and by the constitutional agency alone the laws must be made until the constitution itself is changed. The power to whose judgment, wisdom and patriotism this high prerogative has been intrusted cannot relieve itself of the responsibility by choosing other agencies upon which the power shall be devolved, nor can it substitute the judgment, wisdom and patriotism of any other body for those to which alone the people have seen fit to confide this sovereign trust.[29]

of hand as either strange or impervious, this latter, radically alternative interpretation, is unwarranted.

[28] Joseph Story offers an elaborate account of the Latin maxim *delegata potestas non potest delegari* in his book on agency law: "One, who has a bare power or authority from another to do an act, must execute it himself, and cannot delegate his authority to another; for this being a trust or confidence reposed in him personally, it cannot be assigned to a stranger, whose ability and integrity might not be known to the principal, or, if known, might not be selected by him for such a purpose. . .The reason is plain; for, in each of these cases, there is an exclusive personal trust and confidence reposed in the particular party. And hence is derived the maxim of the common law; *Delegata potestas non potest delegari.*" *Commentaries on the Law of Agency as a Branch of Commercial and Maritime Jurisprudence, with Occasional Illustrations from the Civil and Foreign Law* (Boston: Little, Brown, 1839), § 13. The agency law principle, in Story's rendition, establishes a rebuttable presumption against subdelegation. Namely, delegated authority—especially when conferred in view of the agent's special fitness—cannot, in principle, be re-delegated, unless this power is expressly conferred on the agent or can be fairly implied, for instance, from the terms of the agreement or the usages of the particular trade. That is apparently still the law, 1 *Restatement of the Law of Agency Second* (St. Paul, Min.: American Law Institute Publishers, 1958), § 18: "Unless otherwise agreed, a person cannot properly delegate to another the exercise of discretion in the use of a power held for the benefit of the principal." Story does not transpose the agency law maxim into the field of public law in his constitutional *Commentaries,* perhaps since he would have understood it essentially as an inference from an overly doctrinaire or, in modern categories, 'formalistic' understanding of the principle of separation of powers. Story was, like Madison, a strong advocate of a position which comes closer to what nowadays is called separation of powers "functionalism." According to Story, in an argument similar to Madison's in *The Federalist 47*, the principle can be reduced to a requirement that "the whole power of one of these department should not be exercised by the same hands which possess the whole power of either of the other departments." Lest that would happen, institutional autonomy and mutual checks are the best safeguards of the initial allocation; power counteracts power. *See Commentaries on the Constitution of the United States* (Boston: Little, Brown, and Company, 1891(1833)), Vol. 1, Book III, Chapter VII, "Distribution of Powers," pp. 388–406, § 525.

[29] Thomas McIntyre Cooley, *A Treatise on the Constitutional Limitations Which Rest Upon the Legislative Power of the States of the American Union* (Boston: Little, Brown, and Company, 1868), p. 137.

It is important to point out that, while at the highest level of abstraction a principle of nondelegation as such is relatively easy to justify in a government of limited (divided and enumerated) powers, analysis seems fated to be bogged down at the moment one tries to define, concretize, and give it a certain measure of workable specificity as a doctrine or rule of constitutional law. In the abstract, as a pure exercise of analytical jurisprudence, the discussion can easily revert into tautologies and absurdities. For instance, while the legislature should be in principle prevented from delegating legislative power, legislative power is, by constitutional definition, the only power the American legislature possesses to begin with and—conversely—any power it would delegate to the executive is by definition legislative and non-delegable (since, by the same token, also by constitutional definition, the executive and the judiciary branches only posses and can only exercise executive and judiciary powers, respectively). Does the Constitution then prescribe or assume a purely formal understanding of the 'powers' vested in the respective branches of government, and more particularly of legislative power and legislation or does it require a more substantive or material concept?

To be more specific, the nub of the matter is whether executive and administrative rulemaking, quasi-adjudication, and interpretive discretion or discretionary action in pursuance of a statutory command, no matter how vague the legislative authorization, always constitute only law-execution according to the given statutory terms or whether "the Constitution contains some implicit principle that constrains the scope or precision of otherwise valid statutory enactments."[30]

Accepting *ex hypothesi* that such a principle of limitation on the precision of statutes is supported by the Constitution in turn gives rise to a congeries of subsequent dilemmas. Does nondelegation mean only no legislative abdication or does the prohibition also apply to a delegation of discretion to the enforcement agency? Does a statutory grant of discretion ever equate in substance an unconstitutional abdication of its legislative powers by Congress? Does nondelegation apply only to subordinate executive/administrative rulemaking? Does the application of the doctrine vary in respect of the constitutional context to which it is applied or can a nondelegation standard be identified and applied to all statutory authorizations, irrespective of the nature of the fields to be regulated (an obvious example would be foreign affairs as opposed to purely domestic legislation) or of the given situation (emergency delegations or delegations in normal situations)? Should the

[30] Posner and Vermeule 2002, at pp. 1728–1729, defending the 'naïve view' according to which "a statutory grant of authority is not a delegation"; in the authors' view, the Constitution supports solely a minimalist nondelegation rule, based on which only the delegation of an individual legislator's voting rights would be deemed unconstitutional. *See also* Eric A. Posner and Adrian Vermeule, "Nondelegation: A Post-Mortem," 70 *U. Chi. L. Rev.* 1331 (Fall 2003). Compare and contrast, Larry Alexander and Saikrishna Prakash, "Reports of the Nondelegation Doctrine's Death Are Greatly Exaggerated," 70 *U. Chi. L. Rev.* 1297 (Fall 2003).

constitutionally required level of precision or scope of a statutory enactment vary with respect to the delegate (compare delegation to private parties to delegation to an independent regulatory agency to a delegation to a government department to a delegation to the President)?

An across the board answer to all of these questions is impossible to provide. Part of the analytical quagmire arises from the fact that, as Hans Linde, a particularly perceptive commentator on modern delegation debates, once noted, "[t]here is not just one rule on delegation but several, depending on the relevant constraint."[31] Since the doctrine prohibiting the delegation of legislative power is not an explicit rule of the Constitution, different views on nondelegation constitute inevitably so many inferences regarding legislation, inferences either derived directly from text and structure or read into the text from assumptions regarding background norms of constitutional theory (the rule of law, separation of powers, theories of democracy/representation, and legitimacy, notions which, in their turn, do not by any means lend themselves to easy definition). In delegation-related debates, much confusion arises, therefore, from a failure to make explicit the background assumptions and, consequently, to separate the inferential strands. To this extent, the manifold unreflective uses of the phrase "legislative delegation" constitute, to paraphrase Justice Frankfurter, "an excellent illustration of the extent to which uncritical use of words bedevils the law."[32]

What will follow throughout most of this chapter is a discussion of a historical evolution, an account of the need for delegation as it emerged in modern American political legal history; we will be dealing with a phenomenon and its judicial and theoretical reception. Yet, since theoretical or judicial positions on delegation constitute of necessity the by-product of different assumptions, these need to be first properly identified and disentangled, in order for the discussion to approach a level of clarity which would in turn allow for the account and assessment of events to be properly perceived. At this juncture, in order to get a point of ingress into the constitutional dimension, it will thus be necessary to block out a starting conceptual framework and an introductory taxonomy of what can be reasonably understood by the notion of 'legislative delegation,' in terms of the constitutional considerations underlying the nondelegation doctrine.

Since all the theoretical points to be raised over the next few pages have already been visited more generally in the previous chapter of the book and will be commented on, as need arises, throughout the rest of the argument, only groundwork assumptions and taxonomies more directly relevant to the present discussion need to be re-introduced here.

[31] Hans A. Linde, "Structures and Terms of Consent: *Delegation, Discretion, Separation of Powers, Representation, Participation, Accountability,*" 20 *Cardozo L. Rev.* 823 (1998–1999), pp. 849–850.

[32] Frankfurter, J., concurring in *Tiller v. Atlantic Coast Line R. Co.*, 318 U.S. 54, 68 (1943).

3.1.1.2 Delegation of the Legislative Power in American Constitutional Law: Relevant Conceptual Associations and Constitutional Constraints

A phrase begins life as a literary expression; its felicity leads to lazy repetition; and repetition soon establishes it as a legal formula, undiscriminatingly used to express different and contradictory ideas.

Frankfurter, J., concurring in *Tiller v. Atlantic Coast Line R. Co.*, 318 U.S. 54 (1943)

After a single preambulatory sentence, the Constitution of the United States begins with this simple proposition: 'All legislative powers herein granted shall be vested in a Congress of the United States.' What does it mean?

Douglas H. Ginsburg, "Delegation Running Riot," 18 (1) REG. 83 (1985)

The answer to this question is by no means an easy one. The point should be restated that nondelegation is not an explicit rule of the constitution but an implicit doctrine, inferred from constitutional text and structure, as interpreted in light of background assumptions derived from history and political and constitutional theory. The various takes on delegation reflect this multiplicity of assumptions with respect to distinct relevant constraints on the legislature and legislation. This multiplicity of conceptual associations accounts in turn for the irreducibility of the notion of "legislative delegation" to one single definition.

Delegata Potestas Non Potest Delegari

It is sometimes believed that the constitutional rule of nondelegation in American law derives in a way from or at least is largely informed by a Roman law principle which, insofar as it applied to public law, forbade the sub-delegation of specially conferred jurisdictional authority.[33] If *iurisdictio* (literally translated, "the power to declare rights," embracing the general magisterial power to administer justice) was held as of right, attached to an office, it could be delegated, under the reservation that pure or unmixed *imperium* (*merum imperium,* embracing capital jurisdiction in criminal

[33] Dig. I. 21. 1, *De officio eius, cui mandata est iurisdictio* (*Duties of One to Whom Jurisdiction is Delegated*): "Papiniano libro primo quaestionum. Quaecumque specialiter lege vel senatus consulto vel constitutione principum tribuntur, mandata iurisdictione non transferuntur; quae vero iure magistratus competunt, mandari possunt." ("Any powers specially conferred by statute or *senatus consultum* or imperial enactment are not transferable by delegation of a jurisdiction. But the competence attached to a magistracy as of right is capable of delegation.") Dig. I. 21. 5. "Paulus libro octavo decimo ad Plautium. Mandatam sibi iurisdictionem mandari alteri non posse manifestum est. Mandata iurisdictione privato etiam imperium quod non est merum videtur mandari, quia iurisdictio sine modica coercitione nulla est." ("It is obvious that one cannot delegate to another a jurisdiction which one holds by delegation. When a jurisdiction is delegated to a private citizen, it seems that there is also delegated a power of imperation, albeit not a pure one; for there is no such thing as a jurisdiction without some modicum of coercive power.") The example is given (Dig. I. 21.1.) of the praetor not being able to delegate, when allegation is made that a master has been murdered by his slaves, the task of hearing the case, since jurisdiction over such cases is delegated to him by a *senatus consultum.*

matters) could not be carried by the transfer of jurisdiction, since *merum imperium* was considered to have been delegated itself by special legal grant, and thus was not inherent in an exercise of jurisdiction.[34] Conversely, jurisdiction exercised by virtue of formal and special legal grant from higher authority (through a *lex, senatus consultum, constitutio principis*) could not be sub-delegated, unless sub-delegation would be allowed by statute or convention. The underlying Roman law principle, usually expressed in common law sources through the maxim *delegata potestas non potest delegari* (or *delegatus non potest delegare*), was first incorporated into the common law by Bracton, in his *De Legibus et Consuetudinibus Angliae*. Afterwards it was given another authoritative validation by Coke's *Institutes* and—in more recent times—expounded as an important principle of agency law by Lord Mansfield, Kent, and Story. Finally, it was incorporated into constitutional law, so that an early Pennsylvania case, *Parker v. Commonwealth*, could praise the maxim as expressing "a primal axiom of jurisprudence."[35]

In the most comprehensive and authoritative study tracing the archeology of the Latin maxim in common law sources, Patrick W. Duff and Horace E. Whiteside advanced the argument that, apparently, the popularity of the *delegata potestas non potest delegari* principle in American constitutional law would have been the result of a pure mishap, quite literally a typo in one the early manuscripts of Bracton's *De Legibus*. Apparently, the printer inadvertently substituted a "non" for a "nec" and changed a colon for a semi-colon, changes that in turn radically altered the meaning of the text, from the correct one, *i.e.*, "jurisdiction cannot be delegated by the king in such a way that primary jurisdiction does not stay with other king" (or "the King's power is not diminished by delegation to others") to "jurisdiction cannot be delegated."[36] According to the two authors, Coke allegedly seized on the version distorted by the mistake, took a part of it ("jurisdictio delegata non delegari poterit") out of context, turned it into the first version of the modern maxim, and thus erroneously helped to perpetuate a typographical error into an agency and constitutional law principle: "[W]e thus learn that the 'maxim' which was to serve

[34] Dig. II.1.3 (Ulpianus libro secundo de officio quaestoris): "Merum est imperium habere gladii potestatem ad animadvertendum facinorosos homines, quod etiam potestas appellatur." ("To have simple *imperium* is to have the power of the sword to punish the wicked and this is also called *potestas*.") A transfer of jurisdiction would carry a transfer of mixed *imperium*, since a certain measure of coercion (for instance, the power to impose a fine) was considered as entailed by an exercise of jurisdiction). *See*, more generally, one these issues, David Johnston, "The General Influence of Roman Institutions of State and Public Law," in D. L. Carey Miller and R. Zimmermann, eds., *The Civilian Tradition and Scots Law. Aberdeen Quincentenary Essays [Schriften zur Europäischen Rechts- und Verfassungsgeschichte, Bd. 20]* (Berlin: Duncker & Humblot, 1997), pp. 87–101.

[35] *Parker v. Commonwealth*, 6 Barr. 507. 515, 10 Law Rep. 375 (Pa. 1847), Pennsylvania decision which held unconstitutional, on nondelegation grounds, a local option law which authorized the citizens of a number of counties to decide by local ballot whether the sale of liquors in those counties was to be continued.

[36] *See* Patrick W. Duff and Horace E. Whiteside, "*Delegata Potestas Non Potest Delegari*: A Maxim of American Constitutional Law," 14 *Cornell L. Q.* 168 (1928–1929).

the turn of Coke, to command the respect of Kent and Story, and to leave its mark on the constitutional history of the United States, owes its origin to medieval commentators on the Digests and Decretals, and its vogue in the common law to the carelessness of a sixteenth century printer."[37]

The wholesale analogy of the delegation problem under a modern constitution with the reference to royal jurisdiction in Bracton is to a certain extent undiscriminating in the narrow etymological sense of the word, a failure to make rational distinctions. Unlike the king, who, notwithstanding medieval developments and debates on the difference between person and office and the king's "two bodies," was a concrete person with a concrete will, in the modern legitimacy paradigm (where the delegation problem arises as a problem of limited and limiting government) the people's 'will' is an abstraction, sovereignty. To be sure, sovereignty as such (as a source of public power or 'primary jurisdiction') is, as an unstated final assumption, unlimited and undiminished by the grant (the constitution), which in turn can in both theory and practice be changed by changing the terms of the grant, adopting another constitution or amending the existing one (according to the procedures by which it bound itself and which structure and form its will). But the delegation problem bears on the extent to which the legislature, as an agent restrained within an initial mandate, is legally within the *vires* of the grant, *i.e.,* the written constitution by which sovereignty is limited. Failure to understand and recognize this *as a matter of principle* is equivalent to the opposite statement, namely (to use Marshall's words) that "written constitutions are absurd attempts, on the part of the people, to limit a power in its own nature illimitable."[38] It is thus only as a result of a myopic neglect of first principles that an otherwise well-researched and learned study should come up with the baffling thesis that the nondelegation doctrine in American agency and constitutional law owes its existence to a sixteenth-century typographical error and a number of subsequent happenstances. Contrariwise and obviously enough, the main reason why the Latin maxim was seized upon by judges and commentators is not its ancient pedigree but rather, conversely, the ancient lineage is indicative of the maxim's capacity to condense a simple kernel of truth, which is of the highest relevance to any regime of law-bound exercise of public power. The legislative power under a rigid written constitution, like any power that is not primary but derived, that is delegated, is limited and conditioned in its exercise by the original grant of authority.[39] Hence, the relevant constitutional constraints need to be identified.

---

[37] *Id.*, at 173.

[38] *Marbury v. Madison*, 5. U.S. 137, 177.

[39] Jaffe also dismissed the Whiteside-Duff thesis with characteristic deftness: "But the judges have, I think, merely seized on a convenient legal formula to express the underlying thought of Locke that 'the legislature neither must nor can transfer the power of making laws to anybody else, or place it anywhere but where the people have.'. . .If it be thought that the judges were reading the 'vesting' provision itself, pursuant to the maxim, it may be replied that a maxim enforced by Coke, Story, and Kent over the course of 400 years is far more relevant to the interpretation of a modern document than an unknown reading of a thirteenth century text." Louis Jaffe, *Judicial Control of*

The Vesting Clause of Art. I and the Supremacy of the Constitution Argument

The most limited version of the principle of nondelegation can be justified solely on the basis of the principle of the supremacy of the Constitution[40] and of the Vesting Clause of Art. I: "All legislative Powers herein granted shall be vested in a Congress of the United States, which shall consist of a Senate and House of Representatives."[41] A nondelegation rule derived from the Vesting and Supremacy Clauses would of necessity not differentiate among recipients of congressional power. Since the focus is on the duty of Congress, the nondelegation prohibition, in this version, applies equally to delegations to the executive, the judiciary, independent administrative agencies, states or local governments, voters or private parties, perhaps even congressional committees. The argument is fairly straightforward: since the legislative powers are granted by an original act of sovereignty, by delegating or abdicating them Congress would render the initial allocation a nullity and defeat the purpose of having government limited by a Constitution in the first place.[42]

Hence, Congress is bound by a constitutional duty to exercise its powers. This duty would entail two obvious nondelegation limitations: (a) Congress cannot delegate powers specific enough so that delegating them would very clearly defeat the purpose of assigning responsibility for their exercise to the Congress in the first place[43] and (b) Congress could not delegate to an agency a completely open-ended authority to choose from and pursue any and all federally permissible ends.[44]

Administrative Action (Boston, Toronto: Little, Brown, and Company, 1965), at p. 54. *See also* comments in Barber 1978, at pp. 26–30.

[40] The Supremacy Clause (Art. VI, Paragraph 2) provides that "[t]this Constitution, and the Laws of the United States which shall be made in Pursuance thereof; and all Treaties made, or which shall be made, under the Authority of the United States, shall be the supreme Law of the Land; and the Judges in every State shall be bound thereby, any Thing in the Constitution or Laws of any State to the contrary notwithstanding."

[41] U.S. Constitution, Article I, Section 1.

[42] James Hart, "Limits of Legislative Delegation," 221 *Annals of the American Academy of Political and Social Science* (1941) 91: "Certainly it cannot honestly be denied that this principle (that the creatures of the Constitution may not in their discretion alter its allotment of powers) is necessarily implicit in the constitutional allotment. To deny this would make that allotment meaningless."

[43] Laurence Tribe gives the examples of setting up a special agency outside Congress to ratify treaties (contrary to the requirement of Article II, Section 2, that treaties become effective only upon senatorial ratification by a two thirds majority of present Senators) and setting up a "Federal Court of Impeachment" (contrary to Art. I, Section I "The Senate shall have the sole Power to try all Impeachments"), *American Constitutional Law*, 2nd ed. (Mineola, New York: The Foundation Press, 1988), § 5–17, at p. 363.

[44] *Id.*: "An agency exercising delegated authority is not free, as is Congress itself, to exercise its authority to pursue any and all ends within the affirmative reach of federal authority. Rather, an agency can assert as its objectives only those ends which are connected with the task that Congress created it to perform. The open-ended discretion to choose ends is the essence of legislative power; it is this power which Congress possesses but its agents lack." *See also* James Hart, *The Ordinance Making Powers of the President of the United States* (Baltimore: The Johns Hopkins Press, 1925), for a similar nondelegation argument: there is a constitutionally supported difference between a. legislative power, an almost "full discretion in the premises" and b. "co-legislative power,"

While, as we shall *see* in due course, the latter limitation plays an important role as a nondelegation-related canon of construction in modern judicial review of administrative action, as prohibitions on Congress these two restrictions imagine hypotheticals unlikely enough to have much practical or epistemological value.

Outside these two rather uncontroversial non-delegation restrictions and solely on the basis of the grant of legislative power and the constitutional supremacy clauses, the duty of Congress, in this minimalist version of doctrine, can be reduced to the necessity of making, in the exercise of its enumerated powers, a clear legislative decision among the salient policy alternatives existing at the time of enactment, as registered on the legislative record. This minimalist version of the nondelegation doctrine has been, to my knowledge, only advanced by Sotirios Barber.[45] The thesis is original enough and relatively straightforward: a minimal constitutional rule of nondelegation, the only rule of delegation constitutionally defensible, needs to be a *self-standing* "principle of legalistic inflexibility."[46] The supremacy of the constitution is the last independent *positive legal* argument for nondelegation, remaining after the elimination of germane but conceptually independent constraints (identified as, the separation of powers, theories of representation, the common law agency maxim, and due process). Delegation is permissible, as long as it does not approach abdication, namely, as long as Congress

"discretion as to subordinate premises only." *Delegatus non potest delegare* (*delegata potestas non potest delegari*) would apply only to a. but not to b.

[45] Barber Sotirios, *The Constitution and the Delegation of Congressional Power* (Chicago and London: The University of Chicago Press, 1978).

[46] A similar argument in comparative law was given, in an insightful little exercise in logical positivism, by the Danish philosopher and jurist Alf Ross ("Delegation of Power-Meaning and Validity of the maxim *delegata potestas non potests delegari*" 7 *American Journal of Comparative Law* 1 (1958)). In light of his general jurisprudential project of freeing law and legal thinking from the pernicious influence of metaphysics, the Scandinavian Legal Realist scholar was at the same time puzzled and irked by the persistence in constitutional thought of a notion without (or with scant) support in positive law, which moreover eluded easy definition: "[D]elegation does not appear to be regarded as a functional legal concept, defined by certain observable criteria, but rather as a kind of magical act, the transfer of a magical force, the very 'power to legislate.' The question is not presented as an inquiry as to the legal criteria defining the term 'delegated legislation' (introduced to describe certain juristic acts) but rather as a question whether a juridical magic transfer of power of this kind is in fact possible or not. The maxim *delegata potestas non potest delegari* seen from this angle assumes more the character of an axiomatic truth, a juridical magic law of nature, rather than of an empiric rule of law, conditioned like other rules of law by time and space." (at p. 11) Ross's solution is treating the problem of legislative limits "not in general terms but in relation to the text, presuppositions, and principles of the various constitutions, each in its historical setting." (p. 21) Ross's analysis is ultimately flawed, nonetheless, to the extent that, in an application of his more general theoretical position to the Danish Constitution, he presents as an evident and unproblematic nondelegation limit on the legislature, inferred from Section 63 (courts are competent to review the legality of all administrative acts, including rules pursuant to law): "a prohibition against delegation of such *indefiniteness* that judicial review is eluded." As we shall *see* in due course, however, the delegation-related aspects of normative indeterminacy in modern statutory interpretation are not at all unproblematic exercises of judicial review.

can be fairly said to have made "a clear policy decision among salient alternatives." Judges would enforce this version of the doctrine by poring on the legislative history to determine whether Congress delegates out of indecision, thus unconstitutionally abdicating its duty, or as an incident to making a choice among alternatives.[47] Barber is in a way proposing a 'hard look' (nondelegation) doctrine for congressional enactments.[48] Aside from the separation of powers quandaries it would create by having the judiciary police so intrusively legislative records (to identify only the most problematic among many side-effects one can think of), the problem with this sort of 'hard-look doctrine' version of nondelegation constitutionality review is that the notion of nondelegation as such is incomprehensible

[47] Thus, Congress can make an 'experimental' delegation, incidental to making a future choice, and the delegation would be constitutionally 'saved' by a mandatory review and reenactment provision ('sunset' clause), which binds Congress as an institution and goes through the same legislative process as the initial enactment (bicameralism and presentment): "Through a permissive interpretation of the delegation doctrine, however, delegations from congressional irresolution could be constitutional—at least when measured by the minimal values supporting the rule—if they could be interpreted as instruments of policy decisions yet to be made. A statutory provision for mandatory review and reenactment could be presumptive evidence that Congress had committed itself to decide eventually the issues delegated." (Barber 1978, at pp. 123–124). Barber was aware of the fact that, in the logic of his version of nondelegation, congressional legislative indecision could not be compensated by other methods of review (in his enumeration, the [now defunct] legislative veto, committee oversight, appropriations process), since these methods of control, as substitutes to legislative policy indecision, according to the terms of his nondelegation theory, would pose delegation problems of their own. In view of future formalistic decisions (most notably *INS v. Chadha* and *Bowsher v. Synar*), Barber Sotirios's diagnosis proved to be a good foretelling of doctrinal evolution, even though partially and in a somewhat obverse manner: "[A]s *Chadha* makes clear, once Congress makes its choice in enacting legislation, its participation ends. Congress can thereafter control the execution of its enactment only indirectly-by passing new legislation." *Bowsher v. Synar*, 478 U.S. 714, 733 (1986) (opinion of the Court, per Burger, C.J.). By 'obverse manner' I understand that Supreme Court separation of powers 'formalism' did not directly force Congress to make specific legislative decisions (as Barber's preferred version of the doctrine would have it) but limited Congress's legislative power to the decision made at the time of the enactment, without possibility for further adjustments compensating for the initial delegation-indecision, short of the full-fledged Art. I Section 7 legislative process.

[48] Since this version of nondelegation review is primarily about regulating legislative processes, an analogy could also be drawn with Judge Hans Linde's "due process of lawmaking" approach to the Due Process Clause of the Fifth and Fourteenth Amendments. As commonly known, the Clause protects individuals against federal government (and, respectively, state) deprivation of "life, liberty, and property, without due process of law." In a 1976 article ("Due Process of Lawmaking," 55 *Nebraska Law Review* 197 (1976)), Linde observed that the tests applied by the Supreme Court in substantive due process rationality review are focused on the rationality of the means-ends correlation, whereas—in his view—the real question to be asked was one of legitimacy (i.e., is the choice—the statutory purpose—a legitimate one?), the problem of substance (legitimacy of ends pursued) could be conceptually distinguished from the matter of process, and—last but not least—the Due Process Clause, just as it reads, is primarily concerned with process, not substance. Therefore, asking the due process constitutional question in an instrumentalist key struck him as incorrect and he proposed instead focusing the judicial quest on policing the rationality and consistency of legislative processes.

or vacuous in the absence of the normative constitutional meta-principles that it showcases and stands for.

Representation and Delegation: Accountability, Participation and Deliberative Rationality

Oversimplifying, the basic argument here is that we elect representatives to make, in Lockean terms, "laws and not legislators."[49] Behind the epigram lies, of course, the difficulty of specifying what it means for a legislature to make legislators, in terms of how we understand the constitutional duty of making laws. In Locke's account this difficulty is overcome by reducing the scope of legislation to rules of just conduct and merging two arguments, representation and the rule of law, into one, so that specificity of the mandate renders accountability easy to assess. The specificity of the mandate, in Locke's counterfactual, derives in turn from the way of positing the state of nature, so that the dividing line between private and public, the baseline from which limitations on legislation ("just rules of liberty and property") and thus on delegation would be assessed appears unproblematic, since posited as natural and pre-political. To anticipate further discussion, it is worth pointing out here that understanding of and positions regarding legislation and thus delegation are inextricably linked with assumptions regarding and attitudes towards the proper line dividing between private and public spheres or domains. Laurence Tribe's insightful remark on this matter is particularly apt: "Even the institutions of contract and property can of course be understood as such delegations. A great deal about any legal system's premises may be discerned by observing which exercises of coercive power are regarded in that system as intrinsic to private ordering and which are viewed in the system as delegated by the public."[50] A concrete baseline from which to assess limitations on legislation, hence on delegation, was constituted in America (as in all common law legal orders) by the common law preference for private ordering. This baseline, which was assumed by the pre-New Deal Court as the yardstick for gauging the constitutionally prescribed legislative reservation, nowadays dominates the logic of modern administrative law in all of its constitutive aspects (hearing rights, standing, and reviewability immediately spring to mind).[51]

[49] Par. 141. *See* discussion *supra*.

[50] Tribe 1988, at p. 368, note 26.

[51] *See*, for instance, Sunstein, "Constitutionalism after the New Deal," 101 *Harvard Law Review* 421, 423 (December, 1987), speaking admiringly about the mutation brought about by "the New Deal reformers, [for whom] the common law was neither natural nor prepolitical." For Sunstein, quite expectedly given his more general thesis regarding the socially and legally constructed nature of preferences and rights, limitations on government derive from a more abstractly normative understanding of legality. Hence the penchant on attacking private law baselines for public law arrangements; *see*—for instance—*supra*, at 426: "One of the greatest ironies of modern administrative law-an area whose origins lay in a substantial repudiation of the common law- is its continuing reliance on common law categories." Also, in "Lochner's Legacy," 87 *Colum. L. Rev.*

From a representation-centered perspective on delegation, the main consideration underlying the nondelegation doctrine is, *prima facie*, one of accountability. Once a legislature enacts statutes that, instead of prescribing clear rules of conduct and assigning benefits and burdens authoritatively, delegate lawmaking either *explicitly* (authorizing an external agency to flesh out the actual content of the law through delegated legislation or—to use the American administrative law terminology—rulemaking, pursuant to vague statutory guidance) or *implicitly* (through statutory ambiguities which allow for excessive interpretive discretion),[52] it blurs the lines of accountability, short-circuiting the self-correcting mechanisms of electoral check: "[F]ormulation of policy is a legislature's primary responsibility, entrusted to it by the electorate, and to the extent Congress delegates authority under indefinite standards, this policy-making function is passed to other agencies, often not answerable or responsible in the same degree to the people."[53]

The nub of the matter is not only, however, that, by delegating its power Congress erodes democracy in the sense of simply failing to aggregate and translate properly the common will of a hypothetical people. The people as such, as a subject of public law, were in a way 'relocated' by the Constitution outside government, thus making it impossible for any branch to 'speak' for them and claim a representative monopoly.[54] In fact, throughout the nineteenth and way into the twentieth century, American state constitutional law decisions repeatedly struck down local option laws (or contingent legislation whose entry into force had been made conditional on referenda) on nondelegation grounds. The opinions emphasized, in Madisonian vein, that American constitutions had ordained not simply democracy

873 (June, 1987), at 875: "Numerous decisions depend in whole or in part on common law baselines or understandings of inaction and neutrality that owe their origin to Lochner-like understandings."

[52] "The power of an administrative agency to administer a congressionally created. . .program necessarily requires the formulation of policy and the making of rules to fill any gap left, implicitly or explicitly, by Congress." *Morton v. Ruiz*, 415 U.S. 199, at 231. *See Chevron U.S.A. v. Natural Resources Defense Council*, 467 U.S. 837, at 843–844: "If Congress has explicitly left a gap for the agency to fill, there is an express delegation of authority to the agency to elucidate a specific provision of the statute by regulation. Such legislative regulations are given controlling weight unless they are arbitrary, capricious, or manifestly contrary to the statute. Sometimes the legislative delegation to an agency on a particular question is implicit rather than explicit. In such a case, a court may not substitute its own construction of a statutory provision for a reasonable interpretation made by the administrator of an agency." *See also Food and Drug Administration v. Brown & Williamson Tobacco Corp.*, 529 U.S. 120, at 123: "Chevron deference is premised on the theory that a statute's ambiguity constitutes an implicit delegation from Congress to fill in the statutory gaps." *Also see* Monaghan 1983, at p. 26: "Judicial deference to agency 'interpretation' of law is simply one way of recognizing a delegation of lawmaking authority to an agency."

[53] *United States v. Robel*, 398 U.S. 258, 276 (1967) (Brennan, J., concurring opinion).

[54] "The true distinction between [earlier republics] and the American governments lies in the total exclusion of the people, in their collective capacity, from any share in the latter. . . ." The Federalist No. 63 (James Madison) *See* Gordon S. Wood, *The Creation of the American Republic: 1776–1787* (New York: Norton, 1972, c1969), at p. 599: "All parts of the government were equally responsible but limited spokesmen for the people, who remained as the absolute and perpetual sovereign. . . ."

but representative democracy, a different and qualitatively superior substitute.[55] Hence, the issue seems to be also that, by delegating its law-making functions, Congress defeats the purpose of the intricate mechanisms of accommodation set forth by the legislative process provisions of Art. I (7) and curbs the main advantages of representation, as the Framers saw them: the "filtering effect" and legitimizing role of public deliberation and—the obverse side of the same coin—avoidance of 'factionalism' or private capture of public power. According to the original design, the purpose of the intricate constitutionally-ordained legislative process, which is arguably defeated by passing the buck through shell enactments and vague statutory language, was to raise the cost of law-making and thus increase the quality of legislation, by reducing the incidence of rash, ill-considered or factional enactments; here the argument from representation is fused at the hip with considerations regarding the constitutionally mandated separation of powers.[56] Raising the decision costs of passing laws means of course a less efficient

---

[55] An interesting survey of state decisions on delegations to voters is provided in Duff and Whiteside 1928–1929. For instance, in *Rice v. Foster* 4 Harr. 479 (Delaware 1847), one of the earliest cases of this kind, the following reasons are given by the state supreme court for striking down on nondelegation grounds a local option temperance law: "The proposition that an act of the legislature is not unconstitutional unless it contravenes some express provision of the constitution is, in the opinion of this court, untenable. . ..An act of the legislature directly repugnant to the nature and spirit of our form of government, or destructive of any of the great ends of the constitution, is contrary to its true intent and meaning; and can have no more obligatory force, than when it opposes some express prohibition contained in that instrument. . ..Wherever the power of making laws, which is the supreme power in a State, has been exercised directly by the people under an system of polity, and not by representation, civil liberty has been overthrown. Popular rights and universal suffrage, the favorite theme of every demagogue, afford, without constitutional control or a restraining power, no security to the rights of individuals, or to the permanent peace and safety of society. In every government founded on popular will, the people, although intending to do right, are the subject of impulse and passion; and have been betrayed into acts of folly, rashness, and enormity, by the flattery, deception, and influence of demagogues." Compare, nonetheless, with a contemporaneous Illinois decision upholding a law which made a division and redistricting of a county contingent on local option: "The extent to which this maxim should be applied to a legislator depends upon a proper understanding of legislative powers; upon a proper determination of what may legitimately be done in the exercise of those powers. Is it easy to say that it is the business of the legislature to make laws; but then we must inquire, what kind of laws may be made? Must they be full, complete, perfect, absolute, depending upon no contingency and conferring no discretion?" *People v. Reynolds* 10 Ill. 1 (1849).

[56] *See* for instance John F. Manning, "The Nondelegation Doctrine as a Canon of Avoidance," 2000 *Supreme Court Review* 223, 239: "More specifically, Art. I, Section 7 filters congressional lawmaking powers through the carefully structured process of bicameral passage and presentment to the President. By dividing legislative power among three relatively independent entities, that intricate and cumbersome process serves several crucial constitutional interests: it makes it more difficult for factions (or, as we would put it, 'interest groups') to capture the legislative process for private advantage, it promotes caution and restrains momentary passions, it gives special protection to the residents of small states through the states' equal representation in the Senate, and it generally creates a bias in favor of filtering out bad laws by raising the decision costs of passing any law. The nondelegation doctrine protects those interests by forcing specific policies through the process of bicameralism and presentment, rather than permitting agency lawmaking on the cheap."

legislative process, resulting in occasional stalemates, hence a reduced output, less legislation overall, both good and bad—a risk that was considered in the Founding Era, nonetheless, well-worth taking in view of the benefits.[57]

Although here is not the place for a more thorough elaboration, suffice it to point out that, from a representation-derived perspective, the rule of nondelegation seems to mandate a requirement of legislative specificity and clarity at least with respect to certain policy choices[58] and to create a strong presumption against delegations of subordinate lawmaking to politically unaccountable bureaucracies[59] and private parties.[60] In light of the foundational concern with factionalism, the delegation to

---

[57] The Framers were aware of the trade-off. Madison, discussing the role and value of bicameralism in The Federalist No. 62, argued that, while "the power of preventing bad laws includes that of preventing good ones," "the facility and excess of law-making seem to be the diseases to which our governments are most liable." *See also* No. 73 (Alexander Hamilton), the constitutionally prescribed legislative process guards against the "passing of bad laws through haste, inadvertence, or design."

[58] This position has been most forcefully advanced in recent years by Cass Sunstein, *see*, for instance, *Designing Democracy-What Constitutions Do* (Oxford: Oxford University Press, 2001), Chapter 6-Democracy and Rights: The Nondelegation Canons, arguing that the delegation doctrine properly reverts into canons of narrow construction and judicially mandated requirements of clear legislative specification (clear statement) in constitutionally sensitive areas, a "democracy-forcing judicial minimalism": "What I mean to identify here are the nondelegation canons, not organized or recognized as such, but central to the operation of modern public law in America and many other nations, and designed to ensure clear legislative authorization for certain decisions." (at p. 138) Sunstein's position is not without support in the case-law, *Mistretta v. U.S.*, 488 U.S. 361, 374 n7: "In recent years, our application of the nondelegation doctrine principally has been limited to the interpretation of statutory texts, and, more particularly, to giving narrow constructions to statutory delegations that might otherwise be thought to be unconstitutional." (Blackmun, J.) *See also* Richard Stewart, "Reformation," noting use of the technique of narrow construction of statutes (as opposed to invalidation of congressional enactments: delegation used for 'nullification' purposes) as a nondelegation-related *practice* of the "post-nondelegation doctrine" Court: "Third, courts began to demand a clear statement of legislative purpose as a means of restraining the range of agency choice when fundamental individual liberties were at risk. . .The technique is more discriminating than the nondelegation doctrine; it substitutes tactical excision for wholesale invalidation." pp. 1680–1681.

[59] *See*, for instance, *Printz v. U.S.*, 521 U.S. 898, which struck down as unconstitutional provisions of the Brady Handgun Violence Prevention Act which imposed background check requirements on state officers (chief law enforcement officers (CLEOs) of each local jurisdiction); Congress cannot delegate the enforcement of federal law to state officials, unaccountable to the President, at 922: "The Brady Act effectively transfers [the responsibility to 'take Care that the Laws be faithfully executed'] to thousands of CLEOs in the 50 States, who are left to implement the program without meaningful Presidential control (if indeed meaningful Presidential control is possible without the power to appoint and remove). The insistence of the Framers upon unity in the Federal Executive-to ensure both vigor and accountability- is well known." (Scalia, J., opinion of the Court). *See also* Harold J. Krent, "Fragmenting the Unitary Executive: Congressional Delegations of Administrative Authority Outside the Federal Government," 85 *Nw. U. L. Rev.* 62 (Fall, 1990).

[60] For instance, in *National Association of Regulatory Utility Commissioners v. F.C.C.* 737 F2d 1095, 1143, n. 41: "Recent years have witnessed a renewal of interest in the traditional role of nondelegation doctrine. . . .As attention to this area of our law grows, it refocuses thought on one of the rationales against excessive delegation: the harm done thereby to principles of political accountability. Such harm is doubled in degree in the context of a transfer of authority from Congress to an agency and then from agency to private individuals. The vitality of challenges to the former type of transfer is suspect, but to the latter, unquestionable."

private groups of a publicly-sanctioned power to exercise non-consensual coercion is particularly suspect.

To be sure, what a constitutionally mandated level of specificity is and what the policy choices to which a requirement of legislative clarity is constitutionally attached are questions to which an answer cannot be given in the abstract. The discussion will have to wait concrete exemplifications at a later stage of our analysis. Neither can the constitutional implications regarding delegation of law-making to private actors be clarified at this point. The argument should be re-introduced, nonetheless, that the answer to this latter question is essentially dependent on where the line between public and private is drawn, so that what are essentially public and presumptively non-delegable (as opposed to private) functions can be assessed.[61]

Separation of Powers and Nondelegation: Checks and Balances

> If the effective functioning of a complex modern government requires the delegation of vast authority which, by virtue of its breath, is legislative or 'quasi-legislative' in character, I cannot accept that Article I-which is, after all, the source of the nondelegation doctrine-should forbid Congress from qualifying that grant with a legislative veto.
>
> White, J., dissenting in *I.N.S. v. Chadha*

> Precisely because the scope of delegation is largely uncontrollable by the courts, we must be particularly rigorous in preserving the Constitution's structural restrictions that deter excessive delegations.
>
> Scalia, J., dissenting in *Mistretta v. U.S.*

In the American constitutional context, the doctrine of nondelegation seems to be associated with the principle of separation of powers both conceptually, as an issue of constitutional theory, and functionally, as a matter of legal dogmatics.[62] An argument for a constitutional limitation on the legislative branch can be easily inferred *prima facie* from the doctrine of separation of powers, as derived from the text of the constitution. The introductory ("vesting") clauses of the first three articles read as follows:

> All legislative Powers herein granted shall be vested in a Congress of the United States, which shall consist of a Senate and House of Representatives.[63]

---

[61] *See also* Linde 1999, at p. 847 (note 74): "Much depends, of course, on whether assigning a role to private organizations is characterized as a delegation of public authority or as a legal endorsement of essentially private arrangements. The characterization often reflects unarticulated baselines of public and private functions." The foundational study on this matter is Jaffe's "Law Making by Private Groups," 51 (2) *Harvard Law Review* 201 (December, 1937).

[62] *See*, for instance, *Mistretta v. U.S.*, 488 U.S. 361, at 371 (Blackmun, J., opinion for the Court): "The nondelegation doctrine is rooted in the principle of separation of powers that underlies our tripartite system of government."

[63] US Constitution, Article I, Section 1.

> The executive Power shall be vested in a President of the United States of America.[64]
> The judicial Power of the United States, shall be vested in one supreme Court, and in such inferior Courts as the Congress may from time to time ordain and establish.[65]

Nonetheless, a nondelegation rule derived from the text of the vesting clauses alone, while or perhaps because it constitutes a perfect instantiation of what Roscoe Pound once called "the perennial struggle of American administrative law with nineteenth-century constitutional formulations of Aristotle's three-fold classification of governmental power,"[66] is of scant analytical help. As was already noted, it yields results that are circular and absurd. By constitutional definition legislative power could not be delegated, even though legislative power is the only power the legislature has to delegate in the first place. However, it stands to practical reason that without a certain degree of interpretive discretion and delegated rule-making day-to-day government could not carry on.[67] On the other hand, if the "unreality of formal logic," as James Hart once called a purely abstract treatment of the delegation problem, be abandoned for an analysis which emphasizes scope rather than the intrinsic character of the power under analysis, where, along the continuum ranging from no discretion to abandonment or abdication should the line be drawn which distinguishes constitutional legislation from an unconstitutional delegation of the legislative power?

Some authors, most notably Kenneth Culp Davis,[68] and a few decisions, have invoked the Necessary and Proper (or "Sweeping") Clause,[69] to justify legislative delegations as a matter of constitutional principle. As the argument goes, the

[64] US Constitution, Article II, Section 1, Clause 1.

[65] US Constitution, Article III, Section 1.

[66] Roscoe Pound, *An Introduction to the Philosophy of Law,* pp. 15–16.

[67] Hart 1925, at pp. 131–132: "Furthermore, it may be argued that, since Congress has only legislative powers, any power which it delegates to another organ must of necessity be legislative in nature. The logic of such argument is flawless, but it is with the unreality of such formal logic that we disagree. The very nature of government is such that the legislature cannot always decide every detail. It becomes necessary, therefore, for the courts to distinguish between what it must do to fulfill its function and what it may either do or leave to the administrative department in connection with its execution of the law." *See also* Edward S. Corwin, *The President-Office and Powers 1787–1957 –History and Analysis of Practice and Opinion* (New York: New York University Press, 1957), pp. 122–123: "Nor is it sufficient to urge that executive power is a mere capacity to act within limits set by the legislature. For the obvious answer is that, on this assumption too, the maxim against delegation loses all its virtue unless there is some intrinsic limitation to the capacity of the executive thus to act, which again would render the maxim superfluous."

[68] Davis 1978–1984.

[69] Art. I, Section 8, Clause 18: "Congress shall have Power...[t]o make all Laws which shall be necessary and proper for carrying into the Execution the foregoing Powers, and all other Powers vested by this Constitution in the Government of the United States, or in any Department or Officer thereof." Of course, the present discussion of the Sweeping Clause is relevant to all the nondelegation-relevant debates under review in this chapter.

Necessary and Proper Clause gives Congress the requisite constitutional authorization to decide how much to decide itself and how much to leave out for others to decide. Nonetheless, while in the abstract it is perfectly true that legislation cannot be perfectly self-contained, since any law entails discretion, a certain amount of "deciding oneself" and a certain amount of "leaving out" for others to decide (delegating),[70] as a matter of constitutional principle this argument is unhelpful and misguided. It poses the question wrongly, since a limitation on the legislative scope of Congress has to exist, otherwise a jurisdiction of enumerated legislative powers would become unfettered legislative discretion. And it states the question in form of an answer, shifting at the same time the justificatory nondelegation burden on the Sweeping Clause, since the problem is precisely determining what and how much is, constitutionally speaking, necessary and proper for Congress to decide (which is in essence the delegation question). These matters are ultimately constitutional line-drawing responsibilities for the Supreme Court (not for Congress) to exercise. That exercise, in turn, cannot be carried out solely based on the text and in the abstract; it needs to be informed by underlying constitutional values and more concrete points of reference.

It will be remembered at this juncture that, in Locke's argument, whose distinctions might once again shed some light on the matter, a nondelegation limitation on the legislative branch appeared as a corollary of the limitation of the legislature to the enactment of permanent "rules of liberty and property" addressed to the individual; Lockean legislation is always and only normative (in Lockean language, "general, antecedent, promulgated, standing rules of liberty and property"), not constitutive. Conversely, it should be pointed out that the reverse side of Locke's limitation of legislation to normative enactments was the recognition that there are certain fields of government action and situations that, by their very nature, cannot be regulated in the same manner as the regular domestic regime of liberty and property, by means of rules. Because they are irreducible to legislative prescription, these matters need to be regulated politically and according to discretion. One cannot predetermine by rules, for instance, the actions of foreigners, which are dynamic and unpredictable, whereas their treatment in domestic law is largely subordinated to prudential considerations deriving from foreign affairs imponderables and the pursuit of national interest; the matter is better left to "the prudence of those, who have this power committed to them, to be managed by the best of their skill, for the advantage of the commonwealth."[71] Hence, Locke's

[70] *See* Scalia, J. dissenting opinion in *Mistretta v. U.S.*, 488 U.S. 361, at 417: "The whole theory of *lawful* congressional 'delegation' is not that Congress is sometimes too busy or too divided and can therefore assign its responsibility of making law to someone else; but rather that a certain degree of discretion, and thus of lawmaking, *inheres* in most executive or judicial action, and it is up to Congress, by the relative specificity or generality of its statutory commands, to determine—up to a point—how small or how large that degree shall be." (emphases in original) The delegation question bears precisely on the parenthetical observation "up to a point."

[71] *See esp.* Second Treatise of Civil Government, § 147, cited in full and commented, *supra*.

federative and prerogative 'powers' were treated as analytically distinct from the executive (where by 'executive' he essentially understood non-discretionary or ministerial execution of the law), even though, as a matter of governmental practice, Locke correctly pointed out that the same person or group of people would need in most cases to exercise all three of these 'powers': the executive (in the sense of non-discretionary enforcement of the law), the federative, and the prerogative.

Unlike Locke's legislature, the American Congress shares with the executive branch attributions in fields which Locke considered as essentially non-legislative, such as foreign affairs and war measures, whereas emergency situations are almost completely passed over in the text of the Constitution.[72] By the same token, in spite of theoretical arguments and occasional judicial rebuffs to the contrary,[73] a president, by virtue of his independent constitutional attributions (Chief Executive, Commander in Chief) and of the constitutional power to "take care that the laws are faithfully executed" has a certain original, independent law-making (decree-making) power.

What nondelegation means in the context of separation of powers is dependent on first identifying and defining the relevant among two different theoretical strands, so that the considerations underlying a nondelegation doctrine could be isolated and independently assessed. The conceptual intersections will mainly vary, as we have already noted in the course of the previous chapter, with respect to whether one refers to a constitutive or procedural, checks-and-balances variance of the separation of powers or a rule-of-law or normative, more functionally-oriented, version of the doctrine.

Within the balance version, power has a more dynamic and colloquial meaning (sway, strength, influence)[74] and the major concern is "undue" accumulation or

---

[72] "Article II vests 'the executive power in the president, but only after Article I has given most of the traditional royal prerogatives, or at least a share in them, to one or both houses of Congress." Forrest McDonald, Foreword, *The Constitution and the American Presidency*, (Martin L. Fausold & Alan Shank eds., 1991), at ix.

[73] "In the framework of our Constitution, the President's power to *see* that the laws are faithfully executed refutes the idea that he is to be a lawmaker. . . .And the Constitution is neither silent nor equivocal about who shall make the laws that the President is to execute. The first section of the first article says that 'All legislative Powers herein granted shall be vested in a Congress of the United States. . . .'" *Youngstown Sheet and Tube Co. v. Sawyer*, 343 U.S. 937, 579, 587 (Black, J., opinion for the Court).

[74] A good exemplification of the balance theory can be found in Blackstone, 1 (Ch. 2) *Commentaries* 151, speaking of the benefits of the balance of powers (the two Houses of Parliament and the "crown, which is a part of the legislative, and the sole executive magistrate"): "Like three distinct powers in mechanics, they jointly impel the machine of government in a direction different from what either, acting by themselves, would have done; but at the same time in a direction partaking of each and formed out of all; a direction constitutes the true line of the liberty and happiness of the community." *See*, for a similar argument regarding the two main strands of separation of powers arguments and constraints, Elizabeth Magill, "The Real Separation in Separation of Powers Law," 86 (2) *Virginia Law Review* 1127 (September 2000).

aggrandizement of political power at any one point in the system, threatening monopoly. The balance version or strand of the principle of separation of powers is related mainly to the prevention of tyranny by structural (institutional autonomy and procedural interdependence, checks and balances) arrangements. From this perspective, the main concern underlying the nondelegation doctrine is aggrandizement of the executive by means of open-ended statutory authorizations. As we will see in due course, the modern phenomenon of massive lawmaking delegations tilted the balance in favor of the Presidency and a revival or vigorous enforcement of the rule of nondelegation, it is sometimes believed, would, in the new setting, produce salutary results consistent with the original scheme of distributing power among autonomous institutional actors. In this respect, as Laurence Tribe pointed out, nondelegation would serve the dual purpose of the separation of powers principles underpinning the constitutional allocation of powers, namely that of "simultaneously limit[ing] and protect[ing] congressional power."[75] Conversely and by the same token, the phenomenon of massive delegations of law-making discretion to the executive and the administration produced both a number of new institutional accommodations and a resulting conceptual divergence in separation of powers jurisprudence, arising from modern judicial attempts to grapple with the phenomenon of delegation ('formalist' and 'functionalist' schools).

Separation of Powers and Nondelegation: The Rule of Law Version of Separation of Powers

> [N]ormally the progress of law should be away from discretion toward definite rule.
> Ernst Freund, "The Substitution of Rule for Discretion in Public Law" (1915)

We now come to another version of the nondelegation doctrine, conceptually related to the normative, rule of law strand of the principle of separation of powers. Looked at from this perspective, by delegation is understood a formal statute which grants a vast amount of discretion, whether of rulemaking or (quasi-)adjudication, to the implementing/enforcement agency. Here, the principles or rather values underlying the doctrine are grounded in considerations of justice and dignitary concerns which regard the discrete individual faced with adverse state action. In this understanding and from this perspective, the nondelegation doctrine is related to the fair notice and due process (or 'natural justice') considerations of impartiality and independence underlying the procedural requirements of the due process clause of the Fifth and Fourteenth Amendments[76] and—more directly—to the substantive

---

[75] Tribe 1988, at p. 362. *See also* Verkuil 1989, at 318: "The courts can review the quality of the delegation, to ensure that legislative power is not unintentionally divested. In this role, the Court acts paternalistically, to protect Congress from itself."

[76] *See* Cushman 1941, who, not at all surprisingly given the topic of his study, reduces the rule of nondelegation to a matter of due process (discretion confined by standards): "To permit (. . .) an officer or an agency to exercise legislative power unrestrained by legislative standards is to subject

fair warning requirements of the related void-for-vagueness doctrine or the rule of lenity in criminal law.[77] In the latter, substantive dimension, the doctrine is also germane to the requirements of the First Amendment overbreadth doctrine on the specificity of enactments, even though the area of fundamental rights is more focused and seems analytically and constitutionally distinct from the problem of nondelegation as such. The reason why a high degree of specificity or statutory precision is required in this area is that, otherwise, selective licensing policies (where prior licensing is required), and selective, discriminating or arbitrary enforcement (where sanctions are applied) would achieve indirectly what is not permissible directly, i.e., prior restraints on speech (censorship) or content-based

---

the citizen to the danger of an arbitrary power against which he may have no effective protection. It is but a short step from this to the position that one whose rights have been impaired by the exercise of unrestrained legislative discretion in the hands of an administrative officer or agency is being deprived of liberty or property without the due process of law. In short, the rule against the delegation of legislative power as it is now construed exists not for the purpose of keeping alive an abstract principle of government, but for the purpose of surrounding private rights with a protection just as readily available under the due process clause. In fact, the doctrine of the non-delegability of legislative power could safely be scrapped as long as due process of law remains the effective constitutional guarantee it now is." Robert E. Cushman, *The Independent Regulatory Commissions* (New York: Pentagon Books, 1972 (c1941)), pp. 433–434. Now, of course, as such, a constitutional requirement of legislative standards to guide the delegate can serve both structural (balance version) separation of powers purposes and normative (discretion-related) separation of powers considerations. In this respect, compare *Skinner v. Mid-America Pipeline, Co.*, 109 S. Ct. 1726, 1731: "[S]o long as Congress provides an administrative agency with standards guiding its actions such that a court could 'ascertain whether the will of Congress has been obeyed,' no delegation of legislative authority trenching on the principle of separation of powers has occurred."; and *American Power & Light Co. v. SEC* 329 U.S. 90, 105 "constitutionally sufficient if Congress clearly delineates the general policy, the public agency which is to apply it, and the boundaries of this delegated authority. Private rights are protected by access to the courts to test the application of the policy in light of these legislative declarations."

[77] The void-for-vagueness doctrine supports the same clarity and generality purposes of the rule-of-law version of nondelegation, by requiring, to use Oliver Wendell Holmes's characteristically terse and eloquent definition that "[a]lthough it is unlikely a criminal will consider the text of law before he murders or steals, it is reasonable that a fair warning be given the world, in language the common world will understand, of what the law intends to do if a certain line is passed." In *McBoyle v. U.S.* 283 U.S. 25. To better perceive the correlation, in *United States v. L. Cohen Grocery Co.* 255 U.S. 81 (1921), a grocer was indicted under a provision of the war time Food Control Act, which made it a federal crime, punishable with imprisonment for up to two years "for any person willfully. . .to make any unjust or unreasonable rate or charge in handling or dealing in or with any necessaries." The defendant challenged the constitutionality of the act on nondelegation grounds: Congress had delegated to courts and juries its "legislative power to determine what acts should be held to be criminal and punishable." The court struck down the provision on void-for-vagueness grounds: Congress had not fixed an ascertainable standard of guilt, adequate to present the accused under the statute with the nature and cause of the accusation against them: "to attempt to enforce the section would be the exact equivalent of an effort to carry out a statute which in terms merely penalized and punished all acts detrimental to the public interest when unjust and unreasonable in the estimation of court and jury." (White, J., opinion of the Court, 255 U.S. 81, 89).

restrictions. The following excerpt from a concurring opinion of Justice Brennan is particularly useful for illustrating the constitutional problematics: "Congress ordinarily may delegate power under broad standards. . ..The area of permissible indefiniteness narrows, however, when the regulation invokes criminal sanctions and potentially affects fundamental rights. . .This is because the numerous deficiencies connected with vague legislative directives whether to a legislative committee. . .to an executive officer. . .to a judge and jury. . .or to private persons. . .are far more serious when liberty and the exercise of fundamental rights are at stake."[78] (case citations omitted)

Arguments which approach the problem of delegation from a rule of law perspective are also concerned with the systemic values which would be served by imposing across the board qualitative rule of law constraints on legislation (and on the institutional legislature): a legal system modeled as a framework of rules of just conduct enhances net individual liberty (Hayek),[79] promotes dignitary values (Fuller),[80] enhances both democracy and the authority of law as such (Lowi).[81]

---

[78] *U.S. v. Robel*, 389 U.S. 258 (1967), 274–275, Frankfurter, J., concurring. *See* Tribe 1988 § 12–38, "The Problem of Overbroad Delegation," pp. 1055–1057.

[79] *See* Friedrich Augustus von Hayek, *The Constitution of Liberty* (Chicago: University of Chicago Press, 1978 (c1960)), pp. 212–213: "The trouble with the widespread use of delegation in modern times is not that the power of making general rules is delegated but that administrative authorities are, in effect, given the power to wield coercion without rule, as no general rules can be formulated which guide the exercise of such power. What is often called 'delegation of law-making power' is often not delegation of the power to make rules—which may be undemocratic or politically unwise—but delegation of the authority to give any decision the force of law, so that, like an act of the legislature, it must be unquestioningly accepted by the courts. . ..It is only when the administration interferes with the private sphere of the citizen that the problem of discretion becomes relevant to us; and the principle of the rule of law, in effect, means that the administrative authorities should have no discretionary powers in this respect." *Also see The Road to Serfdom* (London: Routledge, 1991, c1944) and *Law, Legislation, and Liberty-A New Statement of the Liberal Principles of Justice and Political Economy* (London: Routledge, 1993 (c1982)). In the former work, Hayek famously argued that, given the massive exercise of administrative discretion by the administration, pursuant to the open-ended enabling type of legislation characteristic of the twentieth century, the difference between Western democracies and the contemporaneous Nazi Germany or Stalinist Russia was just one of degree. By 'rules of just conduct' Hayek understood the traditional tort, contract, property, and criminal law, which coagulated into a framework of clear guidelines for individual action. As I understand his main thesis, the more legislation departs from this model and allows for administrative discretion which interferes with the private sphere of the citizen, the more individual liberty is displaced by legislatively-mandated discretion. Hayek's preferred model of law is not legislation but common-law, which, by its emphasis on tradition and incremental development by means of analogy and contextual distinctions over time, was, epistemologically, the embodiment of a superior type of rationality than legislation, in Hayek's opinion, a rationalistic, warped, rigid, one-time exercise in a larger post-Enlightenment project of self-subverting rationality.

[80] *See* his *The Morality of Law* (New Haven: Yale University Press, 1969).

[81] *See* Lowi, *The End of Liberalism-The Second Republic of the United States*, 2nd edition (New York and London: Norton, c1979), *esp.* Chapter 5: "Liberal Jurisprudence: Policy without Law," pp. 92–126. The thesis, as I understand it, is that the displacement of the rule of law as a law

Yet these latter considerations are contingent or epiphenomenal, and should not be allowed to detract attention away from correctly comprehending that the principal consideration underlying the nondelegation doctrine from a normative, rule of law-derived separation of powers perspective, is discretion in the sense of arbitrariness, which needs in this account to be at the same time checked and authorized by clear and specific legislative directions.[82] Specific, normative enactments guide administrative action and minimize the incursion of the state in the protected sphere of individual autonomy, since clear legislative guidance (where no discretion equates no delegation) makes it possible in turn for the court to exercise its role of containment. This theoretical account of nondelegation finds in the evolution of American administrative law a paradigmatic instantiation in the historical period identified by Richard Stewart as the "traditional" or the "transmission belt" model of administration, which, according to him, ran until and up to the New Deal and was characterized[83] by "protecting private autonomy by curbing agency power":

---

of "authoritative" rules by statutory grants of discretion accompanied by vague standards obfuscated the distinction between politics and law, by rendering the entire political process "tentative" and thus amenable at all its points to bargaining and horse-trading, therefore subject to capture by the most vociferous or powerful interest-groups: "Liberal jurisprudence is a contradiction in terms. Liberalism is hostile to law.…Interest-group liberalism has little place for law because laws interfere with the political process.…In brief, law, in the liberal view, is too authoritative a use of authority. Authority has to be tentative and accessible to be acceptable. If authority is to be accommodated to the liberal myth that it is no power at all, it must emerge out of individual bargains.…Delegation of power provides the legal basis for rendering a statute tentative enough to keep the political process in good working order all the way down from Congress to the hearing examiner, the meat inspector, the community action superviser, and the individual clients with which they deal. Everyone can feel that he is part of one big policy-making family." pp. 92–93. *Also see*, by the same author, "Two Roads to Serfdom: Liberalism, Conservatism, and Administrative Power, 36 *Am. U. L. Rev.* 295 (Winter, 1987).

[82] Laurence Tribe's caveat is, nonetheless, particularly useful here: "But vagueness is not calculable with precision; in any particular area, the legislature confronts a dilemma: to draft with narrow particularity is risk nullification by easy evasion of the legislative purpose; to draft with great generality is to risk ensnarement of the innocent in a net designed for others." *Supra*, at p. 1033. *See also* Colin Diver, "The Optimal Precision of Administrative Rule" 93 *Yale L. J.* 65 (Nov. 1983), identifying three 'dimensions' of rules, "transparency" (the virtue chiefly celebrated by the delegation doctrine), "accessibility" (the degree to which a rule is accessible to its intended audience and "easily applicable to concrete situations without excessive difficulty or effort"), "congruence" (basically, means-ends correlation) and observing that pursuing change on one dimension will usually require a trade-off on another. The necessity of "transparency" – "congruence" tradeoffs is evident *prima facie*.

[83] Stewart's well-known study identified three periods, roughly, pre-New Deal, New Deal, post-New Deal-especially the 60s and 70s, characterized by three paradigms of administrative law, the traditional (when judicial review was focused on policing and containing discretion), expertise (when judicial deference was justified by the belief in the expertise of the administrator of the statute), and the interest-balancing models of administrative law (judicial review serves the function of reinforcement and balancing of participation or—if you will—representation in administrative rulemaking processes, so that bureaucratic decision making approaches a surrogate micro-legislative process). The periods are slightly overlapping while the 'models' of administrative law have to be understood in the Weberian sense of ideal-types, i.e., explanations that give

"With the possible exceptions of military and foreign affairs functions and times of national emergency, the Constitution recognizes no inherent administrative powers over persons and property. Coercive controls on private conduct must be authorized by the legislature, and under the doctrine against delegation of legislative power, the legislature must promulgate rules, standards, goals or some 'intelligible principle' to guide the exercise of administrative power."[84] The mutually reinforcing considerations of individual autonomy, fairness, and coherence (predictability and consistency) that underlie a rule of law-oriented rule of nondelegation are of course analytically distinct from the nondelegation constraint on legislation as such. What joins discretion and the nondelegation constraint on the legislature is a requirement and an assumption that intrusions into the protected individual sphere are legitimate only if assented to and agreed upon by the people's representatives, through the legislative process, because of the limited mandate that legislation has and—secondarily—since thus the people are taken to impose burdens on themselves. Here, indeed, defining the protected individual sphere (for instance, this protected sphere could be defined along a life, liberty, and property criterion; or just fundamental rights) will be the crucial question for conceptually assessing the level of legislative vagueness that constitutes an impermissible delegation. To put it even more clearly, from the standpoint of conceptualizing a general constraint on legislation and the legislature, the delegation inquiry will ultimately have to be conceptually traced back to the point of identification of a baseline: a stable line of assessment delimiting private autonomy from permissible scope of public (legislative) action. Theoretically, in Locke, for instance, the limit is one of natural and therefore neutral, pre-political rights: the life, liberty, and property triad; legislation is institutionalized natural law. Historically, the common law also presumed both liberty and property rights as a legal baseline for gauging state action in terms of departure from status quo (neutrality) and legislative legitimacy.

At the end of this section and related to what has been remarked above regarding the analytical distinctiveness of rule of law-related concerns with discretion, it should be pointed out that the doctrine can also revert from constraints on legislation and legislative discretion into nondelegation-derived limitations on the administration. Thus, for instance, a derivative nondelegation constraint can be imposed on the administration by judicial requirements to check and confine its legislatively-granted discretion through standards and rules.[85] The logic is apparent: a legislative delegation places on the administration a rule-of-law duty to confine its discretion by delegated legislation which corresponds to the formal justice requirements which we associate with legislation in the first place. In modern American legal theory, this secondary rule of nondelegation is associated with the work of Kenneth

coherence to clusters of judicial review and legislative developments, extracting out of them the dominant paradigm. Richard B. Stewart, "The Reformation of American Administrative Law," 88 *Harv. L. Rev.* 1667 (1974–1975).

[84] *Id.*, at 1672.

[85] *See*, for instance, *Holmes v. New York City Housing Authority*, 398 F.2d 262 (1968).

Culp Davis on administrative discretion. While Davis deemed the nondelegation doctrine as a conceptual excrescence of—in his words—the Diceyan-Hayekian "extravagant notion of the rule of law,"[86] he advanced the argument that courts could impose, in the absence of legislative standards, a sort of 'nondelegation doctrine' on the administration.[87] In terms of actual judicial practices, even as the problem will be revisited, to anticipate further discussion and clarify the pragmatic stakes of the matter, consider the following excerpt from a modern Oregon Court of Appeals decision which required the Oregon Liquor Control Commission to structure and limit its licensing discretion, exercised under the open-ended guidance "demanded by public interest or convenience," through written and published standards and rules; I shall take the liberty of giving a longer citation which, to put it in vernacular, covers all the bases: "A legislative delegation of power in broad statutory language such as the phrase 'demanded by public interest or convenience' places upon the administrative agency a responsibility to establish standards by which that law is to be applied. . . .We recognize the wide discretion vested in the commission by its enabling legislation, but that discretion is not unbridled. It is discretion to make policies for even application, not discretion to treat each case on an ad hoc basis. . . .Finally, and most directly applicable to this case, the parties to a contested case are entitled to judicial review. Judicial review is among the safeguards which serve to legitimatize broad legislative delegations of power to administrative agencies. In the absence of standards, however, the courts are unable to perform that task of judicial review."[88]

[86] Kenneth Culp Davis, *Discretionary Justice- A Preliminary Inquiry* (Westport, CT: Greenwood Press, 1980 (c1969, by Louisiana University Press)), II-The Rule of Law and the Non-delegation Doctrine, pp. 27–51. *See* Stewart 1974-1975 arguing that Davis's derivative version of the doctrine is, unsurprisingly, fraught with the same difficulties, judicial enforcement-wise, as the doctrine itself. *See* Skelly Wright, *Beyond Discretionary Justice* (Book Review; reviewing Davis) 81 *Yale L. J.* 575, 582 (1972): "We need, in short, some standards for when we should require standards."

[87] *Id.*, at pp. 58–59. "I propose that the courts should continue their requirement of meaningful standards, except that when the legislative body fails to prescribe the required standards the administrators should be allowed to satisfy the requirement by prescribing them within a reasonable time. . . .The requirement should gradually grow into a requirement that administrators must strive to do as much as they reasonably can to develop and to make known the needed confinements of discretionary power through standards, principles, and rules. The nondelegation doctrine might also be gradually shifted from a constitutional base to a common law base." (emphases omitted)

[88] *Sun-Ray Drive-In Dairy, Inc. v. Oregon Liquor Control Commission*, 16 Or. App. 63, 517 P.2d 289 (Or. App. 1973). *See* comments in Mashaw et al., p. 82. As a matter of federal law, the D.C. Circuit Court of Appeals held, in a 1999 decision, that the Environmental Protection Agency's failure to limit its statutory discretion under the Clean Air Act by an "intelligible standard" violated the nondelegation doctrine, effecting an unconstitutional delegation of legislative power, and remanded to the agency for adoption of a limiting, permissible construction of the statute (*American Trucking Associations, Inc. v United States Environmental Protection Agency*, 175 F.3d 1027(C.A.D.C., 1999)) Now, as one can *see*, even though the issues are related, in terms of constitutional nondelegation constraints, this interpretation has the matter completely the other way around. The Supreme Court reversed, observing, in a characteristically trenchant opinion by

3.1.2 Legislation and Delegated Lawmaking in American Constitutional History

> From Wiscasset in the district of Maine, to Savannah in Georgia, by the following route, to wit: Portland, Portsmouth, Newburyport, Ipswich, Salem, Boston, Worcester, Springfield, Hartford, Middletown, New Haven, Stratford, Fairfield, Norwalk, Stamford, New York, Newark, Elizabethtown, Woodbridge, Brunswick, Princeton, Trenton, Bristol, Philadelphia, Chester, Wilmington, Elkton, Charlestown, Havre-de-Grace, Hartford, Baltimore, Blandensburg, Georgetown, Alexandria, Colchester, Dumfries, Fredericksburg, Bowling Green, Hanover court-house, Richmond, Petersburg, Halifax, Tarborough, Smithfield, Fayetteville, Newbridge over Downing creek, Cheraw court-house, Camden, Statesburg, Columbia, Cambridge and Augusta; and from thence to Savannah.
>
> Act of February 20, 1792, ch. 7, § 1, 1 Stat. 232, establishing the first post road
> Article I, Section 8, Clause 7, granting Congress the power "[t]o Establish Post Offices and Post Roads."

Contemporanea expositio est optima et fortissima in lege. The excerpt from the 1792 Act of Congress that serves as motto for this introduction is not necessarily meant to unravel, by pointing out the minute enumeration that the statute makes of each single point of transit on the post road, the public-spiritedness of early American legislatures and the public-regardedness of specificity in statutory language. Indeed, from a public choice perspective on delegation, specificity is sometimes indicative, conversely, of interest-group ('factional,' in Madisonian language) legislation.[89] In 1792, being on a post route was one of the most valuable

---

Scalia, J.: "In a delegation challenge, the constitutional question is whether the statute has delegated legislative power to the agency. . . .We have never suggested that an agency can cure an unlawful delegation of legislative power by adopting in its discretion a limiting construction of the statute. . . .The idea that an agency can cure an unconstitutionally standardless delegation of power by declining to exercise some of that power seems to us internally contradictory. The very choice of which portion of the power to exercise –that is to say, the prescription of the standard that Congress had omitted- would *itself* be an exercise of forbidden legislative authority. Whether the statute delegates legislative power is a question for the courts, and an agency's voluntary self-denial has no bearing upon the answer." *Whitman v. American Trucking Association*, 531 U.S. 457, 472–473 (2001).

[89] In "A Theory of Legislative Delegation," 68 *Cornell L. Rev.* 1 (1982–1983), a standard public choice treatment of the nondelegation doctrine, Peter H. Aranson, Ernest Gellhorn, and Glen O. Robinson (AGR), argue that the practice of congressional delegations creates 'public policy lotteries' (by virtue of the irresolution reflected in vague statutory language, politics is moved down the line into the administration of the statute) and 'fiscal illusions' (by not assigning clearly benefits and burdens, the real policy stakes and the actual costs of a given regulatory scheme are obfuscated and delayed, just like in the case of deficit spending) and distributes private goods at public expense. Thus, according to AGR, vigorous enforcement of the nondelegation doctrine would produce more public goods legislation and thus increase aggregate social welfare. But *see* Jerry L. Mashaw, *Greed, Chaos, and Governance-Using Public Choice to Improve Public Law* (New Haven, CT.: Yale University Press, 1997), at pp. 143, arguing that, often enough, it is precisely specific legislation which codifies pork barrel transactions, so that "AGR should advocate a constitutional rule which somehow requires that the legislature be limited to specific

federal goods one's Congressman could deliver and, consequently, the 1792 act might be regarded as no more than an early example of 'pork-barrel politics.' There is an even better reason for referring to this statutory provision. The choice between specificity and generality of the statutory language in this particular case occasioned the first delegation controversy in American constitutional history.

The debates on a postal bill began in the first session of Congress after the ratification of the Constitution. The original version reported to the Committee of the Whole was in effect an enabling act, authorizing the President to decide, at his discretion, the postal routes and the locations of the post offices. This language was stricken when an unnamed representative argued that "this is a power vested in Congress by an express clause of the Constitution, and therefore cannot be delegated to any person whatever."[90] The final version of the bill continued with the Post Office and established the office of the Postmaster General, under the authority of the President "in performing the duties of his office and in forming contracts for the transportation of the mail."[91] The Post Office was afterwards continued by two statutes providing for 1-year extensions until, in December 1791, during the House of Representatives Committee of the Whole debate of the First Session of the Second Congress on a more detailed bill, which, among other new specifications,[92] designated in its first section a particular coastal post road from Maine to Georgia. Representative Sedgwick proposed to strike out the clause which designated the route and insert instead the following language: "by such route as the President of the United States shall, from time to time, cause to be established."[93] Sedgwick noted that the second clause of the bill, as reported by the committee, read: "it shall be lawful for the Postmaster General to establish such other roads as post roads, as to him may seem necessary."[94] Should his motion be deemed unconstitutional on delegation reasons, Sedgwick argued, the second section as reported would also be invalid, "for if the power was altogether indelegable, no part of it could be delegated; and if a part of it could, he saw no reason why the whole could not."[95]

legislation whenever it wants to be vague, and to vague legislation whenever it finds it easier to be specific."

[90] I was able to find the excerpt from the postal act and the reference to this particular legislative debate in Gary Lawson, "Discretion as Delegation: The 'Proper' Understanding of the Nondelegation Doctrine" 73 George Wash. L. Rev. 235 (2005) and Nicholas J. Szabo, "Origins of the Nondelegation Doctrine" (unpublished paper available for download at http://szabo.best.vwh.net/delegation.pdf, last visited August 19, 2005), respectively. The Congressional debates cited here can be found on-line, on the website of the Library of Congress, http://www.memory.loc.gov/ammem/amlaw/lwac.html, Annals of Congress, 2nd Congress, 1st Session, House of Representatives debates, *see* Post Office Bill, pp. 229–235, 237–242 December 1791.

[91] 1 Cong. Sess. I Ch. 16, Act of September 22, 1789, 1 Stat. 70.

[92] The act also formally admitted newspapers to the mails and prohibited postal officials from opening letters.

[93] Annals of Congress (Library of Congress on-line version, *see* URL *supra*) at p. 229.

[94] *Id.*, p. 230.

[95] *Id.*

Moreover, he reasoned, if the duty of Congress to the commands of the Constitution is understood in an absolute sense, to require no delegation in the sense of no implementing discretion whatsoever, why would not members of Congress turn coiners and start minting money, in fulfillment of their Art. I, Section 8, clause 5 duty "[t]o coin Money"? The constitutional difference between legislation and execution cannot be understood as more than a difference between establishing a *principle* and carrying it through by means of administration: "Congress, he observed, are authorized not only to establish post offices and post roads, but also to borrow money; but is it understood that Congress are to go in a body to borrow every sum that may be requisite? Is it not rather their office to determine the principle on which the business is to be conducted, and then delegate the power of carrying their resolves into execution? They are also empowered to coin money, and if no part of their power be delegable, he did not know but they might be obliged to turn coiners and work in the Mint themselves."[96] In a rebuff, Representative Page carried the *reductio ad absurdum* argument to the opposite pole of the continuum: if this much legislative discretion could be constitutionally devolved upon another branch, why could not everything legislative be left to the lights of the Executive and meanwhile Congress might as well adjourn indefinitely: "If the motion before the committee succeeds, I shall make one which will save a deal of time and money, by making a short session of it; for if this House can, with propriety, leave the business of the post office to the President, it may leave to him any other business of legislation; and I may move to adjourn and leave all the objects of legislation to his sole consideration and direction."[97]

One of the supporters of the Sedgwick motion opined in turn that, since the duty of Congress, lying as of necessity it must somewhere between these two extremes, was a matter of degree, unascertainable in a principled manner, how much regulation was constitutionally mandated must in the end be left to the decision of the legislature: "Much has been observed respecting the Legislative and Executive powers, and the committee are cautioned against delegating the powers of the Legislature to the Supreme Executive. Without attempting a definition of their powers, or determining their respective limits, which he conceived it was extremely difficult to do, he would only observe that much must necessarily be left to the discretion of the Legislature."[98] Prudential considerations were also adduced in support of the Sedgwick motion, most notably the necessity of future adjustments in the administration of the law (which would be hampered by making advance statutory provision for a given route) and the superior expertise of the administration.

Most Congressmen spoke vehemently against a delegation to either the President or the Postmaster General, delegation that they regarded not only as unconstitutional as such, in relation to the Art. I legislative duties of Congress, but also as a practice

[96] *Id.*, pp. 230–231.
[97] *Id.*, 233.
[98] *Id.*, 236.

prone to breed in the long run administrative corruption and executive tyranny. The motion was voted down in the session of Wednesday, December 7. One of the most eloquent closing arguments against it, before it was put to the vote of the Committee of the Whole, came from James Madison. He observed that, since the power had been granted in the Constitution, it was the duty of the legislature to exercise it itself, whereas the specificity of the authorization would of necessity vary with the field of regulation and the necessity of further adjustment could be fulfilled by Congress through further legislative action. The fact that a line could not be logically drawn along a continuum of discretion to describe the difference between legislative and executive action was of no consequence, since the matter was not one of abstract logic but of practical government and needed to be perceived in a given context: "Mr. Madison said, that the arguments which are offered by the gentleman [*sic*] who are in favor of the amendment, appear to be drawn rather from theory than from any line of practice which had hitherto governed the House. However difficult it may be to determine with precision the exact boundaries of the Legislative and Executive powers, he was of the opinion that those arguments were not well founded, for they admit of such construction as will lead to blending those powers so as to leave no line of separation whatsoever."[99]

3.1.2.1 The Executive, the Administration, and the Bounds of Legislative Specificity

> Thus we arrive at the fundamental principles of our administrative system: no executive power without express statutory authority-the principle of enumeration; minute regulation of nearly all executive functions, so that they become mere ministerial acts-the principle of specialization; and specific delegation of these functions to separate officers-the principle of diffusion of executive power. In contrast to these we find in Europe executive powers independent of statute, discretionary powers of action and control vested in superior officers, and the concentration of the administrative powers of the government through the hierarchical organization of the executive departments.
>
> Ernst Freund, "The Law of the Administration in America," 9 (3) *Political Science Quarterly* (September 1894)

> [I]n a government by law discretion ought to have a very limited place in administration. Its legitimate function is indicated by the organization of a chief executive power which stands for that residuum of government otherwise subject to law which cannot be reduced to rule.
>
> Ernst Freund, "The Substitution of Rule for Discretion in Public Law" 9 (4) *American Political Science Review* (November, 1915)

> The distinction between administrative power and executive power, a distinction which once had the stature of a first principle, is today on the verge of obliteration, and ready and waiting to replace it is the concept of the unity of the executive power.
>
> Nathan D. Grundstein, "Presidential Power, Administration, and Administrative Law," 18 (3) *Geo. Wash. L. Rev.* 285 (April, 1950)

[99] *Id.* 238.

> THE COURT: So, when the sovereign people adopted the Constitution, it enumerated the powers set up in the Constitution, but limited the powers of Congress and limited the powers of the judiciary, but it did not limit the powers of the Executive. Is that what you say?
> Mr. BALDRIDGE: That is the way we read Article II of the Constitution.
>
> Argument for the Government in *Youngstown Sheet and Tube Co. v. Sawyer*, 343 U.S. 937 (1952) (*The Steel Seizure Case*) (in Alan F. Westin, *The Anatomy of a Constitutional Law Case* (1958)

As Justice Holmes pointed out with characteristic acumen and typical hyperbole, sometimes and on certain points of law "a page of history is worth a volume of logic."[100] *Consuetudo est optimum interpres legum.* While the Sedgwick delegation motion with respect to the Post Office Establishment occasioned fiery opposition and was easily defeated in favor of specific language delineating the administrative attributions of the Postmaster General and even the exact route of the post road, the controlling provisions of two contemporaneous statutes, which created the Foreign Affairs and War Departments, were worded in the following language: "Be it enacted, &c., That there shall be an Executive department, to be denominated the Department of Foreign Affairs, and that there shall be a principal officer therein, to be called the Secretary for the Department of Foreign Affairs, who shall perform and execute *such duties as shall from time to time be enjoined on or entrusted to him by the President of the United States,* agreeable to the Constitution. . .and furthermore, that the said principal officer shall conduct the business of the said department *in such manner as the President of the United States shall, from time to time, order and instruct.*" (emphasis supplied)[101]

The explanation (which presents much interest for our topic) that comports best with historical fact and common historical sense resides in the peculiarly American separation between executive and administrative functions. From the onset, a number of Presidential powers were deemed as essentially executive in nature, where by 'executive' it was understood, *caeteris paribus*,[102] something more in the Lockean sense of 'prerogative' or 'federative' powers or Blackstone's conception of prerogative (*i.e.*, primarily military and foreign affairs attributions).[103]

---

[100] *New York Trust Co. v. Eisner*, 256 U.S. 345, 349.

[101] An Act Establishing an Executive Department, to be denominated the Department of Foreign Affairs, Act of July 27, 1789, ch. 4, 1 Stat. 28, § 1. The War Department Act, § 1 (Act of August 7, 1789, 1 Stat. 49) contains, *mutatis mutandis*, almost identical language.

[102] Namely, 'as qualified by the constitutional institutional (structural) arrangements' (for instance, the Senate foreign affairs role or Congress's power "to declare war" or "grant letters of marque and reprisal").

[103] *See* Arthur Bestor, "Separation of Powers in the Domain of Foreign Affairs: The Intent of the Constitution Historically Examined," 5 *Seton Hall L. Rev.* 527 (1974), at p. 532: "Executive power signified to Blackstone, as it did to the American framers, those powers of decision and action that can be exercised by a chief executive in his name, simply by virtue of the authority granted directly to him by the constitution or the laws. Though the executive may ultimately be held responsible-by impeachment or repudiation at the polls-for executive decisions made or executive actions carried out, executive powers themselves are almost by definition discretionary, and therefore capable of being exercised without the necessity of submitting a proposed course of action to prior legislative deliberation or approval."

The latter's view of the matter, particularly given the influence of the *Commentaries* (as one of the main and most accessible authorities on the common law) on the Framers, presents particular interest in this respect. Its brief summation shall be useful here, for heuristic purposes. Blackstone makes a clear distinction between the prerogatives of the crown "respect[ing]...[England's] intercourse with foreign nations" and those that concern "its own domestic government and civil polity." Regarding the former, the king is "the delegate or representative of his people" and embodies the sovereignty of the nation in relation to other equal sovereigns.[104] Thus, the prerogatives of the King in respect of war and foreign affairs are vast and unchecked by "stated rule, or express legal provision," even though a political check exists in the possibility of impeaching ministers of the Crown. The list of 'external' prerogatives comprises power to conclude treaties, to wage war, send and receive ambassadors, grant letters of safe conduct, power to control the entry and residence of foreigners, who "are under the king's protection, though liable to be sent home when the king sees occasion."[105] Likewise and on the same principle, in the exercise of domestic prerogatives directly related to foreign affairs prerogatives, such as controlling the exportation of arms, Parliament would normally grant the executive broad powers.[106] In purely domestic matters, on the other hand, the

[104] As a matter of political and legal theory, this distinction is usually explained in natural law and the contractarian tradition (the argument comes forth most clearly, though with different emphasis, in both Locke and Hobbes) by the fact that, while the creation of civil government presupposes the giving up of each member's natural right to wage war within the political community (consequently, all-out conflict is contained within), without, states as such remain in the state of nature (which is potentially a state of war). Blackstone seized on this principle, and adduced it to strengthen the argument, in addition to historical (the Crown's residuum of power) and prudential (need for unity and strength) considerations: "For it is held by all the writers on the law of nature, that the right of making war, which by nature subsisted in every individual, is given up by all private persons that enter into society, and is vested in the sovereign power." 1 *Blackstone's Commentaries* (Ch.7-"Of the King's Prerogative") 249.

[105] *Id.*, at p. 252.

[106] *See* for instance 1 *Blackstone's Commentaries* 255, commenting on "the power vested in his majesty, by statutes 12 Car.II.c.4. and 29 Geo.II.c.16 of prohibiting the exportation of arms or ammunition out of this kingdom, under severe penalties." In this vein, consider the argument in *United States v. Curtiss Wright Export Corporation.*, 299 U.S. 304 (1936), where the Court considered a delegation challenge to a congressional joint resolution authorizing the President to prohibit or allow, by proclamation, the sale of arms and ammunitions to countries engaged in armed conflict in the Chaco region, if such prohibition—or allowance—"may contribute to the reestablishment of peace." In a famous opinion, Justice Sutherland (largely in dicta) described attributes of external sovereignty having flowed from the Crown directly to the United States "in their collective and corporate capacity as the United States of America." The President is declared the foremost actor within the domain of foreign relations: "The President is the constitutional representative of the United States with regard to foreign nations." (at 319) Indication of the policy to be followed was deemed to be pertinent to the denial of the delegation challenge, yet the breadth of the delegation is to be assessed under different standards than those applicable to an enabling law dealing with purely domestic matters: "Whether, if the Joint Resolution had related solely to internal affairs it would be open to the challenge that it constituted an unlawful delegation of legislative power to the Executive, we find it unnecessary to determine." (at 315).

prerogative is narrowly limited by statute and right and cannot infringe on the liberty and property of the subject, by creating new obligations and crimes. The king cannot for instance create by proclamation new offices save purely honorary ones, for creating new offices with fees attached or attaching new fees to existing offices "would be a tax upon the subject, which cannot be imposed but by an act of parliament."[107] Neither would Parliament be understood to constitutionally grant extensive discretion with respect to purely domestic matters and the delegation in the so-called *Statute of Proclamations*, 31 Henry VIII. c.8., is described as "calculated to introduce the most despotic tyranny."[108]

Other things being equal, this seems to have been the original understanding in American public law. Thus, while in the exercise of purely 'executive' power, the Executive would be granted broad delegations of authority, since supported by original and autonomous constitutional authority, domestic administration, on the other hand, would to a large extent be perceived as an extension of legislation.[109] Correlatively, the Vesting Clause of Art. II, which would occasion much debate later on,[110] was given a limitative interpretation during the Founding Age and

---

[107] 1 *Blackstone's Commentaries* 262.

[108] 1 *Blackstone's Commentaries* 261.

[109] As late as 1881, a Senate Report drew the distinction between executive power and the administrative authority of departmental officers in the following terms: "The President, and the President alone, is the Constitutional executive; he and he alone is the co-ordinate executive branch of the government. ...The departments and their principal officers are in no sense sharers of this power. They are the creatures of the laws of Congress, exercising only such powers and performing only such duties as those laws prescribe." S. Rept. 837, 46th Cong., 3rd Sess., 1881.

[110] The Vesting Clause of Art. II is, like the Vesting Clause of Art. III and unlike their Art. I counterpart, not qualified by the phrase "herein granted." This difference would occasion a twentieth-century debate on the proper constitutional scope of presidential power between incumbent President Theodore Roosevelt and former President (then Chief Justice) Taft. While the former, unsurprisingly in view of his sanguine and vigorous political career, interpreted the clause (the so-called "stewardship theory") extensively, as granting a President, as a 'steward' of the People, all powers not expressly denied, the latter ("constitutional theory") read the clause as granting only powers expressly granted (as enumerated in the rest of the article). As a matter of constitutional drafting history, it appears that the "herein granted" qualification was a last minute addition made by the Committee of Style, a committee without authority to make substantive modifications, cf. Charles C. Thatch, Jr., *The Creation of the Presidency 1775–1789: A Study on Constitutional History* (1922), cited by Lawrence Lessig and Cass R. Sunstein, "The President and the Administration," 94 *Colum. L. Rev.* 1 (January, 1994) pp. 48–49, FN 203: "When the report of the committee of style was submitted it was found that the legislative grant now read: 'All legislative powers herein granted shall be vested in a Congress.'...Whether intentional or not, it admitted an interpretation of executive power which would give the President a field of action much wider than that outlined by the enumerated powers." Historically, the clause had been consistently interpreted narrowly, as limited to the attributions specifically enumerated in the article. A notable (since disregarded) exception in the Founding Era was made by Alexander Hamilton ("Pacificus," No. 1, June 29, 1793). Yet it should be emphasized that Hamilton's more expansive views of administration (*see The Federalist No. 72*) and strong, energetic executive power (*see* for instance, The *Federalist No. 70*, giving the example of Roman dictatorship and speaking about the occasional necessity for republics "to take refuge in the absolute power of a single man, under the formidable title of a dictator") were largely idiosyncratic in the Founding

throughout the nineteenth century, thought to encompass only the former kind of power and be limited by the attributions specifically enumerated in the other sections of Article II.[111] Hence, in exercising his duty under the constitutional requirement to "take care that the laws are faithfully executed," the President would be essentially an agent of Congress, entrusted only with "powers as to administrative details"[112] and powers indispensable to carrying out his duties under the Take Care Clause.[113] If one accepts the premise of a constitutionally-ordained distinction between administrative and executive powers and of a corresponding institutional distinction between the president and the administration, then, as Nathan Grundstein was keen to point out, "[c]ongressional delegations of power to the President would be tested by different constitutional criteria than Congressional delegations to administrative agencies of its own creation. That is to say, a true question of constitutional separation of powers could arise only with respect to the delegation of legislative power to the President, whose office was not created by Congress, whose enumerated powers were beyond Congressional control, and who was not responsible to Congress."[114] This is all the more true bearing in mind that any delegation of discretion to the President (or to the administration if the

---

Era décor. *See*, more specifically, on these issues, Nathan D. Grundstein, "Presidential Power, Administration, and Administrative Law," 18 (3) *Geo. Wash. L. Rev.* 285 (April, 1950). For a modern theoretical defense of a unitary executive grounded in the more open-ended wording of Art. II's Vesting Clause (like the Vesting Clause of Art. III and as opposed to the Vesting Clause of Art. I), *see*, for instance Steven G. Calabresi and Saikrishna Prakash, "The President's Power to Execute the Laws," 104 *Yale L. J. 541* (December, 1994); Steven G. Calabresi and Kevin H. Rhodes, "The Structural Constitution: Unitary Executive, Plural Judiciary," 105 *Harv. L. Rev.* 1153 (1992).

[111] Frank Johnson Goodnow, *Comparative Administrative Law: An analysis of the Administrative Systems National and Local, of the United States, England, France and Germany* (New York, London: Putnam, 1893), at p. 62: "What the meaning of these words was in 1787 has just been shown. It was that the President was to have a military and political power rather than an administrative power." Also, W. W. Willoughby: "[I]t was undoubtedly intended that the President should be little more than a *political chief; that is to say, one whose function should, in the main, consist in the performance of those political duties which are not subject to judicial review.*" (as found quoted in Lessig and Sunstein, *supra*, at p. 44) (emphasis added)

[112] Frank Johnson Goodnow, *The Principles of the Administrative Law of the United States* (New York, London: Putnam, 1905), at p. 75.

[113] *See Cunningham v. Neagle (In re Neagle)* 135 U.S. 1, 10 S. Ct. 658 (1890). U.S. Marshall Neagle had been appointed by the Attorney General to protect U.S. Supreme Court Justice Field while on circuit duty and, fearing for the latter's life during an altercation, had shot and killed a man. Held that the Take Care Clause was sufficient legal basis and defense to justify issuance of a federal writ of habeas corpus to free Neagle from a California jail where he was held pending trial for murder: "The Constitution, section 3, Article 2, declares that the President 'shall take care that the laws be faithfully executed'....Is this duty limited to the enforcement of acts of Congress or of treaties of the United States according to their *express terms*, or does it include the rights, duties, and obligations growing out of the Constitution itself, our international relations, and all the protection implied by the nature of the government under the Constitution?" (per Miller, J.) These powers would have effect in a court of law if limited to acts of individual application.

[114] Grundstein 1950 at p. 304.

President can effectively control it) entails, because of the veto power, a *de facto* 'retrieval' difficulty. Once a statute effects a departure from the political status quo (inter-branch balance) and delegates power without a 'sunset' clause or a mandatory review and reenactment provision, if the president chooses to veto subsequent changes in the initial statutory authorization (abrogation or amendment), a very likely reaction if the change would result in a diminution of executive power, the law can be passed only under the very stringent requirement of a two-thirds override.[115]

In the exercise of his political powers, a President would not be controlled by the courts, which could not review collaterally, for instance, decisions of the President as to the boundaries of foreign states or the payment of claims based on international awards.[116] Yet, as the first president, George Washington, was to notice in 1793, there was an important legal limitation[117] to the president's original executive powers: they did not have the force of law and thus could not unilaterally impinge upon individual rights at domestic law.[118] The Washington Administration's attempts to prosecute U.S. citizens in violation of the Neutrality Proclamation

---

[115] Confusion between the two issues is common. *See* Posner and Vermeule 2002 at p. 1741, note 81, citing *United States v. Winstar Corporation*, 518 US 839, 873 (1996) ("[A statute] is not binding upon any subsequent legislature.") and concluding that: "Those who disagree with our argument about legislative entrenchment, however, should take into account that the revocability of delegatory legislation leaches out much of the starch from the sort of horrible hypotheticals commonly advanced to support a nondelegation rule." In fact, it does not; this sort of argument confounds and conflates the categories. What is theoretically possible and what is practically feasible or possible, given the 'retrieval difficulty' associated to the veto power, are not one and the same thing. Put otherwise, save from the perspective of the most radical (obtuse?) form of positivism, there is a point at which practical considerations of such magnitude gain dogmatic constitutional value. This is all the more true as the authors defend a pragmatic viewpoint on the matter.

[116] *Foster v. Neilson* 27 U.S. 253 (1829), *U.S. v. Blaine* 139 U.S. 306 (1891).

[117] Other than the political one of having to share foreign affairs attributions with the Senate, which, according to Goodnow, for instance, had been modeled on the colonial precedent of executive councils (in the exercise of these functions, the Senate would be effectively an 'executive council' and not a legislative body; Goodnow observed that the House is actually said to be in 'executive session'), just like the president himself had been granted most of the attributions pertaining to the former colonial governors. *See also* Gerhard Casper, "The American Tradition of Shared and Separated Powers: An Essay in Separation of Powers: Some Early Versions and Practices," 30 *Wm. and Mary L. Rev.* 211 (Winter, 1989), at 261: "Although the special responsibility of the President for the maintenance of foreign relations was understood, neither the President nor Congress assumed that the Executive had what John Locke, in his version of separation of powers, called the 'federative' power, which pertained to foreign relations and was, by him, classified as an executive power." (reviewing separation of powers practices from the Washington Administration).

[118] "The Executive..., in addition to 'tak[ing] Care that the Laws be faithfully executed,' Art II, § 3, has no power to bind private conduct in areas not specifically committed to his control by Constitution or statute; such a perception of '[t]he Executive power' may be familiar to other legal systems but is alien to our own." *James B. Beam Distilling Co. v. Georgia*, 501 U.S. 529 (1991), Scalia, J., concurring. *See* more generally for this distinction discussion and authorities in Henry P. Monaghan, "The Protective Power of the Presidency," *93 Colum. L. Rev.* 1 (January, 1993).

(obliquely, under the common law crime of breach of the peace, as violations of the laws of nations or U.S. treaties) failed until, in 1794, Congress passed the Neutrality Act and expressly made violation of neutrality a federal crime.[119] Nonetheless, legislative authorizations in fields over which the executive was understood to have independent or original constitutional authority would be fairly broad. One such example, from the last year of the Washington administration, 1796, is a statutory grant authorizing the placement of individuals on the invalid list of the army "at such rate of pay, and under such regulations as shall be directed by the President of the United States for the time being."[120] During the Adams Administration, by an act of July 9, 1798, the Executive was delegated the power to license privateers against armed French vessels, giving the captains "commissions…revocable at the pleasure of the President of the United States." The "Act concerning Aliens" of June 25, 1798, and the "Act respecting Alien Enemies" granted the President the power to regulate by proclamation the terms of residence or the deportation of virtually any and all classes of non-citizen residents (or to grant dispensations at his own discretion). Offenders would be brought before the courts to be tried and deported, bonded or "otherwise restrained, conformably to the proclamation or regulations which shall and may be established as aforesaid."[121]

---

[119] *See* Saikrishna Prakash and Michael D. Ramsey, "The Executive Power over Foreign Affairs," 111 *Yale L. J.* 231 (November, 2001).

[120] 1 Stat. L. 450 (1796).

[121] 1 Stat. L. 577. It could be objected that the constitutionality of the Alien and Sedition Acts was contested at the time, that the opposition stirred by the enactments was believed to have led to the election of Thomas Jefferson, and that the acts would be quickly repealed at the beginning of Jefferson's Administration (*see also The Kentucky Resolution* and *The Virginia Resolution*, passed by the legislatures of the two states, condemning the acts; available for download on the site of the Avalon Project at Yale Law School, http://www.yale.edu/lawweb/avalon/kenres.htm). Nonetheless, for our purposes here, the acts are just an extreme manifestation of a constitutional reality, that of very broad delegations and of a very lenient (patent unreasonableness) standard of review in domains understood as traditionally executive. *See*, for instance, *Mahler v. Eby* 264 U.S. 32 (1924) formula to deport aliens based on administrative determination of "undesirability" found constitutional (at p. 40): "Nor is the act invalid as delegating legislative power to the Secretary of Labor. The sovereign power to expel aliens is political, and is vested in the political branches of government. Even if the executive may not exercise it without congressional authority, Congress cannot exercise it effectively save through the executive….With the background of a declared policy of Congress to exclude aliens classified in great detail by their undesirable qualities in the Immigration Act of 1917, and in previous legislation of a similar character, we think the expression 'undesirable residents of the United States' is sufficiently definite to make the delegation quite within the powers of Congress." (opinion of the Court, per Taft, C.J.) *Gegiow v. Uhl* 239 U.S. 3 (1915), narrow scope of review applied to an immigration officer's construction of statutory language ("likely to become a public charge") in a denial of admission (based on the officer's appreciation of the state of the labor market) (at p. 10): "Detriment to labor conditions is allowed to be considered in § 1, but it is confined to those in the continental territory of the United States, and the matter is to be determined by the President. We cannot suppose that so much greater a power was intrusted by implication in the same act to every commissioner of immigration, even though subject to appeal, or that the result was intended to be effected in the guise of a decision that the aliens were likely to become a public charge." (per Holmes, J.).

Obversely, in the administration of domestic legislation, the Executive would have little statutory discretion and—consequently—political control. Even though a measure of political control over the administration was recognized by the so-called "decision of 1789," by virtue of which the President was granted removal power by Congress (in the statutes creating the first three federal departments, Foreign Affairs, War, and Treasury),[122] control over the administration would be limited by the minute specification of administrative attributions in the statutes. It stands to reason that, if the administrative tasks are generally ministerial (or considered so by the reviewing court, which amounts in practice to the same result), the actual political (executive) control is minimal.[123] Correlatively, the courts would police the discharge of statutory duties and the interference of the administration with the rights of the subject under a stringent standard of review. The distinction between executive action (political; exercise of constitutional and statutory discretion) and administration (ministerial, non-discretionary; according to the rule of law) and the consequences thereof on judicial review was first expounded, as it is well known, in *Marbury v. Madison*. Yet neither the actual extent of the presidential political control of the administration by means of the removal power nor the scope of review of administrative acts as a legal check on administrative action were settled matters for a while.[124] For instance, Congress considered the Secretary of the Treasury as its agent so much so that, although the statute had granted removal power to the president, Jackson's dismissal of Secretary Duane from this office, as a result of the latter's failure to execute an order would be later described by Wyman to have been "worth a hundred cases from the law reports."[125] Conversely, in terms of legal

[122] The Constitution gives the President a qualified Appointment Power, Art. II, Section 2 (2): "[H]e shall nominate, and by and with the consent of the Senate, shall appoint Ambassadors, other public Ministers and Consuls, Judges of the supreme Court, and all other Officers of the United States, whose Appointments are not otherwise provided for, and which shall be established by Law; but the Congress may by Law vest the Appointment of such inferior Officers, as they think proper, in the President alone, in the Courts of Law, or in the Heads of Departments." It says nothing about removal.

[123] The other side of the token is that in the case of broad delegations, the half-truth of David Currie's remark becomes apparent: "[J]udicial review is not an end in itself but a means of enforcing (constitutional and statutory) limitations on executive authority; if there are no limitations, there is nothing to review." *The Constitution of the Federal Republic of Germany* (Chicago, Chicago University Press, 1994), p. 131.

[124] Indeed, Postmaster General Kendall did not even appear in the Circuit Court and his return to the writ (to show cause why a mandamus should not be issued, compelling him to pay the balance owed) made the—retrospectively surprising—argument that "the doctrine laid down by the chief justice in *Marbury v. Madison*, never was recognized as law by the executive authority." *U.S. ex rel. Stokes v. Kendall*, 5 Cranch C.C. 163 (C.C.D.C. 1837). *See* discussion of the case, *infra*.

[125] Wyman, *The Principles of the Administrative Law Governing the Relations of Public Officers* (1903), cited by Grundstein 1950 at p. 289. The story can be found in Lessig and Sunstein 1994 at pp. 78–85. In short, much like Nixon was to do later on, in the Watergate affair, Jackson promoted a first Secretary, fired summarily the second (Duane), until a third appointee (the future Supreme Court Justice Roger Taney) finally complied with Jackson's orders to withdraw government money from the Bank of the United States. The first two refused to comply with an order which

authority to direct the conduct of the administration, a completely different answer would obtain during the tenure of the same president, in the case of *Kendall v. United States*,[126] which held that the Postmaster General could be compelled by mandamus to pay the balance owed a number of mail transportation contractors, according to the terms of a special appropriation bill, presidential directives to the contrary notwithstanding: "To contend that the obligation imposed on the President to see the laws faithfully executed, implies a power to forbid their execution, is a novel construction of the constitution, and entirely inadmissible."[127]

Unlike the contemporaneous European practice, American constitutional law, from the very onset, did not make a distinction between material ordinances and administrative ordinances[128]; both were understood to need legislative authorization, in order to be enforceable by the courts.[129] Thus, the ordinances adopted by the President as a result of his independent constitutional power to direct the

---

they perceived as being in derogation of their constitutional and statutory duties. The larger constitutional question was and is whether and to what extent the President can exercise circuitously, by virtue of his removal power, the discretionary power vested (delegated) by statute in an administrative officer.

[126] *Kendall v. U. S. ex rel. Stokes*, 37 U.S. 524 (1838). Willoughby considered the case had finally clarified the meaning of the Constitution on Congress's being "the primary source of administrative power."

[127] 37 U.S. 524, 613.

[128] The former create rights and duties, regulating the relations of private citizens towards one another and towards the state; the latter, the duties of the administration in relation to the law. *See* Hart 1925, at p. 19: "In general, our laws have been based upon a conception of the relation between legislation and administration entirely different from that in vogue in Europe. There, general legislation passed with the knowledge that the Executive has the independent power to supplement statutory generalizations, is the normal method. With us it is conceived to be the function of the legislative department to define with completeness and in concrete terms the right and duties which are to be created, and not simply to set forth a general policy to guide the Executive. The enactments of Congress have accordingly been characterized by concreteness, specificness, detail, the limitation of generalities by provisos, and the anticipation (as far as possible, of all future contingencies." *See also id.*, pp. 53–54, explaining the difference by analogy with the German administrative law distinction between *Rechtsverodnungen* and *Verwaltungsverordnungen*.

[129] Goodnow 1905, at pp. 84–85: "The ordinances which the President may adopt are of two kinds: First, those which are issued simply as a result of the exercise of his power of direction over the officers of the administration and which are sanctioned merely by his power of removal; and second, those ordinances which are intended to have the force of law, which, therefore, will be enforced by the courts and which may bind not merely an officer of the government, but as well an individual who in the proper case may be punished criminally for refusing to obey them." Hart's 1925 study establishes a more comprehensive taxonomy, by analogy with contemporaneous European constitutional-administrative practices, along four criteria: (a) source of authority (constitutional and statutory); (b) scope (autonomous and self-contained, independent of statute, as compared/opposed to sub- or co-legislation); (c) subject-matter (ordinances which constitute material law as opposed to material ordinances); (d) purpose (emergency versus normal situations).

administration would be unenforceable other than by his power of removal.[130] The power to issue normative ordinances, which bind the citizen, needed to be expressly delegated by Congress: "[I]t may be laid down as a general rule, deducible from the cases, that whenever, by the express language of an Act of Congress, power is entrusted to either of the principal departments of the government to prescribe rules and regulations for the transaction of business in which the public is interested, and in respect to which they have a right to participate, and by which they are to be controlled, the rules and regulations prescribed in pursuance of such authority become a mass of that body of public records of which the courts take judicial notice."[131] With the exception of army and navy regulations, where (for reasons which have been already stated) the statutory authorization would be broad and the standard of review more lenient,[132] to the extent that domestic normative regulations would be enforced in the courts in the case of an attempt to punish their violation criminally, the rule of strict construction would be followed.[133]

This distinction between law (administration) and politics (executive) or—even better—between inward office bound by law (ministerial) and outward commission

---

[130] Goodnow 1905, at pp. 84–85 gives the example of a civil service rule promulgated 1896, which forbade the removal for political reasons of officers in the classified civil service of the United States. Courts regarded such an ordinance a matter of pure administration and refused to enforce it "and have declared that the only redress open to one who claims that he has been removed contrary to its provisions, is an appeal to the President to remove the offending officer." *White v. Berry* 171 U.S. 366 (1898).

[131] *Caha v. U.S.*,152 U.S. 211(1894), 222.

[132] *Ex parte Reed* 100 U.S. 13 (1879); *Swaim v. U.S.* 165 U.S. 553 (1897). An officer (and even a civilian in the employment of the navy) may be punished by imprisonment by virtue of a court martial constituted under such regulations, whose sentence would be reviewable by Art. III courts only for clear jurisdictional error. *Swaim* goes as far as recognizing an inherent constitutional authority, resting on the Commander in Chief Clause, to convene general courts-martial "in the absence of legislation expressly prohibitive." (at 558) Wyman considered that the President would have an original decree-making power to issue general regulations which bind the citizen, not delegated by Congress but deriving directly from the commander-in-chief clause (Administrative Law, p. 287 et sequitur).

[133] *See United States v. Eaton*, 144 U.S. 677 (1892). Defendant, a wholesaler, had been prosecuted for failure to keep a book and make a return respecting sales of oleomargarine, to the commissioner of internal revenue, as prescribed by a regulation (under the authority of congressional statutory authorization to make "needful regulations" for carrying the act into effect, the failure to do anything "required by law" made by the act a criminal offense; the statute expressly imposed duties only on manufacturers), in addition to the statutory requirements. The regulation was voided by the Supreme Court as unsupported by the statute: "Regulations prescribed by the president and by the heads of departments, under authority granted by congress, may be regulations prescribed by law, so as lawfully to support acts done under them, and may thus have, in a proper sense, the force of law; but it does not follow that a thing required by them is a thing required by law as to make the neglect to do the thing a criminal offense in a citizen, where a statute does not distinctly make the neglect in question a criminal offense."

bound by practical and political necessity (discretion)[134] was first eroded and blurred by emergencies. The Civil War marked a first sharp increase in executive powers, through both broad anticipatory delegations (enabling legislation) and ex post indemnity bills voted by Congress after the executive had already acted independently, by decree.[135] In terms of anticipatory delegations, to give an example, the Act of Congress of Aug. 6, 1861 made it the duty of the President "to seize, confiscate and condemn all property used in aiding, abetting or promoting the present or any future insurrection against the United States."[136] The Civil War also inaugurated a "short-lived major bureaucratic effort," establishing the precedent of a first attempt at extensive administrative reform, even though a professional, well-structured bureaucracy did not exist and the civil service was still based on the Jacksonian 'spoils system.'[137] This major concentration of power in the executive branch offset the balance existent in the antebellum period, by creating a precedent of executive action the intensity and breadth of which had never been experienced.[138]

The First World War period witnessed a massive grant of crisis lawmaking discretion to the Wilson administration, by means of authorizations given by

---

[134] *See*, in this vein, Carl Schmitt, *La Dictature*, especially the chapter 1 discussion on the relevance of the distinction between an officer and a commissioner in Bodin's *Six livres de la République*.

[135] Making the orders of the President or his immediate subordinates "a defense in all courts," for instance the Acts of March 3, 1863, May 11, 1866, and March 2, 1867, ratifying the unilateral presidential suspensions of Habeas Corpus and (the latter) protecting officers against suits based on *Ex parte Milligan*. According to the Supreme Court, Congress could validly ratify whatever action it could have approved in the first place: "...it is plain that if the President had in any manner assumed powers which it was necessary should have the authority or sanction of Congressm that on the well known principle of law, 'omnis ratihabitio retrotrahitur et mandato equiparantur,' this ratification has operated to perfectly cure the defect." *The Amy Warwick (The Prize Cases),* 67 U.S. 635, 671 (1862).

[136] Public Acts of the XXXVII. Congress, 1st sess., ch. Lx. More generally, *see* William A. Dunning's brief but excellent study on the impact of the Civil War on the Constitution, "The Constitution of the United States in Civil War," 1 (2) *Political Science Quarterly* 163 (Jun., 1886).

[137] The South was governed after 1865 much like a conquered colony, by large numbers of federal civilian bureaucracy employed in the Freedman's Bureaus. The Civil Service (Pendleton) Act inaugurated, in 1883, the partial demise of the spoils system administration and the beginnings of professionalized (merit-based) federal civil service; it was passed partly as a result of the Progressive efforts at reforming the aministration and partly in direct response to the public outcry stirred by the 1881 assassination of President Garfield by a disappointed office-seeker. Jerry L. Mashaw, "Reform" and the Public Service in the United States (New Haven: Yale University Press, 2001), unpublished draft on file with the author.

[138] Herbert Tingstén, *Les pleins pouvoirs-L'Expansion des pouvoirs gouvernamentaux pendant et après la grande guerre*, traduit du Suédois par E. Söderlindh (Paris: Librairie Stock, Delamain et Boutelleau, Publications du Fonds Descartes, 1934), p. 153. *Also see*, Clinton Rossiter, *Constitutional Dictatorship-Crisis Government in the Modern Democracies* (Princeton: Princeton University Press, 1948) and James Hart's study, "The Emergency Ordinance: A Note on Executive Power," 23 *Colum. L. Rev.* 528 (1923).

Congress to issue regulations and orders controlling drafting (Selective Service Act), food and fuel regulation (The Food and Fuel Act of 1917), and reorganize the administration in a way that would render executive action more efficient, including any change in agencies already regulated by congressional acts (Overman Act of 1918). These latter two acts were only passed after long delays and extensive debates in Congress (The Food and Fuel Act was stalled for four months in the Senate and was finally passed after a protracted conference committee), while disgruntled Congressmen brandished epithets like "despotism," "dictatorship," or "absolutism."[139] Fiery parliamentary opposition notwithstanding, it was fairly well understood that these laws, given the clear indication of policy, limited domain of authorization (specific fields: drafting, food control, executive reorganization, etc.), and the practice of built-in sunset provisions, did not constitute "blanket delegations."[140] Exercise of broader powers was comprehended as just temporarily required, in essence a form of what Clinton Rossiter would later call, with a phrase of staying power, "constitutional dictatorship."

The return to normalcy and perhaps also the fact that the war-time strong administrations of Lincoln and Wilson were followed by the lame-duck presidencies of Johnson and Harding, obfuscated for a period of time the changes and disruptions in the original scheme, so much so that most contemporaneous commentators (Goodnow, Hart, Willoughby) treated the emergency enabling act as no more than an exception to the initial constitutional arrangement. What was important, Willoughby concluded, was that the President, outside exercise of strictly 'executive' powers, acted as an administrator, according to the terms of statutory authorizations. The statutes granted "administrative powers of the most comprehensive character," true, but they were administrative powers based on statutory grant, nonetheless. Yet, *definitio fit per genus proximum et differentiam specificam.* Used perhaps, as us humans often are, to employ a given conceptual order long after the factual predicates that first justified it have outgrown initial belief in their validity, these great public lawyers failed to perceive the transformation in the nature of statutory authorizations as such, and what that transformation entailed for the integrity of the whole system. They also failed to grasp the fact that powers exercised during a real emergency may be acquired by prescription and reclaimed in the future under a pretense of emergency and, further, that an emergency may to a certain extent be legally manufactured by the sovereign. This is perhaps the nub of truth in Carl Schmitt's characteristically ambiguous and ambivalent

---

[139] *See* detailed description in Tingstén 1934, pp. 151–174. A taxonomy and analysis of war cases is provided by Clinton Rossiter, *The Supreme Court and the Commander in Chief* (Ithaca, N.Y.: Cornell University Press, c1951).

[140] However, in spite of sunset clauses and a general understanding that official ending of the war would terminate these authorizations, emergency powers were exercised after the cessation of hostilities, for instance, during the 1919 mining strike.

epigraph: "Sovereign is he who decides on the exception."[141] Much better situated in terms of hindsight, Nathan Grundstein later captured, in a brief passage commenting on William Dunning's essay on the constitutional legacy of the Civil War, the crux of the changes that had intervened. The observations are worth citing at length in the conclusion of this section: "Professor Dunning's brief essay cuts to the very bone of executive power as we know it today, and we are on familiar ground when we scan his findings-the concentration of governmental power in the executive, the open recognition of 'popular demand' as a legitimate basis for executive action, the resort to 'general ideas of necessity' as a convenient source of executive authority, the appearance of the principle of 'temporary dictatorship' as an accepted part of our constitutional system, absolute executive discretion as to means in the prosecution of war, the merger of civilian and military power of the President, the breakdown of the distinctions between the executive and legislative functions, and the impotence of the judiciary as against the executive."[142]

3.1.2.2 Administrative Discretion, Legislative Scope, and the Growth of Federal Regulation: "A Law that Takes Property from A. and Gives it to B"

> The state of nature has a law of nature to govern it, which obliges every one; and reason, which is that law, teaches. . .that, being all equal and independent, no one ought to harm another in his life, health, liberty, or possessions.
>
> John Locke, *The Second Treatise of Civil Government* (1690)

> The purposes for which men enter into society will determine the nature and terms of the social compact; and as they are the foundation of the legislative power, they will decide what are the proper objects of it: *The nature, and ends of legislative power will limit the exercise of it*. . ..An ACT of the Legislature (for I cannot call it a law) contrary to the great first principles of the social compact, cannot be considered a rightful exercise of legislative authority. . .a law that takes property from A. and gives it to B.: It is against all reason and justice, for a people to entrust a Legislature with SUCH powers; and, therefore, it cannot be presumed that they have done it. (emphasis supplied)
>
> Chase, J., opinion of the Court in *Calder v. Bull* (1798)

In *Marbury,* Chief Justice Marshall famously remarked, distinguishing political (unreviewable) executive action from judicially reviewable performance of ministerial administrative duties, that "[t]he province of the court is, solely, to decide on the rights of individuals, not to enquire how the executive, or executive officers, perform duties in which they have a discretion."[143] The juxtaposition of individual rights and scope of judicial review reveals another meaning and aspect of discretion

---

[141] *Political Theology-Four Chapters on the Concept of Sovereignty* (*Politische Theologie: Vier Kapitel zur Lehre der Souveränität*), George Schwab transl. (Cambridge, Mass. and London, England: The MIT Press, c1985), p. 5.

[142] Grundstein 1950, at pp. 307–308.

[143] 5 U.S. 137, 170 (1803)

and another dimension of the delegation phenomenon. Here, as noted above, the delegation-relevant disjunction is not the separation of powers between political (executive) and ministerial (administrative) exercises of public power according to distinct constitutional and legislative terms but a rule of law differentiation between rule-bound, legally confined administrative interference with private individual rights on the one hand and discretionary administrative action with respect to state claims and publicly-granted privileges (public rights) on the other. The issues are analytically distinct and, even though there is an obvious conceptual and historic overlap between the two problems,[144] the emphasis or focus at this point is on the rights of the individual faced with intrusive state action and not on the balance struck between the branches of power.

According to the classic constitutional and administrative algorithm, whereas private rights were subject to exceptional, narrow, and limited legislative regulation, public rights and to a certain extent state claims on the individual were the proper matter of administrative discretion.[145] Accordingly, the brief account that follows will approach the phenomenon of legislative delegations from the perspective of increasing governmental interference with liberty and property rights (and with the economic configuration that a given legal definition of property and liberty rights constitutes) and the resulting realignment and adjustment of public power and private right which characterizes the evolution of modern administrative law and sets the terms of debates on the constitutionality of legislative delegations.

I shall try to clarify and concretize these starting points, through the intermediary of a case roughly contemporaneous with and whose factual background is somewhat similar to that of *Kendall v. U.S.*, the Jackson administration adjudication discussed in the context of the historical presentation of presidential control over the administration of the law. In *Decatur v. Paulding*,[146] Susan Decatur, the widow

[144] Richard B. Stewart and Cass Sunstein, "Public Programs and Private Rights" 95 *Harv. L. Rev.* 1193 (April, 1982), at 1232–1233: "*The reservation of a major share of economic life to a system structured through private litigation was a key element in the separation of powers scheme*. . ..The grant of extensive lawmaking authority to administrative bodies deprived the courts of much of their established dominion, granted vast responsibilities to bureaucratic entities not anticipated in the Constitution, and undermined the separation of powers." [emphasis supplied]

[145] The theoretical father of modern constitutionalism, Locke, provides us here with another interesting insight into the matter. The rule of law distinction explored in this section parallels the difference between legislative (stated, antecedent, promulgated rules of liberty and property) and prerogative (§ 160 "[a] power to act according to discretion for the public good, without the prescription of the law and sometimes even against it") powers, just as the separation of powers problems analyzed in the preceding section mirror Locke's disjunction between legislative, executive, and federative powers. Even though it has a political dimension as well, derived from English historical contingencies (the convening and dissolution of parliament was historically an important part of royal prerogative) Locke's prerogative encompasses a larger sphere than that of Aristotelean equity, with which it is sometimes analogized (justice considerations which justify departures from rules according to the needs of individual situations) and is essentially very close to the modern equivalent of "policy-making discretion."

[146] 39 U.S. 497 (1840).

of a Navy officer, sought a writ of mandamus to compel the Secretary of the Navy to pay her, out of the Navy pension fund, both a lifetime pension under the general statute providing for the widows of officers deceased in the naval service and, cumulatively, a second one, granted her personally for five years, under a special resolution passed by Congress on the same day as the general naval pension act. She (reasonably enough under the circumstances) felt entitled to both, while the administration, in the absence of express statutory language mandating disbursement, interpreted the legislative silence on the precise matter of whether the resolution had granted a cumulative indemnification to mean that she had to make a choice between the two. Her request denied by the Secretary of the Navy, Susan Decatur applied for a redetermination of her claim to the President, Andrew Jackson, who concurred with the Secretary and denied the request. The Court, in stark departure from the *Kendall* case, deferred to the administrative interpretation, noting that a head of an executive department, "in the administration of the various and important concerns of his office, is continually required to exercise judgment and discretion. . .in expounding the laws and resolutions of Congress, under which he is from time to time required to act."[147] In his dissent, Justice Catron went further still and doubted whether there was *any* case in which it were proper for the courts to compel disbursement of public money through the prerogative writ of mandamus, since (to sum up his argument in familiarly modern terms) this sort of claim dealt not with an individual right but with issues of policy, outside the judicial purview. Such matters are unfit by their nature for judicial resolution: "It is an invitation to all needy expectants, with pretensions of claim on the government, to seek this superior and controlling power, (the Circuit Court of this District,) and invoke its aid to force their hands into the treasury, contrary to the better judgment of the guardians of the public money."[148]

To be sure, even though it is essential for the integrity of a legal system that a demarcating line should be drawn between them, in a systemic and broader sense 'legal' and 'discretionary'[149] are by no means categories with self-evident meanings attached. As noted earlier, in terms of nondelegation, this distinction needs a line of reference for assessing the legitimacy of legislation as such. The baseline theoretically assumed by classical constitutionalism and historically

[147] *Id.*, at p. 515.

[148] *Id.*, at p. 521.

[149] Which does not mean that sources of discretion as such cannot be identified and tabulated taxonomically, *see*, for instance Stewart 1974-1975, at p. 1676, note 25, identifying three sources of discretion:

i. "the legislature may endow an agency with plenary responsibilities in a given area and plainly indicate that within that area its range of choices is entirely free";
ii. "the legislature may issue directives that are intended to control the agency's choice among alternatives but that, because of their generality, ambiguity, or vagueness, do not clearly determine choices in particular cases"; and
iii. clauses precluding judicial review.

provided as a matter of actual practice by the common law was one of private rights, which were to a certain degree presumed and perceived in both legal theory and actual law as natural and prepolitical.[150]

As Henry Monaghan argued in his article on "*Marbury* and the Administrative Law,"[151] much of early American judicial review of administrative action clustered around the different import of Marshall's admonition in *Marbury v. Madison* that "it is emphatically the duty and province of the judicial department to say what the law is" with respect to state interference with common law, private liberty and property rights and individual claims against the state or "public rights", respectively. The distinction is important since 'what the law is' in both constitutional and administrative matters depends to a certain extent on who gets to define statutory meaning with finality, while at the same time the level of deference accorded administrative statutory interpretations both constitutes and validates, as Monaghan points out, a delegation of lawmaking authority.[152] In the case of governmental interference with private rights of liberty and property, including instances when the judicial process (Art. III courts) would be used for enforcement of the government's claims against private parties, the judiciary would carefully scrutinize the administrative interpretation of the law, just as it would do in controlling the constitutionality of legislation,[153] on a correctness standard or (in Monaghan's phrasing) "independent judgment rule," i.e., substituting its own interpretation for that of the administration if need be.[154]

---

[150] The classic debate on the issue of whether the Constitution reposes on natural law or is just positive legislation is the dispute between Justices Chase and Iredell in *Calder v. Bull* 3 U.S. (3 Dall.) 386 (1798), with Justice Chase's seriatim opinion expounding the natural rights/natural law version. *See* comments in Tribe, *supra*, at 561: "Chase's natural rights were defined in large part reflexively: they were the residue marked out by the limits on government implied by its very reasons for being." Perhaps, to a certain extent, adherence to a final assumption of natural rights or—in Tribe's words—a "residue marked out by the limits on government implied by its very reasons for being" is inescapable for a public lawyer adhering to the idea of limited government, constitutionalism. As a theoretical matter (yet with quite a few practical implications) the question is only what that implied limitation should be at any given time and whether the rule of law wedge one seeks to draw between the state and the individual would be a more *concrete normative* one, such as the generality-life-liberty-property criterion of old constitutionalism or whether one should seek its replacement by an *abstract normative* position of sorts.

[151] Monaghan 1983.

[152] *Ibid.*, at p. 6.

[153] The Court has a monopoly of interpretation of questions of constitutionality, *see*, for instance *City of Boerne v. Flores* 521 U.S. 507 (1997).

[154] Monaghan is only interested in the narrower question of the extent to which the Constitution, i.e., *Marbury*'s definition of judicial review, controls in turn judicial review of administrative legal interpretation of federal statutes and in the resulting allocation of interpretive authority between the federal judiciary and the administration. *See also*, related, Robert Rabin's more expansive history of judicial control of federal regulatory action, "Federal Regulation in Historical Perspective," 38 *Stan. L. Rev.* 1189 (May, 1986). Judicial review of administrative action can also be imagined as defined by a continuum whose poles are *de novo* consideration of law, facts, policy (which was the position of the Court, for instance, in some post-Civil War reviews of rate

Conversely, when non-coercive governmental conduct would be scrutinized, in the case of "public rights," claims by private individuals upon the government (especially governmentally granted benefits, purely statutory creations, such as the pension claim at stake in *Decatur*), the judiciary would review administrative action under a mere rationality or patent unreasonableness standard (in Monaghan's phrasing, "clear mistake"). That is, unless the statutory duty would be so clearly ministerial as to compel another (judicial) interpretation (the situation in *Kendall*), the meaning attributed by the administration to the statute (jurisdictional questions aside) would be awarded a large degree of deference and allowed as a matter of course to control the decisional outcome. Claims by individuals against the government and certain claims of government against individuals (customs duties, taxes) could, theoretically, be resolved by Congress itself, executive officers or specially created "legislative courts."[155] To wit, in the leading 'public rights' case, *Murray's Lessee v. Hoboken Land & Improvement Co.*, the Court held that summary execution on a warrant of distress to levy on the property of a collector of public revenue found by the Treasury auditor to be in default did not constitute (by virtue of failure to go through the judicial process) a denial of due process under the Fifth Amendment. The warrant issued in accordance with the Treasury audit *was* the due process of law required by the Constitution: "For, though 'due process of law' generally implies and includes *actor, reus, judex,* regular allegations, opportunity to answer, and a trial according to some settled course of judicial proceedings, yet, this is not universally true."[156]

While government made little demands (customs and taxes) from and provided little benefits (veterans' pensions, with a big outflow after the Civil War) to individuals, the distinction was unproblematic in thought as in practice. Until the Civil War, most federal activity revolved around subsidizing private enterprise. Even as the West was settled, culminating in the passage of the Homestead Act

reasonableness) and—at the other extreme—a highly deferential model of review, in matters of both interpretation of law and factual predicates for administrative action (*NLRB v. Hearst*). According to Rabin, most frequently, the Court oscillated between two intermediate positions within this range, which he defines as "Right Answer" (the so-called "hard look" review, best exemplified by *Citizens to Preserve Overton Park v. Volpe*) and "Best Efforts", respectively (for instance *Chevron, U.S.A. v. Natural Resources Defense Council*).

[155] A brief historical note may help clarify the matter. Since the central government as such has sovereign immunity against direct suits, unless it chooses to waive it expressly, the initial way of proceeding was for an individual having a claim on the government to petition the legislature for a special appropriation bill, which the *Kendall* case held, as we have noted above, to be mandatory upon the administration (the disbursing officer). In 1855, the Court of Claims was created (now, recreated in 1982, as the U.S. Court of Federal Claims) under Art. I, as a "legislative court." At the beginning, its 'judgments' had no legal effect whatsoever and were drawn up in the form of a bill to be laid before Congress, then it became a real legislative court, its judgments binding on the Secretary of the Treasury, with a possibility of appeal to the Supreme Court. Initially it was given no equity jurisdiction. It still has no jurisdiction over torts committed by the government.

[156] 59 U.S. 272 (1855), 280. *See also Ex parte Bakelite Corporation* 279 U.S. 438 (1929), for an extensive review of developments and enumeration of Art. I courts.

(1862), with huge tracts of land given away to settlers and railroads, neither the states nor the federal government delivered services directly. Responding to a number of catastrophic explosions, federal statutes mandating standards, labeling, licensing and inspection requirements for steamboat boilers (infractions subject to criminal penalties) were passed in 1838 and 1852 under the Commerce Clause. Yet these statutes were legislative oddities in a landscape where, "from a national perspective, commercial affairs took place in a world without regulation."[157] In fact, aside from public works (canal and road building, which were contracted out), the government's paramount function, both state and federal, was largely limited to the facilitation of private development through ensuring property rights.[158]

By the same token, as a constitutional issue, the government's function was limited thus since legislation, both federal and state, was in its turn limited in scope by a restrictive reading of the Commerce Clause and respectively and correlatively by the guarantees of liberty (including freedom of contract)[159] and property. Property and liberty and, consequently, the legitimacy of legislation, were constitutionally defined and limited, in turn, by the background common law legal institutions, in terms of common law rights.[160] As a direct result, constitutionally, the police power of the states was perceived to extend only to *sic utere* (concrete damage to another's property or to health, safety, and morals) equal regulations of property.[161] The limitation on the police power of the states became an explicit rule of positive federal constitutional law with the passage of the Fourteenth Amendment in 1868. Yet, it had been commonly presumed from the very onset that residual legislative power did not mean plenary. To wit, in the classic text of American constitutional law, Justice Story's 1833 *Commentaries,* the common classical assumptions had been resumed and restated with an accuracy and forcefulness which warrant a longer citation: "Whether, indeed, independently of the constitution of the United States, the nature of republican and free governments does not necessarily impose some restraints upon the legislative power, has been much discussed. It seems to be the general opinion, fortified by a strong current of

---

[157] Rabin 1986, at p. 1196.

[158] Willard Hurst 1967, passim.

[159] *Allgeyer v. Louisiana* 165 U.S. 578 (1897), constitutional definition of liberty extends to freedom of contract.

[160] Cass Sunstein labels this interpretation of the constitution and judicial review of administrative action, i.e., from the premise or standpoint of property and liberty rights, and the many property-related constitutional provisions, "Lochner-like premises" (probably because of the pejorative overtones which the label has acquired) and assimilates them to a reactionary-conservative, misplaced or at least obsolete (and now debunked) common law baseline of natural rights and proposes departure from this baseline and its replacement with a new theory of interpretation. In passing, it is unclear in what if any *legal* sense a constitutional provision is "Lochner-like." *See* for instance his *Reconceiving the Regulatory State: After the Rights Revolution* (Cambridge, Mass.: Harvard University Press, 1990).

[161] *Sic utere tuo ut alienum non laedas* (use your property so as not to harm another's).

judicial opinion, that since the American revolution no state government can be presumed to possess the transcendental sovereignty to take away vested rights of property, to take the property of A and give it to B by a mere legislative act. A government can scarcely be deemed to be free, where the rights of property are left solely dependent upon a legislative body, without any restraint. The fundamental maxims of a free government seem to require, that the rights of personal liberty, and private property, should be held sacred. At least, no court of justice, in this country, would be warranted in assuming, than any state legislature possessed the power to violate and disregard them; or that such a power, so repugnant to the common principles of justice and civil liberty, lurked under any general grant of legislative authority, or ought to be implied from any general expression of the will of the people, in the usual forms of the constitutional delegation of power. The people ought not to be presumed to part with rights, so vital to their security and well being, without very strong and positive declarations to that effect."[162]

Against this background, legislative measures such as minimum wage laws or the maximum hours legislation of the type later made famous by the dispute in *Lochner v. N.Y.*, since unsupported by this limited array of reasons (as purely redistributive), would exceed the constitutionally permissible purview. Consequently, such a law would be deemed unconstitutional, being considered as in and of itself—substantively—a deprivation of property and contractual liberty without due process, under the Fourteenth Amendment.[163] This sort of legislation would essentially be, in the words of Chase and Story, the "law that takes property from A. and gives it to B.", against the purposes of the social compact, and hence against justice, nature, reason, and, more importantly, against the Constitution.

Aside from the equal regulation of noxious uses of property (nuisances), understood as the proper constitutional scope of state legislation under the police power, the common law traditionally imposed a price reasonableness and nondiscrimination obligation on certain professions and businesses, either on the ground that their services were held out to the public ("common callings")[164] or because they were "affected with a public interest," within the list of businesses historically recognized as crown prerogatives and as such the beneficiaries of a legal (exclusive

[162] Story, Commentaries (Rotunda and Nowak edition, 1987), pp. 510–511.

[163] *Lochner v. New York*, 198 U.S. 45 (1905) A law restricting to sixty the number of hours bakers could work during a week (a maximum of ten during a day) was declared unconstitutional, since rationally unsupported by any classical police justification (health or safety). Compare with *Muller v. Oregon*, 208 U.S. 412 (1908) where a similar law, limiting the number of hours women could work in laundries and factories was upheld, largely as a result of the Court's being persuaded by the social data in the famous "Brandeis Brief" that physical and social differences between men and women established a public health (police) justification for the law.

[164] Or, in a more modern analogy, because they provided "prime necessities" from the economic vantage point of actual monopoly (public utilities). *See* discussion in Michael Taggart, "The Province of Administrative law Determined?," in *The Province of Administrative Law*, Michael Taggart (ed.) (Oxford, England: Hart Publishing, 1997), pp. 1-20. The common callings still recognized today are the innkeeper, the ferryman, and the common carrier.

grant from the king) monopoly: turnpikes, canals, roads, strategically located seaports and wharfs, bridges and ferries.[165] And, conversely, a property historically considered as affected with a public interest would be entitled to monopoly protection and subjected to regulation by charter, as a prerogative of the crown.[166] The rationale for the reasonableness restrictions on prices applied to legal monopolies and public franchises, as first stated by Lord Chief Justice Hale in the seventeenth-century tract *De Portibus Maris*, is that one who benefits from a public privilege accepts the privilege under terms, with the stated and implied restrictions on his property attached to it, including state regulation of its use and compensation. When one accepts a public benefit, property is no longer merely private (a "common right") but becomes "affected with a public interest."

In the landmark 1787 decision of *Munn v. Illinois,*[167] the Supreme Court upheld a Granger law that imposed a maximum rate on use of grain warehouses and elevators in the state. The actual market position of the business was analogized to that of a "legal monopoly." A "virtual monopoly," the Court held, would also be a proper subject of regulation, as a "business affected with a public interest": "Looking, then, to the common law, from whence came the right which the Constitution protects, we find that when private property is 'affected with a public interest,' it ceases to be *juris privatis* only.'. . .*Property does become clothed with a public interest when used in a manner to make it of public consequence, and affect the community at large.* When, therefore, one devotes his property to a use in which the public has an interest, he, in effect, grants to the public an interest in that use, and must submit to be controlled by the public for the common good, to the extent of the interest he has thus created."[168] (emphasis supplied) In *Munn*, the Supreme Court also accepted as constitutional *ex post legislative* ratemaking on an unchartered business, a grand departure from the original understanding that any price regulation would be imposed by the charter incorporating the business, *ex ante*, as a *contract* between the sovereign and the private enterprise "affected with a public interest." By the same token, in the logic prevailing before *Munn*, what would be affected with public interest and thus subject to regulation by charter was not a matter for arbitrary legislative earmarking but stood defined by the common law.[169]

---

[165] The classic English decision is *Alnutt v. Inglis* 12 East, 527, 104 Eng. Rep. 206 (K.B.1810), in which Lord Ellenborough held that the London Dock Company, a licensed customs house for goods bound for export, being the beneficiary of a legal monopoly, was under a duty to the public of imposing only such charges as were reasonable (at pp. 210–211): "There is no doubt that the general principle is favored both in law and justice, that every man may fix what price he pleases upon his property or the use of it: but if, for a particular purpose, the public have a right to resort to his premises and make use of them, and he have a monopoly in them for that purpose, if he will take the benefit of that monopoly, he must as an equivalent perform the duty attached to it on reasonable terms."

[166] Hovenkamp 1991, at p. 114.

[167] 94 U.S. 113.

[168] Hovenkamp 1991, at p. 126.

[169] *Id.*, "Modern regulation by statute applies more or less equally to all similar firms in a sovereign jurisdiction –for example to all common carriers within the state. But regulation by charter was

In that logic, public interest was considered as an exceptional function of private interest, limitedly confined in terms of enumerated historical categories.

Moreover, the *Munn* Court stated, no one had a constitutional interest in the common law definition of property; legislation could in theory replace determination of prices by private contracts in the case of "businesses affected with a public interest" at any time, since "[i]n fact, the common law rule, which requires the charge to be reasonable, is itself a regulation as to price....a mere common law regulation of trade or business may be changed by the statute. A person has no property, no vested interest, in any rule of the common law."[170] As it is apparent (in part perhaps from the vantage point of hindsight), there are a fair number of tensions in this way of framing the problem. As the author of the dissenting opinion, Justice Field, noted in a strongly worded opinion, once what is "affected with the public interest," as a matter of public regulation, would no longer be determined strictly according to the terms of the common law, the lines of demarcation between private and public would blur and the constitutional protection of property from legislation could potentially become illusory. If a legislature could attach the label "affected with the public interest" to any kind of property and then regulate its use, what is then the constitutional limit on legislation? Would regulation of use not be a substitute for a taking, imposing burdens on few for the benefit of all without any need for all to compensate? As Justice Holmes would later be keen to point out, in the first 'regulatory takings' case, *Pennsylvania Coal Co. v. Mahon*, "When this seemingly absolute protection [of property and liberty of contract under the Fourteenth (and Fifth) Amendment] is found to be qualified by the police power, the natural tendency of human nature is to extend the qualification more and more until at last private property disappears."[171] In practice, protection came from reasonableness review of ratemaking. While the *Munn* Court identified rate regulation as a legislative function, it then proceeded to supervise statutory ratemaking under a strict *de novo* standard of review. While ratemaking would be "essentially legislative," final determination of the reasonableness of a rate, in order to ensure against its becoming arbitrary or confiscatory, would be, by the same token, essentially judicial.[172]

---

specific to the firm....This approach was generally consistent with classical theory, which regarded regulation as rare and not to be presumed. As late as the 1860's and 1870's railroads were chartered with no price regulation whatsoever....As late as 1877, when *Munn v. Illinois* affirmed the constitutionality of rate regulation of an unincorporated enterprise, many believed price regulation was beyond state power unless the firm operated under a charter authorizing the regulation."

[170] *Id.*, at p. 134.

[171] 260 U.S. 393, at 415 (1922).

[172] Rabin 1986, at p. 1210.

3.1.2.3 What Exactly Is a Trust?

> Suppose the great Lawgiver had constructed the Ten Commandments with the same uncertainty. Suppose he had said: "Thou shalt not steal; thou shalt not bear false witness; thou shall not covet-contemporaneously or under substantially similar circumstances and conditions" (laughter); or suppose at the conclusion of the decalogue the following provision had been added: "Provided, however, that upon application. . .persons so designated may be authorized to cheat, steal, bear false witness, or covet, and said commission may from time to time prescribe the extent to which said persons may be relieved from any or all said commandments."
>
> Congressman Weaver, debates on the Interstate Commerce Commission Act (*Congressional Record*, 49th Cong., 2d Sess. 820 [1887]

> Iv all th' great evils now threatenin' th' body politic and th' pollytical bodies, these crool organizations an' combinations iv capital is perhaps th' best example iv what upright an' arnest businessmen can do whin they are let alone. They cannot be stamped out be laws or th' decisions iv coorts, or hos-tile ligislachion which is too frindly. Their desthruction cannot be accomplished be dimagogues.
>
> Th' thrust are heejous monsthers built up be th' inlightened intherprise iv th' men that have done so much to advance pro-gress in our beloved counthry. On wan hand I wud stamp thim undher fut; on th' other hand not so fast.
>
> Mr. Dooley's summary of Theodore Roosevelt's first message to Congress[173]

Constitutional limitations on legislation from the baseline of the common law constituted the legal counterpart of the classical economic system. Similarly, departures from the classical legal arrangement which conceptualized common law rights as pre-political or natural went in lockstep with departures from classical economic thought, which had conceptualized the market as self-correcting outside the limited governmental intervention of enforcing a framework of equal rules of conduct (including equal and limited police power legislation).[174] The railroads were, after the Civil War, one of the most important economic fields, vital to the economic health of the country. After some efforts at state subsidization of competition, by chartering competing railroads, it became more and more clear that the

---

[173] In Willard Hurst 1967, at p. 84.

[174] Tribe 1988, Chapter 8, Model II-The Model of Implied Limitations on Government: The Rise and Fall of Contractual Liberty. For an exploration of the correlation between classical economics and classical legal thought, Herbert Hovenkamp, *Enterprise and American Law 1836–1937* (Cambridge, Mass.: Harvard University Press, 1991). The study seeks to demonstrate that Adam Smith-like economic classicism and legal classical thought were interrelated and marginally overlapping, not in some simplistic deterministic way but rather because: "American political economists and American judges operated in the same uniquely American 'market' for ideas." (at p. 96) Of more direct interest to us here is the observation, at p. 296, that: "[t]he great values of nineteenth-century American lawyers-individualism, liberty of contract, abhorrence of forced wealth transfers- were also the values of classical political economy." More generally on the history and evolution of regulation, Thomas K. McCraw's monograph, *Prophets of Regulation* (Cambridge, Mass, and London, England: Belknap-Harvard University Press, c1984).

laws of competition, assumed to be self-correcting by classical economics, just did not apply to this industry. Because of its characteristics (very large fixed costs with comparatively very little operating costs), if either forced into competition or left unregulated by the state—the orthodox classical economic options—the railroad companies seemed ever "destined to be either filthy rich or perpetually broke."[175] Legally, the railroads were the ideal embodiment of a "business affected with a public interest," as common carriers, historically subsidized by the state (sometimes granted extensive eminent domain privileges). According to the common law, they were under a duty of nondiscrimination and charge reasonableness. In the wake of the Civil War, complaints of rate discrimination and preferential treatment of shippers, merchants, farmers, and localities by the railroads were ubiquitous.[176] After the Supreme Court disabled the states from regulating rates on interstate rail traffic (including its intrastate segment), in the 1886 decision of *Wabash, St. Louis & Pac. Ry. v. Illinois,*[177] Congress would be compelled to regulate instead and, in 1887, the modern federal administrative state was inaugurated by the creation of the Interstate Commerce Commission, fashioned after the state railroad commissions and given the power to issue retroactive, nonpunitive cease and desist orders from conduct deemed in violation of the statute, i.e., unreasonable and discriminatory rates. The Court took a very limited view of the scope of federal regulatory power and read the statute accordingly, regarding the commission as no more than a preliminary referee, whose findings of fact were treated in a judicial proceeding as only prima facie valid. The ICC's interpretation of its governing statute was accorded almost no deference whatever.[178] In his monographic article on the

---

[175] Hovenkamp 1991, at p. 148: "If the railroads were permitted to have unregulated monopolies, rate gouging and large monopoly profits at the expense of the shippers were sure to result. If the railroads were forced to compete with each other and pooling or other forms of cartelization were strictly forbidden, railroad rates would almost certainly be driven to a level too low to cover fixed costs, forcing the railroads into bankruptcy."

[176] An economic and legislative history of the problems leading to the creating of the state and federal railroad commissions can be found in the first chapter of McCraw's monograph. *See also*, Rabin 1986, at pp. 1206–1207: "[W]hat seems most apparent is that virtually no one was happy with the discriminatory practices engaged in by the railroads to secure additional business. Merchants, farmers, regional loyalists, and railroad entrepreneurs all shared the view that federal regulation was essential. Where they disagreed was on the crucial particulars."

[177] 118 U.S. 557 (1886).

[178] E.g., *ICC v Cincinnati, New Orleans & Texas Pacific Railway*, 168 U.S. 11 (1897) In the face of ten years of different ICC practice (and Congressional acquiescence), power expressly conferred in the act to declare rates *unreasonable* was declared by the Court not to imply a power to establish *reasonable* rates; if Congress had wished to confer ratemaking power, it should have done so in express terms. *See also Chicago, Milwaukee, St. Paul Railway v. Minnesota*, 134 U.S. 418 (1889) state legislation giving an agency "final and conclusive" authority over the reasonableness of rates would not control the courts, since rate reasonableness is "eminently a judicial question." In the 1910 case of *Interstate Commerce Commission v. Illinois Central Railroad*, 215 U.S. 452 (1910) the Court would present a different, much more restrained view of the scope of review: "Beyond controversy, in determining whether an order of the Commission shall be suspended or set aside, we must consider: (a) all relevant questions of constitutional power or right; (b) all pertinent

history of federal regulation, Robert Rabin makes the interesting remark that: "[t]he tendency in administrative law to regard the delegation doctrine as the principal judicial tool for determining the legitimate scope of agency authority seems to me to be mistaken. By far, the more common strategy resorted to by the Supreme Court in [the] ICC cases was a persistently narrow construction of the substantive authority conferred upon the agency."[179] In fact, while Rabin's observation is correct in a sociological-statistical sense (i.e., with respect to cumulative practical results and judicial strategy), the two matters of *legitimacy-oriented* constitutional limitations on the scope and precision of statutes and the *discretion-relating* degree of deference accorded administrative statutory interpretation in judicial review of administrative action are conceptually related and reinforcing, since both are related to the concrete baseline of private liberty and property rights, as defined by the common law.[180]

questions as to whether the administrative order is within the scope of the delegated authority under which it purports to have been made; and (c) a proposition which we state independently, although in its essence it may be contained in the previous one, viz., whether, even although the order be in form within the delegated power, nevertheless it must be treated as not embraced therein, because the exertion of authority which is questioned has been manifested in such an unreasonable manner as to cause it, in truth, to be within the elementary rule that the substance, and not the shadow, determines the validity of the exercise of the power." (at 470). According to Rabin, the history of federal regulation explains this change from correctness to a relaxed reasonableness review as a period of acclimatization and accommodation of the Court with administrative innovations.

[179] Rabin 1986, at p. 1215, note 65.

[180] Besides, aside from the fact that the judiciary effectively rendered the Commission's powers almost nugatory through *de novo* review, even as Congress gave the ICC positive power to set maximum rates upon a shipper's complaint that a rate was unreasonable, through the Hepburn Act, in 1906, there was yet not that much administrative discretion granted, within the logic of the classical legal paradigm. The Commission was also given a locomotive inspection function. According to Martin Shapiro, both locomotive inspection and rate setting were perceived as one and the same issue essentially, i.e., "objective, scientific assessements based on exact, nondiscretionary standards." As the locomotive safety standards were set scientifically (since the cost-risk trade-offs incorporated in the standard and based on professional conventions were then unapparent), so too was maximum rate-setting an objective application of science (economics and accounting) to facts (market value): "Economics would determine what a fair rate of return was on investment. That rate was a phenomenon as 'natural', that is, beyond human manipulation, as the transit of Venus. The economist would observe the free market as the astronomer did the heavens, and measure fair rate of return, that is the return that any investment in the market would yield, as the astronomer charted Venus's sidereal movement. The accountant would then determine the amount of the railroad's costs to be properly attributed to the hauling of a particular commodity over a particular track, add the appropriate fair return figure provided him by the economist and arrive at the correct rate. In this realm of accounting, all was quantified and accurately measurable. Nothing was uncertain. Rate regulation was a matter of science rather than discretion." The Frontiers of Science Doctrine: American Experiences with the Judicial Control of Science-Based Decision-Making, EUI Working Papers, European University Institute RSC No. 96/11 (1996). According to Theodore Lowi as well, the nature of ICC became truly discretionary only with the 1920 Transportation Act's granting it power to set "just and reasonable" "minimum rates." This is a very interesting observation in light of the distinct nature of an

Regulation of natural monopolies such as public utilities and the railroads could, after the theoretical issues became clearer, be conceptualized without much effort in common law terms and was, for historic reasons, a lesser challenge for classical economic thought as well. The problem of regulating the *de facto* monopoly as a market failure and 'monopolistic' practices, such as contracts in restraint of trade and dishonest competition practices that undercut the proper functioning of economic laws, would pose, nonetheless, a bigger challenge to both paradigms. At common law, a monopoly was a *legal* monopoly, a grant from the king excluding others from commerce. In classical economic thought, hostility with monopolies was associated with hostility towards mercantilism and its whimsical and wasteful interferences with the laws of the market, while classical legal thinking regarded with just suspicion a privilege.[181] The classical economic and legal idea was that the state should not interfere with the market and not play favorites, a totally different matter than the problem posed by the *de facto* monopoly, namely that the market needed correcting by state interference lest the consumers and small businesses should be coerced by monopolistic prices. Forbidden practices in obstruction of trade, yet another matter, had been in England strictly enumerated and defined with great specificity by the 1552 *Statute against Forestallers, Regrators, and Ingrossers.*[182] As a rule, nonetheless, cartel practices like price-fixing, if non-coercive, were not unlawful, in the sense that, although unenforceable, they could not be challenged by non-(third-)parties to the agreement. A contract in restraint of trade, a third issue still, was a contract by which one limited by covenant one's rights to practice a trade, such as when a grocer would sell a business with an agreement not to engage in the same business in the same locality or within a certain distance. The limitation, lawful if reasonable 'from the point of view of the parties and of the public,' was predicated on public policy grounds having to do with the reasonableness of the self-imposed coercion to the party imposing this limitation on himself and the correlative risk that one who would impose an unreasonable restriction on himself would likely lose all means of livelihood and thus become a public charge.[183] The only trade restrained was, as

---

affirmative power granted in vague terms and exercised in a judicial manner, in an essentially "polycentric" domain: "In effect this meant case-by-case bargaining (called 'on the merits'), the results putting the commission on every side of every issue....this totally altered the meaning of the ICC." (*supra* at 102) .

[181] The constitutional question was whether within the regulatory limits of police powers legislation, the Constitution either implied or forbade (as a Contract Clause impairment and, respectively as a Fourteenth Amendment due process limitation) the conferral of monopoly privileges in public contracts (i.e., corporate charters). The Supreme Court would answer both questions in the negative, Charles River Bridge Case, *Charles River Bridge v. Warren Bridge* 13 U.S. 420 (1837) and *The Slaughter House Cases* 83 U.S. 36 (1872).

[182] 5th and 6th Edw. VI, Ch. 14.

[183] Interpreting the Sherman Act in light of these common law assumptions was the reason for Holmes's argument in his famous *Northern Securities* dissent, where, to the dismay of Theodore Roosevelt, he made the apparently surprising statement that: "[t]he court below argued as if

Holmes would later take pains to emphasize in his *Northern Securities* dissent, the contractor's own. All these rules corresponded essentially to a different economic reality and conceptual template than those reflected in the Sherman Law.

In the politically charged climate of passing the Sherman Law, in 1890, within the context of a very incomplete and muddled understanding of the 'trust' problem,[184] all these problems were 'jumbled' together, in a confused legal formula which replaced the definition of prohibited practices with a vague prohibition stated in the colloquial and moralistic terms inspired by the contemporaneous dislike for the 'trusts.' The act criminalized "every contract, combination in the form of trust, or otherwise, or conspiracy, in restraint of trade or commerce among the several states." Because of the vagueness of the terms and the blanket, no-exception prohibition of the statutory provision, this was rendered in effect a much more serious delegation of authority than the 'unjust and unreasonable rate' one in the Commerce Act, since the terms as such inevitably gave unprecedented policy making discretion to either the Executive or the courts. By the face of the statute, it was not at all clear *what* exactly was prohibited, since every contract is in a sense a restraint of trade, and thus could potentially fall under the statutory sweep. Holmes would later characterize the act, in a 1910 letter to Pollock, as a "humbug based on economic ignorance and incompetence."[185] The "rule of reason"[186]

---

maintaining competition were the expressed object of the act. *The act says nothing about competition.*" At 403 (emphasis supplied)

[184] Brandeis, one of the most vociferous critics of the 'trusts,' personally instrumental in the creation of the Federal Trade Commission, because of his visceral antipathy to 'big business' as such, seems to have been curiously unable to grasp the economic differences in kind between business fields where, because of economies of scale, cartel arrangements would tend towards tight central vertical integration (the 'trusts'), and business fields where, due to easy entry, cartel arrangements would never amount to more than loose peripheral horizontal associations, easy to default on and prone to early demise. He disliked first and foremost the Moloch, big business as such, irrespective of economic benefits derived from operational size, and concentrated his energies on the elimination of unfair trade practices since he correlated 'bigness' (the 'trusts') with unfairness and deceit. Considerations of efficiency and thus consumer welfare came a distant second for Brandeis. During 1911 Congressional hearings, Brandeis states his position bluntly: an efficient firm might nonetheless become "too large to be tolerated among people who desire to be free." Cited by Mark Winerman, "The Origins of the FTC: Concentration, Cooperation, Control, and Competition," 71 *Antitrust L. J.* 1 (2003), at 35. *See* McCraw 1984, "Brandeis and the Origins of the FTC," pp. 80–142. *See also* Ellis Hawley, *The New Deal and the Problem of Monopoly-A Study in Economic Ambivalence* (Princeton, N.J., Princeton University Press, c1966).

[185] Mark DeWolfe Howe, ed., *Holmes-Pollock Letters*, vol. I (Cambridge: Harvard University Press, 1941), at p. 163.

[186] *Standard Oil Co. of New Jersey v. U.S.* 221 U.S. 1 (1911), *see* at 60, for instance, the judicial statement of the problem: "[A]s the contracts or acts embraced in the provision were not expressly defined, since the enumeration addressed itself simply to classes of acts, those classes being broad enough to embrace every conceivable contract or combination which could be made concerning trade or commerce or the subjects of such commerce, and thus caused any act done by any of the enumerated methods anywhere in the whole field of human activity to be illegal if in restraint of trade, it inevitably follows that the provision necessarily called for the exercise of judgment which required that some standard should be resorted to for the purpose of determining whether the prohibition had or had not in any case been violated."

formula by which, analogizing with the common law, the Court sought to narrow down the open-ended terms of the statute, failed to satisfy anybody. The reasonableness test had been developed by the common law to apply to small-scale transactions between individuals in a pre-industrial market and did not fare well applied to huge trust operations in an industrial economy, in the absence of clear legislative guidance.[187] Failure to clarify the statute in terms of received categories through a test of predictable application limiting judicial decision-making presented the danger of a potential arrogation of vast and completely unstructured policy-making discretion by the Court. This was the unprecedented case of legislation which, since impossible to narrow down according to common law categories within the logic of the classic judicial paradigm, could end up either granting unfettered enforcement discretion to the administration (in effect to the Executive, through the Department of Justice), with respect to private rights or else would transform the judiciary into a large-scale policy-maker.[188]

This legal and political quagmire would be momentarily resolved by the conversion of the 'trust-busting' criminal enforcement position of the Sherman Act into a 'fairness of trade practices' corrective administration issue, through the creation, during the Wilson Administration, of the Federal Trade Commission. This solution, of an independent regulatory agency, is generally recognized to characterize the pragmatic and to a certain extent unsystematic American approach to regulation, in both institutional terms and economic strategy.[189] At the time, the commission

[187] The issue was described quite clearly and at an early stage by Gerald Henderson: "It may be conceded that the test is not of itself susceptible of precise and definite application. A court may have good reasons for concluding that it is not proper for a physician to covenant not to practice his profession within 100 miles of the city of York, but they are not very helpful in determining whether or not a consolidation of 40 per cent of the steel industry in the United States is reasonable. At most they suggest the frame of mind into which the judges should put themselves." Gerald Henderson, *The History of the Federal Trade Commission-A Study in Administrative Law and Procedure* (New York: Agathon Press, 1968 (c1924)), at p. 6.

[188] *But cf.* Lowi 1979, at p. 99, the act not a delegation since the object of control was a "numerous but namable collection of companies and identifiable conducts (Therefore, *The* Trusts.)" That may be true in an instrumental, more result-oriented political science sense. From a legal perspective, what is important from a delegation-related perspective is whether or not the new legislation could be narrowed down and interpreted in a consistent manner, through a judicial test which would render the legislative command predictable. Here, Holmes's dissent in *Northern Securities Co. v. U.S.* 193 U.S. 197 (1904), at 402, is pertinent: "[T]he statute is of a very sweeping and general character. It hits 'every' contract or combination of the prohibited sort, great or small, and 'every' person who shall attempt to monopolize, in the sense of the act, 'any part' of the trade or commerce against the several states. There is a natural inclination to assume it was directed against certain great combinations, and to read it in that light. It does not say so. On the contrary it says 'every,' and 'any part.'"

[189] *See*, Giandomenico Majone, *Regulating Europe* (New York and London: Routledge, c1996), for an elaboration on the remark that, categorized with respect to the way in which the proper role of the state and the corresponding place of the market is primarily approached, America is an ideal-typical "regulatory state," since its regulatory function predominates, and to this extent it differs from the welfare state (redistribution function), Keynesian state (stabilization function) or a

formula, already used at the federal level by the Commerce Act, had become a familiar regulatory tool and thus met with almost general approval as a solution to the many dilemmas raised by the unfortunate attempts at enforcing the Sherman Act. It seemed the self-evident answer to the concrete problem posed by the 'trusts.' The extent to which the trust problem and the debates around it constituted a novelty would not be apparent for a while since, in terms of immediate legal developments, the Supreme Court would, in the course of a quick series of decisions, 'interpret away' most of the discretionary powers of the Federal Trade Commission.[190] In 1920, in *Federal Trade Commission v. Gratz*, the Court decided that, while, just as the statute said, "findings of the commission as to the facts, if supported by testimony, would be conclusive" upon the courts, the operating sentence of the FTC Act, "unfair methods of competition," since the meaning of the phrase was in dispute, was *a matter of law* for the court to decide according to the common law.[191] Yet, the conceptual intricacies surrounding the monopoly problem and the various legislative and judicial positions with respect to the matter were the harbingers of a new constitutional paradigm. The essential elements of this new paradigm, many of which constitute the contemporary legal and theoretical template, need to be specified at the closing of this section.

---

combination of the latter two, the Keynesian welfare state: "[T]he regulatory function. . .attempts to increase the allocative efficiency of the market by correcting the various types of market failure: monopoly power, negative externalities, failures of information or an insufficient provision of public goods." That is to say, the state regulates the market policing or substituting for the real life departures from an economic model that supposes a perfect competition, with a perfectly well informed customer and internalization of all the costs.

[190] Usually decisions on appeal from the circuit court of appeals decisions on applications for enforcement or petitions for review of FTC cease-and-desist orders. In a long line of cases, the most representative are *Federal Trade Commission v. American Tobacco Co.* 264 U.S. 298 (1924), rendering nugatory the investigative powers of the FTC; the agency had sought in District Court a writ of mandamus directing the tobacco companies to produce records, contracts, memoranda, correspondence, for making copies and inspection: "Anyone who respects the spirit as well as the letter of the Fourth Amendment would be loath to believe that Congress intended to authorize one of its subordinate agencies to sweep all our traditions into the fire and to direct fishing expeditions into private papers on the possibility that they may disclose evidence of crime. . ..The right to access given by the statute is to documentary evidence-not to all documents, but to such documents as are evidence. The analogies of the law do not allow the party wanting evidence to call for documents in order to *see* if they do not contain it." Opinion of the Court, per Holmes, J.

[191] *Federal Trade Commission v. Gratz*, 253 U.S. 421 (1920), at 427: "The words 'unfair method of competition' are not defined by the statute and their exact meaning is in dispute. It is for the courts, not the commission, ultimately to determine as matter of law what they include. They are clearly inapplicable to practices never heretofore regarded as opposed to good morals because characterized by deception, bad faith, fraud, or oppression, or as against public policy because of their dangerous tendency unduly to hinder competition or create monopoly." Opinion of the Court, per McReynolds, J. The contrast with Brandeis, J.'s dissent is revealing of the clash of paradigms and the issue of delegation as standard of review in statutory interpretation: "Instead of undertaking to define what practices should be deemed unfair, as had been done in earlier legislation, the act left the determination to the commission." (at 436)

In terms of legislative accountability to the electorate (as a representation problem) or regarding Congress's fulfillment of its constitutional lawmaking duty, the general approval with which the new trade commission legislation met reflected precisely the extent to which the legislation constituted a delegation in one of the modern senses of the word, that of irresolution and evasion from responsibility in face of a difficult choice. The vague and broad legislative mandate under which the Commission was meant to operate, prohibition of "unfair methods of competition. . .and unfair or deceptive acts or practices" "in the public interest,"[192] reflected the indecision and lack of agreement on both means and ends surrounding the drafting of the Federal Trade Commission Act. The end product seemed, on the face of it, a statutory cornucopia, able to give all possible things to all possible people which could possibly be affected by the operation of the statute. Small business, big business, consumers, could get protection, advice, good quality of products and lower prices. Bad business would be brought to justice, good business would prosper and thus, under the watchful eye of the commission, everyone would be provided for.

Nobody can disagree, as a matter of principle, with a general proposition, stated in abstract and morally charged terms. Usually, the higher the level of abstraction, the lesser the disagreement; who could ever be, to cite K. C. Davis's characterization of modern legislative mandates, against "the true, the good, and the beautiful."[193] Disagreement comes usually in terms of concrete policy and, by failure to define clearly the critical terms of the statute, "unfair methods of competition," the American Congress broke the path of modern delegations.[194] This legislative direction differed essentially from the Commerce Act, which, initially, had given the Interstate Commerce Commission only power to determine what an unreasonable rate would be, in a quasi-judicial manner, across one industry, proscriptively. Now, even though the method prescribed for the Trade Commission would be quasi-judicial, the task was essentially legislative, to the extent that the commission would need to define what "unfair methods of competition" would mean, across most of the economy, prescriptively, without legislative guidance. It should be pointed out that even the formula "in the public interest," as it found its place in the Clayton and FTC Acts, was no longer freighted with meaning by history and common law. A business 'affected with public interest,' as the reader will remember, had been considered in economic terms one that could be exceptionally

[192] In the Clayton Act, which would also be enforced by the Commission, Congress made an attempt to specify three categories of conduct expressly prohibited: price discrimination, interlocking directorates, exclusionary agreements.

[193] Davis 1969, at p. 20.

[194] Jerry L. Mashaw observed that modern American statutes, even though otherwise replete with technical detail, "often exhibit surprising vagueness precisely at the point of critical policy choice," since "adverbial equivocations" ("feasible," "practicable," "reasonable") render the legislative direction essentially and irresolutely vague, precisely at the point of critical policy choice and this in spite of technical or procedural detail. Mashaw 1997 at p. 135.

excluded from competition and regulated. Conversely, in legal terms, this was an exception from the substantive due process constitutional justificatory burden the government would have to meet when seeking to reach by legislation purely private common law rights. In the FTC Act, "public interest" was standing for a different legislative template, which Jaffe would later call "the illusion of ideal administration," presumed by the "broad delegation model," where, by virtue of collapsing under an open-ended proposition both 'what agencies are and what they ought to be' (namely, regulators in the public interest), the normative burden of assessment is up for grabs and entirely projected on the critic-observer.[195] To put it otherwise, a formula such as 'the public interest,' unless concretized and defined by legislative assignment of burdens and benefits, is in itself lofty and noble-sounding but essentially meaningless abstraction.

Regarding bureaucratic political accountability and closely related to the above observations, at the time, the commission solution as such embodied the expertise-oriented attitude of the Progressives towards administration.[196] At the end of the nineteenth century and the beginning of the twentieth, a belief had surged in legal and political thought that administration could be separated from politics and that regulatory issues could be met with objective, scientific answers. To be sure, in due course, the rightness of Herring's premonitory observation would be proved that "[a]dministrators cannot be given the responsibilities of statesmen without incurring the tribulations of politicians."[197] Since it influenced American administrative law to an important degree and in the longer run, the belief as such in a neat separation of economic administration from politics, is of broader interest to this study. There are

---

[195] Louis Jaffe, "The Illusion of Ideal Administration," 86 *Harv. L. Rev.* 1183 (May, 1973). The main thesis is revealed by the following passage: "The broader the power defined as appropriate for exercise by an administrator, the greater the frustration of the critic who finds that the state of the regulated world is not to his tastes. The assumption that a vague delegation to regulate in the public interest yields a standard which is readily discoverable by an administrator provokes objection when results do not comport with one or another individual's concept of what the 'public interest' requires."

[196] A number of related social-intellectual ideas concerned with social, legal, and institutional reform are brought together under the umbrella of 'progressivism,' a political and intellectual movement influential from the late nineteenth until the first decade of the twentieth century. Daniel T. Rodgers analytically broke the general label of 'progressivism' (and the 'ideology of discontent' characterizing the different positions characterized loosely as progressivism) into three "languages of discontent," epitomizing "three distinct clusters of ideas. . .the first was the rhetoric of antimonopolism, the second was an emphasis on social bonds and the social nature of human beings, and the third was the language of social efficiency." "In Search of Progressivism," 10 (4) *Reviews in American History* 113 (Dec., 1982), at p. 123.

[197] "[T]he control of business remains too controversial and too vital a political issue to be entirely relegated to any commission independent of close control by the policy-formulating agencies of the government." E. Pendleton Herring, *Public Administration and the Public Interest* (New York: McGraw Hill, 1936), at p. 138. *See*, by the same author, a review and analysis of the early political and legal imbroglios of the Federal Trade Commission, "Politics, Personalities, and the Federal Trade Commission," I and II, 28 (6) and 29 (1) *American Political Science Review* 1016 (Dec., 1934) and 21 (Feb., 1935).

two different issues captured under the expertise idea, which concern equally the phenomenon of delegation and its subsequent conceptualization and treatment in legal theory and actual law. If policy making is posited as a matter of expertise, then it seems to be the case that it does not need to be directly controlled politically. More so, *direct* political control would be detrimental, the Progressives believed, since it would bring venality, factionalism and special interest within a realm of objective reason. Regulation by commission was to be in all senses, in the words of a later critic, "regulation without tears."[198] The Progressives were after all, as the word readily shows, progressive, concerned with rapid social change,[199] and thus quite impatient with separation of power theories and their emphasis on forestalling governmental action.[200] As a good litmus test for the temper and stultifying confusion of the times, in this vein, suffice it to point out that a personage of Harvard Law School Dean Roscoe Pound's stature and wit could write in 1920 that: "No one will assert at present that the separation of powers is part of the legal order of nature or that it is essential to liberty."[201] Since as a matter of institutional-procedural design the commissions had been given functions that resembled those of the traditional political branches[202] this became a self-fulfilling prediction about administrative

[198] Marver H. Bernstein, *Regulating Business by Independent Commission* (Princeton, N.J.: Princeton University Press, 1955), at p. 37: "The Progressives had an abiding faith in regulation, expertness, and the capacity of American government to make rational decisions provided experts in the administrative agencies could remain free from partisan political considerations."

[199] *See* Herbert Hovenkamp, "Evolutionary Models in Jurisprudence," 64 *Tex. L. Rev.* 645 (December, 1985). *Also see* by the same author "The Mind and Heart of Progressive Legal Thought" (Presidential Lecture given at the University of Iowa), available for download at http://sdrc.lib.uiowa.edu/preslectures/hovenkamp95/, last visited October 31, 2010). Hovenkamp relates legal Progressivism to the transposition of Darwin's evolutionary theories to social sciences. According to him, *The Descent of Man,* published in 1871, which linked humans to Darwin's general theory of evolution, produced both a right- (Herbert Spencer is here the epitomic example) and a left-wing or Reform Social Darwinism. The Progressives, as Reform Darwinists, believed that the specific difference of the human species is that it can understand and thus control or 'manage' scientifically its evolutionary process.

[200] *See* a review in Vile 1967, X-"Progressivism and Political Science in America," pp. 263–293. Thus the interest and fascination with "efficiency, rationalization, and social engineering" (Rodgers at p. 126)

[201] Roscoe Pound, "Spurious Interpretation," 7 *Colum. L. Rev.* 379 (1907), at p. 384. In short time Pound will experience a spectacular about face, complaining of New Deal "administrative absolutism," just as Landis would later experience his own disillusionment, with the ideas of administrative expertise and objectively attainable public interest. *See*, on these issues, Horwitz, op. cit. Chapter Eight, "Legal Realism, the Bureaucratic State, and The Rule of Law," pp. 213–246.

[202] Even though the initial commissions were not given rulemaking functions, the Federal Trade Commission issued a complaint, enforcing the law ('like' the executive), decided on the merits of the complaint and issued a cease and desist order ('like' a court). Being the institutional heir of the 1903 Bureau of Corporations within the Department of Commerce and of the state 'sunshine' (investigatory) commissions, it also investigated trade practices and compiled data, held trade practice conferences, and made proposals *de lege ferenda* to Congress, functions that resembled (were 'like') those of a legislature.

regulatory independence. This attitude would later be epitomized by James Landis's *The Administrative Process*. Landis, a prominent New Dealer, law professor, and member in the boards of both the Federal Trade Commission and Securities and Exchange Commission, described regulatory administration and the administrative process as such essentially in terms of expertise and as necessary and welcome innovations upon the separation of powers.[203]

In terms of rule of law and judicial review of administrative discretion, should the administrator be deemed an expert in his field of administration, it follows that, as a matter of course, the proper judicial posture should be deference. More so, it would be an unproblematic deference, not the sort involved in the case of judicial submission to the *subjective* legislative and administrative or executive choices of the political branches, in which case the very word, as John Vining put it "calls up lowering the eyes, baring the covered head, laughing at jokes that are not funny."[204] Deference to the *objective* decision of an expert policymaker would pose no such problems, since thus the judge would yield to science and not arbitrariness or whim; properly speaking, there would be in fact no discretion at all, since the administrator would himself be bound by the objective and self-evident result to be achieved.[205] In the general ethos of the time, Ernst Freund's admonition remained largely unheeded, that administration, precisely the other way around, could remain neutral, separate, and expert *if* political decision would specify both means and ends in advance and that "with regard to major matters, the appropriate sphere of delegated authority is where there are no controversial issues of policy or opinion."[206]

---

[203] James M. Landis, *The Administrative Process* (New Haven and London: Yale University Press, 1966 edition with a Foreword by Louis L. Jaffe (c1938)), at p. 15: the administrative process "presents an assemblage of rights exercisable by government as a whole." Yet, the innovation is unproblematic, since (at p. 47): "The desirability of four, five, or six "branches" of government would seem to be a problem determinable not in light of numerology but rather against a background of what we now expect government to do."

[204] Quoted by Michael Taggart in "The Tub of Public Law," in David Dyzenhaus, ed. *The Unity of Public Law* (Oxford & Portland, Oregon: Hart Publishing, 2004), at p. 474.

[205] *See* Stewart 1974-1975, at p. 1678 (commenting on the judicial review consequences of the 'expertise' model of administrative law): "For in that case the discretion that the administrator enjoys is more apparent than real. The policy to be set is simply a function of the goal to be achieved and the state of the world. There may be a trial and error process in finding the best means of achieving the posited goal, but persons subject to the administrators control are no more liable to his arbitrary will than are patients remitted to the care of a skilled physician." In a brief interdisciplinary interlude, consider the 'expertise' model as expounded, in a more chilling formulation, by one of the fathers of modern architecture, Le Corbusier: "The despot is not a man. It is the ... correct, realistic, exact plan... that will provide your solution once the problem has been posed clearly...It is the Plan...drawn up well away from the frenzy in the mayor's office or the town hall, from the cries of the electorate or the laments of society's victims. It has been drawn up by serene and lucid minds. It has taken account of nothing but human truths." (The Radiant City)

[206] Ernst Freund, *Administrative Powers over Persons and Property* (Chicago: Chicago University Press, 1928), at p. 218. The Progressives had borrowed their view of administration as distinct from politics—at least in part—emulating the work of administrative scholars like Freund and

Most importantly, the political and legal contentions over the monopoly problem revealed a deeper cleavage in law and legal thought. As discussed earlier, the classic paradigm of discretion (associated with public law and public rights) and rule of law (associated with judicial determination of private rights) was the result of a sharp distinction between public law and private law, policed by (political) constitutional limitations on legislation on a baseline of natural (pre-political) concrete property and liberty common law rights. In the words of Herbert Hovenkamp: "Classical legal thought was characterized by a rhetoric that viewed the law as coming from a transcendent source, as if it existed apart from the courts and legislatures that formulate the rules. . ..Legal classicism borrowed from William Blackstone, the important eighteenth century writer on the common law, a sharp distinction between private law and public law. In private law the state administered independently established rules, but in public law it *made* the rules."[207] The rules made, we might add, had in turn to be justified in terms of those immanent in the common law and correspond at the point of legislation with the rule of law qualitative requirements on legislation (formal equality, generality, promulgation, prospectiveness, clarity) in order to further minimize state coercion.

Everybody is familiar with Anatole France's mockery of the formal equality of laws which prohibit both the rich and the poor to sleep under bridges and steal bread.[208] In a number of variations on the same theme, the Progressives would turn the tables on the classical paradigm, so that state *non*-interference with the liberty to contract and with property rights would be described as state-sponsored coercion of those subject to actual relations of power underpinned by the structure

Goodnow. The latter had famously drawn a distinction between politics and administration, depicted as a distinction between an expression and the execution of state will. But the difference between these early writers and the 'expertise' model of administrative law is one of kind. What Goodnow and Freund were advocating was not the idea that administration as such could be set apart from politics. Rather, emulating in turn European models of administration, they predicated the instrumental value of professionalized bureaucracy of the 'Weberian' strand, *sine ira ac studio*—in Weber's words—"discharge of business according to *calculable rules*." In this paradigm, the ideal of bureaucracy is a machine, not an expert: "The progress toward the bureaucratic state, adjudicating and administering according to rationally established law and regulation, is nowadays very closely related to the modern capitalist development. The modern capitalist enterprise rests primarily on *calculation* and presupposes a legal and administrative system, whose functioning can be rationally predicted, at least in principle, by virtue of its fixed general norms, just like the expected performance of a machine." [emphasis in original] Max Weber, *Economy and Society: An Outline of Interpretive Sociology* (Berkeley and Los Angeles: University of California Press, 1978), Guenther Roth and Claus Wittich, Eds., at p. 1394. The shift or rather leap of paradigm to the Progressive version of administration is epitomized by Woodrow Wilson's take on the matter, as perhaps best exemplified by his short article on "The Study of Administration," (Vol. II (2) *Pol. Sci. Q.* 197 (June, 1887)) which, not coincidentally, was published in 1887. This is the year that marked the beginning of the modern administrative state, with the establishment of the Interstate Commerce Commission.

[207] Hovenkamp 1995.

[208] Anatole France, *Le lys rouge* (1894).

of property rights.[209] For instance, in a reversion of the contractualist logic upon which the Constitution had been premised, whereby the government is a delegation of society for protection of natural rights of life, liberty, and property, Morris Cohen's influential article on "Property and Sovereignty" described property as a delegation of state power to private individuals.[210]

These arguments had been made much easier by the fact that—at the same time—property as such had been presented as (and perhaps to a certain extent had also become) both "de-physicalized" and "de-personalized." The logic of classical constitutionalism and classical legal thought assumes property to be a relation between a person and a thing. Property, in Locke's *Second Treatise* for instance, is something that I take out of the state of nature and that becomes, by virtue of my 'mixing' labor with it, mine. In a way it is therefore, by virtue of will and intention, an extension of my self. Inherent in the concept of property is the possibility of excluding others, since interfering with my property is equivalent to interfering with me and hence limiting my freedom without my consent. The state cannot legitimately interfere with my property by definition, since the state is my creation for limited and specified purposes, based on consent. We all (pre-politically speaking) only gave it limited powers, for reasons of convenience and uniformity, as our common agent, to interpret the laws of nature, solve undisputedly disputes as to their meaning, and punish transgressions. The same logic can be found in the arch-authority on the common law, Blackstone's *Commentaries,* where the right of property is presented as "that sole and despotic dominion which one man claims and exercises over the external things of the world, in total exclusion of the right of any other individual in the universe."[211] This concrete (physical) and personal notion of property had come under various attacks, such as Gerald Henderson's observation that the Supreme Court's announcement, in review of rates cases, of the rule that rate reasonableness would be a factor of the railroad property's fair market value was in fact circular, since market value was, conversely, a function of the

---

[209] A very good example in this vein is Robert L. Hale's "Coercion and Distribution in a Supposedly Non-Coercive State," 38 (3) *Political Science Quarterly* 470 (September, 1923). *Also see*, for a summation and commentary of relevant debates, Morton J. Horwitz, *The Transformation of American Law 1870–1960 -The Crisis of Legal Orthodoxy* (New York, London: Oxford University Press, c1992), *esp.* Ch. Five-The Progressive Transformation in the Conception of Property, pp. 145–167.

[210] 13 *Cornell L. Q.* 8 (1927).

[211] *Blackstone's Commentaries, supra* 2 (Ch. 1-Of Property, in General). Of course, in both Locke and Blackstone, the final assumption is natural law, i.e., Divine ordinance. In Blackstone the relation between actual practices (positive law) and their foundation in natural law is made very explicit. While "[i]t is well if the mass of mankind will obey the laws when made, without scrutinizing the reasons of making them," if we go to the roots of things, we *see* that the final authority is Divine command, so that the foundation of property is, positively speaking, Genesis 1:28: "In the beginning of he world, we are informed by holy writ, the all-bountiful creator gave to man 'dominion over all the earth.' This is the only true and solid foundation of man's dominion over external things, whatever airy metaphysical notions may have been started by fanciful writers upon this subject."

rates established.[212] Property had conceptually become, in this logic, a legal abstraction, an expectation of gain on the market, protected by state coercion, rather than a tangible thing protected from the state by the constitutional limitations.

By 1933, when an economist and a lawyer, Adolf A. Berle and Gardiner Means, published a book which was called by *Time* magazine "the economic Bible of the Roosevelt administration," it had become harder to argue that the state should not interfere with the individual's natural rights to property and freedom of contract.[213] *The Modern Corporation and Private Property*[214] argued that the main characteristic of modern business corporations was the separation of ownership and management. According to their thesis, the owner-stockholders had relinquished actual control, whereas those in actual control, the managers, had proportionally negligible property-interests in the business and, moreover, were paid salaries often set without a direct correlation with profits made. As a consequence and as the reverse side of shareholder passivity, they exercised real control over other people's property, having at the same time interests partly divergent from those of the actual owners. There seemed to be no reason, in this logic, why the state should not regard all corporations as "affected with a public interest," and legislate to subject them accordingly to "the paramount interests of the community. . .fair wages, security to employees, reasonable service to their public, and stabilization of business. . .."

The Constitution as such had been 'debunked' in 1913 by the Progressive historian Charles Beard, as no more than a 1787 Philadelphia cabal by a handful of self-interested propertied individuals, which sought to selfishly protect their possessions against redistribution, by erecting a legal bulwark against the will of the people.[215] Soon this would be common attitude, to the point when, during the Depression, a state governor would ask in cavalier disregard, when advised that the Agricultural Adjustment Act, a major New Deal piece of legislation, could be declared unconstitutional: "Hell, what's the Constitution between friends?"[216]

In the future, in terms of the proper scope of the legislative reservation, in line with this logic, property would be looking less natural and private and more legally constructed and thus more 'public,' hence more amenable to legislative and administrative discretionary interference. Conversely, what had been in the past deemed as purely legal or public rights would begin to be seen as more like property.

---

[212] "If we reduce your rates, your value goes down. If we increase them, it goes up. Obviously, we cannot measure rates by value if value is itself a function of rates." Cited by Horwitz 1992, at p. 163.

[213] *Cf.* Hovenkamp at p. 360. *See*, relevant for the discussions here, "The Business Corporation in the Post-Classical Era," pp. 357-362.

[214] Adolf A. Berle and Gardiner Means, *The Modern Corporation and Private Property* (New York: Macmillan, 1933).

[215] Charles A. Beard, *The Economic Interpretation of the Constitution of the United States* (New York: Free Press, c1935 (first published 1913)).

[216] *Cf.* Arthur M. Schlesinger, Jr., *The Coming of the New Deal* (Boston: Houghton Mifflin, 1959), at p. 66.

The lines of demarcation between discretionary and legal would shift and blur, with this partial collapse and blending of categories. Most importantly for our purposes, with legislation more discretionary (constitutionally speaking), administration would in time become more lawful and 'constitutionalized.'

3.1.2.4 Assumptions About Legislation, the Nondelegation Doctrine in Court, and the New Deal Constitutional Compromise

> But in the event Congress shall fail to take one of these two courses, and in the event that the national emergency is still critical, I shall not evade the clear course of duty that will then confront me. I shall ask the Congress for the one remaining instrument to meet the crisis-broad Executive power to wage a war against the emergency, as great as the power that would be given to me if it were in fact invaded by a foreign foe.
>
> Franklin Delano Roosevelt, Presidential Inaugural Address, March 4, 1933

> The Constitution of the United States was a layman's document, not a lawyer's contract. *That* cannot be stressed too often.
>
> Franklin Delano Roosevelt, Address on Constitution Day, September 17, 1937

> The mere retreat to the qualifying 'quasi' is implicit with confession that all recognized classifications have broken down, and 'quasi' is a smooth cover which we draw over our confusion as we might use a counterpane to conceal a disordered bed.
>
> Jackson, J., dissenting in *Federal Trade Commission v. Ruberoid Co.* 343 U.S. 470 (1952)

> Procedure is to law what 'scientific method' is to science.
>
> Foster, "Social Work, the Law, and Social Action," cited in *In Re Gault*, 387 U.S. 1 (1967), opinion of the Court, per Fortas, J.

The Legal Doctrine of Nondelegation: A Brief Conceptual Aside

Identifying correctly the poles delimiting the spectrum of a given debate constitutes often a sound heuristic tool. In this case, it may be particularly useful to our proper perception of the historical intersection of the judicial doctrine of nondelegation with the phenomenon of delegation to start the analysis of the crucial constitutional juncture we have reached (the New Deal) with a brief conceptual introduction-reminder.

The logomachy (at times cacophony) of the manifold delegation-related positions in modern and contemporary American public law literature can be reduced to a limited number of sharply polarized standpoints on the precise matter of the proper judicial attitude with respect to the consistent enforcement of a delegation-related constraint, for statutory nullification purposes, in constitutional review of legislation. Since this is the conclusion to a historical analysis and not a literature review and since, moreover, the issue will be revisited once more in the third part, I shall proceed to only exemplify each theoretical benchmark with what I consider to be, for present purposes, its most representative advocates.

At one extreme, there are nowadays those who believe that delegation was and is a viable judicial doctrine (as a matter of positive law), capable of consistent enforcement in constitutional adjudication and in need of resurrection from the legal oblivion into which it has sunk since the New Deal. To exemplify, this position has been expounded more recently in American constitutional theory by John Hart Ely[217] and, in more adamantine fashion, by David Schoenbrod. The proponents of a vigorously enforced nondelegation doctrine believe this judicial attitude would bring a bevy of various benefits. In line with the observations made earlier, it should be pointed out that the envisioned benefits from enforcing a rule of nondelegation differ with respect to one's normative view towards legislation (a constitutionally-mandated legislative choice, a democratic choice, the product of representative deliberation, a constraint on discretion, a limitation on executive power, a rule of liberty, a *public* enactment, etc.). As noted earlier, one's normative assumptions regarding legislation will inevitably determine one's prescriptions on the issue of the constitutionally-mandated legislative reservation and thus also regarding the scope and proper application of a constitutional nondelegation doctrine.

At the other extreme, there are those who believe that the nondelegation doctrine is now defunct. This theoretical stand can be again subdivided. One main position, best typified in my view by an article by Edward Rubin on "Law and Legislation in the Administrative State," urges that, since the practice of modern legislation has drifted apart from our normative view of it (the author makes a universal claim, exemplified with contemporary American practices), and thus modern legislation does not possess "the normative force or metaphysical kick of law,"[218] one would now be allegedly free to legal scholarship and legal technique on the "question of effectiveness," such as (in the American context) the relation between Congress and its executive and independent 'agencies.'[219] The demise of the nondelegation doctrine is, according to Rubin, a very good example of how, in modern American law, normative constraints on legislation have become 'otiose,' since modern legislation is, according to him, best understood and approached as a 'directive addressed to an implementation mechanism.' Rubin asserts that the modern ideal-type of legislation is an "intransitive external statute" (as opposed to its pre-modern 'transitive external' counterpart). This means (in plain English) that modern statutes have become more discretionary and less normative: they delegate discretion (vernacularly, instead of addressing the individual and telling him what to do, they address the administration, telling it what to achieve and how to act) and hence are, in Rubin's preferred jargon, "intransitive."[220] Since, in his view, the category

[217] Who believed an enforceable nondelegation doctrine to be a corollary of his procedural theory of constitutional interpretation, perhaps as an interesting gloss on the inevitable interaction between process and substance-based constitutional theories.

[218] Edward L. Rubin, "Law and Legislation in the Administrative State," 89 *Columbia Law Review* 369 (April, 1989), 379–380.

[219] *Id.*, at 426.

[220] *Ibid.*, at 383: "From the perspective of the implementation mechanism, the statute's degree of transitivity is the mechanism's degree of discretion." Through this pseudo-technical jargon, Rubin means to make the rather simple and apparent observation that modern statutes do not address the individual directly, stating rules for action, they are not *normative*. Modern statues are *constitutive* of administrative discretion. In a condescending comment on and paraphrase of Lon Fuller, Rubin concludes that the 'morality of law' should be properly called, modern legislation-wise, "the morality of transitive external statutes."

'law' is in modern times perforce separated by virtue of practices from the category 'legislation,' Rubin counsels—with surprising yet perhaps somewhat commendable candor—a separate treatment of the matters. To sum up his long and elaborate argument in pedestrian language, legal practice should in general be concerned with practical matters, things in the world, technical issues for the most part, 'category legislation'; legal theory, respectively, with theoretical matters, namely whatever abstract ideas that people may choose to have, 'category law.' The two domains should be separated. The concept and doctrine of delegation would, in this author's view, epitomize best the said cleavage between practices (what legislation is like) and normative assessment (what legal theory tells us law ought to be like) and the consequent need for further separation between the 'categories' 'law' and 'legislation.'

Another version of the 'anti-delegation' stand is yet more radical, since it does not state that the nondelegation doctrine is an obsolescent constitutional constraint but rather affirms that there is no such thing as a delegation-related constitutional constraint on congressional enactments to begin with, and there never was, hence the whole debate is meaningless. This claim is best exemplified by the Posner-Vermeule article already mentioned in the introduction. The title is fairly revealing of the thesis: "Interring the Nondelegation Doctrine."[221] The two authors undertake to demonstrate that, since the doctrine of nondelegation seems instrumentally unfit, maladapted to advance the purposes underlying it, and since the concept as such is a 'metaphor,' 'standing for' and supported by many values and purposes which are both self-standing and hard to disentangle, and thus 'delegation' is irreducible to any single one of them, both the concept and the doctrine are useless. Posner-Vermeule also adduce in support of their thesis the correct observation that the legal doctrine has only been used to strike down statutes twice, during the New Deal, in exceptional circumstances, and thus it should be regarded as an exception to be discarded altogether and relegated to the closet of constitutional oddities, since it confounds clear understanding of actual positive law. There is—in short—no such thing as 'legislative delegation,' conceptually or legally speaking. For centuries, libraries have been stacked with useless writing on a sham topic; redemption comes at last, in slightly more than 41 law review pages.

To be sure, these latter two delegation-related theoretical positions are interesting as such, as events more than as arguments, to the extent that they show how modern legal transformations have impoverished juridical scholarship, divorcing accounts from practices to the extent that legal thought becomes very often, correspondingly, either exclusively quiescent-instrumental or—at the other extreme—divorced from reality, utopian. In our context, it would be easy to dismiss them as caricatures. Rubin's claim could be answered by noting that the fact as such that practices ('category legislation') have departed from normative accounts ('category law') is precisely a good reason for concern and reassessment of

[221] "Interring the Nondelegation Doctrine," 69 *University of Chicago Law Review* 1721 (2002).

practices in terms of the traditional normative constraints. This is especially so since our normative tools, which are sometimes captured under the umbrella concept of constitutionalism, are seemingly the best ones we have at hand. It is unclear otherwise how one could assess legal practices (other than in normative terms) and how one can conceptualize the phenomenon of delegation (except according to the normative framework showcased by the concept).[222] Related, a reasonable rejoinder to the Posner-Vermeule thesis[223] would be that, if nondelegation is a legal concept and a legal doctrine supported by many assumptions and irreducible to any one of them in particular, then so are many other concepts and doctrines of legal theory and of public law: the separation of powers, the rule of law, due process (natural justice), respectively. The Posner-Vermeule thesis is essentially (to paraphrase Lord Reid's *Ridge v. Baldwin* answer to claims "that natural justice is so vague as to be practically meaningless") "tainted by the perennial fallacy that because something cannot be cut and dried or nicely weighed or measured therefore it does not exist."[224]

Yet caricaturized renditions of an issue, even though false, contain a germ of truth distorted by exaggeration. Pointing out the falsity of this latter pole of delegation doctrine-related positions does not, by implication, mean that the former set of theoretical standpoints would be correct. A claim demonstrably false does not become true by standing it on its head. Legislative delegation as a concept is inescapable, since inextricably linked to the idea of constitutionalism, of legislation limited by the conditions of the grant by which government, as an instrument ordained for limited purposes, is itself bound. Since these conditions are captured by the conceptual 'metaphor' legislative delegation, debates generated by the doctrine keep the legal and political stakes under continuous scrutiny, giving unity, consistency and coherence to public law. By the same token, the legal doctrine of nondelegation is inescapable under a written constitution which embodies the idea of government limited by law and whose grants of power are

[222] In this vein, *see*, for a very balanced and thoughtful critique, Peter L. Strauss, "Legislative Theory and the Rule of Law: Some Comments on Rubin," 89 *Colum. L. Rev.* 427 (April, 1989), *esp.* the comment at 427–428, which is worth reproducing at length: "[I]t is in part perhaps because of a failure to *see* that once the conversion has been made from 'transitive' to 'intransitive' statute-making, the question about control-and that question is not only one about Congress's relation to the agencies (the question on which he would have us focus), but also about the people's relationship to both Congress and the agencies; and also about our relationship to the President, and the President's relationship to the agencies. This is, if you like, the separation-of-powers question; one needs to account for the President and the courts as well as for Congress, and for the impact of change in Congress on how we would wish Congress (and our government generally) to be."

[223] Other than the unorthodox argument of authority: too many authors of notice have written too much about it, for the topic to be so easily and cavalierly discarded.

[224] [1964] A.C. 40, at 66, per Lord Reid. Likewise, it would be said in *Maxwell v. Dept. of Trade*, [1974] 2 W. L. R. 338, 349, regarding fairness, that "From time to time, during that period lawyers and judges have tried to define what constitutes fairness. Like defining an elephant, it is not easy to do, although fairness in practice has the elephantine quality of being easy to recognize."

expressed in limited and enumerated manner, in categorical terms.[225] Government as such is an aggregate of delegated power and, as Louis Jaffe puts it, the principle is simple and clear: "[A] delegation of power implies some limit. Action beyond that limit is not legitimate."[226] Nevertheless, the fact that a doctrine of nondelegation is an unavoidable constitutional corollary, does not of necessity mean that it can be judicially enforced through a test of consistent application or that it would be even desirable for it to be enforced, unless perhaps in the most extraordinary of circumstances. Neither does it mean that the deleterious consequences of a modern phenomenon, that of legislative delegations (in the sense of broad interpretive discretion, discretionary action, quasi-adjudication, and rule-making conferred by vague statutory enactments upon the executive and the administration) can be countered or disciplined by a judicially enforced nondelegation constraint on the legislature.

In the following, I will first try to point out briefly that nondelegation tests show fairly well how the doctrine of delegation mirrored judicial assumptions regarding legislation and that, as the character of legislation changed, with the advent of the modern administrative state, corresponding overall less and less to these background assumptions, the nondelegation tests changed in lockstep.

Second, I will show that, to the extent that the notion and legal doctrine of delegation 'capture' or 'showcase' the limitations on legislation and thus on government that are thought constitutionally proper at a given time,[227] the New Deal is indeed exceptional and crucial. It is exceptional not in the sense that it reveals, through the actual example of federal legislation being struck down on nondelegation doctrine grounds, the practical possibility of the doctrine's enforcement. The New Deal is both exceptional and essential because the legislative and judicial practices that marked this watershed constitutional period essentially changed the constitutional baseline along which the legitimacy of legislative enactments would be assessed and thus shifted the boundaries and the essential distinctions along which both constitutional and administrative law had been, as noted earlier, consolidated. By the same token, the famous nondelegation cases of this period, in their grapple with the phenomenon of delegation, mark and announce the essential tensions of the uneasy constitutional compromise along which new practices and debates would be structured.

[225] *Field v. Clark*, 143 U.S. 649 (1892), 692: "That Congress cannot delegate legislative power...is a principle universally recognized as vital to the integrity and maintenance of the system of government ordained by the Constitution."

[226] Jaffe 1965, at p. 320.

[227] *See* for instance Cynthia Farina, "Statutory Interpretation and the Balance of Power in the Administrative State" 89 *Colum. L. Rev.* 452, at 479 (April, 1989): "Nondelegation doctrine served as on the principal battlegrounds upon which the constitutionality of the growth of the federal regulatory authority was tested." Meaning, as I understand her argument, that is served as a battleground since and in the way it structured the major debates on administrative discretion, the proper scope of government, separation of powers, and accountability.

The Nondelegation Doctrine in Court: 216 Bad Years (and Counting)

> Major premise: Legislative power cannot be constitutionally delegated by Congress.
> Minor premise: It is essential that certain powers be delegated to administrative officers and regulatory commissions.
> Conclusion: Therefore the powers thus delegated are not legislative powers.
> Robert E. Cushman, *The Independent Regulatory Commissions* (1941)

> While the Constitution of the United States divides all power conferred upon the Federal Government into 'legislative Powers,' Art. I, § 1, '[t]he executive Power,' Art II, § 1, and '[t]he judicial Power,' Art. III, § 1, it does not attempt to define those terms. . . ..Obviously, then, the Constitution's central mechanism of separation of powers depends largely upon common understanding of what activities are appropriate to legislatures, to executives, and to courts.
> *Lujan v. Defenders of Wildlife* 504 U.S. 555 (1992), opinion of the Court, per Scalia, J.

The title of this section is a paraphrase of Cass Sunstein's 2001 observation that the nondelegation doctrine, as applied to statutes, had by then 211 bad years[228] and one good year (arguably, two). The first motto is taken from a section of Robert Cushman's book on the independent regulatory commissions, where Cushman observed that the Supreme Court had, with the two well-known and notable exceptions, always declared legislative powers as non-delegable, yet constantly evaded the practical consequences of its statement of legal doctrine (i.e., striking down as unconstitutional statutes that delegate legislative power). The usual method of evasion, as Cushman observed, would be the artifice of 'labeling' whatever powers the necessities of government would make Congress devolve upon agencies as non-legislative ('administrative' or 'quasi-legislative' or 'quasi-judicial') and thus delegable.[229]

Yet the Court also sought to confront the matter directly, by enunciating a test separating permissible and constitutional from unconstitutional delegation. As mentioned earlier, the first nondelegation objection to a statute arose in the so-called *Cargo of the Brig Aurora* controversy, where the challenge as such was

---

[228] Sunstein 2001, *supra* note at p. 143. His observation was made in 2001 but the events intervening in the meanwhile, most notably the Supreme Court decision in *Whitman v. American Trucking Assn.*, confirm it.

[229] *Cf.* also Theodore W. Cousens, "The Delegation of Federal Legislative Power to Executive Officials," 33 *Michigan Law Review* 512 (1935), at p. 538: "Summing up the previous cases, without any undue attempt at clarifying that which the Supreme Court itself has left more or less nebulous, two general conclusions may fairly be arrived at:

(1) Wherever a question has arisen as to the validity of the delegation of alleged legislative power it has been uniformly upheld, and
(2) Powers which have been held non-legislative for the purpose of upholding their delegation have for other purposes in other cases (and sometimes in the same case) been held to be legislative or quasi-legislative."

brushed with a quick judicial aside, while the constitutional principle of nondelegation was affirmed.

Field v. Clark,[230] the first actual 'delegation decision,' was triggered by the 1890 Tariff Act's authorization to the President to "suspend, by proclamation...the provisions of this act relating to the free introduction of such sugar, molasses, coffee, tea, and hides" from foreign countries imposing "duties or other exaction upon the agricultural or other products of the United States, which in view of the free introduction of such sugar, molasses, coffee, tea, and hides...he may deem to be reciprocally unequal and unreasonable."[231]

The constitutionality of the act was affirmed, under the delegation test enunciated by an earlier Supreme Court of Pennsylvania decision, coincidentally bearing the theoretically auspicious name *Locke's Appeal*: "Then, the true distinction, I conceive, is this: The legislature cannot delegate its power to make a law; but *it can make a law to delegate a power to determine some fact or state of things upon which the law makes, or intends to make, its own action depend.*"[232] [emphasis supplied] The test enunciated is one of contingent legislation. To a certain extent unsurprising, given the fact that the state case from which the test was 'borrowed' dealt with a contingent local option temperance law. In the case of a statute of contingent application, the delegation-relevant distinction is correctly described as one between making a rule and finding a fact upon which the rule applies; the issues are clearly delineated. Both the fact to be found and the method of finding it are easily determinable. For instance, in *Locke's Appeal*, voting during municipal election would determine whether or not the citizens of the Twenty-second ward of the city of Philadelphia wanted (fact) a further granting of licenses to sell intoxication liquors (rule). The rule applies when the fact obtains. The same demarcation, between a legislative rule and executive ministerial fact-finding according to it had been for good reason pointed out in *The Cargo of the Brig Aurora*, where the President Madison would need to ascertain as a matter of fact whether or not either Britain or France or both of them had revoked their embargo decrees or ceased their hostilities on the high seas against the United States. Nonetheless, upon closer inquiry, one can see that, unlike the statute challenged in *Brig Aurora*, the Tariff Act provision under scrutiny in *Field v. Clark* did not just direct the determination of a state of facts upon the existence of which the application of the law was conditional. It encompassed a value judgment and an element of

[230] 143 U.S. 649 (1892). Delegation by a state statute had already been attacked in the *Railroad Commission Cases*, 116 U.S. 307 (1886). The Supreme Court affirmed the decision of the highest court of Mississippi and maintained that establishing a regulatory commission with supervisory role over the railroads was not contrary to the Mississippi Constitution.

[231] C. 1244, sec. 3, 26 Stat. 567.

[232] "To deny this would be to stop the wheels of government. There are many things upon which wise and useful legislation must depend, which cannot be known to the law-making power, and must, therefore, be a subject of inquiry and determination outside of the halls of legislation." *Commonwealth ex rel. McClain v. Locke et al.*, 72 Pa. 491 (1873)

discretion as to the application of the statutory policy, since comparing tariff structures and assessing whether they are "reciprocally unequal" is not just a matter of finding facts (as the court implied).

The Supreme Court followed the contingent legislation, determination-of-fact rationale as a test in delegation cases until the first nondelegation attack on an administrative agency regulation, in *United States v. Grimaud.*[233] In *Grimaud*, a federal statute granting the Secretary of Agriculture power to make "rules and regulations… to regulate the occupancy and use and to preserve the forests from destruction," violation of the rules made in pursuance of the statute subject to criminal sanctions, was challenged by Pierre Grimaud, a California sheepman charged with grazing his sheep on public lands without having secured the permit required by the regulations. The delegation challenge was that Congress could not constitutionally delegate to the Executive what in fact amounted to the determination, by means of regulations, of the essential elements of a crime. The statute was upheld, on the grounds that: "….when Congress had legislated and indicated its will, it could give to those who were to act under such general provisions '*power to fill up the details*' by the establishment of administrative rules and regulations, the violation of which could be punished by fine or imprisonment fixed by Congress, or by penalties fixed by Congress or measured by the injury done….But the authority to make administrative rules is not a delegation of legislative power, nor are such rules raised from an administrative to a legislative character because the violation thereof is punished as a public offence."[234][emphasis added]

The "fill up the details" test had been 'borrowed' from Chief Justice Marshall's opinion for the Court in *Wayman v. Southard,*[235] an earlier case dealing with a nondelegation challenge to the 1792 Process Act' authorization to the judiciary to establish rules for the service of process and execution of judgments in federal courts. In dicta, Marshall stated that: "It will not be contended that Congress can delegate to the Courts, or to any other tribunals, powers which are strictly and exclusively legislative. But Congress may certainly delegate to others, powers which the legislature may rightfully exercise itself….The *line has not been exactly drawn* which separates those *important subjects, which must be entirely regulated by the legislature itself*, from those of less interest, in which a general provision may be made, and *power given to those who are under such general provision to fill up the details.*" In Marshall's interpretation, as it is apparent from this excerpt, the problem of nondelegation was at the same time unavoidable (according to the letter and spirit of the Constitution, it cannot be contended that Congress could delegate its power), resisting of judicial resolution (hard to draw lines in problems of degree, incapable of principled resolution), and thus best left to practical political adjustment (Congress can delegate to others what Congress can do itself).

---

[233] 220 U.S. 506 (1911).

[234] 220 U.S. 506 at 517, 521.

[235] 23 U.S. 1, at 43 (1825).

The modern nondelegation test was announced in *J. W. Hampton, Jr. & Co. v. United States*.[236] Hampton imported barium dioxide and the custom duty was assessed at a dutiable rate of 6 cents per pound, 2 cents higher than the one set by statute, by a New York custom collector's action, in line with the so-called 'flexible tariff provision' of the Tariff Act of September 21, 1922, which empowered the President to increase or decrease custom duties within a margin of 50% under or above the statutory rates.[237] In exercising his delegated statutory power, the President had to ascertain whether the cost of production in competing countries was equalized by the existing rates with the cost of production in the United States, taking into account, "insofar as he [found] practicable," among other factors, differences in conditions of production, advantages granted the foreign producers by foreign persons or governments, and "any other advantages or disadvantages in competition." The Court stated that the Tariff Act did not constitute an unconstitutional delegation of lawmaking by Congress, under yet another (and the current) nondelegation test: "If Congress shall lay down by legislative act an *intelligible principle* to which the person or body authorized to fix such rates is directed to conform, such legislative action is not a forbidden delegation of legislative power."[238] [emphasis supplied]

David Schoenbrod, perhaps the most outspoken proponent of a revived nondelegation doctrine, considers this a borderline case since, allegedly, with it: "[T]he Court took a giant step toward explicitly allowing Congress to delegate... The Court upheld this statute, citing *Field v. Clark*, but the rationale that the president had only to find facts under a law made even less sense in *Hampton & Co*. The president cannot weigh the equality in costs of production in foreign and domestic industries without first having decided such broad policy question as the appropriate levels of wages and profits in the domestic industry."[239] Schoenbrod argues that, while the test in *Field v. Clark* had been too demanding, since a foreign affairs rationale alone could have saved the statute anyways, the same argument would not apply to *Hampton,* where the president's decision "turned on whether domestic industries earned enough money, rather than on whether foreign affairs charged excessive tariffs."[240] There are some objections to Schoenbrod's claim. In the opinion for the Court, Chief Justice Taft shows that, while the 1890 Tariff Act reviewed in *Clark* had left the judgment upon 'reciprocally unequal and unreasonable' foreign tariffs to the President alone (in practice, of course, to his delegates), the 1922 Act constrained the discretion by procedural safeguards: before action would be taken based on the 'flexible tariff provision,' there would be an initial investigation by the Tariff Commission, with "notice and opportunity to be heard

[236] 276 U. S. 394 (1928).

[237] Sec. 315 of Title III of the Tariff Act of September 21, 1922, 19 U.S.C.S., Sec. 154, 156, 42 Stat. 858 at 941.

[238] 276 U. S. 394, 409.

[239] Schoenbrod 1993, at p. 35.

[240] *Id.*

for all interested parties." Moreover, Taft, C.J., noted, where exactly the line would be drawn when deciding, in a nondelegation challenge, whether Congress had fulfilled its constitutional duty "must be fixed according to the common sense and the inherent necessities of the governmental co-ordination."[241]

Besides, as noted earlier, due to both political and epistemological reasons, there are very substantial differences with respect to the practically attainable and pragmatically feasible degree of statutory precision (and therefore level of discretion) in foreign-affairs related fields. Here, the subject-matter of the statute deals, to put it in Lockean language, with "Leagues and Alliances, and all the Transactions, with all Persons and Communities without the commonwealth."[242] With respect to tariff schemes, "whether domestic industries make enough money" could depend, conversely, on the treatment of foreign industries and the decision on whether they charged excessive tariffs; in a foreign relations paradigm, this policy making problem is a stick that can be grabbed at either end. Here, the "law enforcement model of the Presidency," which constitutes Schoenbrod's assumption, is least tenable and the "protective power of the Presidency" has the upper hand.[243] Moreover and related, it should be noted that the statutory discretionary power at issue was bearing on tariffs, traditionally considered public rights, and did not invade the private rights of the citizen. In 1933, in another Tariff Act case, this time a primarily administrative law statutory interpretation decision regarding the extent to which the Tariff Commission was bound procedurally to function in a court-like fashion, with full disclosure of evidence and opportunity of cross-examination, Justice Cardozo, speaking for a quasi-unanimous Court, stressed the importance of context in determining the constitutionally appropriate level of both legislative and administrative discretion. He also pointed out that the Tariff Act as such was "a delegation, though a permissible one, of the legislative process."[244] Cardozo was

---

[241] 276 U.S. 406.

[242] "This therefore contains the Power of War and Peace, Leagues and Alliances, and all the Transactions, with all Persons and Communities without the commonwealth, and may be called Federative, if any one pleases. So the thing be understood, I am indifferent as to the name." Locke, Par. 146.

[243] Monaghan "The Protective Power of the Presidency," 93 *Colum. L. Rev.* 1 (Jan. 1993)

[244] *Norwegian Nitrogen Products Co. v. United States* 288 U.S. 294 (1933), 305. (in the course of the Tariff Commission process for changing the tariff assessment, initiated at the request of an American competitor that the existing rate, given much higher costs of production in the United States, disadvantaged it) It is interesting to note that Louis Jaffe 1965, at p. 60, note 91, misquotes ("legislative [sic] power" instead of "legislative process") and therefore misinterprets the argument, as an early recognition by Cardozo that legislative power could be delegated but within limits. In fact, within the logic of the decision and Cardozo's argument, he most likely meant what he said and said what he meant. This was a delegation of legislative process, since process is what he was referring to. The argument was that the object of the decision was not legislative in the classical sense of determining rights and duties but rather the determination, according to circumstance, of a mere privilege, by a legislative court. Thus further: "What was once a mere practice [i.e., providing interested parties with a hearing before changing tariff rates] has been converted into a legal privilege. But the limits of the privilege were not meant to be greatly different from those of the ancient practice that had shaped the course of legislation."

literally irate and baffled by the fact that the American subsidiary of a Norwegian nitrite producer would dare request the Commission for production of "every particle of evidence gathered by the Commission or its representatives." The extent of the procedural protections and thus the meaning of the word 'hearing' as used in the Tariff Act depended on the nature of the interest affected: "We are not unmindful of cases in which the word 'hearing' as applied to administrative proceedings has been thought to have a broader meaning. *All depends upon the context*. . . .Whatever the appropriate label, the kind of order that emerges from a hearing before a body with power to ordain is one that impinges upon legal rights in a very different way from the report of a commission which merely investigates and advises. . .. No one has a legal right to the maintenance of an existing rate or duty."[245] [emphasis supplied] While the holding is of course restricted to the facts at hand (since the Tariff Commission was just an investigative body, the final decision on the tariff would rest technically with the President), much can be extrapolated from the facts of the case to the delegation problems discussed throughout the chapter. As one can see, the appropriate levels of administrative statutory and constitutional legislative discretion are seen as cognate and are dependent, as the appropriate level of procedure and appropriate level of judicial intervention (with respect to all these matters), on the nature of the governmental action: essentially political, since relating to foreign affairs; essentially discretionary, since affecting a privilege not a right. Posing the legal problem in terms of the delegation doctrine enforcement induces a generalized and abstract expectation of an across-the-board Congressional nondelegation duty according to the Constitution.

This brief discussion on the tariff cases shows fairly well that, how, and why, even though the concept and doctrine of delegation cannot be 'interred,' since expressive of our fundamental principles and intuitions regarding the nature and scope of government, the doctrine of nondelegation cannot be enforced. Framing the issue in delegation terms, without first separating and unpacking the many assumptive strands which the notion of nondelegation showcases, inevitably obfuscates the problem. That is so because proceeding, as Schoenbrod does, from an assumption of nondelegation, inevitably imposes a heavy normative burden on the critic (or the judge): what is the constitutionally prescribed test of nondelegation depends on first answering, in a general across-the-board manner, the question regarding the constitutionally required 'definition' of legislation.[246]

Posing that question is inevitable, to a certain extent, given the nature of the delegation inquiry, and this reveals also the main problem with the legal doctrine of nondelegation, in terms of enforcement. That is to say, the nondelegation doctrine

---

[245] *Id.*, at 318.

[246] Here I believe Carl Schmitt's early identification of the tensions to be essentially correct, as was his appreciation that the practice of delegations and the judicial invalidation or admission of their constitutionality had cast a new light on the evolution of legislation and of fundamental constitutional principles. Schmitt 1936, at pp. 253–254.

seems unyielding to consistent application, among other reasons, because the delegation inquiry, in and of itself, makes an impossible demand, seeking inevitably an abstract and generalized answer to a question which can only be posed in concrete and pragmatic terms and along specific issues.[247] The doctrine can only, therefore, ultimately be reduced to a legal test which is either too formalistic and normative (as the early tests which sought to distinguish legislation as a constitutional function, essentially distinct from other functions, which cannot be delegated) or too commonsensical ('intelligible principle') to yield a criterion of consistent discrimination application. Nondelegation either conflates in a reductive manner the 'categories' law and legislation, to paraphrase Rubin and echo Kenneth Culp Davis's criticism of the nondelegation doctrine as expressive of "the extravagant version of the rule of law," or reverts the matter of constitutionality into a question of overall legislative decisional precision, of across-the-board constitutionally permissible degree (how much is too much legislative discretion). Either way of posing the problem is—as a rule of judicial decision—essentially useless, since it overtaxes both reality and judicial capabilities.

Moreover, once the delegation doctrine is described as a matter of degree or policy and not of principle, as a rule of judicial decision its enforcement raises, as it has been justly observed, nondelegation problems of its own. As Louis Jaffe noted, "'policy' is like a Chinese puzzle containing the potentialities of an infinite recession of lesser and lesser policies. There is no given line between policy and administration."[248] If there is no way of posing the question in a principled manner, the judiciary cannot enforce the constitutional limitation of nondelegation, since then the "optimal precision" of legislative rules becomes a matter of policy tradeoffs and thus neither amenable nor legitimate for purposes of judicial determination. Statutory precision can only be judicially gauged by reference to more specific constraints and constitutional values, where the question posed is more focused (e.g., what is the constitutionally appropriate/permissible legislative precision and administrative discretion in terms of free speech regulation; or criminal statutes; or taxation), not by virtue of a generalized judicial inquiry into the specificity of statutes.

Observing how, in the nondelegation cases we have reviewed earlier, the tests progressively changed is, nonetheless, of the highest importance, since the inquiry sheds light both on the judicial assumptions regarding the constitutionally appropriate definition of legislation and on the transformations that occurred in the nature

---

[247] This is why nondelegation tests seem, as one author observed, fated to "[restate] the issue to be decided. But while their strength lies in the ability to suggest that, if they are properly applied, everything will be all right, their weakness lies in their inability to generate any consistent application. Legal argument about nondelegation consists of applying these tests to specific delegations of power, applications that generate contradictory conclusions: any delegation both does and does not satisfy the relevant results." Gerald Frug, "The Ideology of Bureaucracy in American Law," 97 *Harv. L. Rev.* 1276 (1984).

[248] Louis Jaffe, "An Essay on the Delegation of the Legislative Power I," 47 *Colum. L. Rev.*, 359, at p. 369 (1947).

of legislation as such. With the advent of the modern administrative state, as judicial presuppositions and understandings regarding legislation no longer easily obtained in reality, constitutional practice found it more and more difficult to come to grips conceptually with these transformations. To wit, the early 'determination of fact' test presupposes an easily identifiable set of normative constraints on legislation. Legislation, in this framework, appears as the epitome of law, a self-contained rule, expressed in general normative terms, addressed to the individual, announcing clear guidance for action, enforceable in a court of law. The administration 'executes' the law (and the judiciary decides its meaning) in a classical paradigm, syllogistically one could say, as a subsumption of rule to facts. The test reflects this paradigm even when in practice the judge formally applies it to a situation falling outside its paradigmatic substantive purview (public rights, foreign affairs-related legislation, where a degree of statutorily authorized administrative discretion had long been recognized as a matter of statutory interpretation).[249] What this implies is that the legislature is, as a default conceptual rule and *theoretically speaking*, constitutionally limited by a certain notion of law, which applies to legislation.

The next judicial step, the 'fill up the details' test, is already a major departure, since now the question is posed differently, more instrumentally, in terms of subject matter and legislative policy. The test is not focused anymore on the 'nature' of legislation as such, as essentially different, distinct in kind from other substantively limited specific state functions and thus non-delegable. As long as the legislature decides the 'important issues' in a statutory scheme, the executive can 'legislate' interstitially.

In the next, 'intelligible principle' test, everything reverts to a question of degree: the constitutionally permissible level of legislative guidance on a continuum of statutory precision. But once the question is posed in this maner, the satsifactory answer is virtually begged in all situations. An 'intelligible principle' can be found in almost every imaginable case, as a result of the very fact that there is a statute passed, empowering a specific agency to act in some way.[250] All statutes can be said to satisfy the constitutional requirements of such a principle. Moreover, the

---

[249] *U. S. v. Vowell. See also supra.*

[250] *See Whitman v. American Trucking Association* 531 U.S. 457 (2001), Justice Thomas, concurring.

"Although this Court since 1928 has treated the 'intelligible principle' requirement as the only constitutional limit on congressional grants of power to administrative agencies, *see J. W. Hampton, Jr., & Co. v. United States*, 276 U.S. 394, 409, 72 L. Ed. 624, 48 S. Ct. 348 (1928), the Constitution does not speak of 'intelligible principles.' Rather, it speaks in much simpler terms: '*All* legislative Powers herein granted shall be vested in a Congress.' U.S. Const., Art. 1, § 1 (emphasis added). *I am not convinced that the intelligible principle doctrine serves to prevent all cessions of legislative power. I believe that there are cases in which the principle is intelligible and yet the significance of the delegated decision is simply too great for the decision to be called anything other than 'legislative.'* As it is, none of the parties to this case has examined the text of the Constitution or asked us to reconsider our precedents on cessions of legislative power. On a future day, however, I would be willing to address the question whether our delegation jurisprudence has strayed too far from our Founders' understanding of separation of powers."

paradigm has already been turned on its head when legislative discretion is implicitly recognized as the rule rather than the exception. In this sense, the evolution of nondelegation tests can be even said to have conceptually anticipated, as a matter of recognizing legislative discretion, the demise of substantive due process during the New Deal. Nevertheless, the New Deal Court, during the only 'good year' of the nondelegation doctrine, will announce the new constitutional compromise between legislative discretion and the constitutional values underlying the nondelegation doctrine, in the course of a rather dramatic inquiry into how much would be considered, constitutionally speaking, too much delegation.

The Blurring of Bright Lines and 'Delegation Running Riot'

> The state would be used as a positive instrument of economic intervention; whether to restore and maintain a competitive system, to aid industrial groups in suppressing competition, or to plan a new industrial order was not clear.
>
> Ellis Hawley, *The New Deal and the Problem of Monopoly* (1966)

> We must lay hold of the fact that the laws of economics are not made by nature. They are made by human beings.
>
> Franklin Delano Roosevelt, "Speech Accepting the Nomination for the Presidency," July 2, 1932

> A national emergency productive of widespread unemployment and disorganization of industry, which burdens interstate and foreign commerce, affects the public welfare, and undermines the standards of living of the American people, is hereby declared to exist.
>
> National Industrial Recovery Act ch. 90, 48 Stat. 195

> This is delegation running riot.
>
> Cardozo, J., concurring in *Schechter Poultry Corporation v. United States* 295 U.S. 495 (1935)

Occasional references to the post-New Deal period as a 'post-delegation' period of American public law often confuse the concept and doctrine with the phenomenon of delegation. As a common story goes, shortly after the New Deal, the Court gave up reviewing the conformity of statutes with the demands of the nondelegation doctrine. Yet, as I hope to have already showed by now, the nondelegation doctrine had nothing to do, instrumentally speaking, with actual constitutional control (judicial review) of legislative discretion. It had never been enforced before 1935 and it defeats, by its very nature, the possibility of consistent and principled judicial enforcement; thus, it is misleading to imply that it would have somewhat fallen from the grace of judicial enforcement in the aftermath of the New Deal.[251] Rather, the limitation on legislation had always been the restrictive interpretation of

[251] For instance, Cass R. Sunstein, "Changing Conceptions of Administration," 1987 *BYU L. Rev.* 927, at p. 945 (1987), defending a certain measure of administrative independence from the President: "Such authorization might also be a necessary quid pro quo for the downfall of the nondelegation doctrine, which has allowed a large rise in presidential power."

constitutional provisions in terms of the common law baseline, with the clear distinctions and associated judicial practices allowed by this baseline (between political and ministerial, public and private). Qualitative restrictions on legislation had been constitutionally possible not because of the enforcement of the nondelegation rule but due to the limitations directly derived from the Contracts, Commerce, and Due Process Clauses. With the traditional boundaries partly collapsed by judicial acquiescence in the New Deal, through the famous line of cases altering the prior constitutional constraints, the nature of the legislation changed and practices were altered, in the sense of increased administrative discretion, an alteration of the traditional balance of powers, and representation-accountability problems.

The line of cases marking the relaxation of these constitutional limitations is well-known and an exhaustive enumeration and description would detract attention from the present argument. Yet, a brief detour is here warranted, for purposes of clarification. It should be mentioned that, before the nondelegation cases were decided, *Home Building & Loan Association v. Blaisdell*[252] had already, by upholding a Minesotta mortgage moratorium law, read an exception into the absolute textual prohibition of the Contracts Impairment Clause, whereas *Nebbia v. People of New York*[253] had averred Justice Field's earlier fears in *Munn,* by upholding a price control statute against a due process and equal protection challenge, upon the rationale that what was considered a 'business affected with a public interest' would be essentially for the legislature to decide, independent of common law categories of acceptable police regulation. The judiciary would only scrutinize the reasonableness or rationality of social and economic legislation on a relaxed means-ends standard of review.[254] This interpretation would effectively trigger the phenomenon of delegation, i.e., more legislative discretion. With the subsequent relaxation of the Commerce Clause limitation on the federal government, the judicial retraction from constitutional review of rationality would validate delegation, in the sense of vast amounts of statutory discretion and a new constitutionally mandated legislative reservation. Thus, effective control of constitutionality would be 'shrunken' to issues of rights and process.

It should be therefore restated that, while the notion of delegation captures well these problems and their associated concerns and helps comprehend and gauge their significance, the legal doctrine had nothing to do with the phenomenon as such and is no cure for the problems raised by it. The nondelegation cases of the period, nonetheless, are constitutionally crucial, since the decisions themselves and the events that led to them reveal both the tenets of the New Deal constitutional

---

[252] 290 U.S. 398 (1934). A Milk Control Board, according to a state statute empowering it to set minimum and maximum prices, had fixed the minimum retail price of milk at 9 cents per quart. Leo Nebbia was convicted for selling two quarts for 18, while throwing in a five cent loaf of bread.

[253] 291 U.S. 502 (1934).

[254] *Id.*, at p. 516: "The phrase 'affected with a public interest' can, in the nature of things, mean no more than that an industry, for adequate reasons, is subject to control for the public good."

compromise and the nature of the tensions and problems that would characterize post-New Deal—contemporary—public law.

Since not one single federal statute had been declared unconstitutional based on a nondelegation challenge before the New Deal, the entire issue had by then come to be considered completely academic. When the 'Hot Oil' Case came before the Court, in a challenge to the National Industrial Recovery Act, the centerpiece of Franklin Delano Roosevelt's legislative program, the delegation question, as Justice Jackson would later report, was "so little anticipated that the governments brief of 227 pages and 200 more of appendix devoted only 13 pages to the topic."[255] Yet, in *Panama Refining Co. v. Ryan*,[256] section 9 (c) of the NIRA, based on which the president was authorized to prohibit the transportation in interstate commerce of oil produced in excess of the limits set by the state quotas ('hot oil'), was struck down as unconstitutional on nondelegation grounds. Louis Jaffe would later observe that, in light of previous nondelegation decisions, the case "involved a narrow power with a somewhat vague but recognizable standard. It should have been upheld and probably would have been if the Court had not been eager to chastise the New Deal's failings."[257] It may very well have been so since, by the time the 'Hot Oil' Case reached the court, NIRA had already been unanimously perceived as a dismal policy failure and a bureaucratic nightmare. Roosevelt himself confessed, around the time of the *Schechter* decision, that 'the whole NIRA business' had become an 'awful headache.'[258] These impressions were only further confirmed by the fact that, as it turned out in court, the main count on which the petitioners in *Panama Refining* were being prosecuted, had already been abrogated because a bureaucratic mistake and, since the Executive Order had not been published, neither the prosecuting attorney nor the courts were aware of this. The event would subsequently lead to the creation of the *Federal Register*.[259] Nonetheless, the power granted as such was arguably, in line of precedents, not excessive, taking into account the fact that the President was effectively limited by the state-determined quotas, incorporated by reference into the federal act.

---

[255] Cited by Barber 1978, at p. 82.

[256] 293 U. S. 388 (1935).

[257] Jaffe 1965, at p. 63.

[258] In Hawley 1966, at p. 130.

[259] Before that, Executive Orders were published yearly with the Statutes at Large. Yet, according to Jaffe, the practice was not unusual of not publishing Executive Orders that a president liked to keep away from public view. In the Federal Register all federal rules, regulations and orders are now officially published, daily, Monday through Friday. According to the Federal Register Act, 49 Stat. 500 (1935), 44 U.S.C. para. 307, no federal regulation, rule, order required to be published, until filed for publication "shall be valid as against any person who has no had actual knowledge" of it. The Code of Federal Regulations, updated yearly (and published on a quarterly basis), codifies the general and permanent rules published by the executive departments and agencies of the Federal Government in the Federal Register. It is organized under 50 titles organized according to subject matter.

The main problem, in the Court's view, was the open-ended declaration of policy in the first section of the act, a "pick and choose" laundry list of often conflicting statutory goals, covering almost any imaginable justification. This was, theoretically, a consistent position, since open-ended policy guidance can mean that there is no 'intelligible principle.' The section reads as follows: "It is hereby declared to be the policy of Congress to remove obstructions to the free flow of interstate and foreign commerce which tend to diminish the amount thereof; and to provide for the general welfare by promoting the organization of industry for the purpose of cooperative action among trade groups, to induce and maintain united action of labor and management under adequate government sanctions and supervision, to eliminate unfair competitive practices, to promote the fullest possible utilization of the present productive capacity of industries, to avoid undue restriction of productions (except as may be temporarily required), to increase the consumption of industrial and agricultural products by increasing purchasing power, to reduce and relieve unemployment, to improve standards of labor, and otherwise to rehabilitate industry and to conserve natural resources." Cardozo, the lone dissenter in the case, noted that as long as discretion had essentially been limited by a standard or procedure, unclear policy direction was not considered fatal in prior delegation cases. According to him, since overproduction was clearly understood as the premise behind state quotas, applying the broad ("hydra-headed" as Louis Jaffe later called it) declaration of policy in Section 1 to the mandate of Section 8 meant a fairly clear policy guideline: protecting persons from competition with illegal producers and avoiding 'demoralizing' prices, that is, prices below costs. Thus, a standard could be read into the section by "reasonable implication." Here, there was therefore no "roving commission to inquire into evils and then, upon discovering them, do anything he pleases."

The true test of delegation would be the unanimous decision in the "Sick Chicken" Case.[260] When the National Industrial Recovery Act granted FDR, as he asked for, 'war powers to fight the Depression,' it soon became clear that nobody quite knew what to do with them, the main reason being that the economic issues (monopoly, unfair trade practices, the relation between them, the size-efficiency correlation) which had been plaguing the Federal Trade Commission and Sherman Act enforcement were still both misunderstood and not agreed upon, policy-wise. Various conflicting 'visions' were thus, in some way or another, incorporated into the act (for instance, codes were exempted from the reach of antitrust laws, yet were 'not to permit monopoly'). In Ellis Hawley's words: "Congress, in effect, had refused to formulate a definite economic policy or to decide in favor of specific economic groups. It had simply written an enabling act, an economic charter, and had then passed the buck to the Administration."[261]

---

[260] *A. L. A. Schechter Poultry Corporation et al. v. United States* 295 U.S. 495 (1935).

[261] Hawley 1966, at p. 33.

Three policy solutions to the 'economic problem' had presented themselves simultaneously: a market-oriented approach, centered on eliminating market dysfunctions, government planning of the economy, and a form of corporatism with government-sponsored cartelization, i.e., (again in Ellis Hawley's words) a rationalized "business commonwealth." The cartelization solution would have the upper hand in the implementation of NIRA. Under Title I, the most important part of the act, trade or industrial associations or groups could apply to the President for approval of initiating a "code of fair competition" for the trade or industry. The President had the statutory duty to ascertain that the groups applying for a code "impose[d] no inequitable restriction on membership" and were "truly representative." The code as such would then be approved, in his discretion, by the President (who could alternatively prescribe his own code), on the sole proviso that it did not "permit monopolies or monopolistic practices" and was not "designed to promote monopolies or to eliminate or oppress small enterprises and will not operate to discriminate against them." The codes set maximum hours and minimum wage provisions, minimum prices, and fair trade practices and were drafted under government mediation through the National Recovery Administration.[262] Once these provisions were agreed upon and approved by the President, through an Executive Order, they would effectively become law, each breach separately subject to criminal prosecution on misdemeanor charges (the penalty being a up to 500 $ fine on each offence).

The facts of the case are simple. The owners of the biggest kosher poultry business in New York, the Schechter brothers, had been convicted under the "Live Poultry Code" of 'fair competition' on a number of counts, among which of interest to us are the code-related ones: violation of the 'straight killing' requirement in the code (which forbade allowing a customer to choose particular chickens from a coop and imposed an obligation to sell only batches of one coop or half-coop) and violating the minimum wage and maximum hours provisions of the code.[263] The court overturned the judgment of conviction, declaring NIRA unconstitutional on delegation and commerce clause grounds. The commerce clause part of the reasoning is of no direct interest here; the court reasoning on delegation can be divided into three different analytical strains, which are all of the highest importance, since they set the groundwork of and thus announce the modern constitutional settlement. While the Executive made the plea of necessity an argument for upholding the constitutionality of the act, the Court declared that emergency justifications, albeit "conditions to which power is addressed are to be always considered when the exercise of power is tested," do not effectively "create or enlarge constitutional power."

In terms of accountability, the court observed, this was not a delegation of 'privileges and immunities' to voluntary trade or industrial associations but in

[262] In fact, since the deputy administrators were drawn from business circles as well, the result would be in effect "little more than a bargain between business leaders on the one hand and businessmen in the guise of government officials on the other." Hawley 1966, at p. 57.

[263] The others were in relation to violations of N.Y. municipal ordinances and regulations and charges of conspiracy.

effect a delegation of 'coercive exercise of lawmaking power' to private groups.[264] Soon afterwards, in *Carter v. Carter Coal Co.,*[265] one of the codes (the Bituminous Coal Code), which had been re-passed by Congress as an act (Bituminous Coal Conservation Act of 1935), would be invalidated, upon a rationale that stresses also (besides the obvious accountability problems) the rule of law implications. There as in *Schechter*, weekly wages and hours could be set for all by a majority of miners and producers in a district or group of districts. The *Carter Coal* court emphasized that a statute that delegated to a majority of private parties the power to impose their will, sanctioned by state coercion, on others, was not only deeply suspect as a matter of accountability-representation but also as a denial of due process (an "intolerable and unconstitutional interference with constitutional liberty and property"): "The power conferred upon the majority is, in effect, the power to regulate the affairs of an unwilling minority. This is legislative delegation in its most obnoxious form; for it is not even delegation to an official or an official body, presumptively disinterested, but to private persons whose interests may be and often are adverse to the interests of others in the same business. . . .The delegation is so clearly arbitrary, and so clearly a denial of rights safeguarded by the due process clause of the Fifth Amendment, that it is unnecessary to do more than to refer to the decisions of this Court which foreclose the topic. *Schechter Poultry Corp. v. United States,* [etc.]"[266]

As the *Schechter* court noted next, there was no legislative guidance to the Executive, other than the laundry list of rationalizations provided by the first section of the act. Moreover, and this was stressed, unlike the FTC Act, which gave *an administrative body* power to regulate "unfair competition," NIRA conferred on *the President* power to determine "fair competition."[267] In effect, the court made two nondelegation arguments, one related to separation of powers proper and the other to its cognate rule of law strain; the executive and the administration.

To start with the administrative discretion argument, as its was noted earlier, public rights could (in the logic of the classical constitutional paradigm) be subject

[264] *See* Stewart 1974-1975, at p. 1796, notes 579–581 and associated text, pointing out the fact that, after the demise of the N.I.R.A., direct and formal interest representation "has fallen into disrepute in the United States and Great Britain, in part because of a tendency to associate it with fascist corporate state programs" and giving an account of the actual operation of NIRA code-making practice similar to that provided by Hawley. In effect, the codes represented a government-sponsored bargain between big industry and organized labor interests at the expense of consumers and smaller employers.

[265] 298 U.S. 238 (1936)

[266] At. 311.

[267] *See* Hawley 1966, at pp. 127–130 for an interesting description of the circumstances of the case. Anecdotically, Brandeis would reportedly tell one of Roosevelt's advisors, after the reading of the decision: "This is the end of this business of cartelization, and I want you to go back and tell the President that we are not going to let this government centralize everything. It's come to an end." A. Schlesinger, *The Politics of Upheaval,* cited by Peter H. Aranson, Ernest Gellhorn, Glen O. Robinson, " A Theory of Legislative Delegation," 68 Cornell L. Rev. 1 (November 1982), FN 35.

to administrative determination as to both fact and law, by means of legislative courts, exception being made for *de novo* review of all questions regarding the so-called 'constitutional' or 'jurisdictional facts,' which determine the agency's power to act.[268] Private rights would contrariwise go for exclusive determination to the regular courts of law, with all the guarantees of judicial process; the administration would be accorded no deference. The departure from this paradigm and the terms of the compromise had been already acquiesced in *Crowell v. Benson,*[269] when the court upheld against a due process challenge the Longshoremen's and Harbor Workers' Compensation Act, under which the administrative method was used to determine compensation awards, i.e., the liability of an individual to another (employer-employee). The court, noting the extensive procedural protections in the act, observed that nothing would preclude Congress in the future from using the administrative method in some such cases, with final administrative determination as to the facts, provided that questions of law and 'fundamental' or 'jurisdictional' facts would be re-determined by the courts, in reviewing the 'quasi-judicial' determinations of these bodies. *Schechter* complements these statements by a broad *constitutional 'quid pro quo'* statement. The Court emphasized that the words "unfair competition" had a meaning in common law and were a "limited concept." By authorizing the Federal Trade Commission a certain measure of discretion as to the determination of the broader term "unfair methods of competition," Congress had structured that discretion, since the Commission was "an expert body" authorized to act quasi-judicially (in light of a specific and substantial public interest, according to a special procedure (formal complaint, notice and hearing, findings of fact supported by adequate evidence, judicial review of the *vires*)).[270] What was essentially alluded to was that, while the court accepted the departure from the common law constraints in what concerned the legitimacy of legislation (as a matter of constitutionally acceptable legislative reservation requirements), broad and discretionary statutory provisions would need to be constrained at the level of administrative implementation by administrative procedure and judicial review. The example of the newly created Federal Radio (future Communication)

---

[268] *Ohio Valley Water Co. v. Ben Avon Borough et al.* 253 U.S. 287 (1920), the rate determination made by a utility can be reviewed by a court (independent judgment) when charge would be made that the rate is confiscatory, statutory provisions ousting judicial review notwithstanding: "In all such cases, if the owner claims confiscation of his property will result, the state must provide a fair opportunity for submitting that issue to a judicial tribunal for determination upon its own independent judgment as to both law and facts; otherwise the order is void because in conflict with the due process clause, Fourteenth Amendment." (at 289) *Ng. Fung Ho v. White, Commissioner of Immigration*, etc. 259 U.S. 276 (1922) (judicial redetermination of the question of citizenship if raised in an immigration deportation proceeding). *Johnson v. Robison* 415 U.S. 361 (1974), a Veterans' Administration determination of eligibility for educational benefits, if challenged under the equal protection clause of the Fifth Amendment, would be reviewed de novo, clause precluding judicial review notwithstanding.

[269] 285 U.S. 22 (1931).

[270] *Schechter*, at 844.

Commission was also given; while the act gave flimsy guidance (grant licenses "as public convenience, interest or necessity requires"), administrative discretion had been contained by expertise (nature of communication industry; allocation of frequencies on the spectrum) and procedure (hearing and evidence). The President was constrained by neither of these limitations.[271]

To be sure, experts and judges or those institutional actors that are 'like' them are best kept independent from politics, for obvious rationality and impartiality considerations. The meaning of these delegation-related distinctions would be clarified in the same day, as the *Humphrey's Executor v. United States*[272] decision was rendered. In *Humphrey*, the Supreme Court took away much of what had been said nine years before in *Myers v. United States,*[273] prohibiting Franklin Delano Roosevelt's removal of a Federal Trade Commissioner, without cause, before the end of his seven-year statutory term, for his uncongeniality with the President's politics. The appointment had been made by the statute subject to limitations (malfeasance, neglect of duty, inefficiency) and the question was whether Congress could constitutionally insulate such an officer from Presidential supervision. Given the nature of the function performed by a Commissioner, the case at hand was essentially distinct from *Myers,* where a statute providing for Senatorial concurrence to the removal of a Postmaster had been declared unconstitutional, as imposing undue limitations on the President's executive duties. The statutory attributions of the Commissioner were, the Court observed, mixed, "quasi-judicial" and "quasi-legislative," and the Commission exercised a mere "executive function," incidental or contingent to these essential functions, rather than being a part of the executive branch. The expertise and impartiality rationales are fused in the reasoning: "The commission is to be non-partisan; and it must, from the very nature of its duties, act with entire impartiality. It is charged with the enforcement of no policy except the policy of the law. Its duties are neither political nor executive, but predominantly quasi-judicial and quasi-legislative. . .a body of experts 'appointed by law and informed by experience."[274] Therefore, the argument of unitary executive derived from *Myers* was found unapplicable, since the nature of the office at hand required a higher degree of insulation from political control. The decision in *Humphrey's Executor* gave thus both a legal validation and an essential qualification to the modern administrative state. The President would not be allowed to control by unfettered executive interpretation (and thus implicit law-making) these vast delegations of legislative power to the administration.

---

[271] *Id.*, at 848: "In view of the scope of that broad declaration and of the nature of the few restrictions that are imposed, the discretion of the President in approving or prescribing codes, and thus enacting laws for the government of trade and industry throughout the country, is virtually unfettered."

[272] 295 U.S. 602, at 624 (1935).

[273] 272 U.S. 52 (1926).

[274] 295 U.S. 624.

3.2 The Constitutional Problem of Delegation in Pre-WWII Parliamentary Jurisdictions

3.2.1 The General Problematics of Delegation in Parliamentary Systems

All the jurisdictions which will come under scrutiny below (the Westminster model, France and Germany until the WWII) have a number of common characteristics with respect to the delegation problem that distinguish them from the American counterpart. Before proceeding to specifics, group similarities should be identified.

In mature parliamentary systems, the institutional delegate is a government politically responsible to and thus dependent on the confidence of the legislature. By the same token, the theoretical delegate controls in practice the delegator-legislature, also in the exercise of the latter's law-making functions. Nineteenth century parliamentarism still evidenced a measure of individual MP autonomy from the party machine and also a degree of parliamentary faction independence from the government in power. As the electoral and party systems came of age, departing gradually from the initial 'Burkean' assumptions regarding representation,[275] the delegation problem began to embrace a common form which in the US is not present to the same extent. American distinctiveness is due to both the institutional self-sufficiency of the political branches of power (a constitutional criterion) and the perpetuation of a 'primitive' electoral and party system (a political peculiarity).[276]

In a parliamentary system, by contrast, law-making is most commonly initiated and effectively controlled by the government, whereas the bill is usually drafted by experts in a ministry. To be sure, this state of facts is not an argument against a constitutionally prescribed legislative reservation opposable to the parliament. To a certain extent, the case against delegation may even be stronger. The legislative process ensures publicity, openness, and transparency of decisionmaking. Thus, a constitutionally entrenched reservation, at least in important matters, even aside from the general legitimacy and rule of law benefits, also becomes an institutional guarantee. It protects the rights of the parliamentary minority, which would

[275] "The theory of parliamentary representative government is built on the assumption of the early-nineteenth-century restrictive electoral system." Sajó 1999, at p. 112, generally, "The Transformations of Parliament," pp. 103–121.

[276] The qualification "primitive" is not used here in a pejorative sense but only to point out the fact that the individual Congressman is still dependent much more on his constituency than upon the party. Since the American electoral and party system did not fully evolve into common modern forms (streamlined decisionmaking, rigid party discipline), members of Congress enjoy a much larger degree of autonomy.

otherwise be routinely sidestepped by the majority through expedited procedures, including shell enactments delegating subordinate legislation to the executive.[277] This role of the legislative reservation in ensuring the rights of the minority and promoting democratic and rule of law values associated with parliamentary publicity and transparency is still highly relevant nowadays.

Limitations on the specificity and subject-matter of statutes (and consequently on delegations) were often introduced in European post-war constitutions as a direct response to the collapse of parliamentarism before WWII. Article 80 of the German *Grundgesetz*, for example, according to which the "content, purpose, and scope" (*Inhalt, Zweck und Ausmaß*) of an authorization to adopt subordinate legislation (*Rechtsverordnungen*) have to be determined by the parliament in the enabling act, is a clear reaction to the vagaries of the Weimar parliaments. Most particularly, it is a constitutional response to the *Ermächtigungsgesetz* of March 1933, by virtue of which the Reich government (*i.e.*, Hitler) was given a blank cheque, for an indefinite future, to adopt executive legislation. Likewise, Art. 13 in the French Constitution of 1946, stating that "[t]he National Assembly adopts legislation alone. It cannot delegate this right"[278] was a response to the authorization given Marshall Pétain by the last parliament of the Third Republic to adopt measures of legislative effect and even change the constitution itself by means of executive decree. Whether these post-war provisions have in fact accomplished the functions they were expected to fulfill and whether they fill in a different role in the general structure of contemporary European constitutionalism than that of the nondelegation doctrine in US constitutional law is a general question for the fourth chapter of this book.[279] But whether the constitutionally-required models of legislative reservation, up until the great law and state transformations of the late nineteenth to early twentieth centuries, did serve a different constitutional function in the European context (and therefore whether the contemporary constitutional response properly addressed the posed phenomenal question) is a historical matter that must be grappled with at this analytical point.

---

[277] *See* Jérôme Trémeau, *La réserve de loi-compétence législative et Constitution* (Aix-en-Provence: Presses Universitaires d'Aix-Marseilles, 1997), at p. 38. *Also see* for a similar and earlier argument Tingstén 1934, at p. 208.

[278] "L'Assemblée nationale vote seule la loi. Elle ne peut déléguer ce droit."

[279] French post-war developments under the Fourth Republic (1946) Constitution will however be discussed in this sub-chapter, since they are in effect a continuation of the constitutional paradigm and constitutional-political problems of the Third Republic. The actual moment of contemporary break with the past, in French constitutional context, is the Fifth Republic Constitution (of 1958), which will be therefore addressed in the next section of the book.

3.2.2 "The Paradox of Supremacy": Phenomena and Rules, Causes and Effects

The common mutations of late nineteenth to early twentieth century parliamentary systems (speed and streamlining of political decision-making, control of parliaments by the government in power, control of the parliamentary process by the strongest faction, sham publicity of parliamentary debates doubled by backroom haggling and party machine dictatorship, etc.) were exacerbated by pre-WWII constitutional orders. They ultimately degenerated into a particularly volatile and malignant form, by virtue of "the paradox of parliamentary supremacy."[280] Peter Lindseth coined this inspired turn of phrase. The paradox referred to is that an omnipotent parliament turned out in the end to be powerless, sliding on the slippery slope toward its own demise and executive dictatorship. But the context and way in which Lindseth used the expression are exemplary of a common conceptual conflation of the phenomenon of delegation, on the one hand, and the constitutional rules with respect to delegating enactments, on the other. Therefore, since the issue is of the highest analytical importance at this juncture, and even at the risk of anticipating somewhat future discussions, his argument must be briefly engaged. He showed, in an extensive comparative study on the matter, how in Third and Fourth Republic France and under the German Weimar Constitution, parliamentary supremacy effectively relegated normative non-delegation arguments to the field of theoretical-academic speculation, political debates, or background norms of parliamentary practice. Lack of review of constitutionality and various institutional deficiencies combined in the result that a legislative reservation could not be effectively opposed to the parliament as a matter of constitutionality.

In his study, Lindseth makes the related causal argument that those systemic problems had as a direct consequence made it easier to delegate vast amounts of discretion to the executive in times of crisis, thus subverting the constitutional system. But the author also seems to advance the more doubtful correlative thesis that the lack of a constitutional nondelegation limitation on the legislature, *as such*, had a direct effect on practices and contributed to the demise of liberal democracies. Contrariwise, nondelegation provisions, after the war (the "postwar constitutional settlement," as Lindseth calls it), would have contributed to the stabilization of these democracies.

Although oversimplifying Lindseth's more elaborate general argument, I will provide a longer citation, to help exemplify at the same time the reasons for my doubt as to his causal claim and the relevance of this discussion for the present study: "It was this *notion of unlimited parliamentary power*, in particular as it

---

[280] Peter L. Lindseth, "The Paradox of Parliamentary Supremacy: Delegation, Democracy, and Dictatorship in Germany and France 1920s-1950s" 113 *Yale L. J.* 1341 (May, 2004). Lindseth Peter L., The Contradictions of Supranationalism: European Integration and the Constitutional Settlement of Administrative Governance, 1920s-1980s (Ph.D. dissertation, Columbia University, Department of History, 2002 [on file with the author]).

related to the permissible *scope of legislative delegation* to the executive, that distinguished the French and German interwar constitutional experiences from the American one....By 1933 and 1940 respectively, the *practice* of unchecked delegation in Germany and France led ultimately to the collapse of the parliamentary system into one in which all effective governmental power would, as a matter of constitutional doctrine, be fused in the person of the national leader.... In postwar West Germany and France, rather, the development of *enforceable, yet flexible, delegation constraints* marked an important constitutional innovation, one essential to the reconciliation of historical conceptions of parliamentary democracy with the reality of executive power in an age of modern administrative governance. The emergence of flexible delegation constraints after 1945 reflected a constitutional commitment to preserve—despite delegation—a mediating role for elected legislatures along with the conception of representative government that they embodied."[281] [emphases supplied]

The author, in support of his thesis, extensively cites Carl Schmitt's claim, advanced in the latter's 1936 "Legislative Delegations" article, that the contemporaneous practice of delegation showed without doubt an irreconcilable tension between practices and "the concepts of legislation and constitution peculiar to separation-of-powers regimes" and "an insurmountable opposition between the concept of legislation in a parliamentary regime and the evolution of public life over the course of the last decades." This tension was then for Schmitt (for obvious reasons, given the time when made and the political propensities of the author) a clear sign that liberal constitutionalism needed to be discarded altogether. Schmitt's argument is contrasted by Lindseth with the recognition by a much more restrained Schmitt, made in the latter's 1943 piece on "The Plight of European Jurisprudence," that: "in the changing situations we preserve the basis of a rational human existence that cannot do without legal principles such as: a recognition of the individual based on mutual respect even in a conflict situation; a sense for the logic and consistency of concepts and institutions; a sense for reciprocity and the minimum of an orderly procedure, due process, without which there can be no law."[282]

The general reasoning leaves the reader with the misleading impression that there would be a direct correlation and close link between delegation-related constraints (or the lack thereof) at the level of the constitution, the phenomenon of crisis legislation, and the fact that dictatorship came about in Europe by means of enabling laws. Aside from revealing the lawyerly habit of overrating somewhat the problem-solving capacity of positive legal measures, this only goes to show the extent to which, while the notion of delegation captures under the assumption of a concept of legislation the most fundamental intuitions about limited government (since it showcases the various constitutional concerns underlying nondelegation constraints), indiscriminate use of the notion as such can easily lead to a failure of

[281] *Id.*, at p. 1353.

[282] Carl Schmitt, "The Plight of European Jurisprudence" ["Die Lage der europäischen Rechtswisseschaft" 1943/44], G. L. Ulmen transl., 83 *Telos* 35 (Spring 1990), p. 67.

separating both the various strains of debate. It can also lead to an undiscerning conflation of the constitutional-political phenomenon from legal concepts and positive rules. What Schmitt actually had said (description-wise) was that the assumptions regarding legislation failed to translate in legal practices. This only indicated the extent to which the system did not correspond to its presuppositions.

The practices of liberal democracies were as a matter of fact realigned along a retrenchment of their presuppositions after the war, in ways responding to the concerns voiced by Schmitt (and many other critics of unfettered parliamentarism) in 1943. To wit, distortions in the political process and institutional power imbalances had been caused by the fact that antebellum constitutionalism had failed to master its facts, since parliamentarism still functioned, before WWII, on the Burkean assumption of an independent representative, i.e., in a general format designed for a much more restrictive electoral system. This was an anachronism at stark variance with the transformations brought by the emergent mass democracy, with its disciplined party systems, where the individual member of parliament resembles a cog in a monolithic party-machine much more than the lofty portrayal of an independent representative in the "Letter to the Electors in Bristol." Given the splintered nature of the contemporaneous political spectrum and the constitutional institution of political responsibility, this contradiction had created in practice staggering systemic instability, with frequent overthrows of governments. In response to this problem, after the war, parliamentarism would be stabilized ('rationalized') by means of institutional changes, for instance by introducing the mechanism of the 'constructive vote of no-confidence' in the German Basic Law and giving up the pre-war unalloyed proportional representation. Thus, the fragmentation and fluidity of the political spectrum were considerably reduced. Likewise, whereas, before the war, rights guarantees were not opposable to the legislator as such (proposals to introduce American-style control of constitutionality had been constantly rejected), legislation would be afterwards disciplined by the adoption of various judicial forms of enforcing constitutional limitations (the French Constitutional Council, the German Federal Constitutional Court, etc.). To counter at the sub-constitutional level the major rule of law displacements produced by the relatively more open-ended character of modern legislation, constitutionality review was paralleled by more intensive ('activist') inroads into the traditional fields of administrative discretion, by means of "activist" judicial review of administrative action.[283] In British Commonwealth jurisdictions, bolder forms of judicial control of the administration (also by way of Privy Council decisions on appeal)

[283] *See* the account of this evolution (comparison between American and English administrative law) in Bernard Schwartz, *Lions Over the Throne-The Judicial Review of English Administrative Law* (New York and London: New York University Press, c1987) and Bernard Schwartz and Henry William Wade, *Legal Control of Government: Administrative Law in Britain and the United States* (Oxford: Clarendon Press, 1972).

partly substituted for the absence of enforceable constitutions an emergent form of common law constitutionalism.

But it is fair to infer that, instrumentally speaking, express nondelegation limitations or the lack thereof *as such* have and had little if anything to do with either the demise or the rebirth of constitutional democracies. Furthermore, leaving aside the common difficulties of establishing grand historical lines of causation, it may reasonably be surmised that a delegation limitation in the constitution is not in any way preventive of dictatorships. Besides, the phenomenon of delegation is related to the problem of emergencies only incidentally and partially. The transformations in the nature of legislation and government that culminated in the present administrative states had been underway long before the major crises of the twentieth century. The impact of these transformations on public law is still evident nowadays, albeit in less dramatic and malignant forms, long after the totalitarian peril was fended off in the respective democracies. Thus, crisis legislation is systemically related to the phenomenon of delegation and both to dictatorship only, perhaps, in the sense captured by Hugo Black in the *Steel Seizure Case*: "[E]mergency powers…tend to kindle emergencies." What is presumptively acceptable in an emergency can create the precedent of pleas of necessity in circumstances where the plea is less justified. How this real problem is to be remedied by means of positive fundamental law is a great contemporary quagmire, a systemic riddle still awaiting its solution.[284] But to expect a nondelegation constitutional provision to solve in any way the sort of problems and disruptions associated with the arrival of dictatorship in Germany is expecting too much of constitutions and judges. It is also confusing an effect with the cause itself: the practice of delegations simply revealed in a dramatic way the shortcomings of the entire constitutional-political systems as such. As Justice Jackson wrote in his unpublished *Steel Seizure* draft: "No thing is more certain than that in the political regime power is attracted by competence and gravitates away from indecision and mediocrity. The autopsy on the Hitler regime in which we participated at Nürnberg leaves a firm conviction that dictatorship in Germany did not seize power because of the strength or competence of the man or clique that headed it, but was suffered to take over by the mediocrity, inertia and disintegration of the Reichstag, a legislative body whose partisan divisions, sectionalism, and inertia let power slip through its fingers."[285]

Before the war, debates on delegation had reflected a clash of paradigms, deriving from the fact that legislation as a practice was gradually failing to correspond with its normative premises, the fundamental classical constitutionalist normative assumptions regarding legislation. Those assumptions had rested on social and economic presuppositions that, across legal orders and on both sides of

[284] *See* András Sajó, "From Militant Democracy to the Preventive State?," 27 *Cardozo L. Rev.* 2255 (2006), on the interaction between welfare-state- and counter-terrorism-related patterns of risk-prevention.

[285] In Schwartz 1987, p. 206.

the ocean, had started to creak and then fail more and more visibly towards the second half of the nineteenth century, under the weight of an industrial, technically advanced and standardized, mass society. The upheaval had changed political (parliamentary and electoral) systems to the point where institutions built upon obsolete ideal-typical justifications and practical presuppositions were functioning in full disagreement with their changed environments and eventually collapsed. In strictly juridical terms, a discrepancy was gaping between the constitutional guarantees of fundamental legal institutions and the reality of their instantiations. We have already tracked the uneasiness of the constitutional protections of common law with the emergence of the trusts and the modern "monopoly" in the United States. Albeit the judicial-constitutional dramatics of the American events was not paralleled elsewhere, similar developments and debates occurred in all major democracies.

All justifications of foundational juridical institutions are of course idealized legal fictions. But they must also be ideal-typically fictional; at a certain point of departure from the reality of things the justification has to yield and the practice must be changed or at least qualified. It is, to give just one example, hard to maintain and constitutionally hold as sacrosanct the idea of a contract as "law between the parties," "meeting of the minds," "free fusing of volitions," when the ubiquitous practical example is the sale or provision of standardized goods and services under a standardized form, over the content of which one of the parties has routinely no say.[286] As legislation consequently changed to cope with these transformations, in more or less abrupt patterns of intervention, this departure from accepted understandings and practices regarding the constitutionally premised legislative reservation was labeled "delegation." Many reactions under this label had at the time an ideological, "reactionary" component, i.e., sheer aversion to governmental encroachment upon social and economic areas previously regarded as off-limits. But the change in the nature of legislation also raised more serious and perennial concerns, which have to do with the possibility of constitutionalism and constitutional adjudication to redraw the lines of assessment and replace those initial presuppositions and practices with workable substitutes. These concerns are still valid at present, since they pertain to the foundations of public law adjudication and legal rationality and, therefore, with the systemic capacity of constitutions to constrain power, enable collective agency, and ensure freedom.

After the war, irrespective of their form, attempts to regulate constitutionally the legislative reservation simply translated, as a matter of judicial enforcement of delegation provisions in constitutions, the new legislative reservation, namely fundamental rights. This happened in all Western democracies, in America as well as in Europe. The question whether this new legislative reservation is a functional substitute for the disappearance of the classical presuppositions and distinctions has to be kept in abeyance and await its answer in the fourth chapter

[286] Ernst Forsthoff, *Die Verwaltung als Leistungsträger* (Stuttgart und Berlin: W. Kohlhammer, 1938), *esp*. 38 ff.

of this book. The claim as to delegation debates and practices reflecting the departure from a normative notion of legislation will be exemplified in what follows.

3.2.3 Sole and Despotic Dominions*: The Common Law and Parliamentary Sovereignty*

3.2.3.1 Hewart's Interjection!

> Between the 'Rule of Law' and what is called 'administrative law' (happily there is no English name for it) there is the sharpest possible contrast. One is substantially the opposite of the other.
>
> Lord Hewart of Bury, *The New Despotism* (1929)

At the peak of post-revolutionary Whig constitutionalism, William Blackstone described both property and the sovereignty of Parliament as absolute, in an eerily symmetric, mirror-image manner. Property is "a sole and despotic dominion" exercised by a man over a thing in complete exclusion of the entire universe and ultimately derived from the divine ordinance in *Genesis* 1: 28, whatever "airy metaphysical notions may have been started by fancy writers upon this subject."[287] Likewise, Parliament has an "absolute despotic power" to undertake legally anything that is possible naturally. Nothing can stay in the way of its untrammelled will: "true it is, that what parliament doth, no authority in the world can undo."[288] The Holmesian "page of history" will help us understand how these two despots came into conflict and why this conflict raised at the same time serious, ongoing constitutionalist concerns and loud but ultimately futile cries of unconstitutional delegation.

In England, the distinction between legislation proper and the independent normative authority of the King's Council crystallized around the formal requirement of consent by the three estates. During the reign of Edward III, the practice began to settle in that further modifications of the *jus terrae*, the so-called *statuta nova*, needed to obtain the consent of all three estates, while all other matters could be regulated independently by the king, through the means of ordinances and proclamations. It also began to be an accepted practice, from the thirteenth century onward, that enactments of a permanent and general nature ("que sont perpetuels," dealing with "pointz a durer") as opposed to those of a particular or local character ("que non sont mye perpetuels"), need to be assented by the three estates, passed in

[287] 2 *Blackstone's Commentaries* 3 (1979 Chicago original facsimile edition).

[288] 1 *Blackstone's Commentaries* 156.

the form of a statute, and are to be selected and entered upon the Statute Roll, for the cognizance of the courts of justice.[289]

The practice slowly became entrenched[290] and the only major known departure prior to the Revolution dates back to the Tudor period, when Parliament delegated the power to legislate, i.e., to unilaterally depart from and modify the common law through royal proclamations, to Henry VIII: "The King, for the time being, with the advice of his Council, or the more part of them, may set forth proclamations under such penalties and pains as to him and them seem necessary, which shall be observed as though they were made by Act of Parliament; but this shall not be prejudicial to any person's inheritance, offices, liberties, goods, chattels, or life; and whosoever shall willingly offend any article contained in the said proclamations, shall pay such forfeitures, or be so long imprisoned, as shall be expressed in the said proclamations; and if any offending will depart the realm, to the intent he will not answer his said offence, he shall be adjudged a traitor."[291]

The act was quickly repealed in the reign of Edward VI[292] and this kind of particularly offensive and unorthodox practice subsequently subsided.[293]

---

[289] The older rules of prospective application, *statuta vetera*, enacted in the aftermath of the Magna Charta, were deemed to be part of the law of the land irrespective of the originating authority. *See*, on these issues, Rudolph Gneist, *The History of the English Constitution*, Philip A. Ashworth translation (New York: G. P. Putnam's Sons, 1886), Vol. II, *esp.* pp. 19–25. Gneist considers 15 Edward II to be the first express recognition of Parliament as a legislative assembly: "Revocatio novarum ordinationum anno 1223; les choses, qui serount à establir, soient tretées accordées et establies en parlaments par notre Sr. le Roi et par l'assent des Prelats, Countes et Barouns et la communaulté du roialme." (FN 3, at p. 21). *See also* Charles Howard McIlwain, *The High Court*, at p. 313 and François Pierre Guillaume Guizot, *History of the Origin of Representative Government in Europe*, Andrew R. Scoble translation (London: Henry G. Bohn, 1852), at pp. 482–483: "Ordinances were not inscribed, like statutes, upon the rolls of Parliament; they were less solemn in their character, although their object frequently had reference to matters equally legislative and of equally general interest, such as the enactment of jurisdiction or of penalties. It is not more easy to clearly distinguish ordinances from statutes, than great councils from Parliaments properly so called. All that we can say is, that less importance and stability were attributed to this class of legislative measures."

[290] The statute of York, in 1322, already provides that "thenceforward all laws respecting the estate of the crown, or of the realm and people, must be treated, accorded, and established in Parliament by the king, by and with the assent of the prelates, earls, barons, and commonalty of the realm." In Guizot, *supra*, at p. 461.

[291] 31 Henry VIII., c. 8 (1539). One can *see* that the "delegation" is actually checked by a fair number of legal safeguards, even by modern standards. For a study of the legislative activity of the Parliament during the reign of Henry VIII, challenging with many examples the received view that the Parliament was brow-beaten into submission by the king, *see* S. E. Lehmberg, "Early Tudor Parliamentary Procedure: Provisos in the Legislation of the Reformation Parliament," Vol. 85 (No. 334) *The English Historical Review* 1–11 (Jan. 1970).

[292] Stat. I Edw. VI. C. 12.

[293] Blackstone is particularly critical of the practice: "Indeed, by the statute 31 Henry. VIII. c. 8. it was enacted, that the king's proclamations should have the force of acts of parliament: a statute, which was calculated to introduce the most despotic tyranny; and which must have proved fatal to the liberties of this kingdom, had it not been luckily repealed in the minority of his successor, about five years after." 1 Blackstone's *Commentaries on the Laws of England* 261 (Facsimile of the First Edition, Chicago & London: Chicago University Press, c1979).

Nonetheless, two caveats are important, if these historical references are to be perceived in their proper context. First, the royal pretensions of inherent normative authority grounded in prerogative were hedged in more slowly and finally curbed only by an incremental evolution, marked, on its crucial points, by the authoritative pronouncement of Lord Chief Justice Coke in the 1610 *Case of Proclamations,*[294] the abolition by Parliament of the Star Chamber in 1641, and the developments surrounding and following the Civil War. Dicey gives the interesting example of Lord Chatham's attempt, as late as 1766, to prohibit the importation of wheat by means of a proclamation. This unrestrained executive assertion was immediately sanctioned by Parliament, which passed in the same year an Act of Indemnity to remedy the otherwise ensuing illegality on the part of the Crown.[295]

Second and more relevantly for our inquiry, parliamentary sovereignty does become an undisputed tenor of the constitution both in law and in fact once the last Stewart king, James II, is rushed with short ceremony from the throne by the Glorious Revolution. But Parliament itself was to take a longer time to become a primarily legislative body, a law-making assembly proper, in the sense we now understand it. Lord Bacon's insightful admonition that "[n]ew laws are like the apothecaries' drugs; though they remedy the disease, yet, they trouble the body"[296] reflects fairly well the activity of the British Parliaments up to the first half of the nineteenth century. The eighteenth and early nineteenth-century Parliaments, far from epitomizing the Lockean ideal of bodies relegated to the enactment of general rules of prospective application, preserved a primarily medieval, judicial character, fairly evident in the character of the acts that were passed. For instance, even though the particularly objectionable practice of attainder bills would lapse after

[294] *Case of Proclamations* (1610) 12 Co. Rep. 74, K. & L. 78. In this landmark case, Coke's opinion was demanded by the Crown in Privy Council as to whether the king could regulate by proclamations, under a penalty of a fine and imprisonment, the trade in starch and building restrictions in London. In a major inroad on royal prerogative, Coke advised that the king can, by proclamation, "for the Prevention of Offenses," only require the subjects to obey the law (and then the proclamation *ad terrorem populi* would constitute an aggravating circumstance) but cannot create new crimes, enlarge the criminal jurisdiction of the Star Chamber or exceed a specific statutory authorization by an *ultra vires* act: "But a thing which is punishable by the Law, by fine and imprisonment, if the King prohibit it by his Proclamation, before that he will punish it, and so warn his subjects of the peril of it, there if he commit it after, thus as a Circumstance aggravates the Offence; but he by Proclamation cannot make a thing unlawful, which was permitted by the Law before; And this was well proved by the ancient and continuall form of Indictments, for all Indictments conclude, *Contra legem & consuetudinem Angliae*, or *Contra leges & statuta*, &c. but never was seen any Indictment to conclude *Contra Regiam proclamationem*."

[295] A. V. Dicey, *Introduction to the Study of the Law of the Constitution* (London; N.Y.: Macmillan & Co., 1965), at pp. 50–54.

[296] Francis Bacon, *The Works of Francis Bacon* [7] (Newcastle: Cambridge Scholars Publishing, 2010), p. 251.

1697, judicial decrees in the form of a statute were very common throughout most of the eighteenth century.[297]

A perusal of the Statute books can provide us with the most interesting and edifying examples. The one for the year 1770 contains ninety-nine acts, out of which only four are of a general law-making character. The rest of them, even if not technically tabulated as Private Acts, concern purely local or private matters (road improvement here, canal-building there, the repair of Magdalen Bridge, in Oxford, naturalizations, change of names, divorces, etc.).[298] In this vein, Maitland would famously remark later that the eighteenth-century British Parliament "seem[ed] afraid to rise to the dignity of a general proposition."[299] Among contemporary observers, Blackstone, in the *Commentaries,* despaired of the legislative drafting techniques or better yet the lack thereof, while Bentham was exasperated by the incapacity of Parliament to simply legislate the Crime of Theft rather than pass a law about stealing turnips, one about stealing horses, another about stealing turnips at night and a fourth one concerned with stealing horses during day-time.

Part of the reason why this strange situation obtained could be found in the institutional autonomy of Parliament, the corresponding relative distrust of the Crown, and—moreover—the sheer lack of government as such, in the present-day acceptance of modern, professional, streamlined administrative machinery. On a related point, the familiarly modern Benthamite notion that things can be done, changed, prompted, by legislative means, was so strange and unappealing that Lord

[297] In 1697, capital punishment for treason was meted on Sir John Fenwick by an Act of Parliament *Act 8 & 9 Will. III c. 4. See* discussion on attainder in F. W. Maitland Maitland, *The Constitutional History of England* (Cambridge: Cambridge University Press, 1963), p. 386, giving later examples of bills of pains and penalties, which will continue to be used even after the harsher practice of attainder bills is discontinued (the banishment of Atterbury in 1720, the 1876 disfranchisement for bribery, by act of parliament, of certain voters for the City of Norwich). More generally on attainder, "The Bounds of Legislative Specification: A Suggested Approach to the Bill of Attainder Clause" Note, 72 *Yale Law Journal* 330 (1962–1963).

[298] *See*, for a detailed list, the statistics in P.S. Atiyah, *The Rise and Fall of Freedom of Contract* (Oxford: Clarendon Press, 1979), pp. 91–95. *Also see* Maitland 1963, at p. 383, for an equally edificatory taxonomical breakdown of the Statute book for the year 1786: "There are 160 so-called public acts, and 60 so-called private acts. But listen to the titles of a few of the public acts: an act for establishing a workhouse at Havering, an act to enable the king to license a playhouse at Margate, an act for erecting a house of correction in the Middlesex, an act for incorporating the Clyde Marine Society, an act for paving the town of Cheltenham, an act for widening the roads in the borough of Bodmin. Fully half of the public acts are of this petty local character. Then as to the private acts, these deal with particular persons: an act for naturalizing Andreas Emmerich, an act for enabling Cornelius Salvidge to take the surname Tutton, an act for rectifying mistakes in the marriage settlement of Lord and Lady Camelford, an act to enable the guardians of William Frye to grant leases, an act to dissolve the marriage between Jonathan Twiss and Francis Dorrin....One is inclined to call the last century the century of *privilegia*." Similar statistics and comments relevant to our argument are also provided by the introduction to David Lieberman's *The Province of Legislation Determined-Legal theory in eighteenth-century Britain* (Cambridge: Cambridge University Press, 1989), pp. 1–28.

[299] Maitland 1963, at p. 383.

Mansfield is reported to have said: "What! Pass a judgment to do mischief and then bring in a bill to cure it!"[300] And yet, in spite of the legislative shortcomings, the legal system as such corresponded to the Lockean ideal of a general framework of public, uniform, predictable, normative rules. But this was primarily a function of the common law, which developed as a predictable standard of private conduct in spite of or perhaps in part due to legislative inactivity. With the exception of the 1601 Poor Law, protective, corporatist, and interventionist provisions in the extant feudal legislation were either interpreted restrictively by the courts or, simply left unenforced administratively and judicially, eventually fell into obsolence. Parliament seldom interfered with this evolution, save in order to occasionally repeal legislation restrictive of private ordering and freedom of contract.[301] The sixteenth century Statute of Artificers, last bastion of feudal protectionism, was abolished in 1814.[302] But, as soon as feudal restrictions were fuly swept aside, the situation began to slowly change in the opposite direction, in lockstep with the growing importance of the Commons and the maturing of the modern parliamentary system.

Whereas in 1741 Walpole had refused to step down upon losing the confidence of the Commons, 1782 marked the first cabinet (Lord North) entirely replaced by a vote of non-confidence; in 1803, Pitt settled the modern convention that the leader of the majority in the Commons forms the Cabinet. The Reform Act of 1832 is the crucial landmark, since, from that year onward, Parliament lost its medieval, judicial character completely, becoming a modern legislative machine. The Poor Law Amendment Act of 1834 is not only an excellent example of a modern statute but also a "delegating" enactment, at least in one of the senses legislative delegation is understood nowadays: administration of the poor laws passed from the county justices to commissioners given large discretion to make general prospective regulations pursuant to the statutory authorization. The overall character of legislation changed suddenly after the Reform Act: the Statute Book for the year 1844, for instance, comprises 113 Public General Acts, out of which a total of 55 are of a general, public-regarding character.[303]

By this time, nonetheless, it becomes somewhat misleading to say that Parliament "makes" the law that the executive enforces, since the executive is now in true fact becoming more and more the primary initiator and the original drafter of legislation. If in 1836 Lord Melbourne could still venture to say that "the duty of the Government is not to make legislation but to rule," a mere decade later, in 1847, the Prime Minister is reminded by Sir George Lewis that "the business of legislation is now more exclusively in the hands of the government than at any previous time."[304]

Walter Bagehot's nineteenth-century account of the English Constitution, a snapshot of the constitutional changes occurring prior to the Reform Act of 1867,

---

[300] *Fletcher v. Lord Sondes*, unreported decision, cited by Atiyah, *Rise and Fall*, at p. 96.

[301] Atiyah, p. 69 ff. Grimm, *Recht und Staat*, pp. 170–175, 195 ff.

[302] Grimm, p. 174.

[303] Atiyah, at pp. 250–255.

[304] *Id.*, at pp. 253–254.

captured all these transformations by describing both the mixed and balanced constitution and the separation of powers as obsolete concepts, redolent of a false Constitution ("the literary theory," in his words).[305] In the real one, he stated, by virtue of practical developments, the former prerogatives of the Crown had been diminished to the point of irrelevance by legislation, legislation had come to be in fact primarily exercised by the House of Commons, while the referred power (the executive, the Cabinet), fused at the hip with the Commons, had become the real law-maker. From that point onward, any notion of a balanced constitution would be built on recondite chimeras. The developments noted by Bagehot subsequently matured, as it is commonly known, in the Parliament Act of 1911, by virtue of which the Lords are reduced to the practical status of—to use Dicey's contemporary quip—a "Debating Society."[306]

Therefore, when Lord Chief Justice Hewart published his acidulous tract in 1929, suggesting that Parliament was delegating its legislative powers to the Executive, prompted by and as part of a surreptitious attempt by the Executive to use parliamentary sovereignty in order to undermine both Parliament and the Rule of Law, and, further, that the Executive itself was gullibly at the hands of a subterraneous bureaucratic cabal, which he resoundingly stamped as a "new despotism," his argument was flying in the face of all the transformations noted above.[307] The Committee on Ministers' Powers, promptly appointed at the request of the Lord Chancellor, dismissed the conspiratorial charge on the bona fides of the Civil Service, for lack of evidence, and issued an extensive report on the matter of secondary legislation.

As a practical issue, the Committee opined, any root-and-branch condemnation of delegation as such had already become unwarranted, given the sheer scope of modern government, and the corresponding lack of parliamentary time, fluctuating nature of the domains to be regulated, and technical, expertise-intensive subject-matters of modern legislation. If by delegation one would understand the sheer need and amount of subordinate legislation pursuant to initial statutory authorization, as such, delegation was to be condoned as a practice "indispensable, inevitable, legitimate and constitutionally desirable for certain purposes, within certain limits, and under certain safeguards."[308] If delegation-related arguments were meant to

---

[305] Walter Bagehot, *The English Constitution*, revised American edition (New York: D. Appleton & Company, 1892).

[306] *See*, for a thorough discussion, Vile 1967, Chapter VIII, "The Rise and Fall of Parliamentary Government," pp. 212–238.

[307] Rt. Hon. Lord Hewart of Bury, *The New Despotism* (London: Ernest Benn, 1929). For a more restrained contemporary pamphlet, *see* Carleton Kemp Allen, *Bureaucracy Triumphant* (London: Humphrey Milford: Oxford University Press, 1931).

[308] "The truth is that if Parliament were not willing to delegate law-making power, Parliament would be unable to pass the kind and quantity of legislation which modern public opinion requires." *Committee on Ministers' Powers Report*, H.M.S.O. (Cmd. 4060) (1932), at p. 23. For contemporary comments on the Report, *see* John Willis "The Delegation of Legislative and Judicial Powers to Administrative Bodies-A Study of the Report of the Committee on Ministers' Powers," XVIII *Iowa Law Review* 150 (1932–1933) and Arthur Suzman "Administrative Law in

express rule-of-law concerns with administrative discretion, then, as rule-of-law and accountability-oriented remedies, the practice of extensive secondary rule-making and quasi-adjudication pursuant to enabling legislation needed to be reined in by a variety of safeguards, such as better publication standards, parliamentary scrutiny, and general access to judicial review of the vires. Certain practices were deemed to be particularly problematic and the Committee urged their more cautious usage for the future: delegation of the power to modify an Act of Parliament,[309] privative clauses (exclusion, by the enabling act, of the reviewing power of the courts), delegation of the power to legislate on matters of principle, and delegation of the power to impose taxation.

As a *constitutional* argument, nonetheless, Lord Hewart's attack could be very easily dismissed and the refutation is as clear and valid now as it was in 1932. To state, as he had, that "it is the task of Parliament to make the laws, and the real business of the Executive is to govern the country in accordance with the laws which Parliament has made"[310] constitutes, in light of the constitutional premises of the British parliamentary system, at best a political or ideological argument, with little if any legal-constitutional clout, and at worst a meaningless tautology. Given the flexible, unwritten nature of the constitution and the state of normative quasi-irrelevance to which the prerogative has been reduced,[311] no substantive legal baseline exists along which one could assess what would constitute legislation proper. In light of the main tenet of the British Constitution, parliamentary sovereignty, Parliament itself is under no constitutional obligation to legislate with a certain degree of specificity or on certain specific matters. Thus, the notion of delegation as such is unintelligible from a legal-constitutional standpoint, as

England: A Study of the Report of the Committee on Ministers' Powers," XVIII *Iowa Law Review* 160 (1932–1933).

[309] Sometimes referred to as "Henry VIII clauses," these are provisions in statutes allowing for the modification of the enabling act by secondary legislation (statutory instruments), without parliamentary authorization. *See* discussion above.

[310] Hewart 1929, at p. 75. *Also*, in Kemp 1931, at p. 8: "In all these matters, legislative and judicial, what is really happening is that Parliament is getting rid of its own responsibilities. It is a short and easy method of legislation to delegate wide and ill defined powers to subordinate bodies, etc."

[311] The prerogative, to which we have already referred, is the sovereign and original power of the Crown to legislate, by Order in Council, independent of the authority of the Houses of Parliament. It was used in the past to legislate for a newly conquered territory and could still be invoked to regulate trade and commerce during war-time (e.g., the 'Second Reprisals Order,' of 16th of February 1917, an Order in Council establishing a blockade of enemy territory), although the most common modern means of dealing with emergencies of all kinds is the sweeping enabling act. The judiciary could historically be relied on, moreover, to remind the Executive that the Crown cannot alter the law of the land by Order in Council (*see*, for instance, *The Zamora* [1916] 2 A.C. 77).

opposed to a polemical-political benchmark.[312] The only constraints on legislation are those of manner and form; as a matter of constitutional law, no normative constraints on the legislature itself could be envisioned. Thus, the constitutional problematics related to the validity of the enabling law per se reverts into a second-order, administrative law problem: a presumption against sub-delegation, statutory interpretation in substantive review of the *vires*, and due process ("natural justice") constraints on the exercise of discretion.

3.2.3.2 Dicey's Dilemma

The problem had already been put to legal test in the course of an appeal from Canada. Since Canada was constitutionally, until the 'Patriation' of the Constitution in 1982, under the British North America Act (the Constitution Act) of 1867, a claim could be theoretically made that the constitutional limitation on the Dominion would be exceeded not only by a federal 'interdelegation,' whereby transfers of authority upset the federal division of powers[313] but also when the Dominion Parliament or the legislatures of the provinces "delegate" excessive discretion and thus legislative power to the respective executive branches (the Governor General, Ministers, Federal Boards at the federal level or Lieutenant Governors, Provincial Ministers, Provincial Boards at the provincial level, respectively), by failing to legislate with specificity.

This contention was rejected in 1883, by a Privy Council decision on appeal. The appellant, Archibald Hodge, proprietor of a tavern in the city of Toronto, was held by a police magistrate in breach of a police resolution of the License Commissioners of Toronto (he had kept his shop open after seven o'clock

[312] For instance, a Royal Commission on Carrots, empowered by an Act of Parliament to make regulations and issue quality standards respecting carrots, to inspect carrot farms, and prohibit the commercialization of substandard carrots, the observance of its rules and regulations made a misdemeanor subject to a fine, is not a delegate of Parliament in a constitutional sense, since Parliament is under no constitutional obligation to either legislate at all or legislate in a substantively recognizable way or with a given degree of specificity. Conversely, without parliamentary authorization, the Commission could not have existed in the first place. In the unlikely case such Commission would have been created by a prerogative Order in Council, its nosy inspectors could have been legally chased off the farm and even shot for trespass by a hypothetical carrot farmer. For this lively exemplification and a score of other helpful comments and sobering conversations, I am indebted to Stephen Scott, Professor Emeritus of Constitutional and Public Law (private conversation, McGill University, Winter 2003).

[313] The Constitution Act of 1867 primarily governs the division of legislative powers between the Federal Government and the Provinces. Inter-delegation (between the legislatures) was declared unconstitutional in a decision by the Supreme Court of Canada on a complementary delegation to effect a cooperative provincial-federal old age pension scheme. *Nova Scotia Inter-delegation* case of of 1950, *Attorney-General of Nova Scotia v. Attorney General of Canada* [1951] S.C.R. 31. *See* comments in Peter W. Hogg, *Constitutional law of Canada* (Scarborough, Ont.: Carswell, c2003), 14-Delegation, pp. 327–356.

at night on a Saturday, 'suffering billiards to be played therein,' against the regulation), fined twenty dollars and, in case of non-payment, ordered to be imprisoned for fifteen days with hard labor. The resolution had been passed on the basis of a provincial temperance law (Liquor License Act), which gave commissioners power to pass regulations on licensed houses. Hodge claimed, among other things, that the Act was unconstitutional since the provincial legislature, by virtue of its being a delegate of the Imperial Parliament, had to make the law itself and was not to delegate its delegated (through the B.N.A. Act of 1867) legislative power to a municipal body. The Privy Council rejected this particular claim with rather short ceremony: "It appears to their Lordships, however, that the objection thus raised by the appellants is founded on a misconception of the true character and position of the provincial legislatures. They are in no sense delegates of or acting under any mandate from the Imperial Parliament. When the British North America Act enacted that there should be a legislature for Ontario, and that its legislative assembly should have exclusive authority to make laws for the Province...it conferred powers in no sense to be exercised by delegation from or as agents of the Imperial Parliament, but authority as plenary and as ample within the limits prescribed by sect. 92 as the Imperial Parliament in the plenitude of its power possessed and could bestow....It was argued at the bar that a legislature committing important regulations to agents or delegates effaces itself. That is not so. It retains its powers intact, and can, whenever it pleases, destroy the agency it has created and set up another, or take matters directly in its own hands. How far it shall seek the aid of subordinate agencies, and how long it shall continue them, are matters for each legislature, and not for Courts of law, to decide."[314]

This goes to introduce the nature of the Diceyan dilemma and show why modern administrative law in most common law jurisdictions is still, to paraphrase a modern Canadian commentator, a more than "slightly dicey business."[315] I must

[314] *Archibald G. Hodge v. The Queen* (1883), 9 AC 117, at 132. In one of the war-time 'delegation' decisions, *In Re Gray*, 57 S.C.R. 150 [1918], an Order in Council passed under the authority of the War Measures Act of 1914, was attacked on nondelegation grounds, since derogating from a statutory provision in the Military Service Act of 1917. The Justices of the Supreme Court of Canada, while sustaining the executive measure, indicated that, in principle, 'abandonment,' 'abdication' or 'surrender' by Parliament of its legislative powers would, nonetheless, be unconstitutional: " Parliament cannot, indeed, abdicate its functions, but within reasonable limits at any rate it can delegate its powers to the executive government." (Per Fitzpatrick, C.J.). *But cf.* Hogg 2003, at p. 330: "In effect, the War Measures Act transferred to the federal cabinet virtually the whole legislative authority of the parliament for the duration of the war. The Court held that even a delegation as sweeping as this one was valid....[S]ince none of the majority judges regarded the War Measures Act as an unconstitutional abdication, abandonment, surrender, it is not easy to imagine the kind of delegation that would be unconstitutional. Nor did the judges indicate how their suggested limitation was to be reconciled with the Hodge doctrine of plenary and ample power; or, to put the question in another way, what principle of constitttional law dictated the suggested limitation."

[315] W. H. Arthurs, "Rethinking Administrative Law: A Slightly Dicey Business," 17 (1) *Osgoode Hall Law Journal* 1 (April 1979).

begin by stating that my own use of the quip is not to be understood in a pejorative sense. Although contemporary commentary reviles Dicey as a matter of course for having "effectively interred the idea of administrative law in England by denying its existence,"[316] this ritualized profession of academic antipathy is largely misdirected. Dicey essentially pointed out an inescapable trend in modern law and the tensions that would arrive from it.[317] Blaming him for pointing out the troubles to come does seem somewhat unfair, much like the proverbial shooting of the messenger.

Albert Venn Dicey's classic, *The Introduction to the Study of the Law of the Constitution*,[318] presents the characteristics of the English rule of law as involving "three distinct though kindred conceptions": legal equality ("the universal subjection of all classes to one law administered by the ordinary Courts"; the state as such has the position of an individual in any legal proceeding); the 'inductive' character of English constitutionalism (the general principles of the constitution derive gradually and spontaneously from adjudication "as to the rights of given individuals," so that individual rights are the source of the constitution rather than the opposite); and, most importantly, the avoidance of arbitrariness by virtue of the fact that "no man is punishable or can be made to suffer in body or goods except for a distinct breach of law established in the ordinary legal manner before the ordinary Courts of the land."[319] For Dicey, as for Locke, legislation is essentially a rule with normative force, addressed to the individual. The primary implementation mechanism is a court (conversely, law is defined as "any rule which will be enforced by the courts"). In consequence, the executive (the government) is reduced to a ministerial (non-discretionary) role: "[The rule of law] means…the absolute supremacy or predominance of regular law as opposed to the influence of arbitrary power, and excludes the existence of arbitrariness, of prerogative, or even of wide discretionary authority on the part of the government."[320] Dicey presented the essential legal elements of the English constitution in a somewhat duplicative manner. They resided in the sovereignty of Parliament, the rule of law, and the inductive-incremental development of the constitution itself by means of adjudications on rights rather than, as was the case on the Continent, by deduction from pre-established rules.

One of the main considerations which he thought distinguished starkly British law from the continental system of administrative law, whose very name was

---

[316] Paul R. Verkuil, "Crosscurrents in Anglo-American Administrative Law," 27 *Wm. & Mary L. Rev.* 685 (1986), 686: "In his influential 1908 treatise, A. V. Dicey, Vinerian Professor of English Law, effectively interred the idea of administrative law in England by denying its existence."

[317] For a more sympathetic reception, *see*, for instance, John A. Rohr, "Dicey's Ghost and Administrative Law," 34 (1) *Administration and Society* 8–31 (March 2002).

[318] A. V. Dicey, *Introduction to the Study of the Law of the Constitution* (Indianapolis: Liberty Fund, 1982 (1915)).

[319] *Id.*, p. 110.

[320] *Ibid.*, p. 120.

according to him unknown to common lawyers in "countries which, like the United States, derived their civilization from English sources" (as he famously put it, "the want of a name arises at bottom from our non-recognition of the thing itself"), was equality of all subjects before the law. No special legislation and no privileges would be acceptable under the English Constitution. A public servant would come before the court like a private person; if if he should act outside the limits of his power, with no authority, then official status alone would not bind the court in any way.[321] There was in England no public interest in the sense that the administration would sit in independent judgment on it, like a court of law. The interest of the state would be decided by the court on an equal basis with and in opposition to the interest of the individual. Dicey, when condemning the *droit administratif* of France, was fully aware of (and had in fact laudatory words with respect to) the evolution of the French Council of State into a judicial body bound by a consistent system of principle and precedent. It was rather the principle of the state being given special status as a guardian of the public interest that he mostly reviled.[322] Martin Shapiro, describing Dicey's position, sums it up aptly, as follows: "Government could not act against individuals when it pleased, how it pleased, or for whatever reason it pleased. It could only act according to preexisting general laws passed by a representative body like Parliament or Congress. For Dicey, one of the central features of the rule of law was that, when a dispute arose between government and an individual about whether government had acted according to law, that dispute would be submitted to the regular courts as a normal law suit. The government would be treated as simply one of the parties, granted no more consideration by the judge than any other party. In this way, the rule of law could be enforced on government as it was on individuals, by the courts."[323]

What held these assumptions together was a concept of legislation that would soon become untenable. The law can be generally characterized as a rule if legislation is in fact most of time limited to the regulation of questions of rights as between individuals (torts, property, contracts) or claims of wrong by the state against an individual (criminal law). Dicey defined, after all, law and legislation as being one and the same thing, namely "any rule which will be enforced by the courts." What would soon happen was that the first element of his constitutional paradigm (sovereignty of Parliament) would enter into conflict with the second (the Rule of Law), posing big problems to the third (adjudication).

In 1915, Dicey would write an article entitled suggestively "The Development of Administrative Law in England," in which he made the observation that a recent

---

[321] "[An English official] who exceeds the authority given him by the law incurs the common law responsibility for his wrongful act; he is amenable to the authority of the ordinary courts." *Law of the Constitution 389*.

[322] Martin Shapiro, *Who Guards the Guardians-Judicial Control of Administration* (Athens and London: Georgia University Press, c1988), at p. 37: "What condemned continental administrative law in the eyes of English liberals was that it provided a special status for the state."

[323] *Id.*, at p. 36.

decision of the House of Lords, *Local Government Board v. Arlidge*,[324] had been "a considerable step to the introduction among us of something like the *droit administratif* of France."[325] *Arlidge* dealt with an order of the Hampstead Borough Council that had closed a dwelling house as "unfit for human habitation," based on the authority given borough councils by the Housing and Town Planning Act of 1909. Arlidge followed the procedure in the act and appealed to the Local Government Board (a government department headed by a Minister), which had been given power by the act to determine its procedures as to appeals, provided that appeals were not dismissed without holding a public inquiry. A public inquiry was subsequently held by an inspector appointed by the board, who then made a report confirming the borough council's decision (the closing order). Arlidge repaired the house, again appealed, and after another public inquiry the order was again confirmed. Arlidge had asked to be given reasons (to see the report made), to have the actual decision maker in the board disclosed to him, and to be authorized to present his case orally (to be heard). He had been denied all these requests and sought *certiorari* on these grounds. On appeal in the House of Lords he ultimately lost his case. The Lords decided that since the Minister, the head of the board, was politically responsible to Parliament, members of the board were not compelled to act like judges.

The problem with this argument, according to Dicey, was that property being a common law right, an interference with it, albeit in exercise of—to use the American consecrated term, for purposes of comparison and reminder—police power, was understood as requiring the highest substantive and procedural (natural justice) protections. The common law had functioned on the understanding, expounded so forcefully by Dicey's classic, that interferences with rights would be diminished by the protection of the full set of substantive and procedural guarantees awarded by the judicial process. Conversely, non-normative issues, such as claims of privilege (for instance a liquor license) and political matters (for instance a deportation order) would meet with minimal judicial interference with the decision maker, since they are discretionary in their nature. Bringing in a political justification for non-disclosure, the House of Lords had upset settled understandings as to what would be political and discretionary and what would be legal and determined according to the judicial process: "This reference to the so-called ministerial responsibility is somewhat unfortunate. It is calculated to promote the belief that that such ministerial responsibility is a real check upon the action of a Minister or Cabinet when tempted to evade or override the law of the land. But any man who will look plain facts in the face will see in a moment that ministerial liability to the censure not in fact by Parliament, nor even by the House of Commons, but by the party majority who keep the Government in office, is a very feeble guarantee indeed against the action which evades the authority of the

[324] [1915] AC 120 (Eng. HL).

[325] 31 *Law Quarterly Review* (1915) 148–153.

law courts. A Cabinet is rarely indeed tempted to defy the wishes of the majority of the House of Commons, since it is the support of that majority which keeps the cabinet in office. If a Minister or the Government is tempted to evade in some form or other the authority of the law, the temptation must arise from the fact that that his action is desired, or at lowest will not be censured, by the majority of the House of Commons."[326]

Since the sovereignty of Parliament is legally unlimited, in face of a statute granting discretion explicitly, the judge is essentially bound by the legislative command and limited to the testing of the outward limits of discretion, hence the Diceyan dilemma of reconciling the rule of law with the sovereignty of parliament in the case of a head-on collision.[327]

Dicey and Hewart are commonly associated by contemporary critics, their positions deemed to be part and parcel of the same, ultraconservative and knee-jerk reflexive enmity to the modern welfare state. Yet the two had distinct standpoints and their arguments have different conceptual-legal stakes and weights. Hewart's shrill cries of delegation and acrimonious accusations of bureaucratic conspiracies were then (and are all the more in hindsight) a mere ideological interjection, a product of failure to understand change and seek legitimate ways to adapt to it. But not all worries about the future are expressions of desire to go back to a condemned past and not all irreversible changes have to be welcomed simply because they are inevitable. A few Victorian idiosyncrasies notwithstanding, Dicey's dilemma is in its core a subtle and emphatically legal argument, and insofar it is still fully pertinent to us today. What he observed was a blurring of the received legal categories and the impact of this confusion of distinctions and criteria on judicial practices. Once policy and political considerations are accepted as legitimate arguments in the judicial determination of rights, the end-result may well be a legalization of discretionary policy and politics. But it could equally signify the politicization of justice and the instrumentalization of freedom.

[326] *Id.*, at p. 152: *See*, in the same key, *Dyson v. Attorney-General* [1911] 1 K.B. 410, at p. 424: "If ministerial responsibility were more than the mere shadow of a name, the matter would be less important, but as it is, the Courts are the only defence of the liberty of the subject against departmental aggression." (per Farwell, L.J.).

[327] "In the Diceyan, common law understanding of the rule of law, the legislature has a monopoly on law-making authority, while the judges have a monopoly on interpretation....However, the judges' interpretive monopoly is still subordinate to the monopoly on legislation. Judicial interpretations of the law must always defer to clear expressions of parliamentary intent-the common law will give way to legislation, no matter how offensive the statute is to the values of the common law or to moral sensibilities. Indeed, the common law has ultimately the same extra-legal guarantees against legislative disruption as general moral sensibilities, for when the common law does have to give way to statute, the remedy for the disruption to its order is to be found outside the law, in the source from which the disruption emanated-in democratic politics."David Dyzenhaus and Evan Fox-Decent, "Rethinking the Process/Substance Distinction: *Baker v. Canada*" 51 *U. Toronto L. J.* 193 (Summer, 2001), at p. 198.

3.2.4 France: Law as the Expression of General Will

> Mais là ou n'existe pas une semblable constitution, la délégation du pouvoir législatif, quoique critiquable rationellement, ne soulèvera point d'objection juridique, elle sera possible en droit. Dans un tel milieu en effet le pouvoir législatif statue librement, souverainement, sur n'importe quel objet. Il peut modifier les relations des divers pouvoirs publics, il peut librement retoucher et modifier la Constitution. Ne peut-il faire moins, intervertir momentanément les rôles que celle-ci a distribués?
>
> Adhémar Esmein, "De la délégation du pouvoir législatif-A l'occasion du projet dit 'des pleins pouvoirs' presente par M. Crispi au Parlement italien" *Revue politique et parlementaire*, 1894[328]

> En effet, la délégation du pouvoir législatif, comme de toute autre prerogative que la Constitution attribue aux Chambres, est juridiquement impossible.
>
> Adhémar Esmein, *Éléments du droit constitutionnel français et comparé* 1921[329]

France's archetypal constitutional model of legislation, inherited in equal measure from the legacy of Rousseauian sovereignty-related aphorisms, the inexperience in governing of the 1789 revolutionists, and the post-revolutionary distrust of the king, rests on the idea of a complete subordination of the executive to the command of the law. The decree of November 3, 1789 already provided that the executive could not adopt any self-standing normative ordinances, but only enforcement "proclamations" consistent with the letter of the law.[330] Even the regulation of the military and navy was done exhaustively through parliamentary legislation. This attempt to suppress all independent executive decree-making authority culminated in the Jacobin constitution of 1793, whereby the whole exercise of state power had to be legislatively mediated by the National Convention. The force of facts eventually took revenge on this extreme example of doctrinal Rousseauian purism and power soon completely reverted to the Committee of Public Safety. This is, to cite George Jellinek's wisely prudent words, a good if particularly brutal example for the way in which "constitutions and statutes cannot decree away the nature of the State, since they alone cannot gainsay that legislation (*Gesetzgebung*) can never replace government (*Regierung*)."[331] Albeit such an extreme understanding of the supremacy of parliamentary legislation yielded to more pragmatic arrangements, this general principle remained an undisputed central tenet of French

---

328 [Where such a constitution does not exist, the delegation of legislative power, however criticizable rationally, will raise no juridical objection, and thus will be legally permissible. In such a [constitutional] context the legislative power disposes liberally, in a sovereign manner, over whichever subject. It can modify the relationship between the public powers, it can freely amend and change the constitution. Why could it not also do less and momentarily interchange the roles assigned by the said constitution?]

329 [In effect, the delegation of legislative power, just like the delegation of any other constitutional prerogative, is juridically impossible.].

330 Georg Jellinek, *Gesetz und Verordnung: staatsrechtliche Untersuchungen auf rechtsgeschichtlicher und rechtsvergleichender Grundlage* (Freiburg I.B.: Mohr, 1887), p. 85 ff.

331 *Id.*, at p. 90.

constitutionalism. When Charles X tried in 1830 to break with constitutional conventions and common understandings and suspend the freedom of the press by ordinance, based on Article 14 of the *Charte constitutionnelle* of 1814, the result was in fact a huge public outcry, revolution, the ousting of the king, and the instauration of the July Monarchy. The reviewed Charter of Louis-Philippe explicitly limited the ordinance-making power of the monarch to provisions that would neither suspend nor derogate from the law ("sans pouivor jamais ni suspendre les lois elles-mêmes ni dispenser de leur exécution").

The two mottoes at the beginning of this section are excerpts from two works of the famous French constitutionalist Adhémar Esmein, in which he advanced the argument that, unlike the sovereign parliament of England, the French one was bound by the constitution (the 'constitutional laws,' in fact) of 1785. He was relying, in support of his claim, on the express grant of power in the *Loi constitutionnelle du 25 fevrier 1785, rélative à l'organisation des pouvoirs publics*, which read, similar to the U.S. Constitution Vesting Clause of Art. I: "Le pouvoir législatif s'exerce par deux assemblées: la Chambre des députés et le Sénat." ("The legislative power shall be exercised by the two houses, the Chamber of Deputies and the Senat.") He was also relying on the precedent in the 1795 Directorial Constitution, whose Art. 45 expressly prohibited delegation: "En aucun cas, le Corps législatif ne peut déléguer à un ou plusieurs de ses membres, ni à qui que ce soit, aucune des fonctions qui lui sont attribuées par la présente Constitution." ("Under no circumstances shall the Legislative Body delegate, either to one or a plurality of its members, or to any other body, either of the functions which are attributed to it by the present Constitution.") That meant, for most French theorists, that executive legislation, in the sense of autonomous normative decree-making power, would be possible only as a strictly delineated exception. The claim had grounding in constitutional history and practices. But most of all Esmein relied, just like his English colleagues, on a normative ideal and practice of legislation, which would be soon put to the test.

The Great Depression brought about the practice of *décrets-lois*, law-decrees, rules of derogatory force, through which statutory provisions could be amended or abrogated. The decree-laws were first used during the WWI and afterwards entrusted to the Poincaré government during the transition to peace-time conditions. They 'entered into normality' during and after the overproduction crisis.[332] A *décret-loi* is based on an initial authorization by the parliament through a *loi de pleins pouvoirs*, authorizing the government to legislate within the confines of a defined subject-matter and prior deadline. With the passage of time, the domain of authorization became more generous and the parliamentary checks more symbolic. While the initial procedure provided for control by obligatory ratification and hence parliamentary incorporation (if the decree laid before parliament were

[332] *See* Bourdeau 1995, at pp. 366–385.

approved) into the legislative order, this practice was soon to be abandoned in fact.[333]

As mentioned, according to the traditional logic of post-revolutionary France, the executive enjoyed almost no independent normative decree-making power, except for limited domains like rules of administration and colonial matters. Private rights would be determined by *loi* and only secondary or effective implementing measures could be determined by *règlements d'administration publique* (decree of public administration). As the laws started 'delegating' in matters traditionally considered the domain of legislation, the cleavage between the normative (and constitutional) constraint on legislation (*loi materielle*) and the reality of formal legislation (*loi formelle*) whose actual substantive content was in fact fleshed out by the executive gave rise to a set of both constitutional-theoretical and practical legal quagmires. The 'constitutional theory,' as represented in constitutional theory by Esmein, considered delegations as flat-out unconstitutional.[334]

Another set of opinions maintained that enabling laws were not 'delegations of legislative power' but in fact 'attributions of competence' and thus permissible (this playing around the problem by means of linguistic labeling is redolent of the American debates discussed above). To wit, Léon Duguit, the main exponent of this position, argued nonetheless that a number of constitutional limitations would need to restrict the scope and content of the enabling act, thus: (1) the criminalization of conduct; (2) taxation; restriction on individual liberty in the general sense and comprising physical liberty, freedom of contact, commercial freedom, freedom of work; (3) restrictions on property.[335]

A third set of positions claimed that *delegations* were in fact a form of *legislation*. In the logic of this standpoint on the matter, if executive decrees passed under the authority of an enabling act would be considered a form of delegated legislation, this would in effect mean that no judicial review of administrative action was

---

[333] As Maurice Duverger describes the evolution: "[C]elui-ci [the parliament] ne veut pas prendre de responsabilite à cet égard, sachant qu'il est impossible d'abroger les décrets-lois et n'acceptant pas de les cautioner. Les décrets-lois continuent donc à s'appliquer sans être ratifiés." Also, further "Le procédé des décrets-lois est contraire à la Constitution, car les compétences ne se délèguent pas en droit public: le Parlement n'a pas le droit de déléguer son pouvoir legislatif au gouvernement. La nécessité pousse à modifier ainsi la Constitution par l'usage, par la coutume, et les décrets-lois finissent par être considérés comme normaux." Maurice Duverger, *Le système politique français* (Paris: Presses Universitaires de France, 1990), pp. 125–126. *Also see* a more thorough legal analysis in Joseph Barthélemy and Paul Duez, *Traité de droit constitutionnel* (Paris: Librairie Dalloz, 1933), "Le Règlement," pp. 772–782. *See also*, more generally, Otto Kirchheimer, "Decree Powers and Constitutional Law in France under the Third Republic," 34 (6) *American Political Science Review* 1104 (Dec., 1940).

[334] The common problem is of course specifying what delegation means in a given context, given that a certain amount of discretion is indispensable.

[335] Léon Duguit, "Des règlements faits en vertu d'une compétence donnée au gouvernement par le législateur," *Revue du droit public et de la science politique en France et à l'étranger*, p. 313–349, at p. 327.

available, since the *Conseil d'Etat* could not review the constitutionality of legislation.

The modern evolution of French administrative law and its increasing effectiveness in curbing administrative arbitrariness and executive power, in contrast to the traditional fleetingness of French constitutionalism, do much justice to Otto Mayer's well-known observation that "constitutional law passes, whereas administrative law stays."[336] An action for excess of power (*recours pour excès de pouvoir*) came before the Council of State in 1907, in relation to a government modification of the terms of a public contract made with a number of railroad companies. The government had taken measures by a 1901 decree of public administration, on the legal basis of two laws, of 1842 and 1845, enabling the government to adopt by regulation 'necessary measures for the police, safety, conservation, usage, and exploitation of railroads.' The 1901 decree had modified an earlier *règlement d'administration publique,* from 1846. The railroads argued that the earlier decree had exhausted the legal basis and the government would need to go to the parliament for another enabling act and that their contractual rights, as guaranteed by the earlier regulation, had been infringed. The alternative position would have been that the Council could not review the decree, since it was equivalent in constitutional status to its legislative authorization and thus unreviewable per se in *contentieux administratif.* In *Compagnie des chemins de fer de l'Est et autres*, while rejecting the action of the railroads on merits, the Council, to the dismay of theoretical purists, called the act a legislative delegation and declared the decree annullable as a regulation. It mattered not what the terminology was. As long as an act would emanate from the administration, it would always be reviewable on an 'organic criterion' (*critère organique*), based on the nature of the promulgating organ: "Considering that, whether the acts of the Head of State constituting public administration regulations are carried out by virtue of a legislative delegation and consequently include the full exercise of powers attributed by the legislature to the Government in this particular case, they are however not by virtue of this fact shielded from review, since these are the acts of an administrative authority; and it is the purview of the Council of State, in its jurisdictional capacity, to examine whether the acts adopted by means of public administration regulations are within the limits of legality."[337]

Yet the judicial method, while amenable for determinations of claims of right, cannot be generally expected to solve political and systemic problems, aside from the fact that, as David Currie pointed out, judicial review "is not an end in itself but a means of enforcing (constitutional and statutory) limitations on executive

---

[336] "Verfassungsrecht vergeht, Verwaltungsrecht besteht." Otto Mayer, Deutsches Verwaltungsrecht, 3. Aufl. 1924, Vorwort.

[337] C.E. 6 déc 1907, Rec. 913, concl. Tardieu, reported and commented in M. Long, P. Devolvé, G. Baibant, P. Weil, B. Genevois, *Les grands arrêts de la jurisprudence administrative* (Paris: Sirey (Éd. Dalloz), 10th edition, 1993), pp. 100–105, at p. 100.

authority; if there are no limitations, there is nothing to review."[338] Discussing, in 1931, the implications of the constitutional transformations, which had intervened by means of the changing nature of parliamentary enactments, on a constitutionally tenable concept of law, Raymond Carré de Malberg systematically showed that the only distinctions between legislation (*loi*) and executive (*règlement* or *décret-loi*) remained by then, of necessity, those of a formal (and not a material) nature. In terms of constitutionality, the law prevailed over executive decree by virtue of its superior place in the normative hierarchy and its benefit of spontaneous and initial delimitation of a legislative framework within which the executive would subsidiarily flesh out secondary rules.[339] The end of the Third Republic came about abruptly, through a legislative delegation to Marshall Pétain, giving him power to amend the constitution itself or adopt a new one.[340]

In response to these events, an express constitutional limitation would be thus set forth by Art. 13 of the 1946 Constitution: "L'Assemblée nationale vote seule la loi. Elle ne peut déléguer ce droit." ("The National Assembly has an exclusive right to adopt legislation. It cannot delegate this right.") In spite of this provision, delegation would persist throughout the Fourth Republic. Institutional instability, coupled with the need for efficient government after WWII, gave way to just more elaborate manners of bypassing the constitutional prohibition. The Fourth Republic developed two more delegation instrumentalities: the framework-law (*la loi-cadre*) and the extension of regulatory power (*extension du pouvoir règlementaire*). A framework-law would only set forth the general principles of a particular subject matter, while leaving the manner and details of application to the discretion of the executive. If parliament does not nullify the decrees within a certain deadline, the decrees would be assimilated with an act of legislation. An 'extension of the regulatory power' is, as revealed by its name, a provisional "de-legislation" of a specific domain. Since the regulatory field is "de-legislated," decrees could even modify the existent legislation in the specified area, since this would proceed by virtue of parliamentary sanction. The justification was that parliament could, at any rate, intervene and override the decree by express legislation. This latter procedure was declared by a 1953 *Avis* of the Conseil d'Etat as within the boundaries set by the Constitution, as long as two conditions were duly observed: (1) delegation should not impinge on matters which are reserved by constitution or tradition to legislation (most importantly fundamental rights, reserved to the legislative domain by the 1789

---

338 Currie 1994, at p. 131.

339 Raymond Carré de Malberg, *La loi, expression de la volonté générale* (Paris : Sirey, 1931), at p. 74 : "A un premier point de vue déjà, il ressort du concept actuel de la loi que la puissance législative n'est pas susceptible en soi d'être déléguée. D'après la Constitution, elle a, en effet, pour l'un de ses caractères spécifiques d'être une puissance initiale, s'exerçant spontanément, d'un seul jet, et d'une façon autonome. Une puissance déléguée ne peut donc plus être de la puissance législative. Ainsi, dès que l'on constate que le pouvoir réglementaire ne peut se mettre en mouvement qu'à la suite de et en vertu d'une habilitation, il devient manifeste que le règlement ne rentre plus dans la notion constitutionnelle de pouvoir législatif."

340 Ross 1958.

Declaration and by the Preamble to the 1946 Constitution); and (2) the delegation could not be completely open-ended, as to effect an abdication. Yet delegation went on unabated and the end of the Fourth Republic witnessed even a revival of the particularly disreputable Third Republic practice of *décrets-lois*.

3.2.5 Legislative Reservation in Germany-State and Society

> Je weniger die Teilhabe am Staate sich verwirklichte, desto wichtiger wurde die Freiheit vom Staate.[341]
>
> Ernst Forsthoff, *Deutsche Verfassungsgeschichte der Neuzeit* (1961)

3.2.5.1 Legislative Reservation in the Constitutional Monarchy: The Advance of Society

Old Germanic law defined law-making as resting on an agreement between king or emperor and estates. One of Charles the Bald's *Capitularia* contains thus the indicative sentence: "Law is made by the consent of the people upon the institution of the king." (*Lex consensus populi et constitutione regia fit.*). The king could, on his own authority, edict only "administrative regulations" (*Amtsrecht*) but not law proper (*Volksrecht*), i.e., rules of a legislative character, immediately binding the subjects.[342]

As the political power of the emperor diminished, the application of this principle became a gradually exacerbated feature of the Holy Roman Empire. Towards the end, especially after the Peace of Augsburg, the Imperial Estates (*Reichsstände*) began increasingly to claim not just a right to express consent to the imperial "institution" but also full authority to participate in the act of legislation proper. Eventually, even the decree-making authority of the emperor was relegated to exceptional and restricted implementing orders.[343] With the rise of territorial sovereignty and the correlative decline of the political relevance of the Empire into what Pufendorf would emotively describe as a "monstrosity", territorial rulers acquired a general law-making competence, which was only unequally and to a relatively limited extent checked by the local estates.[344] Indeed, territorial sovereignty and legislative competence begin to be associated in characteristically

---

[341] The less political participation in the State was actualized, the more important was freedom from the State.

[342] Edictum Pistense, a. 864, § 6, In Jellinek, at p. 101.

[343] *Id.*, pp. 101–102.

[344] The rationalization of German absolutism was however checked, until the end of the Holy Roman Empire of German Nation, by the imperial courts, which functioned on a medieval (acquired rights) template. Grimm, *Recht und Staat*, p. 88.

modern absolutist fashion; the eighteenth century jurist Johann Jacob Moser conflates them in his definition: "Who has territorial sovereignty (*Landeshoheit*), has law-making authority (*Gesetzgebungsrecht*), and who has legislative authority, has territorial sovereignty."[345] Exceptionally, in certain principalities, the provincial medieval parliaments managed to preserve portions of autonomy and assert participatory rights. In Eastern Frisia, Württemberg, and Mecklenburg, for instance, the estates exercised their rights to assent to (or in the case of Ostfriesland to take part in the making of) new legislation or amendments of old laws.[346] But, on the whole, no clear and general principle can be derived with respect to the distinction, according to either subject-matter or normative form, between the independent law-making authority of the territorial rulers and law-making with the consent of the medieval estate parliaments, respectively.

Under the influence of the Enlightenment and modern natural law ideas, commentators seek to impose on this disordered, partly medieval and partly modern framework, a coherent template, some rational normative criterion against the yardstick of which the incoherent growth of practices could be evaluated and rationally rearranged. Already in the period of German enlightened absolutism, the idea of separation between the person of the sovereign monarch and the state as sovereign entity led gradually to a general theoretical requirement of the supremacy of law and, consequently, of powers organized and divided according to natural law dictates. But none of the compartmentalizations of state power into analytically distinguished functions or the definitions of law according to an abstract criterion seemed to explain or account for reality, in an even remotely satisfactory way. The early defenses of separation of powers have all the rationalistic pathos of the Enlightenment. In Kant's *Metaphysics of Morals*, for emblematic example, the state is the ideal unity of the three separated powers, each of which is in turn "a moral person" characterized by a dominant trait. The legislative is "irreproachable" (*untadelig*), the executive is "irresistible" (*unwiderstehlich*), whereas the "sentence of the Supreme Judicature" (*Rechtsspruch des obersten Richters (supremi iudicis)*) is marked by its finality (*unabänderlich*). These powers complement each other and act in concert in the form of a syllogism. The legislative rule constitutes the major premise, enforcement of the rule by the executive the minor premise, whereas the judge concludes the syllogism with a right decision in a given case.[347] But even as late as the early nineteenth century, Carl von Rotteck's *Lehrbuch des Vernunftrechts und der Staatswissenschaften* (*Textbook of Rational Natural Law and State Sciences*), for instance, divides state functions into only two, law-making, which would proceed by establishing rules in an abstract way (according to concepts, *nach Begriffen*) and administration, which only executes, enforces those rules according to context and individual circumstance. This division

[345] *Ibid.* p. 103.

[346] *Ibid*, note 15, p. 104.

[347] Immanuel Kant, *Metaphysik der Sitten*, § 45–49.

appeared to him inevitable, since "every directive proceeding from the State power is either of a general and temporally indefinite nature (i.e., thought of in a abstract conceptual way) or constitutes a definite act (adjusted to a concrete case)."[348]

All such abstract logical exercises could of necessity lead nowhere, since they were too remote from both the reality of things and the practical requirements of government. To wit, defining law as a general act and dividing all state functions into administrative and legislative would have at the same time qualified some universal attributions of the legislature as administrative-executive in nature (most notably, the budgetary ones) and completely deprived the executive of its traditional, prerogative regulatory powers over the military, bureaucracy, and foreign affairs.[349] But, whereas the extreme theoretical demands of rational natural law (*Vernunftrecht*) were ricocheting from the reality of state practices, the old medieval methodology of defining state functions according to the traditional attributes of sovereignty (*regalia*) had also become unsatisfactory and anachronistic. Meanwhile, a constitutive rearrangement of government and thus the constitutional decision on the legislative reservation was, so to speak, left in suspension by the force of events. This serves to introduce a German particularity, namely a steady and deep disconnect between the requirements of constitutionalism and the representations of legislation and separation of powers in state and constitutional theory, on the one hand, and the reality of state practice, on the other. Georg Jellinek famously and insightfully quipped that: "all life scorns upon the categories forced upon it from the outside."[350] But this rift, in German constitutional context, is not just a result of the general difficulty of seizing upon the diversity of life through abstract-rational tools; it reflects in equal measure the late, fragmentary, and unequal path of constitutional modernization.

The general ambiguity is already apparent in the way in which legislation is referred to in the late eighteenth century Prussian codification, the *Allgemeines Landrecht für die preußischen Staaten,* where the provisions regarding law-making are products of both late absolutist conceptions (law is the emanation of sovereign will) and the contractualist natural law/rational law representations of the age (law as a general enactment, law as a rule directed at the attainment of common welfare, etc.).[351] In the final text, references to police regulations and legislation are interchangeable. Paragraph 6 of the codification defines thus the right to "give or abrogate laws and general police regulations as well as the authoritative interpretation of the law" as a sovereign right (*Majestätsrecht*), whereas paragraph 7 gives the head of state the right to authorize exemptions (*privilegia*) from the general laws. Under the influence of the French Revolution, moreover, the initial, more liberal

---

[348] Böckenförde, *Gesetz und gesetzgebende Gewalt*, at p. 108.

[349] *See* general discussion on the nineteenth century German and Austrian state law (*Staatsrecht*) commentaries regarding the proper constitutional "nature" of budget laws (legislative or executive-administrative) in Georg Jellinek, *Gesetz und Verordnung*, pp. 169–177.

[350] "Alles Leben spottet der von Außen an dasselbe herangebrachten Kategorien." *Id.*, at p. 223.

[351] *Id.*, pp. 79 ff.

versions were drastically curtailed and extensively qualified, which resulted in further incoherence. The 1784 draft (*Entwurf eines allgemeinen Gesetzbuchs für die preußischen Staaten*), for instance, defines (§ 50) "the general welfare" as basis for or reason of the laws.[352] The version from 1791 already rewrites this sentence in a more cautious, statist manner. Now, the corresponding paragraph reads: "The welfare of the State in the first place, and of its inhabitants more particularly, is the purpose of the civil society and the general aim of the laws."[353] In the final, 1794 version of the code, the paragraph is elided altogether, as are many other similarly more liberal provisions in earlier drafts.[354] Further reactionary reflexes would delay the evolution of constitutionalism as such and the development of German parliamentarism into a characteristically modern form.

The German Federal Act, adopted as legal basis for the confederation established after the defeat of Napoleon, declaimed pithily: "All Confederal states will be given an estate-based constitution (*landständische Verfassung*)" (Art. 13). The fact that no specific term, procedure or guideline was attached to the mandate, together with the multifarious interpretations to which the phrase *landständische Verfassung* lent itself, made it from the very onset unclear whether the requirement was for a return to the old estate-based, medieval representations or for the adoption of new, modern constitutions with modern representative legislatures.[355] Even though the constitutions newly adopted until 1848 were a partial break from the past (and some states, especially the southern principalities, introduced modern representative assemblies), they only qualified absolutism, did not usher in a fully new arrangement. Most importantly, this qualification introduced a new type of legitimacy but did not displace the old. Representation simply took an uncomfortable and uncertain second place right next to the monarchic principle. By contrast, in the rest of Europe, even the restoration of monarchy after revolutions, stylistic and declamatory paraphernalia notwithstanding, had to acknowledge and accommodate a completely new order of legitimacy. To wit, the struggle for supremacy had been settled with finality in England during the Civil War. The initial Stuart restoration only delayed an inevitable course of events and, immediately after the Glorious Revolution, William and Mary already took the throne upon clear constitutional conditions set down by Parliament. Even though, in form, the returning Louis XVIII only condescended to bestow ("octroyer") a constitutional charter on the French, those pretensions were made in full and cautious knowledge that he had inherited a different France after the Revolution.[356] More revealing still,

[352] § 50 Das allgemeine Wohl ist der Grund der Gesetze.

[353] § 77 Das Wohl des Staates überhaupt, und seiner Einwohner insbesondere, ist der Zweck der bürgerlichen Vereinigung, und das allgemeine Ziel der Gesetze.

[354] In Conrad, *Die geistigen Grundlagen*, at p. 47. *See* general discussion in same, *passim.*

[355] Forsthoff, *Deutsche Verfassungsgeschichte*, 93 ff.

[356] *See* Jellinek, *Gesetz und Verordnung*, p. 94: "Der ganze Bau der Staatsverwaltung bleibt so bestehen, wie ihn die Revolution vorbereitet und bereits das Consulat ausgeführt hatte. Insofern war es allerdings eine hohle Phrase, wenn Ludwig XVIII. die aus seiner Gnade entspringende Verfassung anknüpfen wollte an die legislatorische Thätigkeit seiner Vorfahren von Ludwig dem Dicken bis Ludwig XVI."

Napoleon III and nineteenth century Italian kings were reigning "by the Grace of God *and* the Will of the Nation."[357] Obversely, in all the German states, even those that had been exposed to French-modeled constitutionalism prior to the defeat of Napoleon and the Restoration, the monarchical principle was paramount and undisplaced. The Bavarian Constitution from 1818 formulated the principle, in Title II, §1, as follows: "The King is the Head of the State and joins in his person all the rights of state power, exercising them according to the stipulations established by him in this constitutional document."[358] Under these general conditions, legislation was, in principle and residually, the product of the sovereign's will, to which as a matter of exception the consent of the legislature would be required in specified fields. How extensive the portion of authority carved out in this way was differed from place to place, albeit, as a general rule, it is now set forth that laws affecting the property and liberty of the subjects cannot be adopted, abrogated, amended, or authoritatively interpreted without the agreement of the representative assembly or, the estates, respectively. The Constitution of Bavaria provided for instance that: "Without the counsel and agreement of the kingdom's estates no new general law concerning personal freedom or the property of the citizens can be adopted, nor can an existing one be amended, authentically interpreted, or abrogated."[359] Some constitutions further included procedural law and organization law, exceptionally even law concerning the military, in the subject-matters to which the consent of the representatives must be required. In all cases, the right of initiative belonged to the monarch.

The next wave of constitution-making, around and after the 1848 revolution, gave a right of initiative in law-making to the legislatures and generalized the modern representative assembly model.[360] Art. 62 of the 1850 Prussian Constitution provided: "The legislative power shall be exercised jointly by the king and the two houses. The agreement of the king and the houses is necessary in each case," whereas Art. 45 attributed the executive power to the king and expressly recognized the latter's authority to adopt implementing decrees. Nonetheless, legislation proper still remains at this stage an exceptional normative activity and it is relegated to a confined normative domain. This is a result of the fact that the king posseses original decreemaking (legislative) power within the fields that are regarded as executive in their nature, primarily the bureaucracy and the army. Within this area, deemed to constitute the core of the State, legislative and thus judicial interference

---

[357] *Cf.* Dietrich Jesch, *Gesetz und Verwaltung: Eine Problemstudie zum Wandel des Gesetzmäßigkeitsprinzipes* (Tübingen: J.C.B. Mohr (Siebeck), 1961), p. 83.

[358] Grimm, *Deutsche Verfassungsgeschichte*, p. 114 ff.

[359] Böckenförde, *Gesetz und gesetzgebende Gewalt*, p. 71 ff, Grimm, *Deutsche Verfassungsgeschichte*, p. 113 ff., Jellinek, *Gesetz und Verordnung*, p. 110.

[360] The normative division between ordinances and legislation in the imperial constitution of 1871 (*Verfassung des Deutschen Reiches*, commonly referred to as *Bismarksche Reichsverfassung*) reflected the federal partition of power between the Reich and the member states. It is therefore of no relevance to this argument.

is not admissible. A normative dichotomy was thus created, by virtue of which the representative assembly and parliamentary legislation occupied constitutionally a sphere separated from the state proper. The result was a clear-cut delineation between law and discretionary power, legislation and administration, monarchical principle and popular representation, state and society: "Executive and Parliament, State and society, monarch and people are antipodes; both spaces are separated from each other and, in the inner core of their respective purviews, mutually free from encroachments or external influence. The inner space of the executive is free from the society just as the society itself is protected from inroads into the protected area of freedom and property."[361]

3.2.5.2 The Qualified Retraction of the State

As we have already seen in the case of the other jurisdictions, the constitutional guarantee of the classical legislative reservation and therefore the rationality of the fundamental legal distinctions predicated upon it depended not only on the restriction of legislation to a constitutionally specified normative field and subject-matter. It also required, as a "mirror" or flip-side premise, the retraction of the administration and the executive from the field of legislation proper into the confines of their newly defined purview. To put it another way, just as the society and the legislature were constitutionally permitted to carve a defined space of legal regularity into a normative domain previously occupied by the absolutist state, the administration was also constitutionally required to progressively relinquish control over this societally secured area of property and freedom and withdraw to the newly delimited confines of the state.[362] This realignment correspondingly resulted in a clear delineation between law and politics, i.e., between ministerial administration according to the law and discretionary powers unchecked judicially, respectively.

Already in the *Allgemeines Landrecht* one can detect the beginnings of an incipient contradiction or at least clear rift between the older purview of police power, the promotion of general welfare and public felicitousness (*Glückseligkeit*, *cura promovendae salutis*), and the modern constitutional paradigm. In the logic of the latter framework, individual welfare is a matter for individual and social (self-) regulation, whereas the police prerogative of the administration in this respect is reduced to policing *stricto sensu*, i.e., preventing for the future and generally noxious uses of private liberty and property (*cura advertendi mala futura*).[363]

---

[361] Jesch, *Gesetz und Verwaltung*, p. 91.

[362] Thus related and insightfully, Maier, *Die ältere deutsche Staats- und Verwaltungslehre*, p. 248: "Man mag im Nachhinein geneigt sein, festzustellen, dass die Bindung an das Gesetz als generelle abstrakte Norm (und damit die Entstehung einer Verwaltungsrechtswissenschaft, die wesentlich den rechtsstaatlichen Gesetzesvollzug zum Inhalt hatte) erst möglich wurde mit der Eliminierung des Wohlfahrtszwecks und der Beschränkung der Polizei auf bloße Gefahrenabwehr."

[363] Maier, at p. 245.

The tasks of the state are described extensively in the 1794 codification, in the eudaemonistic key characteristic of the absolutist state: "...to ensure for the establishment of institutions, through which the inhabitants are provided with the means and the opportunity to develop their powers and abilities, and to use those powers to the development of their welfare."[364] But the power of police is already defined in a restrictive, modern way, as the authority to protect the public and prevent public nuisances: "The necessary means to preserve public peace, safety, and order (*Erhaltung der öffentlichen Ruhe, Sicherheit, und Ordnung*) and to prevent dangers to the public or individual members thereof constitute the police power (*das Amt der Polizei*)."[365] This rift between the older and newer conception of police will deepen together with the slow process of constitutionalization. Its decisive turning point is the 1882 "Kreuzberg Decision" of the Prussian Superior Administrative Court.[366]

In 1879, the Royal Police Presidium of Berlin had adopted a regulation concerning the protection of a monument erected in 1878, on a slope of the Kreuzberg Hill, to commemorate victory in the anti-Napoleonic Wars of Liberation from 1813 to 1815. The regulation provided for an administrative building approval procedure, so that the view overlooking the city from the foot of the monument and from the city up to the monument would not be obstructed by civil constructions. A landlord whose application for a building permit had been rejected (only the construction of smaller, mansion-type buildings could be authorized on his plot, in order not to block the view) sought judicial redress against the Police Presidium and eventually won. The defendant Police Presidium relied both on the extensive interpretation of the state purview in the *Allgemeines Landrecht* and, more particularly, on two provisions of Title 8, Part 1 according to which "no construction shall be undertaken that would damage or imperil the public good or deface the cities and public squares" (§ 66) and "streets and public squares are not to be narrowed, polluted, or otherwise defaced", respectively. The court observed however that property had become a fundamental right by virtue of the Constitution of the Kingdom of Prussia, whose article 9 read: "Property is inviolable. The use of property can be restricted or property can be taken only for reasons of public utility, against just compensation according to the law, paid in advance or, in exceptional cases, at least preliminarily determined." Accordingly, the police powers of the administration were to be interpreted restrictively, as directed strictly at the attainment of "public order, peace and safety," rather than extending to "ideal goods" and general esthetic

---

[364] § 3 II 13 ("...für Anstalten zu sorgen, wodurch den Einwohnern Mittel und Gelegenheit verschafft werden, ihre Fähigkeiten und Kräfte auszubilden, und dieselben zur Beförderung ihres Wohlstandes anzuwenden.").

[365] § 10 II 7. *See* discussion in Peter Badura, *Das Verwaltungsrecht des liberalen Rechtsstaates* (Göttingen: Otto Schwartz & Co., 1967), pp. 34–35.

[366] There are in fact two decisions (*Erkenntnisse*), of June 10, 1880 and June 14, 1882, respectively. In *Preußisches Verwaltungsblatt* (1) 1879/1880, S.401 ff. and (3) 1881/1882, S. 361 ff. They are cited here from the reprint in *Deutsches Verwaltungsblatt* DVBl, 1985, 216, 219.

values. An extension of police power exercise to the views of an institution about the general esthetic harmony of the monument's architectural surroundings was also held to be unjustified. The provisions regarding the "defacement" of public spaces did not imply an administrative legal prerogative of appreciating the beauty of the city but rather had to be restrictively interpreted, as referring strictly to any given building as such and applying solely to "a serious defacement" caused by a particular construction. If the state wanted to undertake an extensive restriction of property, such as the one impugned by the plaintiff, it could only do so by means of either seeking special legislation in parliament or by way of the regular expropriation procedure set forth in the Takings Law, under a showing of public utility and the advance payment of just compensation.[367]

Thus was decided with finality that the administration could not intervene in the sphere of society, i.e., in the constitutionally-secured area of "liberty and property" other than in calculable, legislatively predetermined ways. In 1895, the first edition of Otto Mayer's epoch-making administrative law textbook coined the defining trait of the rule of law administration and hence also determined the proper scientific object of administrative law: *Eingriffsverwaltung* (intervention administration). By evident contrast with the police administration of the absolutist state, the actions of the rule of law state in the field of administration are defined as strictly measurable against the yardstick of parliamentary legislation, by means of applications for judicial review. Furthermore and correlatively, Mayer defines legislation as generally and essentially coextensive with legal norm (*Rechtssatz*), namely with general rules of normative force addressed to the individual: "The most important feature of the constitutionally valid legislation. . .is its intrinsic capacity of speaking in norms. The legal norm is a normative determination addressed to everyone, defining what action is right or wrong, in terms of a generally described factual hypothesis."[368] The imagery as such is revealing, such as for instance when the author describes, through a suggestive analogy, the intervention of the administration in the private sphere, on the basis of the law. A law is not just a restriction of administrative power but also "an enlargement of it to an area, from which until that moment it had been excluded; *the door is therefore opened to the administration*, so that it now can act correspondingly *in that particular, previously closed space*. This effect is attached intrinsically to each law that undertakes an interference with liberty and property." [emphases supplied][369] Therefore, in Mayer's account, the archetypal type of administrative action is the administrative act (such as a notice of tax assessment), which interferes in and with the private sphere, on the basis of a clear legislative rule, in a calculable and readily predetermined manner, ultimately subject to a thorough judicial determination.

---

[367] *Id.*, p. 222.

[368] Otto Mayer, *Deutsches Verwaltungsrecht*, dritte Auflage, unveränderter Nachdruck (Berlin: Duncker & Humblot, (1924) 2004), at p. 66.

[369] *Id.*, p. 72.

This constitutional-administrative withdrawal of the state from the field of society proper was however, as the title of this subsection indicates, a qualified one. The final cause of this qualification is the general historical evolution of the country, its *Sonderweg,* as an overused cliché goes. Unlike in the rest of Europe, both the emancipation of private law and society from feudal restrictions and the general liberalization of the economy were undertaken to a large extent by the state, namely, by the in roughly equal measures liberally- and state-minded bureaucracy. The limitation of the state was in Germany largely self-imposed and, especially in Prussia, the progressive emancipation of the private sphere from public control constituted a top-down, bureaucratically engineered process: "In contrast with England or France, no coalition between natural law and society against the monarch ever came into being [in Germany]. A pact was made rather between the officialdom and philosophy, whereas the latter became a philosophy of state (*Staatsphilosophie*), in both senses of this term."[370] But even in Southern Germany, where this emancipation was ostensibly undertaken in the first two decades of the nineteenth century, by introducing modern-style representative assemblies and rights charters, the relative lack of attributions rendered parliamentarism rather decorative. Its lack of real power and dearth of responsibilities meant in practice that it could, in Ernst Forsthoff's caustic characterization, "keep arguing on the cheap (*billig räsonieren können*)."[371]

By the same token, it was precisely due to the neutral but unquestionably superior position of the state that the economic impetus of the late nineteenth century could be administratively managed and extensive social protectionism could be introduced.[372] In fact, interventionism by way of trade protectionism and the state support of extensive cartelization (a phenomenon Ralf Dahrendorf appositely called "industrially feudal society") went hand in hand with a peculiar type of social welfare measures (to use Dahrendorf's countervailing quip, the "authoritarian welfare state"). The "New Economic Politics (*Neue Wirtschaftspolitik*)," inaugurated by Bismarck in 1879, through the introduction of the protective tariff, was closely followed by health insurance (1883), accident insurance (1884), and invalidity and old age insurance (1889) legislation.[373] This idiosyncratic German mixture of economic interventionism and authoritarian welfarism coupled with a strict separation between state and society had as a direct legal consequence an extensive and systematic neglect of even larger areas of administrative discretionary powers than in other jurisdictions. Germany acquired a social welfare and administrative state *avant la lettre,* while preserving the administrative law means of the nineteenth century to control it. The separation of state and society and its correlative legal avatar, the dichotomy of lawful

---

[370] Grimm, *Recht und Staat*, p. 90.

[371] Forsthoff, *Deutsche Verfassungsgeschichte*, p. 110.

[372] *See generally*, Ralf Dahrendorf, *Gesellschaft und Demokratie in Deutschland* (München: Piper & Co., 1965).

[373] Grimm, *Recht und Staat*, pp. 150-151

"intervention administration" vs. purely discretionary executive and administrative attributions not subject to legal control, resulted, along this general evolution of state, economy, and society, in the uncontrolled growth of large areas of administrative action. These zones of state action were fully devoid of judicial supervision or even legal-scientific evaluation: "Where state action is equated with sovereign action, only that kind of exercise of authority which addresses the citizens in a "normative command backed by sanction" (*hoheitlich*) mode fits the theory. Where that was not the case, the purity of the public law was paid for with a narrowing of its view range (*Blickverengung*): all the activities of the state which did not embrace a mandatory form, namely the social welfare functions and the promotion of culture, economic aids, etc., escaped the attention of legal science. Administrative authorities profited from this neglect, since they could thus see themselves to a large extent freed from legal controls."[374]

Even though the separation between the imperial state and the Wilhelmine society was shattered by the Great War,[375] the full constitutional-political import and the greater constitutional and administrative law consequences of the intervening transformations remained obscured during the short-lived Weimar democracy. This occurred on the one hand by virtue of the fact that the presidential office substituted to a certain extent the monarchic principle, and thus the essential constitutional relationship between legislation and administration remained unchanged. Moreover, the state of almost uninterrupted emergency in which the Weimar Constitution operated made recourse to Art. 48 (which enabled the adoption of emergency presidential decrees with legislative force and effect) and open-ended enabling laws inevitable. A parliamentary litany of ever more extensive authorizations preceded the Enabling Law of 1933. The *Ermächtigungsgesetz* of October 13, 1923, for instance, authorized the government of the Reich (in fact the Streseman Cabinet) to adopt delegated legislation derogating from fundamental rights until the end of the cabinet's term or until the dissolution of the political coalition supporting it in the *Reichstag*.

3.3 Rules and Changes

Classical constitutional law presupposed a partial overlap and—within the overlapping area—synonymity between legislation as a practice and the normative category law. This presupposition rested, in terms of its ultimate natural-law

374 Grimm, *Recht und Staat*, p. 103. *See generally*, Badura, *Das Verwaltungsrecht des liberalen Staates* and Forsthoff, *Verwaltung als Leistungsträger*.

375 Forsthoff, *Deutsche Verfassungsgeschichte*, p. 185: "Constitutionally speaking, the autonomy of the civil society (*bürgerliche Gesellschaft*) came to an end during WWI. The clear separation between state and society, the dialectical relationship of togetherness and conflict, between the society based on natural human inequality and the state based on civil equality, did not reemerge after the war."

justifications, on the premise of the "natural" character of society and on a level of societal separation from the state proper. Legally, this paradigm required an intense constitutional protection of the general conditions of societal self-regulation of life, liberty, and property.

The nondelegation proviso expressed this foundational and structural expectation, namely that the essential legal framework regulating private conduct would be formed of normative rules of Lockean pedigree (i.e., prospective, general, stable, and clear rules of private and criminal law). A constitutional limitation of the legislature to the enactment of rules of just conduct further implied that what was deemed essentially private could be categorically and systemically separated from what was considered properly public. From this requirement derived a flip-side implication. Just as the sphere of society, and thus of private conduct, was constitutionally sheltered from excessive political discretion, some areas of state action were premised as irrelevant from a judicial public law standpoint. The relational indifference of public law adjudication towards decisions regarding matters deemed essentially political in nature was expressed by way of categorically distinct tests and standards of review in constitutional and administrative law. This resulted in a clear division between areas of law proper and areas of political discretion and in a cluster of germane legal dichotomies between discretionary and ministerial administration, right and privilege, external affairs and internal matters, hence (ultimately) between the mutually exclusive domains of politics and law.

These foundational divisions were both constitutive of fundamental legal practices and reinforced (in the case of the US Constitution) by means of fundamental law. As we have seen, irrespective of what fundamental presuppositions a paradigmatic constitutional system started from (supremacy of the Constitution in the US, monarchical principle in Germany, parliamentary sovereignty in England and related Westminster jurisdictions, preeminence of legislation coupled with the denial of original normative attributions to the executive in France), these presuppositions eventually yielded to or accommodated in various forms the central requirement of separating neatly in terms of public law adjudication between "law proper" and political (administrative and executive) discretion. This requirement was showcased by the delegation notion and, in the US constitutional context, it was also legally expressed by means of the nondelegation doctrine.

The classical constitutional paradigm had been underpinned by general social, economic, and political premises whose correspondence with reality was increasingly more often and ever more intensely put into question during the second half of the nineteenth and the beginning of the twentieth century. The character of legislation changed, reflecting the political, economic, and social changes brought about by the rise of mass society, mass democracy, and standardized, concentrated late capitalism. Once significant discretionary powers devolved upon the executive and administration to intervene, within the wide interstices of open-ended parliamentary mandates, in fields previously regarded as off-limits to unmediated political decision, an immediate political and ideological reaction was to accuse parliaments. These were castigated for "delegating their powers" in alleged dereliction of their constitutional duties. A later and more sober constitutional reflection attempted to bring constitutionalist presuppositions into line with those phenomenal changes, by imposing on parliamentary enactments a constitutional requirement of specificity and clarity. In the United States, the constitutional reflection and the immediate reaction to contemporaneous change coincided perfectly, as the Supreme Court enforced the nondelegation doctrine in order to sanction specific legislative excesses of the New Deal. In Europe, nondelegation constitutional limitations were a part of the general package of post-WWII "rationalizing" solutions to the pre-war crisis of parliamentarism.

The next chapter of the book will inquire into the functional needs intended to be served by this kind of constitutional rules and into whether limitations on delegation were an adequate constitutional response to the general phenomenon of delegation. The next articulation of this argument will also ask whether and under what conditions a positive rule of fundamental law can compensate for systemic transformations in the nature of constitutionalism.

Chapter 4
Delegation and Contemporary Implications: The Erosion of Normative Limits

> Nicht der Inhalt sucht sich seine Form, sondern die über der inhaltlichen Entleerung des Gesetzesbegriffs erhalten gebliebene Form sucht sich (wieder) den ihr angemessenen Inhalt.[1]
>
> Ernst-Wolfgang Böckenförde, Gesetz und gesetzgebende Gewalt – Von den Anfängen der deutschen Staatsrechtslehre bis zur Höhe des staatsrechtlichen Positivismus (Nachwort, zweite Auflage, 1981 (1958)).

4.1 (Non)Delegation Redux: Constitutionalism, Reason, and Rationality

4.1.1 Nondelegation Redux: The Limits of Reason

But before we proceed further with the inquiry at hand, into whether a positive rule of constitutional law can compensate for systemic changes in the structure of the liberal constitutional state, pause must be taken to retrace, up to this junction, the essential course of the book's argument. Delegation, as we have seen, is a term whose immediate and indiscriminate use in observing and assessing constitutional phenomena is commonly misleading. This is due to the intertwined and irregularly overlapping multiplicity of assumptions informing the notion. Unless careful analytical observance is paid to the relevant presuppositions, proper understanding, and thus also the epistemologically fruitful use of the delegation concept in theoretical debates, can easily be preempted by hasty prejudgment or ideological prejudice.

[1] Not the content searches for its proper form, but rather the emptied form preserved after the disappearance of the initial legislative purview seeks (once again) an appropriate [constitutional] substance.

DOI 10.1007/978-3-642-22330-3_4,

Furthermore and related at a more pragmatic-technical level, the conceptual complexity and irreducibility of the notion inevitably affects the operation of constitutional law rules purporting to check the practice of delegation by way of substantive limitations on the constitutionally permissible scope and precision of parliamentary enactments. If positive legal rules cannot be reduced to their operating principles, adjudication will be unable to devise intelligible tests for consistent application. An extrapolation from Albert Venn Dicey's observation is particularly pertinent in this context, that "every law or rule of conduct must, whether its author perceives this fact or not, lay down or rest upon some general principle. . .if a law fails at attaining its object, the argument lies ready to hand that failure was due to the law not going far enough, i.e., to its not carrying out the principle upon which it is founded to its full logical consequence."[2] The inverse consequence is equally detrimental. An inability to reduce nondelegation rules to a manageable delegation principle will either render the effect of such provisions nugatory or will result in an inconsistent, haphazard application of the rules. Needless to say, this general observation holds true in all legal fields. But its veracity in constitutional law is exponentially compounded by the nature of fundamental legal questions and the premise of constitutionalism as a political-philosophical and historical backdrop for the operation of constitutional law proper. What is true in general of legal doctrine (the dependence of written, positive law, on extra-textual notions) is all the more true of constitutional doctrine. The open-ended references of fundamental law provisions render many constitutional law rules and institutions intrinsically reliant, if they are to be at all intelligible, on political theory and constitutional history.[3]

Thus, as it was argued throughout the text, the delegation concept, as a foundational notion of modern, normative constitutionalism, must be accounted for by way of tracing its constitutional-philosophical and historical genealogy. The conceptual lineage of delegation, as we have seen, places this construct at the constitutional-philosophical crossroads between older understandings of fundamental law and the modern paradigm. Unlike the pre-modern, "descriptive" and "organic" fundamental law of the Middle Ages and also unlike currently emerging post-modern trends (e.g., more fluid notions such as "governance" or "transnational (societal) constitutionalism"), modern constitutionalism is intrinsically and structurally reliant on the idea of delegation and hierarchically structured, delegation-related patterns of justification. In his book on the constitutive role of the feud in

[2] A.V. Dicey, *Lectures on the Relation Between Law and Public Opinion in England During the Nineteenth Century*, 2d ed. (London: Macmillan, 1962), pp. 41-42, quoted after Robert Bork, *The Antitrust Paradox: A Policy at War with Itself* (New York: The Free Press, 1993 (1978)), pp. 421-422.

[3] *See generally*, on the interdependencies between political theory and constitutional law, Christoph Möllers, *Gewaltengliederung; Legitimation und Dogmatik im nationalen und internationalen Rechtsvergleich* (Tübingen: Mohr Siebeck, 2005) and the abridged and revised version of the argument, *Die drei Gewalten: Legitimation der Gewaltengliederung in Verfassungsstaat, Europäischer Integration und Internationalisierung* (Weilerswist: Velbrück Wissenschaft, 2008).

medieval constitutionalism, Otto Brunner made the observation, particularly apposite to illustrate this point, that "the derivative nature of public authority, the delegation [of the exercise of public power by the sovereign], even if only in the concealed form of a implicitly recognized usurpation, became a characteristic of public law in the modern sense. The comprehension of the delegation sequence fulfilling this derivation of authority is essential to the understanding of the inner structure of the state."[4] In modern meliorist projects, this recognition of an ultimate source of authority, from which all legal and legitimate exercises of public power derive, also entails the presupposition of a profession of faith to the ultimate source of authority ("general will", "the sovereignty of the people"). However, since the will of the delegator is an abstraction and can be manufactured and ascribed fictitiously by the delegate, the chain of delegation becomes a logically inescapable but practically perverse formality. In the logic of constitutionalism, contrariwise, the structure of delegation pervades, as a matter of legality and legitimacy, both the architecture of structures of justification and the logic of fundamental legal relations. Under limited government, all exercises of delegated public power are held in trust and confined within the limits of the specified authorization.

Aside from the observation regarding the centrality of delegation to constitutionalism, a second insight, equally useful to our current inquiry, can be derived from the general analytical context of the quoted fragment. Brunner's general argument regarding the foundational role of the feud in medieval constitutionalism[5] was a retort to the recurring tendency of public law scholars to read modern or contemporary ideological representations into past constitutional realities, rather than seeking to properly understand past realities and concepts in their own terms and according to their own logic. In his study on the law of the feud (*Fehderecht*), he proposed, more particularly, that only an unhistorical and anachronistic understanding of constitutionalism could either regard the Middle Ages as devoid of a constitution or impress retroactively upon that period the procrustean models of nineteenth century liberal constitutionalism ("state", "the rule of law", etc.). To Brunner, such exercises were reductively stultifying and ideologically charged. Thus read in an anachronistic key, everything in the past that did not fit the adventitious modern mold could be disregarded as normatively irrelevant facts,

---

[4] Otto Brunner, *Land und Herrschaft: Grundfragen der territorialen Verfassungsgeschichte Österreichs im Mittelalter* (Wien, Wiesbaden: Rudolf M. Rohrer Verlag, 1959 (vierte, veränderte Auflage)), p. 145: "Ja die Ableitbarkeit, die Delegation, wenn auch selbst in der verstecken Form einer stillschweigend anerkannten Usurpation, wird geradezu zu einem Charakteristiken des öffentlichen Rechts im neuzeitlichen Sinne. Für die Erkenntnis der inneren Struktur dieses Staates ist die Einsicht in den Delegationszusammenhang wesentlich, in dem diese Ableitung sich vollzieht."

[5] The book's supporting historical research is ostensibly restricted to medieval developments in the territories of present-day Austria and Bavaria. But *see* Howard Kaminsky, "The Noble Feud in the later Middle Ages," 177 *Past and Present* 55 (2002), arguing that the essential argument of *Land und Herrschaft* can be easily extrapolated to the constitutional situations of medieval England and France.

lawless brutality, the "rule of the fist" and suchlike. Contrariwise, as Brunner argued, once it is noticed that the exercise of the medieval right to wage feuds had been fettered within a juristically ritualized and highly formalized structure (i.e., formal letter of challenge—*diffidatio*, rules regarding the terms of engagement, the inclusion and exclusion of third parties in the feud, the personal, temporal, and 'subject-matter' exemptions regarding the actual carrying out of the conflict, the formal way of closing disputes—*Urfehde*—and the formalized consequences thereof, etc.), a different conclusion was inescapable. The right to wage feuds had constituted in its constitutional environment the means within the confines and constraints of which a medieval man essentially pursued—ideal-typically—a quest for law and justice. Anachronistic analysis had, according to Brunner, missed the essence of a constitutive element of pre-modern constitutionalism: behind the alleged "law of the fist" stood "one of the strongest moral forces of all social life, namely the passionate sense of justice (*Rechtsgefühl*) of the individual."[6] Whether or not one fully agrees with the historical specifics, the argument draws on a keen insight that applies with equal force to our current inquiry. Thinking about constitutional institutions in abstract terms, defining them by means of *genus proximum* terms of comparison, and approaching them within an anachronistic framework of reference, is an exercise that usually misses the essence of constitutional phenomena.

The notion of delegation that sheds proper light on the contemporary import of positive delegation-related constitutional rules can be unraveled only within the context from which such constitutional limitations arose, that of the conceptual and phenomenal conditions of the possibility of classical constitutionalism. As it was argued here, the normative constitution was from the onset a Janus-faced achievement of the Age of Enlightenment. On the one hand, the project of synthesizing the essential rules of a polity and thus legally predetermining, potentially in perpetuity, the political life of the state, is highly indebted to the dominating philosophical/ideological theme of the eighteenth century. The written constitution poses very intensive demands of and on rationality and, in this respect, normative constitutionalism marked a stark departure from its earlier, "descriptive" and "organic," pre-modern counterparts.[7] On the other hand, as the discussions of Rousseau and Bentham in the first part of the book have argued, the intellectual presuppositions of classical constitutionalism avoided the Enlightenment-derived extremes of reason unbound. Thus, to paraphrase Kant's 1784 metaphor, the "walking aids" of reason (*Gängelwagen der Vernunft*) were not fully removed in the philosophy and practice of liberal constitutionalism.[8] Classical liberal constitutionalism has straddled from the onset the pre-modern belief and systemic presupposition in "natural" or unquestionable boundaries to the operation of rationality and the newly emerging faith in the power of human reason, now liberated

[6] *Id.*, at p. 109.

[7] Grimm 1988, 2005.

[8] Immanuel Kant, "Beantwortung der Frage: Was ist Aufklärung?" in: *Berlinische Monatsschrift*, Dezember-Heft 1784, S. 481-494.

from past hindrances, to master and reshape the world. The normative constitution and the constitutional systems of the late eighteenth and nineteenth centuries managed to reconcile in their operation the inevitable contradictions arising from this antinomy.

As we have seen in the previous section, classical constitutionalism operated, not only at the level of justifications but also in terms of the actual operation of the legal system, on the essentialist presupposition of natural, pre-political—and thus pre-constitutional—limits to state action. This premise was most evident in the review of the US developments. In the American case, the distinction between the core "natural" and "private" rights to personal security, i.e., "a person's legal and uninterrupted enjoyment of his life, his limbs, his body, his health, and his reputation",[9] personal liberty (i.e., freedom from imprisonment or restraint without due process), and property, on the one hand, and, on the other, the legally constructed "public" or "political" rights, can be easily substantiated not just as a matter of theory but also in actual constitutional law practice. The "natural" rights implied full recourse to the protection of the law, in the sense of engaging to their defense the entire panoply of judicial guarantees. Correlatively, the constitutional protection of private rights perceived as pre-constitutional implied as well the presupposition—as of constitutional right—of "Lockean" legislative rules, "a standing rule to live by, common to every one of that society and made by the legislative power erected in it, a liberty to follow my own will in all things where the rule proscribes not and not to be subject to the inconstant, uncertain, arbitrary will of another man."[10] Obversely and by categorical contrast, in the case of the second category, "adjudication" of "political rights" was to be had primarily, if at all, in the political branches. [11] These foundational and structural presuppositions of substantively differentiated degrees of requisite legislative specificity and categorically distinct levels of judicial protection represented precisely the understanding of nondelegation in the classical age of liberal constitutionalism. If looked at against this background of conceptual-historical context, the meanderings and apparent inconsistencies of US constitutional jurisprudence on delegation are relatively easy to reconcile.

The delegation question cannot be answered in formal terms, because the text as such, without the overhanging classical constitutional context and worldview, invites precisely a formal question but is at the same time of very little help in addressing it: "The Federal Constitution is written as if the 'legislative Powers' vested in Congress, the 'executive Power' vested in the President, and the 'judicial Power' vested in the federal courts are Platonic forms. But efforts by modern formalists to define these separate powers founder on the fact that all three branches

---

[9] 1 Blackstone's *Commentaries* 129.

[10] Second Treatise, Par. 22.

[11] Caleb Nelson, "Adjudication in the Political Branches," 107 (3) *Colum. L. Rev.* 559 (April 2007).

perform similar functions."[12] Asking the question in formal terms and across the board resulted throughout the nineteenth century in a constitutional affirmation of the doctrine as such and the correlative denials that it applied to the cases at the bar, whenever the particular provisions impugned did not fit the classical ideal-type of law and legislation 'proper'. As we have seen, the court's nondelegation tests as such were formulated in substantive terms, mirroring the ideal-typical, substantive understanding of legislation as private rule of just conduct that dominated classical constitutional thought. The tests posited parliamentary enactments as self-sufficient rules of just conduct, whose enforcement would be more or less automatic (the executive does not make the rule but determines the factual background upon which enforcement is contingent) or whose implementation would be relatively unproblematic (the implementing decree only "fills in the details").[13]

The point is in need of restatement that this ideal-typical vision of legislation evoked by the courts in fashioning nondelegation tests did not (and did not need to) fully correspond to the reality of legislative practice (to give the most conclusive example, common law rules are "found" by judges). Relatedly, the English developments were edifying, where, as we have seen, accusations of delegation started to be vented precisely when Parliament became a well-functioning, disciplined and industrious law-making machine. The latent but essential question was not the ostensible and formal one, i.e., what kind of legislation should the legislature pass, in the sense of how unspecific a law should be before it would constitute an unconstitutional delegation, but what kind of trespass would automatically trigger a constitutional duty of judicial protection. To put it differently, delegation was understood as unprincipled public intervention in a domain of legal relations regarded as essentially private and presumptively protected by constitutional law from unjustified interference by way of public regulation. The limitation of the legislature with respect to the private sphere presupposed as a flip-side corollary the legislative freedom to assign discretionary implementation and enforcement powers in areas considered "public" in nature. Therefore, in the US, both the nondelegation tests and their application simply mirrored the classical foundational presuppositions that there were fields of state action where a certain degree of legislative/legal vagueness was "natural" and thus pursuant discretion was legitimate and fields of private action where the state had a clearly confined duty of safeguard and calculable, exceptional intervention.

This systemic essentialist structure of classical constitutionalism was not difficult to observe in the analysis of the American developments, due to the evolutive, uninterrupted simultaneity of constitutionalism, constitutional law, and constitutional adjudication. But its main features are evidenced by relatively analogous constitutional patterns in other jurisdictions. For instance, the constitutional progression of the German dichotomy between state and society up to its legal crystallization in the 1882 "Kreuzberg Decision" served the same purpose of

---

[12] *Id.*, p. 561.

[13] Congress may not delegate "powers which are strictly and exclusively legislative," *Wayman v. Southard*, 23 U.S. (10 Wheat.) 1, 42 (1825).

differentiating in kind areas of state action fully and "naturally" governed by law proper, where public interference had to correspond to clearly defined normative standards, and areas of discretion, where the state "made" the rules more or less freely and administered them discretionarily. Classical constitutional law could be defined as a science discerning the natural limits of the state from the axioms of individual freedom. In turn, classical constitutional review was—thus aptly Edward White—"guardian review",[14] judicial policing of those principled, immutably drawn systemic boundaries. This is how judges themselves perceived their purview: "[judges] make no laws. . .establish no policy, [and] never enter into the domain of public action. . .[t]heir functions. . ..are limited to seeing that popular action does not trespass upon right and justice as it exists in written constitutions and natural law."[15]

The 1928 enunciation by the US Supreme Court of a formal delegation test, according to which a congressional enactment must contain an "intelligible principle" (i.e., it must have a constitutionally requisite degree of precision) marked the implicit recognition of an upheaval in foundational structures. It expressed the transition from substance to degree. This legal transformation, which was fostered by and gave expression to mutually reinforcing processes of structural social-economic change and overlapping worldview and ideological metamorphoses, had by then long been underway. As we have previously seen, various tendencies of the Progressive movement had announced, already during the waning decades of the nineteenth century, a new social-scientific "mood" in partial response to the reinforcing phenomena of massive urbanization and standardized, concentrated, technologically advanced capitalism. This new world of the urban and industrial machine needed to be regulated with bureaucratic-scientific methods and law (understood as general rules with normative force, addressed to individuals) was perceived as an important but by no means paramount instrument in the social-scientific toolbox. Expert modalities of social and economic control, namely, the bureaucracy and new means of technocratic administration, seized the progressive imagination with much greater appeal than rules and courts. In the new paradigm "[t]he focus had shifted from essences to actions," from the individual to the social group, and from essentialist truth to "truth as a process."[16] As we have seen, the liberal constitutional system reacted unsurely to both a new reality of overwhelming industrial, economic, and social concentrations and the ideological impetuses for change foisted on it by critics of those processes. This reactive insecurity translated into vague legislative mandates and the initially hesitant trial of new bureaucratic methods to implement those tentative, relatively open-ended provisions. In the case of the Interstate Commerce Commission Act, a genuine

---

[14] G. Edward White, *The Constitution and the New Deal* (Cambridge, Massachusetts and London, England: Harvard University Press, 2001).

[15] Justice David Brewer, "The Moment of Coercion," 1893 address before the New York State Bar Association, quoted in White, *id.*, p. 206.

[16] Robert H. Wiebe, *The Search for Order, 1877-1920* (New York: Hill and Wang, 1967).

battle was fought in Congress over the implementation method. Only after protracted debates were regulation by commission and a broader legislative mandate favored over narrower rules and enforcement by private damage suits in federal court.[17] But after the adoption of the 1914 Clayton and Federal Trade Commission Acts an understanding had begun to settle in that such kinds of legislative mandates and administrative innovations were already securely entrenched and there to stay. By 1916 Elihu Root felt justified to proclaim that a point of no return had been reached: "There will be no withdrawal from these experiments. We shall go on; we shall expand them, whether we approve theoretically or not; because such agencies furnish protection. . .[which] cannot be practically accomplished by the old and simple procedure of legislatures and courts. . . ."[18]

Although at different constitutional paces, similar and roughly contemporaneous observations were being made by continental lawyers. In a brief yet path-breaking 1938 study, Ernst Forsthoff argued that the inability of the classical state and law to grapple with new phenomena was largely due to the increasing inadequacy of the dominant classical presupposition of private individual/social autonomy to address new kinds of structural dependency created by technologically advanced industrialization. True, contemporary man had acquired a historically unparalleled range and expanse of capabilities (his "effective space" had been extended by widening possibilities to travel and communicate). This freedom to project one's existence into ever wider spaces had nonetheless been gained at the price of and was increasing in proportionally inverse lockstep with deepening dependence on the external provision of the basic preconditions of existence (in Forsthoffian jargon, the "controlled space" of human existence was continually shrinking).[19] The distance between the average individual and the state had been quite literally much wider a mere century before, when, even though most human beings died a few hundred yards from the place where they had been born, they controlled to a much higher degree the general conditions of their livelihood (took water from the well, grew their own food, lived on the land, etc.).[20] Forsthoff concluded that the classical dichotomies of German administrative law, as canonized by Otto Mayer's notion of exceptional "intervention administration"

[17] The Reagan bill, reported by the House Commerce Committee in 1878, provided for treble damages suits, filed in federal courts by the aggrieved shippers and, for each offense, 1000$ fines against the railroads, the amount to be divided between the state and the "informant." *See* the study on the ICC Act adoption by Morris Fiorina, "Legislator Uncertainty, Legislative Control, and the Delegation of Legislative Power," 2 *J. L. Econ. & Org.* 33 (1989).

[18] Quoted in Wiebe 1967, pp. 295-296.

[19] Forsthoff 1938.

[20] The interdependence of economic conditions and constitutionalism finds ample support in eighteenth-century literature. For instance, Jefferson believed that republican government was only possible in America, where, due to the wide sparsely populated spaces and the abundance of arable lands, most men literally depended, for their survival, on the cultivation of their lands and characters. *See* Stanley Katz, "Thomas Jefferson and the Right to Property in Revolutionary America," 19 *The Journal of Law & Economics* 467 (1976).

(*Eingriffsverwaltung*) and the assumption entailed by it, namely exceptional public interference with the autonomous private-social sphere, no longer offered a satisfactory conceptual and practical legal way of grappling with the new conditions of social life. Private social-economic and legal arrangements had themselves suffered structural changes, which could no longer be related to their initial individualistic assumptions. The replacement of the contract as a "meeting of the minds" by the reality of standardized contracts had for instance substituted systemic coordination and risk-allocation purposes for the initial individual-centered premises of the juridicial institution. These changes from individualistic essence to structural-systemic degree, as Forsthoff opined premonitorily, even though more fluid or opaque in nature and thus more difficult to define legally, were inescapable and would inevitably reshape the law: "The adaptation of the modern man to the technical world results in a juristically less easily definable, and yet for that reason no less effective, curtailment of the juristic autonomy of the individual."[21] The responsibility of the state for the provision of public services necessary to sustain life (*Daseinsverantwortung des Staates*) such as water, waste disposal, transportation, provision of electricity, etc. and consequently an administrative duty of intervention had to replace the failing, fictitiously and factitiously presumed collective responsibility of the nineteenth century. The new relation between the state and the individual had to be reassessed theoretically and reconceived constitutionally.[22] But this practical and theoretical reassessment would prove much more difficult than the realization that society vs. state, "liberty and property" constitutionalism had come to an end.

4.1.2 Delegation Rephrased: A Degree of Rationality

The reminder is useful at this point, that nothing in the argument should be understood to imply a sentimental-elegiac melancholy and surreptitious longing for a "golden age of constitutionalism" or—much less so—the latent desire to return to prior terms of reference. A historically empathetic understanding of shifts in constitutional paradigm cautions only striving for the detached posture of the observer,

[21] Forsthoff 1938, p. 39.

[22] Given the time when the book was published, this conclusion may strike a cynical chord in the English language reader. Since, unlike his one-time mentor Schmitt, Forsthoff's work is untranslated and relatively unknown outside of Germany, the note is justified that the 1938 argument was untainted by National-Socialist ideology. In the Bonn Republic, Forsthoff pursued (unsuccessfully and with an increasing degree of dissatisfaction) his attempt to reconceive administrative law through the conceptual lens of *Daseinsvorsorge*. He tried to give the concept the same doctrinal consistency and pivotal role that Otto Mayer had achieved for *Eingriffsverwaltung*. *See* Forsthoff's classic monograph, *Lehrbuch des Verwaltungsrechts*, 10. Auflage (München: C.H. Beck, 1973). *See generally*, Florian Meinel, *Der Jurist in der industriellen Gesellschaft. Ernst Forsthoff und seine Zeit* (Berlin: Akademie Verlag, 2011).

neither embracing change enthusiastically as liberating nor deploring as a loss inevitable transformations that cannot be undone. No normative conclusions are made here with respect to contemporary constitutional law. My argument has simply been that classical constitutionalism operated according to a legality and legitimacy model which, like all ideal-types, never fully corresponded to the justified and regulated realities but functioned, up until the end of the nineteenth century, with a reliable degree of consistency. Constitutionalism could master its facts and, therefore, as long as both the constitutional system of reference and the referenced reality corresponded, foundational legal assumptions could appear to those living within their intellectual confines as natural.

To be sure, the disenchantment of constitutionalism, namely the erosion of the preconditions for and the corresponding demise of belief in the existence of natural limits to constitutional and legislative intervention, has made it possible to perceive law and adjudication as essentially political exercises. From the vantage point of the metamorphosis, it became possible, for instance, to recreate "triumphalist narratives" within an ideological framework of reference, reinterpreting and denouncing or praising past practices by ex post attribution of noble or nefarious motives. This instrumentalist key in which fundamental law is approached or through which its history can be ideologically rewritten in hindsight is a conspicuously contemporary phenomenon: "[C]haracterization of the general performance of individual Supreme Court justices in ideological terms did not exist in commentary during the nineteenth century."[23] The phenomenon is relevant to our current inquiry, since it evidences a crisis, namely a systemic inability to make sense coherently of fundamental legal practices, without either falsifying the reality observed or simplifying the normative framework of reference in a rudimentary-procrustean way. The detachment between law as a practice and the normative plane, i.e., an inability to relate the two dimensions other than either at the technical level of mere description or in the distorted normative terms of instrumental manipulation/normative misconstruction, tells a relevant structural story about the state of fundamental law and about the possibilities of constitutional science. A refreshingly terrestrial example will help illustrate this point.

The ambivalence with which turn of the century regulation pioneers, lawmakers, and courts approached the new phenomenon of industrial concentrations in the United States was discussed at some length in the preceding part of the book. As we have seen, the political and legislative debates giving birth to the Sherman, Clayton, and Federal Trade Commission Act, and the contradictory tendencies in the New Deal approach to the problem of monopoly, evidenced that generalized sense of hesitancy. This widespread foundational irresolution was due not only to the multifarious and interacting pragmatic considerations and yet unsolved questions (was 'bigness' always bad, as Brandeis certainly believed? was it always the fruit of

[23] G. Edward White 2001, p. 272. *See generally* the discussion of this general problematic in Chapter 9 "The Canonization and Demonization of Judges," 269 ff. *Also see* by same, "The Lost Origins of American Judicial Review," 78 *Geo. Wash. L. Rev.* 1145 (September, 2010).

predation?, did it always foster predatory behavior? etc.) or to the understandable human fear of the unknown. Obversely, these secondary tensions reflected the irreconcilable dissonance between the political, legal, and economic presuppositions of the system and the looming reality of an increasingly de-individualized, seemingly impenetrable and inescapable economic reality. As Judge Learned Hand would later put it in his famous *Alcoa* dictum, referring to the "belief that great industrial combinations are inherently undesirable, regardless of their economic results": "In the debates in Congress Senator Sherman himself. . .showed that among the purposes of Congress in 1890 was a desire to put an end to great aggregations of capital because of the helplessness of the individual before them."[24] And yet what to do about this helplessness and how precisely to do it escaped Hand just as much as it had eluded Theodore Roosevelt, the pioneer "trust buster," half a century before. Once the initial knee-jerk reaction of assigning blame by way of primitive ideological cliché ("the evil trust") had yielded to an understanding that an irreversible but somewhat untractable change had occurred, a new legal question found itself always on everyone's table, industry included.[25] The challenge to be addressed was how one could maintain the optimal measure of 'honest' competition without hobbling the economy.

Indeed, the provisions of the competition laws (tentative, broadly formulated, sometimes announcing conflicting goals, in short: "delegations") evinced from the onset this general perplexity and the ensuing inability to grapple with the phenomena. Courts inevitably joined in the general conundrum, interpreting antitrust law in an equally tentative and therefore often inconsistent manner. This was to be expected; in the absence of a common normative standard of reference, one way of solving the problem of conflicting goals is to try to reconcile them ad hoc. Another possibility, legal-rationally more consistent (and perhaps, in view of judicial limitations, also a more institutionally legitimate way out of the dilemma), is the reduction of the uncertainty by postulating one purpose as the dominant criterion of implementation. Robert Bork's 1978 monograph on the topic influentially advocated the latter option, both anticipating and spurring the future path of antitrust in the US (and the EU).[26] *The Antitrust Paradox* cut the Gordian knot by arguing that the only cogent solution to the jurisprudential quagmire was to apply the criterion of consumer welfare as a yardstick for the enforcement of antitrust legislation, to the complete exclusion of competing goals, most notably industrial deconcentration as a purpose in itself or the welfare of small competitors. By consumer welfare Bork understood the increase in productive efficiency effected by the impugned industrial and commercial practices, whenever a productive efficiency increase would offset countervailing decreases in allocative efficiency (productive efficiency increases consumer welfare by reducing costs and thus, potentially, prices).

[24] *United States v. Aluminum Co. of America*, 148 F. 2d 416, 428 (2d Cir. 1945).

[25] William H.Page, "The Gary Dinners and the Meaning of Concerted Action," 62 *SMU L. Rev.* 597 (2009).

[26] Bork 1978.

Consequently, for example, a monopoly position achieved by purely internal growth (as opposed to one resulting from a recent merger) would be economically and legally unimpeachable,[27] as achievement of monopoly status by "natural" internal growth constitutes by definition the proof of superior efficiency.

Bork's analytically crystalline, undoubtedly brilliant argument is replete with criticism, often amounting to scathing disdain, aimed at defenders of the non-economic, "social and political purposes of antitrust." According to Bork, the defenders of this "jumble of half-digested notions and mythologies" with their "loosely Jeffersonian" hopes for "the preservation of a sturdy, independent yeomanry in the business world"[28] had only been muddling the law—while harming the economy in the process—and leading courts astray from their proper function. In the 1978 "Summation" to the book and the "Epilogue" to the 1993 reprint edition, Robert Bork conjured and saluted, respectively, in retrospect the aptitude of courts to "speak the language of economics rather than pop sociology and political philosophy."[29] This entreaty, its colloquially dismissive tone notwithstanding, is in line with the general tenor of the book, which makes a strong claim to scientific objectivity and methodological neutrality. If one heeds the propounded efficiency-oriented method, prior shamanistic judicial incantations about "small dealers and worthy men" oppressed by "big business" would be inevitably replaced with sound professional analysis, consistent and predictable in its application. At the same time, interestingly, the author felt compelled to use political-philosophical arguments in support of his theses. Throughout the book, he extemporizes in tropes recognizably drawn from the classical linguistic arsenal of the individual vs. the state constitutional tradition. Thus, the post-1978 jurisprudential swerve towards efficiency is praised as a move away from "populism", "statism", "the authoritarian ethos" and "equality of outcome" and towards the rosier horizons of "liberty", "the general welfare", and "the ideal of equality of opportunity": "The regime of capitalism brings with it not merely unexampled economic performance and a social and cultural atmosphere that stresses the worth of the individual, but, because of the bourgeois class it creates, trains, and raises to power, the possibility of stable, liberal, and democratic government."[30]

This encomium goes to exemplify both the depth of the rift between practices and justifications and the inevitable tendency towards falsification embedded in attempts to conceal this fissure. It may be inevitable that "Christmas tree" legislation, given the methodological and institutional limitations of adjudication, ought to be reduced to a dominating principle and thus to a clear, rationally manageable test. It may also very well be that there is no other way out of the dilemma, either at the level of norm-application or at the level of predictable and

[27] "Antitrust should have no concern with any firm size or industry structure created by internal growth or by a merger more than ten years old." *Id.*, p. 406.

[28] *Id.*, at p. 54.

[29] *Ibid.*, p. 427.

[30] *Ibid.*, p. 425.

thus efficient economic regulation. But this legally and economically necessary simplification of a delegation comes at a price and the trade-off must be soberly seen for what it really is. Equality of opportunity, liberty, and desert according to individual merit are, when applied wholesale to the reality of standardized and concentrated capitalism, the terms of a somewhat different world. They do not find full substantiation in a reality dominated by overweening aggregations of industry and capital. Besides, the possibility of manufacturing consumer choice can render the general coordinates of efficiency much more lax than Bork explained or perceived, in a way which parallels transformations of the relationship between voters and representatives in modern mass democracies. All these mutations are epiphenomenal manifestations of "the unsetteldness of the individual ...in an environment dominated by large-scale systemic structures."[31] In short, social and economic transformations entail legislative metamorphoses, which in turn make structural judicial trade-offs all but inevitable. While these processes are as such perhaps inescapable, an embellishment of the ensuing tensions, cloaked in the language of a bygone age has a reductive and disingenuously obfuscating character. Neither the Founding Fathers nor even the drafters of the Sherman, FTC, and Clayton Act were *neo*liberal in their foundational beliefs and premises.

This observation about the incapacity of an inherited constitutional vocabulary to satisfactorily describe current practices leads us to the contemporary problematic regarding the constitutional regulation of legislative delegations. When the distance between foundational justifications and legal practices, on the one hand, and the political, social, and economic realities, on the other, became impossible to bridge, the liberal constitutional system had to undergo foundational transformations. In America, the change was effected "within" the old constitution, by means of interpretation, namely through the transition from the "guardian review" of classical constitutionalism to the post-New Deal "bifurcated review." The judiciary redrew the baseline, adopting as of principle a blanket presumption of constitutionality in the review of democratic legislation. That presumption would be in the future questioned only in enumerated and exceptional cases.[32] In other jurisdictions, the retrenchment was a result of post-WWII constitution-making. In these latter cases, delegation-related provisions were part of the general attempt to preserve and recreate equilibriums devised prior to the emergence of the modern administrative state, by readjusting constitutional rules to fit an older horizon of normative expectations (about individual autonomy under the rule of law, the representativeness and accountability of legislative decisions, the legitimacy of

[31] Ernst Forsthoff, *Der Staat der Industriegesellschaft. Dargestellt am Beispiel der Bundesrepublik Deutschland* (München: C.H. Beck, 1971), p. 160 "Die Folge ist die Verunsicherung des Einzelnen. Er sieht sich in einer Umwelt, die von Großstrukturen besetzt ist und beherrscht wird. Diese Großstrukturen, in denen sich die Industriegesellschaft darstellt, sind seinem Verständnis unzugänglich, da sein Lebens- und Erfahrungsbereich nicht an sie heranreicht."

[32] *United States v. Carolene Products Co.*, 304 U.S. 144 (1938). *See generally* Edward White 2001, *passim.*

executive and administrative decisions, and the separation of powers) to the new realities. The success of this attempt depends in no small measure on the extent to which normative constitutionalism can be severed from its initial systemic presuppositions.

If the argument thus far is correct, the entire structure of classical normative constitutionalism was underpinned by the existence of constitutive limitations on the operation of constitutional rationality. Such limitations are fused at the hip with the institutional and legal-rational constraints of public law adjudication. The relationship between adjudication and procedurally formalized reason is the stock in trade of a jurist. Any lawyer worth his salt knows, if only intuitively, that the entire architecture of the legal system is tailored toward the attainment of juristic, i. e., rationally cognizable (and within rational limits manipulable) truth. The correlative implication, as Lon Fuller's classic piece on the topic reminds us, derives from the implicit limitations of judicially administered rationality: "Adjudication is, then, a device which gives formal and institutional expression to the influence of reasoned argument in human affairs. As such it assumes a burden of rationality not borne by any other form of social ordering. A decision which is the product of reasoned argument must be prepared itself to meet the test of reason. This higher responsibility toward rationality is at once the strength *and the weakness* of adjudication as a form of social ordering"[33] Fuller argued that the intrinsic merits of adjudication as "a process of decision that grants to the affected party a form of participation that consists in the opportunity to present proofs and reasoned arguments"[34] were linked with its limits. As a direct consequence of the contingency of adjudication upon a rationalized procedure and rational patterns of argumentations, he derived the need to restrict this kind of institutionalized decision-making to the resolution of countervailing and individualized claims of right and duty, more amenable to rational solution. Obversely, "polycentric" matters, namely, issues whose consideration 'ricochets' into a web of interrelated problems, would be more amenable to resolution by political choice. A majority vote or an executive decision grounded in prudential considerations are types of decision-making much less subordinated to formal rationality needs.

The overarching constitutional implications of this need to separate law from politics by legal-rational means have been anticipated already during the review of nineteenth century constitutional transformations. Public law adjudication functioned with a very high degree of predictability and consistency as long as judges could relate the solution of constitutional claims to essentialist categories (internal/external and public/private). Those underlying structural dichotomies helped tabulate decisions from the onset as falling within the category of law proper or politics, respectively. Consequently, the degree of judicial control could be adjusted accordingly, in terms of how intrusively the judge would probe the substance

---

[33] Lon Fuller, "The Forms and Limits of Adjudication," 92 *Harv. L. Rev.* 353, at p. 367 (December, 1978) [emphasis in original].

[34] *Id.*, at p. 369.

(merits), legality, and procedural propriety of the decision subject to review. This categorical way of relating to public action concerned the decisions of the legislature as well. By the same token, as the survey of nondelegation-related US Supreme Court decisions has showed, the nondelegation doctrine did not police those distinctions but simply reflected, at the expressive level, the existence of substantive boundaries internal to the constitutional system and external to constitutional regulation.

The general essentialistic-relational approach to the constitution concerned also fundamental rights adjudication. The claim of constitutional right did not receive a "preferred status," that is, an independent, self-standing existence but was equally contingent upon systemic line-drawing. All students of American right/privilege distinction developments know the two Holmesian one-liners on the subject, trenchantly written in his characteristic epigrammatic-apodictic manner. In *McAuliffe v. Mayor of City of New Bedford* Holmes dismissed with very little ceremony the free speech claim made by a police chief fired according to a regulation restricting his political activities: "The petitioner may have a constitutional right to talk politics, but he has no constitutional right to be a policeman. There are few employments for hire in which the servant does not agree to suspend his constitutional rights of free speech as well as of idleness by the implied terms of his contract. The servant cannot complain, as he takes the employment on the terms which are offered him. On the same principle the city may impose any reasonable condition upon holding offices within its control. This condition seems to us reasonable, if that be a question open to revision here."[35] In *Commonwealth v. Davis*, he gave equally short shrift to a claim of right to exercise free speech on the Boston Common, in violation of an ordinance which forbade public speaking without a permit from the mayor: "For the Legislature absolutely or conditionally to forbid public speaking in a highway or public park is no more an infringement of the rights of a member of the public than for the owner of a private house to forbid it in his house."[36] This reasoning found a contemporaneous German counterpart in the notion of "special relationships of subservience" (*besondere Gewaltverhältnisse*), according to whose exquisitely Manichean logic a citizen entering a special relationship with the state, whether by obligation (prisons, the military, public schools) or by volition (public servants) would forfeit or relinquish his fundamental rights at the doorstep of the state, upon leaving the sphere of society.[37]

But the issue of essentialist boundaries to rights ran deeper and had a more sophisticated constitutional dimension than the all or nothing pigeonholing

---

[35] 155 Mass. 216, 29 N.E. 517, 517-518 (1892), per Holmes, J.

[36] 162 Mass. 510, 511, 39 N.E. 113, 113 (1895), aff'd, 167 U.S. 43 (1897).

[37] According to the current doctrine, fundamental rights have effect in the case "special legal relationships" (*Sonderrechtsverhältnisse*), although special legal restrictions may be justified in the context. *See*, for instance, the 2003 "Headscarf Decision" of the Federal Constitutional Court, BVerfGE 108, 282 (*Kopftuch-Urteil*).

according to the law/politics (right/privilege, state/society) set of affiliated distinctions. The constitutional limits of the rights were drawn by the judges and justified by constitutional theorists by means of a "police powers" structure of analysis, symmetrically identical with the determination of limitations on noxious uses of property. For instance, in Christopher Tiedeman's celebrated late nineteenth century treatise on police power limitations, the author conceded, not without a measure of regret, that both the First Amendment and underlying prudential considerations concerning the susceptibility of censorship to abuse would preclude prior restraints to "newspapers, in whose columns we find arguments and appeals to passion, designed to incite the individual who may be influenced thereby to the commission of crimes, appeals to 'dynamiters,' socialists and nihilists, and all other classes of discontents, who believe the world has been fashioned after a wrong principle, and needs to be remodeled."[38] Nonetheless, as Tiedeman hastened to add at the close of the section, while prior censorship as such was barred by the Constitution, this would not protect those availing themselves of the constitutional right in an abusive manner. Socialists, "dynamiters", and nihilists would have eventually found their due desert meted out to them after printing "inflammatory appeals to the passion of discontents", since "he who used [the liberty of the press] was to be responsible in case of its abuse; like the right to keep fire-arms, which does not protect him who uses them for annoyance and destruction."[39] Speech tainted by its "bad tendency" "to injure public morals or private reputation or to lead to other socially injurious acts" would therefore receive no constitutional protection.[40]

Constitutional rationality functioned in a predictable and thus institutionally legitimate manner while it was moored to clear and systemically uncontested premises and dichotomies. It is true that the constitutional changes that accompanied the transition to the modern administrative-bureaucratic state partly took into account the emerging impossibility to keep law fully insulated from politics. This acknowledgement was implicit, for instance, in the explicitly ambivalent design of the newly created European constitutional courts, whose members are, unlike the ordinary judiciary, politically appointed for fixed and often nonrenewable terms of office. It was also implicit in the post-*Carolene Products* retreat of the Supreme Court from the field of social and economic legislation. But these institutional and doctrinal changes have to take into account the systemic demands of normativity and do not compensate for a substantive loss of legal consistency and predictability. The hackneyed description of public law as "political law" only means that administrative and constitutional law are situated at the interface between law and politics and deal with politically and ideologically charged subject-matters. But unless one can confine constitutional and administrative adjudication to a clearly

[38] Christopher G. Tiedeman, *A Treatise on the Limitations of Police Power in the United States* (St. Louis: The F. H. Thomas Law Book Co., 1886), at p. 190.

[39] *Id.*, at p. 192.

[40] White 2001, p. 132. ff.

delineated domain, separated from ordinary law, public law adjudication is subordinated to the usual institutional demands on and of rationality.

Post-war constitutions and post-New Deal constitutionalism had to find a structural replacement for the disappearance of the set of concrete presuppositions and substantive limits within whose framework classical constitutionalism had functioned. Fundamental law provisions limiting the degree of specificity of statutes are attempts to take over, by means of express constitutional regulation, the function of those constitutional systemic presuppositions which had, up until the twentieth century, regulated constitutionalism itself. As it was argued, even in the peculiar case of the US Constitution, where the affirmation of this limitation long preceded the New Deal and the subsequent constitutional upheaval, the nondelegation doctrine as such had been simply reflective of nondelegation assumptions, not an enforceable instrument used in the policing of those presuppositions. When the substantive, essentialistic premises started to change, so did the reflection. The "intelligible principle" test anticipated the transition to occur a mere decade later, by expressing an emergent uncertainty about prior distinctions. As it was also already intimated, what is intelligible, i.e., how specific a statute has to be, is not a question that admits of a clear answer in the form of an enforceable principle, unless one relates 'intelligibility' to a normative background standard of legislation. The Supreme Court used this degree-based test to strike down New Deal legislation and post-WWII constitutions in Europe adopted, as we will further see, analogous institutions. The question of this last chapter is whether such delegation-related provisions can predetermine consistent constitutional adjudication on the matter. A negative answer would reflect not only on the constitutional applicability of this particular type of rule; a deeper implication revealed by the impasse would be the erosion of normativity in contemporary constitutionalism.

The argument thus far was that a constitution as enforceable, supreme law depends on extra-constitutional normative assumptions and that constitutional law operated predictably as long as fundamental law constituted a form of posited natural law.[41] Only with this strong caveat can one say with Niklas Luhmann that the modern, written, normative constitution replaces older, "external" criteria of legality and legitimacy deriving from natural law and natural right with "its own transcendental-theoretical kernel of self-referentiality evinced by the reflexive reason (*die sich selbst beurteilende Vernunft*)."[42] Reason and "reflexive reason" are categorically different things. The replacement of external criteria by positive law was, as we have seen, only partial and remained structurally dependent on a particular natural law/natural rights paradigm. In other words, classical constitutional reason functioned relationally and was itself 'constituted' by natural law/rights presuppositions. The overarching question of contemporary constitutionalism, as revealed by the problem of delegation-related provisions, is precisely

---

[41] Grimm 1970.

[42] Luhmann 1990, at p. 187.

whether constitutional rationality can double back on itself or, to put it in more exacting terms, whether constitutional law can supplant constitutional metaphysics.

4.2 (Non)Delegation After *Schechter*: The Prerogatives of Obscurantism

> The agencies certainly have a good deal of discretion in expressing the basis of a rule, but the agencies do not have quite the prerogative of obscurantism reserved to legislatures.
>
> *U.S. v. Nova Scotia Food Products Corp.*, 568 F.2d 240 (1977), per Gurfein, Circuit Judge.

The political-constitutional background of nondelegation in American fundamental law raises at the institutional level a somewhat different functional problematic than that posed by delegation-related provisions in European constitutions. To begin with, the separation of powers effects of a delegation have immediately apparent distinct implications. Unlike in the case of European parliamentary democracies, where governments are theoretically the agents of parliaments and practically their political masters, under the US Constitution the President and Congress are, by virtue of composition, staggered terms of office, and distinct constituencies, fully autonomous actors in political reality as well as at constitutional law. This inevitably affects both the motivations of Congress (inasmuch as we can attribute intentionality to any collective body) in delegating law-making discretion to the executive and the actual balance of powers consequences resulting from the practice of delegation. For instance, a degree of institutional tension is built into the system by virtue of the presidential veto power, which acts as an implicit disincentive to delegate law-making power that, once delegated, is more often than not lost to Congress. This risk of loss is due not only to the obvious imbalance resulting from the much higher transaction costs of preference formation and aggregation in legislative decision-making but also to the already-mentioned veto-related retrieval difficulty. In order to reverse a previous delegation to the executive, Congress may have to override a likely presidential veto, through an onerous procedure that rarely succeeds.[43]

Furthermore and related, the unitary or plural character of the executive branch is, as we have already seen, constitutionally contested matters. An idiosyncratic modern tendency concerning the institutional identity of the delegates is for instance the "fourth branch of government," *Humphrey's Executor*-related

[43] Between 1789 to 2004, out of 2250 presidential vetoes (regular and pocket), only 106 had been overridden. US Congressional Research Service. Presidential Vetoes, 1789-present: A Summary Overview (CRS Report 98-148, April 7, 2004), by Mitchell A. Sollenberger. Text in: Congressional Research Service Reports, http://democrats.rules.house.gov/archives/crs_reports.htm (accessed August 28, 2011).

peculiarity of the US balance of powers.[44] The practical implications of this constitutionalized difference should of course not be exaggerated. On the one hand, there is an entrenched degree of bureaucratic autonomy from the executive in Europe, just as a counter-tendency towards increasing executive control over the administration, including the autonomous agencies, has been observed in the US.[45] On the other hand, the general problematic of administrative autonomy from politics, predicated upon expertise and/or impartiality ("independent agencies") has by now long ceased to be an American constitutional idiosyncrasy, given the generalized tendency to "neutralize" the administration, i.e., to insulate increasingly more kinds of decisions from the routine control of majoritarian democratic politics through the political branches.[46]

But even with respect to the "ordinary", executive departments, the control over law administration is a contentious matter. After all, Congress could theoretically abolish any office under the Presidency and the Vice-Presidency, which are expressly mentioned in the text of the Constitution. This assertion certainly drives the point to a reality-blind extreme of positivistic formalism; the normative power of the factual is very much at home in constitutional law. Nonetheless, the truth behind the observation is apparent: since all executive departments are statutory creations, statutory language and the allocation of subsequent interpretative authority will confine or not administrative attributions. Consequently, the precision of a delegation as well as the identity of the delegate are also factors of (the predictions regarding) the degree of presidential and congressional control of the administration, respectively. Therefore, the constitutional battle over the meaning of delegation is also part of a larger institutional contest over the control of the administration. By the same token, judicial decisions regarding the requisite degree of statutory specificity as well as the related question of who will decide authoritatively statutory meanings have inevitable repercussions on the balance of power in the administrative state. Deference to the administrative interpretation/implementation of vague statutory provisions is for example a form of judicial acquiescence in or validation of delegation. At the risk of slightly anticipating further discussion, Monaghan's keen observation needs to be cited to substantiate this claim: "A statement that judicial deference is mandated to an administrative 'interpretation' of a statute is more appropriately understood as a judicial conclusion that some substantive law-making authority has been conferred upon the

[44] *Mistretta v. United States*, 488 U.S. 361 (1989), upheld against a nondelegation challenge the Sentencing Reform Act of 1984, authorizing the United States Sentencing Commission, an independent agency 'located in the Judicial Branch,' to create uniform sentencing guidelines for federal offenses.

[45] This tendency can be aggravated but is not necessarily determined by the degree of legislative and judicial control over Congressional delegations. *See generally* Farina 1989 and Elena Kagan, "Presidential Administration," 114 *Harv. L. Rev.* 2245 (2001).

[46] *See* Frank Vibert, *The Rise of the Unelected: Democracy and the New Separation of Powers* (Cambridge: Cambridge UP, 2007). Linz, Juan J. "Democracy's Time Constraints," 19 (1) *International Political Science Review* 19 (1998).

agency."[47] Law-making authority also means relatively unfettered policy discretion and, since political decision inevitably 'moves in' to occupy these fields, the branch most capable by design and capability to profit from this form of judicially sanctioned delegation is inevitably the executive.[48] According to a number of commentators, this danger was increased by the invalidation of the legislative veto in *INS v. Chadha*, which deprived Congress of one of the principal means by which it could have checked delegations *ex post*.[49] But the complementary argument can also be made. Formalistic decisions such as *Chadha*, *Bowsher v. Synar*,[50] *Metropolitan Washington Airports Authority v. Citizens for the Abatement of Aircraft Noise Inc.*,[51] or *Clinton v. City of New York*,[52] insisting on the punctilious observance of the constitutionally requisite procedural proprieties regarding congressional law-making and law-implementation and interpretation, respectively, may function as substitutes or surrogates, compensating for the unenforceability of the substantive nondelegation doctrine.[53]

Conversely, the structural effects deriving from the enforcement of a nondelegation rule would also be different than in other jurisdictions. Arguably, due to the relatively much more lax party discipline in Congress, the enforcement of a nondelegation rule could likely have the immediate consequence of delegating

---

[47] Monaghan 1983, at p. 6.

[48] *But cf.* Sanford N. Caust-Ellenbogen, "Blank Checks: Restoring the Balance of Powers in the Post-Chevron Era," 32 *B.C.L. Rev. 757*, at pp. 813-814 (1990-1991) (the President exercises no control over the independent agencies and relatively little over the executive ones; the agencies are in effect either "laws unto themselves" or captured by the regulated interests) and Jerry L. Mashaw, "Structuring a 'Dense Complexity': Accountability and the Project of Administrative Law," *Issues in Legal Scholarship*, The Reformation of American Administrative Law (2005): Article 4. http://www.bepress.com/ils/iss6/art4 (arguing that the post-"interest balancing" attempts, notably represented by Kagan 2001, to provide a new comprehensive explanatory model for administrative law practices overstates their case, at p. 4: "That Ronald Reagan campaigned on regulatory relief for the automobile industry was as legally impotent in *State Farm* as Bill Clinton's Rose Garden 'authorization' of the FDA's regulation of tobacco in *Brown and Williamson*. *'Presidentialism' may have more descriptive than normative significance*." (last emphasis supplied, citations omitted)).

[49] 462 U.S. 919 (1983). Yet, the opinions on both the practical import of the legislative veto and on the effect of the decision as such are by and large divided. Corwin, in his 1957 study on the Presidency, considered the legislative veto as the main if not the only Congressional delegation-related control mechanism on the Executive. So did, with more reservation, Sotirios, in his delegation study. *But cf* Tribe, § 2-6, pp. 141-152, arguing that the effects of *Chadha* were overall beneficial, raising the quality of the legislative process, enhancing responsibility, heightening visibility.

[50] 478 U.S. 714 (1986).

[51] 501 U.S. 252 (1991).

[52] 524 U.S. 417 (1998).

[53] *See* John F. Manning, "Textualism as a Nondelegation Doctrine," 97 *Colum. L. Rev.* 673 (1997), arguing that procedural guarantees function as "structurally enforced nondelegation doctrine" and substitutes for "executory delegations": "In contrast with legislative self-delegation, the transfer of some policymaking discretion to agencies and courts is understood as a matter of constitutional necessity, and as less amenable to control through judicially administrable standards." (at p. 725).

legislative power from the floor to the committees, therefore to powerful committee and subcommittee leaders, and thus ultimately to interest groups.[54] Woodrow Wilson's 1885 study on congressional government is now primarily remembered because of Wilson's frequently cited quip about Congress in session being "on public exhibition", whereas Congress in its committees had allegedly been "Congress at work."[55] But a few pages farther down in the book, one can find a more sobering remark with respect to the shortcomings of congressional committee work: "I know not how better to describe our form of government in a single phrase than by calling it a government by the chairmen of the Standing Committees of Congress."[56] The correctness of this latter statement was not fully vindicated during the presidential tenure of the former Bryn Mawr professor and, in the wholesale form it was made, it is certainly not true in the present age of strong presidential administrations. Yet, irrespective of how the US government as a whole has evolved in the meanwhile, the decision-making process of Congress itself is still dominated by committee leaders and this bias could be aggravated by a rule shifting more power from the floor.[57] All redistributions of power have systemic ripple effects and produce long-term unintended consequences; but this general tendency is aggravated in a system of multiple autonomous institutional actors and a relatively less streamlined political process.[58]

---

[54] Strauss 1989.

[55] Woodrow Wilson, *Congressional Government: A Study in American Politics* (Cleveland, OH: Meridian Books 1956) (1885), p. 69.

[56] *Id.*, at p. 82.

[57] *See* Fiorina 1986, at p. 45 "[M]any substantive committees are overpopulated by 'interested' congressmen." Fiorina argues more generally that delegation is a function of a number of interacting factors i. the breadth of the language and therefore discretion; ii. the identity of the delegate (courts or administration); iii. the post-adoption expectations of strategically located committee members and chairpersons to control implementation. Strategic behavior would often be according to the author more explanatory of delegation than the complexity of governmental processes. *Also see*, regarding the impact of congressional structural biases on the control of statutorily conferred administrative discretion, J.R. DeShazo and Jody Freeman, "The Congressional Competition to Control Delegated Power," 81 *Tex. L. Rev.* 1443 (2002–2003).

[58] Arthur Macmahon's 1943 cautionary warning still carries therefore the same purchasing power: "The hazard is that a body like Congress, when it gets into detail, ceases to be itself; it acts through a fraction which may be a faction." Cited by Strauss 1989 at p. 434. *See generally* the study by David Epstein and Sharyn O'Halloran, *Delegating Power- A Transaction Cost Politics Approach to Policy Making Under Separate Powers* (Cambridge: Cambridge University Press, c1999), arguing that the imposition of across the board constitutional restrictions on the practice would produce perverse effects, shifting power from the floor to the committees and thus to powerful committee and subcommittee leaders and ultimately also to interest groups; the reasoning is summated in this paragraph: "[D]elegation is not only a convenient means to allocate work across the branches; it is also a necessary counterbalance to the concentration of power in the hands of the committees. In an era where public policy becomes ever more complex, the only way for Congress to make all important policy decisions internally would be to concentrate significant amounts of authority in the hands of powerful committee and subcommittee leaders, once again surrendering policy to a narrow subset of its members. From the standpoint of floor voters, this is little better

If the structural implications of (non)delegation present these jurisdiction-specific particularities and potentialities, the normative and rationality-related functional aspects of the nondelegation doctrine are perfectly comparable to the problematic of delegation-related constitutional provisions in the other jurisdictions under review.

4.2.1 Schechter *Obscurantism: Where is the Constitutional Limit?*

> There is no analytical difference, no difference in kind, between the legislative function—of prescribing rules for the future—that is exercised by the legislature or by the agency implementing the authority conferred by the legislature. The problem is one of limits.
>
> *Amalgamated Meat Cutters v. Connally*, 337 F.Supp. 737 (D.C. Cir. 1971), per Leventhal, J.

> We ought not to shy away from our judicial duty to invalidate unconstitutional delegations of legislative authority solely out of concern that we should thereby reinvigorate discredited constitutional doctrines of the pre-New Deal era.
>
> *Industrial Union Department, AFL-CIO v. American Petroleum Institute* 448 U.S. 607, 686 (1979) per Rehnquist, J., concurring in the judgment.

The retreat of the Supreme Court from the review of social and economic legislation implied the authorization of legislatures to speak in "Delphic" commands with respect to matters not affecting fundamental rights and thus a partial retrenchment of the pre-New Deal, property-liberty line of constitutional assessment. Yet, nondelegation was not directly associated with substantive due process (remember that *Schechter* was a unanimous decision) and, moreover, the values purported to be served by enforcing the doctrine (separation of powers, democracy, the rule of law) are not related to any ideological propensity for or against free markets.[59] The doctrine was therefore spared from the brunt of post-New Deal "demonization" narratives and maintained relatively sound constitutional credentials and an aura of respectability in the administrative state. To wit, the issue of delegation was recurrently brought up in the platforms of several presidential

than complete abdication to executive branch agencies. As it now works, the system of delegation allows legislators to play committees off against agencies, dividing the labor across the branches, so that no one set of actors dominates. Given this perspective, limits on delegation would not only be unnecessary, they would threaten the very individual liberties they purport to protect." (at pp. 237–238).

[59] *But cf.* Sandra B. Zellmer, "The Devil, the Details, and the Dawn of the 21st Century Administrative State: Beyond the New Deal," 32 *Ariz. St. L. J.* 941 (2000) (arguing that nondelegation is inextricably linked to the *laissez faire* judicial propensities of the early New Deal).

campaigns (of political persuasions as distinct as those of Carter and Reagan)[60] and the concept has been central to the arguments of equally diverse political scientists and constitutional scholars (e.g., John Hart Ely, Marci Hamilton, Gary Lawson, Theodore Lowi, Martin Redish, David Schoenbrod, etc.).[61] Furthermore, the rationales adduced by advocates of a stricter enforcement of nondelegation are procedural and ideology-blind, such as the frequently iterated democratic argument. As its essential logic runs, by passing vague statutes Congress evades responsibility for hard political choices. Legislators are thus enabled to pass the buck to the administrators, claiming credit with their constituencies for having voted for the law, while at the same time shifting the decision and the blame for future unpopular choices to the bureaucrats charged with fleshing out the substantive rules.[62] A rule against nondelegation would unmask this structural exercise in hypocrisy, forcing the representatives to make the hard choices themselves and allowing the voters to assign credit properly or place the blame where it should lie. Since, especially in jurisdictions where a representative is more dependent on his constituency than upon the party, voting can only fulfill its functions upon the predicate of a certain degree of normative commitment "[it] seems reasonable to demand as the prerequisite for legislative action some meaningful level of normative political commitment by the enacting legislators, thus enabling the electorate to judge its representatives. . ..Statutes that fail to make such a commitment, instead effectively amounting to nothing more than a mandate to an executive agency to create policy, should be deemed unconstitutional delegations of legislative power."[63] Hence, representative democracy and the ensuing values of legitimacy, accountability, and transparency of decision-making would be served by the doctrine.

This is a respectable, relevant, and coherent concern, in the best tradition of constitutionalism. More often than not, criticism aimed at the democracy-related tenets of this position caricaturizes the seriousness of the general argument and unfairly dismisses the constitutional stakes. Censors can be ascribed to two main strains, the line of pragmatism (adopted by those who respond with no-nonsense arguments to normative objections) and that of normative agnosticism (standing for the position that general concepts are multi-faceted, they admit of too many understandings to be of any use when immediately applied to doctrinal problems).

---

[60] Fiorina 1986 p. 35 FN 3 (Wallace in 1964, Wallace and Nixon in 1968, Carter in 1976, and Carter and Reagan in 1980).

[61] *See supra*, the general discussion in the section on conceptual associations and constitutional constraints at p. 80f.

[62] David Schoenbrod, "Politics and the Principle that Elected Legislators Should Make the Laws," 26 *Harv. J. L. & Pub. Pol'y* 239 (2003).

[63] Martin Redish, *The Constitution as Political Structure* (NY: Oxford University Press, 1995), at 16, 137, quoted after Patrick M. Gary, "Accommodating the Administrative State: The Interrelationship between the Nondelegation and *Chevron* Doctrines," 38 *Ariz. St. L. J.* 921 (2006), at p. 939.

For instance, exemplary of the first category is Jerry Mashaw's commonsensical response to the Ely-Schoenbrod line of critique about broad delegations hampering electoral accountability. Mashaw retorted that voters could just as well sanction their representatives for broad delegations as they do for clear choices, so the nondelegation position, as stated, would be fatuous.[64] But this argument, underneath its apparent matter-of-factness, makes unrealistic demands of electoral accountability. This is due first to the fact that democracy does not operate on the presumption that the median voter disposes of the same levels of philosophical sophistication, political acumen, and knowledge of government, constitutional, and administrative affairs as possessed by Yale Law School Sterling Professors. We usually hold people accountable for punctual "first-order decisions," i.e., in the case of representatives, voting for or against something specific. To hold them accountable for not making a salient choice about a choice (a "second-order decision," namely a decision about the primary, substantive decision about an issue) is something altogether different. This redefined accountability mechanism expands exponentially, and democracy-wise to an illusorily taxing degree, the knowledge and time demands (both decision-specific and about the general environment of the decision-making process) that are made of the mean voter.[65] Second, more important, and related, one cannot expect individuals to be able to solve by means of discrete and intermittent decisions structural systemic deficiencies, since the individual's choices are themselves warped, distorted, and conditioned by the systemic bias, which can only be corrected at the relevant level, by a structural systemic decision (such as—in this case—an enforceable nondelegation rule).

Dan Kahan's debunking attack on the use of the concept of 'democracy' as "the trump card in the antidelegation hand"[66] is representative of normative agnosticism. According to Kahan, the concept of democracy is of little normative use in nondelegation debates, since "democracy" is an emphatically polysemantic concept and no meaning of the notion (as he identifies them: market-pluralist, populist pluralist, and the dialogical and communitarian varieties of civic republicanism) can be given *a priori* normative precedence. Thus, all conceptions will have a role in the assessment of each delegation, since any delegation will serve a concept of democracy (say, populist pluralism) and disserve another (for instance, dialogical). A concept of democracy that would reconcile these semantic offshoots would be equally unavailing. It could not be brought to bear on institutional structure

[64] Jerry L. Mashaw, "Prodelegation: Why Administrators Should Make Political Decisions," 1 *J. L. Econ. & Org.* 81 (1985), at p. 87: "The dynamics of accountability apparently involve voters willing to vote upon the basis of their representative's record in the legislature. Assuming that our current representatives in the legislature vote for laws that contain vague delegations of authority, we are presumably holding them accountable for that at the polls. How is that we are not being represented?".

[65] On first- and second-order decisions, *see* Cass R. Sunstein and Edna Ullman-Margalit, "Second-Order Decisions," 110 (1) *Ethics* 5 (Oct. 1999).

[66] Dan Kahan, "Democracy Schmemocracy," 20 *Cardozo L. Rev.* 795 (1998-1999).

problems since "an ecumenical conception" cannot establish orders of precedence, it is not a meta-concept. Establishing a ranking among these assumptions would of necessity be a function of subjective normative preference, not of normative imperative. Only complete legislative abdication would be clearly detrimental to all possible conceptions and assumptions informing them but that is, opines Kahan with some good reason, "hyperbole bordering on hysteria."[67] Since democracy is "an essentially contested concept" and can tell us little about institutional structure and due to the fact that the Constitution favors neither facet of the general open-textured concept, Kahan proposes assessments in terms of particular policy constellations ("the normative priority of policy to democracy").

Deconstruction with a touch of "no-nonsense" pragmatism and a whiff of relativism is a relatively undemanding endeavor. Knowledge-wise, however, the exercise brings in meager pittance. To begin with, confining normative judgments to micro-policy implications does not do away with the normative problematic as such, since "efficiency expectations are conditioned by normative representations."[68] Related, an "ecumenical concept of constitutional concepts" does not break the normative circle due to the conceptual priority of "normativity over policy." The use of concepts in constitutional jurisprudence and doctrine is not so unconstrained as in a philosophy seminar. Notions have to be subordinated to the idea of limited government under a written constitution and, therefore, one does not have the intellectual leisures of the 'God perspective,' the unbounded spaces, the unconstrained view from above. It is not political–philosophical democracy that would be served by a nondelegation limitation in the arguments of nondelegation advocates, but representative democracy as constrained by the constitutional duties resulting from the limited mandate of Congress. The constitutional limitation takes normative and analytical precedence over the representative democracy-enhancing effects. The actual implications of vigorous nondelegation enforcement are a policy matter, open to many plausible speculations and impossible to predict with certainty. In normative terms, however, the argument against delegation is compelling, irrespective of which feature of representative democracy is emphasized and independent of policy representations.

That the constitutional concept is not just chimerical, a product of fanciful-dogmatic imagination, answers in no way the question as to its practical legal feasibility. The concept of delegation is inescapable in normative constitutionalism due to the overarching idea of legally limited government, to which the notion of representative democracy proper to constitutionalism is in turn subordinated. Thus, once the assumption of a normative limitation on government was thought through

[67] *Id.*, at p. 803: "Indeed, my guess is that no democratically organized community would ever enact a delegation scheme that couldn't be seen as making its government more democratic under some plausible conception of that term."

[68] "Leistungserwartungen sind von Geltungsvorstellungen geprägt." P. Graf Kielmannsegg, "Legitimität als analytische Kategorie", in *Politische Vierteljahresschrift* 12 (1971), 367 (393), quoted after Möllers 2008, at p. 14.

to its inevitable conclusion, this corollary was inescapable in Locke's argument. For symmetrical reasons, the notion is unavoidable in constitutional theory and constitutional law proper: it responds, as Gary Lawson trenchantly observed, to "very fundamental—indeed, almost primal beliefs…To abandon openly the nondelegation doctrine is to abandon openly a substantial portion of the foundation of American representative government. That is a price that most people are unwilling to pay in return for the modern administrative state but it is not surprising that people would look for a way to reduce that price—or at least persuade themselves that they have not really paid it."[69] We cannot relinquish the concept, as long as we want to hold fast to the notion of normatively limited government. But the crucial practical legal question nowadays is whether the limitation on government provided in classical constitutionalism by substantive criteria can be replaced by a formal, positive constitutional limitation on legislation applying across the board. This limitation would have to constrain the legislative choice by virtue of a principled, rule-bound test, which would at the same time constrain judicial discretion, for instance by establishing a constitutional presumption regarding the priority of rules over goals-statutes[70] or the requisite specificity of legislative choices.

Several decisions of the Supreme Court, where, although the majority did not use nondelegation to strike down broad provisions, the opinions mentioned the doctrine as a viable rule of constitutional law, gave credence to hopes for a revival of *Schechter*. In *Benzene*,[71] for instance, the Supreme Court decided that, to the extent that a statutory provision enabled the Secretary of Labor "… in promulgating standards dealing with toxic materials or harmful physical agents … [to] set the standard which most adequately assures, to the extent feasible, on the basis of the best available evidence, that no employee will suffer material impairment of health or functional capacity,"[72] the mandate imposed on the administrator a duty to refrain from prescribing very large burdens on the industry for trivial gains. The court derived from the provision a corresponding obligation to demonstrate "significant risk of harm" before adopting an exposure standard and noted in dicta that, if the interpretation given by the administrator had been correct, the impugned provision "might" have been vulnerable to a nondelegation challenge.[73] Moreover, Justice Rehnquist would have preferred to strike down the

---

[69] Lawson 2002, at p. 332.

[70] *See* David Schoenbrod, "Goals Statutes or Rules Statutes: The Case of the Clean Air Act," 30 *UCLA L. Rev.* 740 (1982-1983) and Schoenbrod 1993.

[71] *Industrial Union Department, AFL-CIO v. American Petroleum Institute* 448 U.S. 607 (1979). *See also* "Cotton Dust", *American Textile Mfrs. Inst. v. Donovan*, 452 U.S. 490 (1981). In both cases, the majority considered that the locution "to the extent feasible" supplied a limiting standard and saved the statute from a nondelegation challenge, whereas Rehnquist's dissents countered that precisely the insertion of that phrase had "rendered what had been a clear, if somewhat unrealistic, statute into one so vague and precatory as to be an unconstitutional delegation of legislative authority to the Executive Branch" (Rehnquist, J, dissenting, 452 U.S. 490, at p. 545).

[72] Section 6 (b) (5) of the Occupational Safety and Health Act of 1970, 84 Stat. 1590.

[73] 448 U.S. 607, at 646 (1979).

provision for delegating legislative power, as he argued in an impassioned concurring opinion that glossed extensively on John Locke's political-theoretical defense of the nondelegation principle. Rehnquist stressed that the nondelegation test ("intelligible principle") was reliable enough to allow for predictable enforcement of the doctrine and added that broad statutory vagueness was only justified in the general regulation of fields marked by rapid technological change, where the fluidity of the domain made a clear legislative command impossible or undesirable. Once a value choice was brought to bear on technological uncertainty (as in the case of setting standards of exposure to dangerous chemicals, where the dose-response curve cannot be established), Congress had to choose between the conflicting values of saving statistical lives and safeguarding the economic health of an industry. Whereas Rehnquist admitted that an amount of delegation and therefore discretion in execution of the law was inevitable, he pointed out that the selective enforcement of the doctrine according to the "intelligible principle" test would promote political responsibility, the accountability of the administration, and viable judicial review of administrative action.[74]

But even when the court held the doctrine inapplicable in the particular case at bar, it did so in carefully worded arguments that distinguished the specific situation as exceptional but did not question the viability of the nondelegation rule as such. For instance, in *Touby v. United States,*[75] the Court held that an expedited procedure in the Controlled Substances Act, enabling the Attorney General to schedule temporarily "controlled substances" when temporary scheduling was "necessary to avoid an imminent hazard to public safety" (the procedure was necessary in order to combat the problem of "designer drugs") did not violate the nondelegation doctrine. Legislative certainty in that context would have easily defeated the purpose of the criminal act, allowing traffickers to deflect prosecution by slight modifications in the chemical composition of a drug, as to make it different from those already scheduled. Moreover, as the court noted, there was a procedure for contesting the scheduling and provision for incidental judicial review in the course of the criminal prosecution: "[temporary scheduling] does not preclude an individual facing criminal

[74] 448 U.S. 607, at 685-686: "As formulated and enforced by this Court, the nondelegation doctrine serves three important functions. First, and most abstractly, it ensures to the extent consistent with orderly governmental administration that important choices of social policy are made by Congress, the branch of our Government most responsive to the popular will. . .Second, the doctrine guarantees that, to the extent Congress finds it necessary to delegate authority, it provides the recipient of that authority with an 'intelligible principle' to guide the exercise of the delegated discretion. . .Third, and derivative of the second, the doctrine ensure that courts charged with reviewing the exercise of delegated legislative discretion will be able to test that exercise against ascertainable standards."

[75] *See Touby v. United States*, 500 U.S. 160 (1991), at pp. 165-166: "Petitioners suggest. . .that something more than an 'intelligible principle' is required when Congress authorizes another Branch to promulgate regulations that contemplate criminal sanctions. They contend that regulations of this sort pose a heightened risk to individual liberty and that Congress must therefore provide more specific guidance. Our cases are not entirely clear as to whether more specific guidance is in fact required." *See* comments and discussion in Mashaw et al., at pp. 77–78.

charges from bringing a challenge to the temporary scheduling order as a defense to prosecution."[76] In other cases, such as areas where the President has independent constitutional authority the nondelegation argument was addressed in received and orthodox delegation categories. In *Loving v. United States*,[77] for instance, the promulgation by the President of aggravating factors in court-martial cases (under his statutory authority over military criminal procedure), factors leading to the imposition of capital punishment, was held constitutional against a nondelegation challenge: "There is nothing in the constitutional scheme or our traditions to prohibit Congress from delegating the prudent and proper implementation of the capital murder statute to the President acting as Commander in Chief... The delegated duty, then, is interlinked with duties already assigned to the President by express terms of the Constitution, and *the same limitations on delegation do not apply 'where the entity exercising the delegated authority itself possesses independent authority over the subject matter....'*"[78] [emphasis supplied].

Given the careful treatment of and occasional sympathetic judicial nods towards the doctrine, the U.S. Court of Appeals decision in *American Trucking*, initially appeared to vindicate the hopes for a revival of the doctrine.[79] In 1999, the D.C. Circuit invalidated, on nondelegation grounds, an interpretation of the Clean Air Act by the Environmental Protection Agency. At issue was a provision of the act directing the EPA to set primary pollution standards (national ambient air quality standards or NAAQS) for certain pollutants as "requisite to protect the public health" with "an adequate margin of safety."[80] Pursuant to this mandate, the agency had issued a regulation on ozone and particulate matter, replacing a previous 0.12 ppm standard, based on 1-h average concentration levels, with a more stringent 0.08

---

[76] 500 U.S., at 161.

[77] 517 U.S. 748 (1996).

[78] *Id.*, at pp. 769-771. *See* "Steel Seizure", *Youngstown Sheet & Tube Co. v. Sawyer*, 343 U.S. 579 (1952), holding that independent constitutional authority does not extend to restriction on civilian property (seizure of steel mills by Executive Order), in times of domestic peace, without express congressional authorization. Compare with the effects of congressional "silence" in foreign affairs, especially executive control of international claims settlement, *Dames & Moore v. Regan* 453 U.S. 654 (1981) and the more recent *American Insurance Association v. Garamendi, Insurance Commissioner, State of California*, 539 U.S. 396 (2003), which held that the president can settle claims of American nationals with foreign governments (and foreign corporations), through executive agreements (which do not need to be ratified by the Senate or approved by Congress) and can preempt state legislation. *See First National City Bank v. Banco Nacional de Cuba*, 406 U.S. 759 (1972), emphasizing "the lead role of the Executive in foreign policy." *See* Alfred C. Aman, *Administrative law in a Global Era* (Ithaca, N.Y.: Cornell University Press, 1992), for an exposition of and an argument regarding the way in which the 'Global Presidency' of more recent times influenced delegations and more generally imbalanced inter-branch relations.

[79] *Am. Trucking Ass'ns v. EPA*, 175 F3d 1027 (D.C. Cir.), *modified in part and reh'g en banc denied*, 195 F.3d 4 (D.C. Cir. 1999), *and rev'd in part sub nom. Whitman v. Am. Trucking Ass'ns*, 531 U.S. 457 (2001).

[80] Clean Air Act, § 109 (b) (1), (d), 42 U.S.C. § 7409 (b), (d) (1994).

ppm standard, based on 8-h measurements. The agency explained the chosen concentration value by pointing out that, although science could not pinpoint a cutoff limit, a threshold under which a concentration would be absolutely safe, a lower standard (0.07) was close to concentrations of ozone produced by non-anthropogenic sources and "[t]he most certain O3-related effects [at 0,07 levels] are transient and reversible."[81] Unusual in the DC Circuit's decision was its unorthodox use of nondelegation. Instead of invalidating the congressional enactment for vagueness and thus delegation, the Court of Appeals remanded the regulation to the EPA and directed the agency to supply an "intelligible principle" to constrain its own implementing discretion. The nondelegation part of the decision was however reversed on appeal by the Supreme Court and thus "[f]or many administrative law scholars, the most awaited case of the year [quickly] turned out to be the most disappointing."[82]

In an opinion written by Justice Scalia, the Supreme Court explained why the nondelegation-related disappointment was inevitable. The opinion noted that the intelligible principle was a limitation on Congress; the very idea that a congressional dereliction of constitutional duty could be substituted by the agency was a contradiction in terms. The question had always been and still remained whether this limitation could be judicially enforced against Congress. But, whereas Justice Scalia provided a litany of examples to show that the provision at issue (section 109 of the Clean Air Act) was not much broader than past, sustained "delegations", he also hinted at the deeper causes of the unenforceability of the constitutional limitation: "It is. . .not conclusive for delegation purposes that, as respondents argue, ozone and particulate matter are 'nonthreshold' pollutants that inflict a continuum of adverse health effects at any airborne concentration greater than zero, and hence require the EPA to make judgments of degree. '[A] certain degree of discretion, and thus of lawmaking, inheres in most executive or judicial action.'"[83]

The intricacies, both knowledge-wise and axiological, lurking in the background of both *Benzene* and *Whitman*, go to underline with particular forcefulness the difficulties posed by such modern kinds of delegation. The administration of vague provisions in these areas (of technology forcing risk-regulation) boils down to the need to put a price on (statistical) human life. Since science is of little help to such choices, be it only due to the unreliability of data or the limited usefulness of extrapolations from experiments, the solution to the problem does not appear to lend itself to principled or normative line-drawing, least of all at the constitutional level.[84] Unless a background normative constraint supplies a principle for gauging

[81] National Ambient Air Quality Standards for Ozone, 62 Fed. Reg. at 38,868.

[82] Lisa Schultz Bressman, "Disciplining Delegation after *Whitman v. American Trucking Ass'ns*," 87 *Cornell L. Rev.* 452 (2001-2002), at p. 452.

[83] *Whitman v. Am. Trucking Ass'ns* (quoting *Mistretta v. United States*, 448 U.S. 361, 417 (1989)), 531 U.S. 457, at 475 (2001).

[84] *See generally* the study by (now Justice) Stephen Breyer, *Breaking the Vicious Circle: Toward Effective Risk Regulation* (Cambridge, Mass.: Harvard University Press, 1993), arguing in essence for a primarily political solution (through a committee under the supervision of the Executive Office of the President) to such problems.

the form and specificity of legislative norms, the kind of normativity resorted to in practice (rules, rules with exceptions, standards, presumptions) depends entirely on considerations of regulatory policy.[85] On a more general note, on questions of degree, substantive intelligibility is a matter of policy and/or viewpoint. To put it more bluntly, one man's intelligibility is another man's unprincipled delegation. Taking the above examples, short of the absurd solution of forcing Congress to come up with a reasoned standard itself, which is absurd not only due to prudential institutional considerations but also due to epistemological reasons, all remaining imaginable positions present Louis Jaffe's "Chinese puzzle" dilemma: "policy . . .contain[s] the potentialities of an infinite recession of lesser and lesser policies."[86] In the absence of a normative constitutional "metric for [statutory] clarity,"[87] entrusting the judge with such tasks at the level of constitutional law would overtax the institutional demands and possibilities of the judicial function. Instead of disciplining discretion, the enforcement of a nondelegation limitation would simply transfer unconstrained policy discretion to the judges under the guise and with the imprimatur of constitutional principle, but without any of the democratic safeguards and safety valves provided by the political and administrative processes. This would displace, rather than solve, and possibly aggravate the nondelegation problem. The difficulties of enforcing a nondelegation limitation would be, moreover, complicated even further if one imagines the nondelegation doctrine analysis to consist of two steps, namely (1) an inquiry into the level of constitutionally requisite statutory clarity, beyond which a provision would be held to "delegate" law-making and, dovetailing with it, (2) a second inquiry into whether Congress delegated due to an acceptable cause (technology-forcing legislation, for instance) or a nefarious irresolution motive (credit-taking, blame-shifting; carelessness; indolence). This structure is implied in a decisive proportion of academic proposals to reinstate nondelegation, insofar as most critics do not want to make wholesale accusations against the administrative, welfare- and risk-management state but seek only to separate the good delegation wheat (delegations that are needed to optimally run the administrative state) from the bad delegation chaff (delegations that undermine representative democracy). The law has trouble enough determining individual intentionality (indeed, it often bridges gaps by way of fictional attributions). Determining the collective 'intent' and 'motivations' of large groups of individuals raises insuperable difficulties and moves tremendous discretionary policy decisions to judges who are neither legitimated nor qualified to exercise them.[88] It is therefore

[85] *See* Diver 1983 and Cass R. Sunstein, "Problems with Rules," 86 *Cal. L. Rev.* 953 (1995).

[86] Jaffe 1947, at p. 369.

[87] Frank Easterbrook, "The Role of Original Intent in Statutory Construction," 11 *Harv. J. L. & Pub. Pol'y* 59, at p. 62 (1988).

[88] *See* Richard Pierce, "The Role of Constitutional and Political Theory in Administrative Law," 64 *Tex. L. Rev.* 469 (1985-1986), arguing that nondelegation tests —"based on some combination of the relative importance of the policy decision and the relative necessity of the legislature's failure to make that decision" (p. 505)—would endow judges with a "thinly disguised putatively

little wonder that the judiciary consistently refuses the invitation to shoulder these burdens.

A secondary question remains, namely, whether the impossibility of enforcing a rule-bound, across the board nondelegation doctrine could not be substituted by a second-best alternative. The Supreme Court itself alluded to this possibility, with a casual *Mistretta* remark tucked away safely in a footnote: "In recent years, our application of the nondelegation doctrine principally has been limited to the interpretation of statutory texts, and, more particularly, to giving narrow constructions to statutory delegations that might otherwise be thought to be unconstitutional."[89] A number of prominent theorists have also advocated nondelegation-based canons of statutory construction as a palliative for the phenomenon of overly broad statutory mandates. The most representative argument is Cass Sunstein's defense of nondelegation canons as a form of "democracy –forcing judicial minimalism, designed to ensure that certain choices are made by an institution with a sufficient democratic pedigree."[90] Since the classical doctrine asks a question of degree, it cannot be enforced at the constitutional level by the judiciary against Congress. Enforcement via nullification, large-scale and across the statutory board, would, says Sunstein "violate its own aspirations to discretion free law" and possibly aggravate the administrative state pathologies (rule of law, accountability, legitimacy deficits) its proponents strive to cure by this means.[91] But the strategic judicial deployment of a set of nondelegation-derived clear statement rules, i.e., restrictive interpretations of broad statutory mandates, requiring an unambiguous legislative decision in a number of sensitive areas, would not be fraught with the same perils. In the case of restrictive interpretations of statutory mandates on the basis of nondelegation principles, the delegation-related distinction is qualitative, since "courts ask a question about subject-matter, not a question about degree."[92] A subject matter question is emphatically amenable to normative specification and thus to principled judicial determination. Moreover, since a clear statement rule only invalidates the decision of the agency, it does not create the same tensions

constitutionally based policy dictatorship" (p. 503). According to Piece, the test would pose already insurmountable problems at step i, since: "there is no objective test for distinguishing 'fundamental' policy issue from other policy issues. The characterization of a policy issue as fundamental inevitably is influenced by each judge's values and ideology. Something that is 'fundamental' to a political conservative, for instance, may not be 'fundamental' to a political liberal." (at p. 502).

[89] *Mistretta*, 448 U.S. at 373 n 7.

[90] Cass R. Sunstein, "Nondelegation Principles," in Richard W. Bauman and Tsvi Kahana (Eds.), *The Least Examined Branch-The Role of Legislatures in the Constitutional State* (New York: Cambridge University Press, 2006), 139-154, at p. 140.

[91] *Id.*, at p. 143.

[92] *Ibid.*, at p. 152.

as invalidation, which denies a legislative choice in categorical terms. In the case of canons, Congress can make the choice itself and is, indeed, required to do so.[93]

This observation, that the optimal form for nondelegation nowadays is that of canons of restrictive statutory construction in order to require clear statements from the legislature, is not only validated by the *Mistretta* aside, but also implied by a long string of decisions. In *Kent v. Dulles*,[94] for instance, the Court held that, absent explicit legislative authorization, the Secretary of State had no authority to promulgate regulations under which a passport would be denied on the basis of Communist affiliation, furthering Communist causes, or on the basis of the applicant's refusal to clarify the issue of affiliation in an affidavit.[95] Given the constitutional value at stake, the right to travel, a part of the Fifth Amendment "liberty," Congress alone could speak in the matter. Similarly, in *Hampton v. Mow Sun Wong*,[96] it was held that the United States Civil Service Commission could not presume authority to restrict access to civil service federal jobs, by adopting a citizenship eligibility requirement (and thus discriminating against aliens). Congress and the President have constitutional power to restrict eligibility but the restriction would need to be specific and express.[97] Similar results have been reached in other constitutional sensitive areas. Thus, it was held that the power to tax,[98] to promulgate

[93] *Also see* Sunstein "Law and Administration after *Chevron*," 90 *Colum. L. Rev.* 2071(1990), arguing that 'nondelegation canons' are not rendered inapplicable by the adoption of the 'rule of deference' in *Chevron* with respect to an agency's interpretations of its enabling act, since they relate to constitutional issues distinct from the principle of agency deference, demanding contrariwise "explicit *congressional* authorization before certain results may be reached." (at p. 2113) *See also* Tribe 2000, at pp. 1010-1011.

[94] 357 U.S. 116 (1958).

[95] *Id.*, at p. 129: "Since we start with an exercise by an American citizen of an activity included in constitutional protection, we will not readily infer that Congress gave the Secretary of State unbridled discretion to grant or withhold it.... And, as we have seen, the right of exit is a personal right included within the word 'liberty' as used in the Fifth Amendment. If that 'liberty' is to be regulated, it must be pursuant to the lawmaking functions of the Congress.... And if that power is delegated, the standards must be adequate to pass scrutiny by the accepted tests. Thus we do not reach the question of constitutionality. We only conclude that s 1185 and s 211a do not delegate to the Secretary the kind of authority exercised here." *See also Greene v. McElroy* 360 U.S. 474 (1959).

[96] 426 U.S. 88 (1976).

[97] *Id.*, at p. 105: "We may assume with the petitioners that if the Congress or the President had expressly imposed the citizenship requirement, it would be justified by the national interest in providing an incentive for aliens to become naturalized, or possibly even as providing the President with an expendable token for treaty negotiating purposes; but we are not willing to presume that the Chairman of the Civil Services Commission, or any of the other original defendants, was deliberately fostering an interest so far removed from his normal responsibilities."

[98] *National Cable Television Ass'n, Inc., v. U.S.* 415 U.S. 336 (1974) The Federal Communications Commission could under its organic legislation impose a fee on cable television companies (CATV's) for services equaling the value of its services to the recipients but was not authorized to tax; taxation cannot be presumed to have been delegated by Congress: "Whether the present Act meets the requirement of *Schechter* and *Hampton* is a question we do not reach. But the hurdles

retroactive administrative rules,[99] and to apply federal law extraterritorially[100] could not be assumed or presumed by Congress' agencies but need to be exercised by means of actual (express) and specific congressional intent. In light of the heightened legitimacy and rule of law concerns raised by delegations to private parties, emphasized in both *Schechter* and *Carter Coal*, a nondelegation canon of construction would attach with particularly good reason to a delegation to private groups of the power to impose private preferences through the use of public coercive authority.[101] This issue has been of actuality in recent years, due to the 'withdrawals' of the state from previously regulated areas (deregulation) and the controversial privatization of some traditionally public functions (contracting out, privatization). Private prisons and the provision of state-funded medical or vocational services by private contractors are conspicuous examples. From this perspective, the problems with delegation are, in the American constitutional context, heightened by the fact that private parties escape constitutional restrictions, due to the limited reach of the "state action" doctrine.[102]

The problem with nondelegation principles or canons as a substitute for the nondelegation doctrine is the impossibility of extracting from the descriptive analysis a workable normative dimension. True, Sunstein provides a taxonomy, distinguishing among canons derived from constitutional principles (such as the rule of lenity or the presumption against retroactive application of statutes), sovereignty-inspired nondelegation canons (such as the presumption against extraterritoriality or the presumption that agencies cannot use statutory ambiguity to waive sovereign immunity) and canons based on public policy (such as the *de minimis* limitation on health and safety regulations, requiring agencies to avoid imposing large expenditures to deter insignificant risks, at issue in the restrictive statutory interpretation in *Benzene*). The problem is that, even though this may well be an accurate description of what the courts have in fact done, no meta-principle(s) can

---

revealed in those decisions lead us to read the Act narrowly to avoid constitutional problems." (at 342). *See also* Tribe, at p. 987, note 30, observing that: "*National Cable Television* was particularly notable because the policy of clear statement was triggered not by some threatened infringement of a constitutionally protected substantive right or liberty –except perhaps a freedom from 'taxation without representation'- but by the delegation doctrine itself." *But cf. Skinner v. Mid-America Pipeline Co.* 490 U.S. 212 (1989), upholding delegation of the taxing power.

[99] *See Bowen v. Georgetown University Hospital,* 488 U.S. 204 (1988).

[100] *EEOC v. Arabian American Oil Co.*, 499 U.S. 244 (1991).

[101] *See*, for instance, *Florida Lime & Avocado Growers, Inc. v. Paul*, 373 U.S. 132 (1963), where a federal regulation was held not to preempt overlapping state law, due to the fact that the content of the federal regulation had been in fact decided by a group of local avocado growers rather than by "impartial experts in Washington or even in Florida." (cited and commented in Tribe, *supra*, at pp. 991–993, *esp*. note 49).

[102] David M. Lawrence, "Private Exercise of Governmental Power," 61 *Ind. L. J.* 647 (1985-1986), Gillian E. Metzger, "Privatization as Delegation," 103 *Colum. L. Rev*. 1367 (Winter, 2003), Ira P. Robbins, "The Impact of the Delegation Doctrine on Prison Privatization," 35 *UCLA L. Rev*. 911 (1988), and Jody Freeman, "The Private Role in Public Governance," 75 (3) *N.Y.U. L. Rev*. 543 (2000).

be derived, to provide courts with a limitative normative criterion for the selection and interpretation of these canons. The insurmountable challenge of the nondelegation doctrine is that of cutting the spectrum of policy degree based on a rule-bound, normative criterion; nondelegation makes a hegemonic constitutional claim on statutory clarity but fails to support it with a normative limitation. Conversely, the problem of canons is too much normative fragmentation. There is, to be sure, a viable, subject-matter explanation for each judicial choice and discrete decisions can be tabulated under a number of broader conceptual categories, just as Sunstein has magisterially done. But, except for a limited number of constitutionally-mandated requirements of specificity such as lenity (which are at any rate normatively self-standing) no common normative-constitutional grammar exists, to guide judges in the enforcement and development of these canons as a countervailing general solution to the systemic problems that led to the revival of interest in the doctrine.[103] Thus, the revival of nondelegation debates reveals itself as a normatively commendable and unavoidable, and yet—from a practical point of view—ultimately fruitless manifestation of a search for normativity in the modern state, a mere epiphenomenon of deeper tensions.

4.2.2 Chevron *Agnosticism: Where is the Legislative Meaning?*

> Congress has been willing to delegate its power broadly—and the courts have upheld such delegation—because there is court review to assure that the agency exercises the delegated power within statutory limits.
>
> *Ethyl Corp v. EPA*, 541 F. 2d 1, 68 (D.C. Cir. 1976) (Leventhal, J., concurring).

> Thus, if Congress declines to make policy decisions and to reflect those decisions in meaningful substantive standards, the judiciary can play no constructive role in constraining agency discretion to make political decisions.
>
> Richard Pierce, "The Role of Constitutional and Political Theory in Administrative Law," 64 *Tex. L. Rev.* 469 (1985–1986).

[103] The argument here is not similar to that made by John Manning, related to unadministrability due to the interpretive burdens. *See* John F. Manning, "Lessons from a Nondelegation Canon," 83 *Notre Dame L. Rev.* 1541 (2007-2008), at p. 1563, n. 63, making the subtle hermeneutical claim that "holding one's method of interpretation constant, it entails arbitrary line-drawing to identify the level of background ambiguity at which statutory outcomes cross the line from congressional choice to statutory discretion." My criticism of nondelegation canons is both simpler and more foundational. It relates, namely, to their lack of normative cohesiveness/coherence: nondelegation canons offer disparate and untractable prudential answers to a structural-normative question. *See*, for a parallel criticism in analogous context (of Sunstein's theory of interpretation canons), Richard Stewart (Book Review of Cass R. Sunstein, *After the Rights Revolution*, Cambridge, Mass., Harvard University Press, 1990), "Regulatory Jurisprudence: Canons Redux?," 79 *Cal. L. Rev.* 807 (1991).

> Administrative law is not for sissies.
>
> Antonin Scalia, "Judicial Deference to Administrative Interpretations of the Law," 1989 *Duke L. J.* 511 (1989).

Although often ridiculed as roughly equivalent to medieval scholastic inquiries into how many angels can dance on the head of a pin, contemporary proposals to revive the nondelegation doctrine are not just aloof 'academic' musings. They are also not exclusively related to the constitutional instantiation of first principles (the quality of representative and accountability mechanisms, systemic rule of law implications, etc.). Contrariwise, the attempt to find the proper normative constitutional limit of legislation expresses also foundational concerns about constitutionalism and constitutional law with very pragmatic, down to earth administrative implications. Whether or not it is possible to constitutionally enforce a nondelegation limitation, the stake of the modern search for delegation limits also derives from and translates into practical considerations about the proper role of public law adjudication. As it was argued thus far, public law is an exercise in structurally controlled rationality. In other words, administrative and constitutional law categories rely on normative distinctions and presuppositions, in the absence of which public law adjudication cannot function rationally, that is, in consistent and predictable ways and structurally free from political and ideological biases.

By the same token, the attempt to substitute pure juridical technique for normativity, i.e., procedure for substance, is fated to disappoint. Procedure, as Jeremy Bentham, the master technician himself, astutely observed, is "adjective law."[104] Like all adjectives, it presupposes a noun in need of suitable qualification. That is to say, it has no meaning without a substantive referent (e.g., "blue sky"). For purposes of introductory exemplification into the conceptual complexities at issue, an elegant and elaborate attempt to justify modern constitutionalism in a procedural key is the comparative study of the German law professor Christoph Möllers.[105] The author stipulates, in Rousseauist-Kantian note, that liberal constitutional democracy rests on self-determination (*Selbstbestimmung*), whose complementary individual and collective manifestations presuppose each other (my liberty depends on the collective freedom of my fellow citizens, whereas the 'general will' cannot have an authentic meaning without my being given the possibility to act as a free moral agent). The writer derives from this liberal-democratic equilibrium a theory of the balance of powers (*Gewaltengliederung*) that instantiates and reflects the tension and complementarity between individual and collective self-determination, respectively. Adjudication, on one end of the spectrum, is legally constrained, retrospective, and bound by the individual and concrete character of

[104] "Of the adjective law, the only defensible object, or say end in view, is the maximization of the execution and effect given to the substantive branch of the law." J. Bentham, *The Principles of Judicial Procedure*, in 2 *Works of Jeremy Bentham* 1, 6 (J. Bowring ed. 1838-1843), quoted after Gerald J. Postema, "The Principle of Utility and the Law of Procedure: Bentham's Theory of Adjudication," 11 *Ga. L. Rev.* 1393, at p. 1396 (1976-1977).

[105] Möllers 2005, 2008.

specific rights-determinations. Law-making, conversely, is less constrained by norms, bears on general objects, and "looks" to the future. The executive function is positioned in the middle of the spectrum—therefrom deriving also its 'segmented' and dual, "in-between" character. Separation of powers results therefore as a continuum or "scale, in which the normative constraints (*Rechtsbindungen*) are more intensive, when individual self-determination is more directly concerned, and more open-ended, when the decision regards the possibility of law-creation for the purposes of collective self-determination. This process of concretization (*Konkretisierungsvorgang*) ultimately has also a temporal dimension, reaching from the future-oriented democratic decision to the judicial disposition of an individual case. In this process of progressive ascertainment one can already recognize the trajectory of law-production from the legislative over the executive all the way to the individual decision of a court of law."[106] The practice-oriented analytical coherence of Möllers' account allows his theory to have a measure of normative mooring to reality and therefore a certain grip on the evaluation of constitutional practices. The *Chadha* decision of the US Supreme Court, which famously invalidated the ex post disposition by the legislature (a one-house veto resolution) of immigration determinations made by the Attorney General, is praised as a correct constitutional intuition of the proper role of a democratic legislature: "thus [i.e., by means of the legislative veto] the closed political law-making process would have been repoliticized for the purposes of an individual case."[107] By the same token, substantive limitations such as nondelegation are declared by the author as impossible and redundant: "There is no general rule prescribing the normative cast of an ideal statute. One could even say, democratic procedures were developed precisely because there is no such ideal type."[108] And yet, in the end, procedure cannot function well without substantive presuppositions. Short of *Chadha*-like clear-cut situations, how individualized or general should the procedure be (and therefore whether we ought to subject a given determination to adjudication or a political decision) are questions which, when the applicable rule of law does not offer clear guidance, the procedure alone cannot satisfactorily address. Whereas Möllers's theoretical justification corresponds broadly and ideal-typically to the way in which we perceive the separation of powers, it helps us relatively little exactly where answers are most ardently needed and tensions are most acute. In that it explains both too much and too little, its analytical elegance notwithstanding, from a doctrinal point of view the argument shares the procrustean fate of closed analytical systems when they are put to hard practical work.[109] But it is not only global attempts at theorizing contemporary law that glide over the surface of juridical phenomena. By the same

[106] Möllers 2008, p. 90.

[107] *Id.*, at p. 130.

[108] *Ibid.*, at p. 127.

[109] Mashaw 1997, at p. 1, quotes an apposite jibe that Picasso is rumored to have thrown at common friends, in response to their uncomplimentary remarks regarding the accuracy of his Gertrude Stein portrait: "[N]ever mind, in the end, she will manage to look just like it."

token, positive law in itself is often of little help in addressing practice-oriented theoretical conundra.

The post-New Deal intricacies and tribulations of constitutional due process are richly revealing of the general dilemma. As we have seen, the older property-liberty presuppositions of the classical liberal state had already become increasingly untenable before the 1930s but a dogged judicial attachment to the liberty and property, right/privilege distinction was impossible to maintain after the New Deal transformations. As a judicial reaction to the unprecedented expanse of the administrative state, procedural due process safeguards were therefore slowly extended to various forms of 'new property.'[110] The constitutional high tide of these new developments was the characterization of welfare benefits, in the 1970 case of *Goldberg v. Kelly,*[111] as a form of 'property' under the Fourteenth Amendment, which needed to be secured, prior to administrative deprivation, with almost the full panoply of due process protections provided by a judicial process.[112] Forms of state largess, which in the past had been considered "privileges" subject to determinations fully discretionary in nature, would now be accorded constitutional 'property-like protection.' And yet, the characterization of government benefits as a "new form of property," although a deft metaphor, overstates in style its analogical, practical and conceptual, possibilities. To wit, if one would consistently judicialize administrative procedures, so that the administrative deprivation of a social welfare benefit would follow a full court-like procedure, the wheels of government would immediately grind to a halt. Falling back *consistently* on the old distinctions appears however, in light of the intervening transformations, illegitimate.[113] Both the majority decision in *Goldberg v. Kelly* and the dissenting judges' accusations of

[110] Charles A. Reich's article, "The New Property," 73 *Yale L. J.* 733 (1963-1964), was the theoretical forerunner of the subsequent judicial developments, arguing that, to the extent that government — both federal and state — had become a major employer and dispenser of largesse, the traditional right-privilege distinction and the *constitutional characterization of a right in common law*, had become untenable. Government largesse needed to be seen as a new property to which Fifth/Fourteenth Amendments constitutional procedural protections would attach.

[111] 397 U.S. 254 (1970).

[112] *Matthews v. Eldridge*, 424 U.S. 319, at 333 (1976): *Goldberg* required a "a hearing closely approximating a judicial trial."

[113] This is not to deny the fact that, in a limited government, the presumption is necessarily negative, that is, against government intervention. This presumption reflects itself in practices and does indeed render current practices coherent. *Cf.* Nelson 2007, at p. 564: "Indeed, to the extent that the Supreme Court's current approach to these issues has any structure at all, that structure comes from the traditional framework [i.e., the difference between 'private' and 'public' rights]. Nonetheless, the acknowledgement of practical necessity does not necessarily lead to a normatively satisfactory justification. *But cf.* Williams 1983 defending "the Constitution's underlying vision of the proper relation between the state and the individual" (p. 4) by a revamped version of the "liberty and property" boundary as "degree of preclusion of private alternatives." Enough has been said so far to indicate that "degree of preclusion," like all matters of degree, presents a very different justificatory/normative configuration than "natural rights."

"unreality"[114] are therefore, to a good measure, equally compelling and perplexing. But no middle way out of the paradox seems to present itself.

Charles Reich's influential article, on the conceptual structure of which the *Goldberg* decision was reliant, argued in familiar realist key that both older and newer forms of property were positive creations of society, thus categorically differentiated constitutional treatment and a presumption of non-intervention based on natural law justifications were unwarranted.[115] Reich's answer to the right/privilege distinction and its associated natural/positive law divide was primarily procedural and across-the-board: "The post-Realist creation of rights in 'new property' would not depend on traditional, natural rights ideas but on the positive creation of procedural limitations on governmental power."[116] But pursuing the "new property" logic to its conclusion, as the court did in *Goldberg*, analogizing a welfare benefits deprivation with a court procedure, would have made a full mockery out of the administrative process. By the same token, compromise solutions to this deadlock, albeit inevitable, have been of little doctrinal and relatively ambivalent practical comfort. First, recourse to default reliance on positive law for the definition of the protected liberty or property has a pronounced tautological character (one looks to the constitution precisely in order to find supplementary procedural protections). [117] Second, the jurisprudential attempt to fine-tune the level of due procedure by means of a "balancing" test is, like all instrumental responses to analytical-categorical questions, a conceptually unsatisfying surrogate. In *Mathews v. Eldridge,*[118] the effects of the holding in *Goldberg* were significantly 'toned down' by entrenching the now familiar three-prong test used in order to decide the level of constitutionally required procedural protection to be accorded a given interest: "First, the private interest that will be

[114] "It somewhat strains credulity to say that the government's promise of charity to an individual is property belonging to that individual when the government denies that the individual is honestly entitled to receive such a payment." *Goldberg v. Kelly*, 397 U.S. 254 (1970), at 275, per Black, J., dissenting.

[115] Horwitz 1992, at p. 246, arguing that the *Goldberg* decision "prominently relied" on Reich's article. *Also see*, Stephen F. Williams, "Liberty and Property: The Problem of Government Benefits," 12 *J. Leg. Stud.* 3 (1983).

[116] *Id.*, p. 245.

[117] Consider the following definition by Jack Beerman, "The Reach of Administrative law in the United States," in M. Taggart (ed.) 1997, at p. 184: " In all cases raising a due process claim that the government has not employed fair procedures, there is a threshold requirement that the plaintiff establish that he or she has a protected interest, usually liberty or property, at stake. The existence of the protected interest, except when constitutionally defined liberty is involved, is determined by looking to an external source of law, such as the statute governing the benefits programme or regulating the government employment. The existence of a protected interest in such cases involves the purely positive law question of whether governing law creates an entitlement to the benefit or employment. If the benefit is purely a gratuity or if the employment is governed by the at-will rule under which an employee may be discharged without notice, then there is no protected interest and no procedural rights attach." *See Board of Regents v. Roth,* 468 U.S. 564 (1972).

[118] 424 U.S. 319 (1976).

affected by the official action; second, the risk of an erroneous deprivation of such interest through the procedures used, and the probable value, if any, of additional or substitute procedural safeguards; and finally, the Government's interest, including the function involved and the fiscal and administrative burdens that the additional or substitute procedural requirement would entail."[119] But, whereas, balancing makes a generous, almost cornucopian promise of professionalism, no-nonsense pragmatism, and policy flexibility—seeming "functionally oriented and quasi-scientific in its methodology"[120]—it delivers in the end unpredictability and unprincipled adjudication. Since (pace Bentham & intellectual progeny) there is no objective, quantitative means of assessment of optimality in law-application, such tests tell us nothing about the way in which the factors ought to and will be pondered in adjudication. The test constrains the judge only marginally and discursively, in the weak methodological sense of imposing a formally structured framework of decisional justification.[121]

These problems, namely the irreducible complexities posed by the adjustment of constitutionally mandated procedural protections to a displaced and ambivalent fundamental, meta-constitutional normative configuration, have been mirrored by symmetrically analogous difficulties at the level of administrative law proper. As commonly known, the main post-war legislative event, essential for understanding contemporary American developments in administrative law, was the passage of the Administrative Procedure Act (APA) in 1946. The final version replaced with a milder form an initial variant, the 1939 Walter–Logan Bill (inspired by Roscoe Pound's American Bar Association report of 1938 and vetoed by President Roosevelt). The ABA-sponsored Pound proposal had reflected pre-New Deal presuppositions about the proper division of labor between courts and administrative bodies to such an extent that Louis Jaffe sarcastically referred to it as "A Bill to Remove the Seat of Government to the Court of Appeals for the District of Columbia."[122] The enacted form, still "a highly conventional lawyer's view of how to tame potentially unruly administrators,"[123] institutes a number of procedures for administrative rule-making and adjudication, as a "default" or "residual" set of provisions to fill the procedural gaps of the organic statutes establishing various federal programs. The APA provision which ended up having the biggest

[119] *Id.*, at 335 (citation omitted).

[120] Jerry L. Mashaw, *Due Process in the Administrative State* (New Haven, CT: Yale University Press, 1985), at p. 102.

[121] T. Alexander Aleinikoff, "Constitutional Law in the Age of Balancing," 96 *Yale L.J.* 943 (1987). For a trenchant and sophisticated critique of the "instrumentalist" deficiencies intrinsic in *Eldrige*-like due process balancing, *see* Mashaw 1985, Chapter 3, "The Model of Competence," pp. 102-157.

[122] Horwitz 1992, at p. 238.

[123] Rabin 1986, at p. 1265: "The APA is, in essence, a highly conventional lawyer's view of how to tame potentially unruly administrators. It divides the universe of administrative action in two general decisionmaking categories, rulemaking and adjudication."

impact on contemporary practices is arguably section 553, setting forth the so-called "notice and comment" rulemaking procedural requirements. According to the section, an agency must, as a default procedure for adopting legislative rules, first issue a "general notice of proposed rulemaking," which is published in the Federal Register. Subsequently, comments are provided by interested persons "through submission of written data, views, or arguments, with or without opportunity for oral presentation." The final rule is published in the Federal Register accompanied by a "concise statement of basis and purpose."[124] This was—and still is, compared, for instance, to the standard European rule-making process—a major innovation on administrative rulemaking procedure.[125] Fallback procedural safeguards appended to rulemaking were considered all the more necessary due to the fact that, while administrative adjudication had always been deemed subject to the constitutional requirements of procedural due process, rulemaking, considered legislative in nature, traditionally evaded procedural guarantees.[126]

---

[124] Sections 554, 556 and 557 specify the procedural requirements to be followed in adjudicatory actions and require a functionally related separation between the prosecutorial and adjudicatory officers (now Administrative Law Judges) of an agency.

[125] American administrative law emphasizes participation, differing from the standard European patterns, which stress judicial protection of rights (or/and judicial policing of legality as such). *See*, Susan Rose-Ackerman, "American Administrative Law under Siege: Is Germany a Model?," 107 *Harv. L. Rev.* 1279 (1993-1994), arguing that German (and more generally European) administrative law could not be a model for the US, due to its de-emphasis on participation. Proposals have also been made to the contrary effect, namely, arguing for an importation of the American participatory processes, most notably notice-and-comment rulemaking, into European (both domestic or E.U.) administrative law. Whether and how that could be achieved, given the distinct nature of the legislative process and democratic will formation in Europe, is a more problematic matter. *See* Theodora Ziamou, *Rulemaking, Participation and the Limits of Public Law in the USA and Europe* (Aldershot, England: Ashgate, 2001) and Francesca Bignami, "Accountability and Interest Group Participation in Comitology: Lessons from American Rulemaking," European University Institute Working Paper, Robert Schuman Centre No. 99/3 (1999).

[126] The distinction between actions that are judicial in nature and to which, therefore, due process protections attach and those of a legislative character, exempted from the constitutional requirement of due process, was drawn by the Supreme Court in two landmark cases. In *Londoner v. City and County of Denver* 210 U.S. 373 (1908), the Supreme Court voided a tax assessment regarding a street paving in the City of Denver, to be levied on the individual landowners abutting the street, on the ground that the individuals had been deprived of their constitutional due process rights (the assessment had been made behind closed doors and the individuals had not been heard prior to the decision but only been granted the possibility to present objections in writing): "[W]here the legislature of a state, instead of fixing the tax itself, commits to some subordinate body the duty of determining whether, in what amount, and upon whom it shall be levied, and of making its assessment and apportionment, due process of law requires that, at some stage of the proceedings, before the tax becomes irrevocably fixed, the taxpayer shall have an opportunity to be heard, of which he must have notice, either personal, by publication, or by a law fixing the time and place." (at 286) In *Bi-Metallic Investment Co. v. State Board of Equalization* 239 U.S. 441 (1915), the Court held, conversely, that when a decision concerns a large number of equally affected individuals, due process rights do not attach (in that case, the Colorado Board of Equalization and the Colorado Tax Commission ordered the valuation of all taxable property in the City of Denver to be increased by forty percent): "Where a rule of conduct applies to more than a few

The APA also set up different and graduated standards of review, distinguishing in principle a more stringent "substantial evidence on the record as a whole", standard for formal administrative action, and a more limited (or less intrusive) "arbitrary and capricious" for the review of the informal administrative decisions. This distinction, requiring a more stringent review for decisions made on a record, was meant to reflect the essential nature of the New Deal compromise, as announced in *Crowell v. Benson* and *Schechter*, that, to the extent that individualized decision-making would be partly taken out of the regular courts, governmental intrusions into the private liberty and property domain would need to be accompanied by judicial-type procedures, so that the displacement would be minimized and the legality, soundness, and procedural regularity of administrative action could be subsequently effectively reviewed by the courts.[127] Largely absent from the initial template was a clear position on discretionary agency action. If anything, there appears at first sight to be a contradiction in the statute, between Section 701, which explicitly exempts from review "agency action committed to agency discretion by law" and Section 706 (2) (A), according to which "[t]he reviewing court shall...hold unlawful and set aside agency actions, findings, and conclusions found to be...an abuse of discretion." In spite of its nominal dissonances, APA generally appeared to contemporary observes as an overall success, a sub- and quasi-constitutional settlement for the new administrative state. In 1950, Justice Jackson referred to it thus, in terms with clear constitutional undertones: "The Act ...represents a long period of study and strife; it settles long-continued and hard-fought contentions, and enacts a formula upon which opposing social and political forces have come to rest."[128]

The fragment continues in less lyrically-inclined, less Pollyannaish fashion to concede the possibility of imperfect drafting: "It contains many compromises and generalities and, no doubt, some ambiguities. Experience may reveal defects."[129] But the evolution of the APA turned out to be relatively little predetermined by its

people, it is impracticable that everyone should have a direct voice in its adoption. The Constitution does not require all public acts to be done in town meeting or an assembly of the whole. General statutes within the state power are passed that affect the person or property of individuals, sometimes to the point of ruin, without giving them a chance to be heard....There must be a limit to individual argument in such matters if government is to go on." (at 445, per Holmes, J.)

[127] For a concise and illuminating rendition of the APA 'compromise,' *see* Alfred C. Aman, "Administrative Law for a New Century," in Taggart (ed.) 1997, at p. 93: "Prior to the Administrative Procedure Act (APA), there was no generally accepted alternative procedural model to the adversary model provided by the courts, even when policy issues were predominant. Procedures, of course, have substantive effects, as well. The more adversarial the procedures, the fairer the process might appear, particularly to those who objected to the substance of the regulation to be implemented in the first place, but the more difficult and costly it was to carry out the governmental programmes involved....It was, thus, a major step simply to be able, constitutionally speaking, to move adjudicatory proceedings from the courts to administrative agencies, to which the Supreme Court gave its constitutional blessing in *Crowell v. Benson* in 1932."

[128] *Wong Yang Sung v. McGrath*, 339 U.S. 33, at p. 40 (1950).

[129] *Id.*, at pp. 40–41.

formal, technical distinctions. Standards of review as such are, as Jaffe observed with trenchant wit, not determinative in themselves but rather indicators of the "spirit or mood in which judges should approach their task."[130] Moreover, even regarded as rough heuristic proxies, the nominal standards have failed to anticipate outcomes in an even marginally satisfactory way. To wit, theoretically, the four primary scope of review standards, (1) arbitrary and capricious, (2) substantial evidence, (3) clearly erroneous, and (4) de novo review,[131] are supposed to provide a sliding scale or "telescopic" degrees of review, from the most generous ("arbitrary and capricious") to the most intrusive (de novo) review.[132] But this formal differentiation has not been reflected by the interpretation of specific standards in actual adjudication. The Supreme Court famously required, for instance, a "probing, in depth review"[133] and a "hard look"[134] in the application of the nominally deferential "arbitrary and capricious" standard. More relevantly, the "scale of review scope" has failed to discipline practices. This discrepancy was evidenced repeatedly by aggregate impact differentials reflecting the application of various standards on discrete fields of administrative action. Some nominally strict

---

[130] Louis Jaffe, "Judicial Review: 'Substantial Evidence on the Whole Record,'" 64 *Harv. L. Rev.* 1233, at p. 1236 (1951). *Cf.*, similar, Martin Shapiro, "Administrative Discretion: The Next Stage," 92 *Yale L. J.* 1487 (1982-1983), at p. 1490: "Standards for judicial review are notoriously vague. The degree to which a court will substitute its judgment for an agency's is neither determined nor expressed by the formula it announces." *See also*, Rabin 1986, at p.1266: "[T]he Act spoke in the broad terms of a charter-'substantial evidence,' 'arbitrary and capricious,' 'statement of basis and purpose,' and so forth-employing language sufficiently vague to allow the greatest leeway in the scope of administrative discretion to fashion regulatory policy in a particularized context."

[131] The scope of review in general is specified in Sec. 706 (2) Scope of Review. The first two and the last standard are derived from this section, (A), (E), and (F): "The reviewing court shall. . .hold unlawful and set aside agency action, findings, and conclusions, found to be:

(A) arbitrary, capricious, and abuse of discretion, or otherwise not in accordance to the law;
(B) contrary to constitutional right, power, privilege, or immunity;
(C) in excess of statutory jurisdiction, authority, limitations, or short of statutory right;
(D) without observance of procedure required by law;
(E) unsupported by substantial evidence in a case subject to section 556 and 557 of this title or otherwise reviewed on the record of an agency hearing provided by statute; or

unwarranted by the facts to the extent that the facts are subject to trial de novo by the reviewing court."

[132] Paul R. Verkuil, "An Outcomes Analysis of Scope of Review Standards," 44 *Wm. & Mary L. Rev.* 679 (2002-2003), at p. 682: "Think of the word 'scope' in 'scope of review' as a contraction of 'telescope.' Like a telescope, scope of review offers either a narrow aperture to limit the breadth of judicial scrutiny, thereby increasing the area of agency discretion, or a wider lens to expand judicial oversight, thereby decreasing agency discretion."

[133] *Citizens to Preserve Overton Park v. Volpe*, 401 U.S. 402, at p. 415 (1971).

[134] *Motor Vehicle Manufacturers Association v. State Farm Mutual Automobile Ins. Co.*, 463 U.S. 29 (1983).

standards have resulted in lenient application, whereas, vice versa, theoretically lenient standards have been applied by judges draconically.[135]

In fact, the administration of the APA provisions has reflected a closer relation to the judicial search for normative substance, echoing overarching philosophical-ideological tendencies and waves of social-economic transformation. The formal distinctions of positive law have been overshadowed by the judicial attempt to find some cohesive, overarching account or explanation, an unifying criterion of justification behind the multiplicity of forms, to guide the substantive and procedural posture of the judge towards these new realities of the administrative state. The initial position, deference to experts, corresponded with the inherited beliefs in social science and bureaucratic solutions to collective problems. In the pre-APA *N.L.R.B. v Hearst Publications,* [136] the Court notoriously deferred to a National Labor Relations Board's interpretation of the term "employee" in its organic act to cover 'newsboys' employed by a number of major newspapers. The administrative interpretation, adopted for the purpose of directing the papers to collectively bargain with the said newsboys, was in clear contradiction to the common-law definition of the legal term "employee." Yet the court bowed, in keeping with New Deal orthodoxy, to the expertise of the board and the broad remedial purposes of the Congressional enactment.[137] Nonetheless, belief in expertise soon waned with an increasing realization of the disconnect between New Deal ideals and the realities of agency 'capture' and manipulative administrative behavior during the McCarthy era. It crumbled altogether with the disasters of the Vietnam War.[138]

Procedure as such, now divorced from a substantive justification, immediately became an ideological-instrumental tool in the new power struggles, following a general realization, on both sides of the ideological aisle, that not only is "one man's delay another man's due process" but one mans' due process can very easily become, once a court can be persuaded to lend a sympathetic ear, another man's sorrows. Procedure also became a passe-partout for administrative practices. In his 1975 classic, "The Reformation of American Administrative Law," Richard Stewart described the contemporaneous province of American administrative law in primarily procedural key, through the conceptual placeholder of the "interest

[135] Verkuil 2002-2003, on the basis of a statistical analysis of field-specific scope of review outcomes, notices that, although, for instance, Social Security Administration are reviewed under a substantial evidence standard, the actual, much more stringent, remand rate (50%) would more accurately correspond to de novo review, whereas Freedom of Information Act reviews, nominally de novo, are reversed at the diminutive rate of 10%, corresponding in fact to extremely deferential, arbitrary and capricious review.

[136] 322 U.S. 111 (1944).

[137] *See also Switchmen's Union of North America v. National Mediation Board*, 320 U.S. 297 (1943).

[138] *See* general discussion at p. 242 ff in Horwitz 1992. ("But above all, disillusionment with the 'best and brightest,' those arrogant technocrats who had confidently predicted a quick victory in Vietnam, produced a deep reaction to claims of expertise.", at p. 242). *See generally*, on administrative pathologies undermining the "expertise" model, Bernstein 1955.

balancing model." That is, the tendencies he then observed revealed a strong judicial bent and emphasis on taming the administrative process through interest representation. The drive towards provision of the broadest possible participation in administrative processes was, indeed, so pronounced that the administration as such had, according to Stewart, begun to resemble an aggregation of mini-legislatures providing a form of "surrogate political process."[139] Both his description and diagnosis are well summated by a passage, which warrants a somewhat longer citation:

> [T]he problem of administrative procedure is to provide representation for all affected interests; the problem of substantive policy is to reach equitable accommodations among these interests in varying circumstances; and the problem of judicial review is to ensure that agencies provide fair procedures for representation and reach fair accommodations. *These difficulties are ultimately attributable to the disintegration of any fixed and simple boundary between private ordering and collective authority.* The extension of governmental administration into so many areas formerly left to private determination has outstripped the capacities of the traditional political and judicial machinery to control and legitimate its exercise. In the absence of authoritative directives from the legislature, decisional processes have become decentralized and agency policy has become in large degree a function of bargaining and exchange with and among the competing private interests whom the agency is supposed to rule. Private ordering has been swallowed up by government, while government has become in part a species of private ordering. Where the governmental and private spheres are thus melded, administrative law must devise a process, distinct from either traditional political or judicial models, that both reconciles the competing private interests at stake and justifies the ultimately coercive exercise of governmental authority. The notion of adequate consideration of all affected interests is one ideal of such a process.[140] [emphasis supplied]

Stewart characterized the paradigm shifts of American administrative law as a series of "model" transitions, from classical "transmission belt" (the administration implements faithfully clear legislative mandates), through Progressive Era- and New Deal-style "expertise" (the bureaucratic experts carry out detachedly general legislative goals), and finally to the then current "interest balancing" model. Those transitions had marked, according to Stewart, an increasing degree of separation and aloofness of the administration from the legitimate channels of classical politics, ranging from presumptively complete dependence, passing through the ambivalence of autonomous administrative expertise, and finally culminating in the administrative reality of a multitude of parallel quasi-political fora, reflecting a myriad of interests. "Interest balancing" consisted in the "*essentially legislative process* of adjusting the competing claims of various private interests affected by agency policy."[141] The new task of the judge would be to umpire and prod this representative process.

---

[139] Stewart 1975, at p. 1670: "Increasingly, the function of administrative law is not the protection of private autonomy but the provision of a surrogate political process to ensure the fair representation of a wide range of affected interests in the process of administrative decision. Whether this is a coherent or workable aim is an open issue. But there is no denying the transformation."

[140] *Id.*, at pp. 1759-1760.

[141] *Ibid.*, at p. 1683.

Even though his argument has often been read in a rosier normative light, a strong undertow of ambivalence and even pessimism careens the article.[142] Stewart's account is still deservedly recognized as a classic because it has the mark of authenticity and the make of first-rate scholarship. It indicates with perfect timing a new phenomenal configuration, points to a fundamental tension and fissure in the structure of public law, and confronts juridical practices with the serious and ideologically unattached normative poise of true scholarship. As Stewart did not fail to intuit, the notion of administratively cognizable "interest" has recognizably fluid denotations and implications. "Interests" are, much like the abuse of "civil society" solutions nowadays, an ambiguous substitute for representative democracy and therefore a questionable palliative for democracy deficits.[143] Moreover and related at a more mundane level, the paradigm of interest balancing imposes very high burdens on the judges, who have to rationally account for the aggregation of these interests in the absence of any common normative scale. In the classical political process, the balance of interests and the substantive rationality of the political decision resulting therefrom are intrinsic in the process. They can be taken by the judge more or less at 'face value' and measured against a rule of law, for instance, a constitutional limitation. Contrariwise, balancing "interests" without a scale in the administrative process provides no stable line of assessment, either procedurally or substantively; indeed, procedural and substantive consistency become complementary tautologies. Therefore, a judicial posture of asking the administrator to take "all affected interests" into consideration and requiring a degree of consistency and rationality in terms of decisional substance, against the background of statutory ambiguity, easily reaches the point of assuming a 'synoptic' judge and a 'synoptic' administrator, while simultaneously undercutting any possibility of achieving rational synopsis.[144] What Stewart was describing in effect, lurking behind the kaleidoscopically splintered imagery of the interest balancing model, was the increasing failure of administrative practices to function according to constitutional presuppositions. A model of administrative process severed *ex hypothesi* from any imaginable connection with the legislative impetus cannot be accounted for constitutionally, since the kind of accountability proper to the classical liberal constitution presupposes normative recursiveness and a global

[142] *E.g.*, Ziamou 2001 (relying on Stewart's account to defend the proposal to adopt US-minted pluralist rulemaking models in Europe). *But cf.* Mashaw 2005, at p. 2 "There is no escaping the overall impression left by *Reformation*. Understood as a project of making administrators accountable to the legislative will, administrative law was failing. The old transmission belt model was in tatters; and, whether others could *see* it or not, Stewart was clearly predicting that its successor, interest representation, would suffer a similar fate."

[143] *See* the "Lisbon Decision" of the German Constitutional Court, for a thoughtful (and skeptical) judicial gloss on the possibilities of substituting "representative associations" and "civil society" participation (Art. 11 Lisbon TEU) to compensate for representative democracy deficits, BVerfG, 2 BvE 2/08 vom 30.6.2009, at para. 290 ff (English translation, at http://www.bundesverfassungsgericht.de/entscheidungen/es20090630_2bve000208en.html).

[144] Shapiro 1988.

sense of consistency of practices and concepts. It presupposes the possibility of tracing public action back to its sources, that is, to a presumptively uninterrupted chain of delegation. Obversely, the archetype of administrative interest balancing, described by the last sentence of Stewart's article as the challenge of "dense complexity," could offer countless ludic possibilities for segmented, fragmentary, ad hoc innovation (and exploitation). After all, the demise of all hierarchical structures has liberating side-effects and implications. But this new reality no longer lent itself to regulation through a constitutionally predetermined kind of normativity. It escaped thus the normative promise of constitutionalism: the possibility of rational control within a meaningful framework for reconciling individual autonomy with collective action.[145]

The expectable judicial reaction was to seek a measure of consistency in a compromised and partial retrenchment towards more stable baselines, in order to thus make this newer administrative paradigm normatively manageable within the framework of limited government. Tellingly, the most coherent attempt at an answer the Supreme Court has given to these pluralist challenges is an administrative law 'mirror' to nondelegation, an administrative law doctrine that seeks a comprehensive reassessment of the judicial positions in the field of policy and value imponderables.[146] In *Chevron U.S.A. Inc. v. Natural Resources Defense Council Inc.*,[147] the Supreme Court was faced with an interpretation by the EPA of the term "stationary source" in the Clean Air Act Amendments of 1977. A statutory provision that required "new or modified major stationary sources" to comply with permit requirements had been reinterpreted to mean an entire plant rather than each individual source of pollution. The EPA had adopted the "bubble concept"

[145] *Cf.* Mashaw 2005, arguing that the major flaw in Stewart's essay was "that article's tendency to take the transmission belt metaphor too seriously –to assume that administrative accountability and administrative legitimacy must flow from or be oriented towards a single source of political authority rooted in electoral processes" (at p. 37). According to Mashaw, accountability is a complex, multifaceted notion. Its conceptual use invites questioning assumptions, whereas its practical instantiations invite complex institutional trade-offs. Mashaw profers therefore, as a counterpart to Stewart's complexity, the complexity of "administrative law as institutional design," in recognition of the fact that "any institutional form is likely to respond to multiple sources of influence and constraint, and thus to participate simultaneously in multiple accountability regimes" (at p. 38). This may be so but Professor Mashaw's answer is the open-ended, managerial challenge of a demiurge, of *constitution-making* even (and one may suspect that he would only relish its complete joys in a world of like-minded demiurges, otherwise the multiplicity of free-floating assumptions, both institution-making and theoretical discussion-wise may veer out of any manageable control). Stewart's question is situated in a completely different paradigm, namely within the conceptual and practical constraints of normative constitutionalism.

[146] Analogous steps back (in the procedural field) are the developments in standing law after *Lujan v. Defenders of Wildlife*, 504 U.S. 555 (1992), holding that pure (mere) "regulatory injury" is not a sufficient standing predicate and (in the field of administrative law proper) *Vermont Yankee Nuclear Power Corp. v. NRDC*, 435 U.S. 519 (1978), putting an end to the "hybrid rulemaking" innovations of lower courts.

[147] 467 U.S. 837 (1984).

(so called since it regards a cluster of buildings as sitting together under a "bubble," for the purpose of applying the permit requirements) primarily for political reasons. During Carter's preceding presidency, "stationary source" had been interpreted to mean each piece of equipment (a furnace, for instance), whereas the "bubble" reinterpretation reflected a comprehensive undertaking by the new Reagan administration to cut the industry a more generous regulatory break.[148] This newer administrative interpretation permitted the installation or modification of individual pieces of equipment that did not meet the standards, as long as the sum total resulting from trade-offs inside the regulatory "bubble" did not exceed the pollution emissions limits.

Apparently breaking with the *Marbury* convention that the "province, to say what the law is" belongs as of right to the judiciary,[149] the Supreme Court announced that questions of law and policy would be reviewed under a standard of deference, comprising a two-step test:

(i) A preliminary determination of "whether Congress has directly spoken to the question at issue"[150];
(ii) A secondary determination of reasonableness. In the absence of a clear congressional statement, "permissible" interpretations given by a federal agency to the statutes it administers would be given deference, meaning that the court would not substitute them with its own (the administrative interpretation will thus, in effect, control the decisional outcome).[151]

That this administrative law statement has constitutional relevance and that its fundamental law import may reside in a relationship between *Chevron* and the delegation doctrine are twin intuitions which have not escaped too many commentators.[152] The heaps of literature over the case express a generalized

---

[148] *Id.*, at 857-858.

[149] Elizabeth Garrett, 101 *Mich. L. Rev.* 2637 (2002-2003) ("One of the most significant administrative law cases, *Chevron v. Natural Resources Defense Council, Inc.* is routinely referred to as the "counter-Marbury." (at p. 2637). Chevron was, ironically, roughly contemporaneous with the "Bumpers Amendment" to the APA which came very close to be adopted in Congress (it passed though the Senate unanimously). The Bumpers Amendment would have required courts to do precisely the opposite to what Chevron directs them, i.e., to decide "independently" (de novo) "all questions of law."

[150] *Chevron*, at 842-843: "First, always, is the question whether Congress has directly spoken to the precise question at issue. If the intent of Congress is clear, that is the end of the matter; for the court, as well as the agency, must give effect to the unambiguously expressed intent of Congress" (footnote omitted).

[151] "If, however, the court determines that Congress has not directly addressed the precise question at issue, the court does not simply impose its own construction on the statute, as would be necessary in the absence of an administrative interpretation. Rather, if the statute is silent with respect to the specific issue, the question for the court is whether the agency's answer is based on a permissible construction of the statute." At 843 (footnotes omitted).

[152] *See* thus Richard Pierce, "Reconciling *Chevron* and Stare Decisis," 85 *Geo. L. J.* 2225 (1996-1997), for whom Chevron is "one of the most important constitutional law decisions in history,

conviction that *Chevron* is momentous and that its importance may lie in the fact that it relates in a foundational way to (1) the practice of "delegation" of power or discretion from Congress to the agencies; (2) the implications entailed by these practices with respect to judicial review of administrative actions; and (3) the nondelegation doctrine and its respective constitutional implications. But the strength of intuition has not resulted in a measure of doctrinal agreement or at least overlap. Indeed, where and wherein that *Chevron*/delegation kinship resides are nebulous matters, judging from the multiplicity of contradictory positions expressed in the literature.[153] Even the practical issue of whether the interrelationship between an unenforced or unenforceable constitutional nondelegation limitation and an explicit judicial admission of deference to administratively delegated "law-making" produces positive or negative effects is under generalized contention. In this latter respect only, contestability and intensity of opposed positions, *Chevron*-related discussions seem to echo nondelegation debates.

Laurence Tribe, for instance, views *Chevron* as a parallel and equally detrimental methodological choice, an example of judicial abdication similar to the failure of nondelegation: "It remains to be seen whether the institutional arrangements with which we are familiar can long survive both *Chevron* and the relaxation of the nondelegation doctrine."[154] To other writers, *Chevron* represents consistency and is therefore simply the logical conclusion to nondelegation. Once the courts allowed the legislature practically unlimited constitutional leeway, they could do no other at the administrative level. As Patrick Garry argues, *Chevron* is perhaps problematic but nonetheless unavoidable once the "institutionalization of ambiguity" was permitted at the constitutional level: "Thus, even though *Chevron* marks a dramatic departure from traditional legal principles, and even though it poses separation of powers concerns, it flows logically and necessarily from the jurisprudential evolution of the nondelegation doctrine."[155] Other authors perceive *Chevron* as

---

even though the opinion does not cite any provision of the Constitution" (at p. 2227). According to Pierce, Chevron provides a better method of enforcing the nondelegation doctrine, by replacing the failed "use of command and control regulation of Congress" (i.e., direct enforcement of the doctrine, by constitutional invalidation of "delegating" statutes) with a "reconstitutive strategy" that changes the institutional incentives (Congress knows now that the administration of vague statutes will be controlled by the President and this provides the legislature with a strong incentive to legislate with specificity) (at pp. 2230-2232).

[153] *See* Thomas W. Merrill and Kristin Hickman, "*Chevron*'s Domain," 89 *Geo. L. J.* 833 (2000-2001), for an elaboration (and a review of the literature on the diverse positions) on whether the status of Chevron is that of i. a constitutional law doctrine, deriving from the separation of powers; ii. a statutory-level doctrine deriving from Congress in the form of a presumption about congressional intent; iii. a common-law-level, judicial norm (canon) of statutory construction.

[154] Tribe 2000 (Vol. I, Third Ed.), at p. 1002. The literature on Chevron is enormous; citations of general positions are provided here for general exemplificatory purposes only, insofar as they serve the needs of this book's argument.

[155] Patrick M. Garry, "Accommodating the Administrative State: The Interrelationship Between the *Chevron* and Nondelegation Doctrines," 38 *Ariz. St. L. J.* 921, at p. 959 (2006).

representing primarily a propitious *judicial* self-limitation, similar to the demise of nondelegation. Both judicial postures commendably express countervailing admissions of epistemological, methodological, and institutional limitation. As this line of arguments runs, the *Chevron* court admitted that judges have no rational, and thus judicial, instruments for reducing structurally determined statutory vagueness. Attempting to provide a judicial solution to the problems of normative and policy conflict created by open-ended statutes would have been in effect judicial law-making, politics by another name, and therefore an illegitimate abuse of the judicial office. Deferring means, in the logic of this interpretation, appropriately stepping back and leaving the space free for politics.[156] To other critics, *Chevron* is good, well-crafted technique: it represents an optimal administrative response to the downfalls that have plagued the enforcement of nondelegation. *Chevron* combines deference when proper, at step one (no clear position by Congress) with a severe rational probing of the administrative motives and reasoning, where judicially possible and appropriate, at step two (reasonableness of the agency interpretation).[157]

As expressed, the doctrine seems clear enough. Furthermore, the *Chevron* Court has gone to great lengths not only to simplify the deference test as such but also to elaborate on its wider foundations and implications, in a way that would help clear out in advance the morass of potential ambiguities in implementation. In a long passage, the Court explains, for instance, that the "intent" of Congress has no motivational-anthropomorphic undertones for the purpose of determining "whether Congress ha[d] directly spoken to the question at issue." It mattered not, as the majority opinion stressed, whether the legislature had considered the meaning of "stationary source" and whether it had taken a second-order position, if any, on the issue: "[T]he decision involves reconciling conflicting policies. Congress intended

---

[156] *See* Pierce (1985-1986), according to whom *Chevron* is a positive, fourth-way alternative to the other (flawed) possibilities of disciplining the policy-making powers of agencies under meaningless statutory standards. Unlike the three other alternatives (the meanwhile invalidated legislative veto; de novo review; revival of nondelegation), deference is both judicially legitimate and politically commendable, shifting policy-making power to the President. *Cf.* partly similar Douglas W. Kmiec, "Judicial Deference to Executive Agencies and the Decline of the Nondelegation Doctrine," 2 *Admin. L. J.* 269 (1988), at p. 290: "Administrative discretion even under the practically attenuated, but constitutionally recognized, supervision of an elected president, seems more in keeping with our constitutional structure than judicial legislation. Lawmaking at the hands of an unelected judiciary raises more questions than it answers against a backdrop of separated powers." *Cf.* also Kenneth W. Starr, "Judicial Review in the Post-*Chevron* Era," 3 *Yale J. on Reg.* 283 (1985-1986), at p. 312: "Policy, which is not the natural province of courts, belongs properly to the administrative agencies and, ultimately, to the executive and legislature that oversee them."

[157] *E.g.*, Lisa Schultz Bressman, "Disciplining Delegation after *Whitman v. American Trucking Ass'ns*," 87 *Cornell L. Rev.* 452 (2001-2002), arguing that "the [*Whitman*] Court should be understood as shifting the delegation inquiry from constitutional law to administrative law" (at p. 469) and noting that administrative standards, therefore a narrowing and disciplining of delegated discretion, can be imposed under step two of *Chevron*.

to accommodate both interests, but did not do so itself on the level of specificity presented by these cases. Perhaps that body consciously desired the Administrator to strike the balance at this level, thinking that those with great expertise and charged with responsibility for administering the provision would be in a better position to do so; perhaps it simply did not consider the question at this level; and perhaps Congress was unable to forge a coalition on either side of the question, and those on each side decided to take their chances with the scheme devised by the agency. For judicial purposes, it matters not which of these things occurred."[158] It continued to gloss, in dicta, on the relative levels of expertise and kinds of accountability of the judiciary and the Chief Executive, respectively. The court bowed to an unclear mix of "technical" knowledge and political choice, in a passage exemplary of unusual, almost apophatic, judicial modesty: "Judges are not experts in the field, and are not part of either political branch of the Government. Courts must, in some cases, reconcile competing political interests, but not on the basis of the judges' personal policy preferences. In contrast, an agency to which Congress has delegated policy-making responsibilities may, within the limits of that delegation, properly rely upon the incumbent administration's views of wise policy to inform its judgments. While agencies are not directly accountable to the people, the Chief Executive is, and it is entirely appropriate for this political branch of the Government to make such policy choices-resolving the competing interests which Congress itself either inadvertently did not resolve, or intentionally left to be resolved by the agency charged with the administration of the statute in light of everyday realities."[159]

It is therefore all the more surprising that, all other things being equal, *Chevron* seems to have been of little avail in simplifying and clarifying the field of administrative law. To begin with, the Court has developed an increasingly sinuous jurisprudence around the limits of *Chevron* itself. The resulting "step-zero" conditions (namely, the prior inquiry into whether *Chevron* deference; or no deference; or more complex, multi-factor, pre-*Chevron* deference, applies) are anything but clarificatory of the statutory predicate, reach, and circumstances of deference.[160] Even decisions that seek to gloss on *Chevron* in an ostensibly rule-like manner are riddled with so many qualifications that in the end they appear to have brought, instead of clarity, an even more byzantine confusion to the field. The 2001 case of *United States v. Mead Corporation*, for instance, denied deference to a "ruling letter" by the US Customs Office Headquarters. At issue was whether a ruling letter classification of three-ring binders as "bound diaries" subject to tariff, in opposition to a consistent prior practice of classifying such planners as duty-free, deserved automatic deference. The Court began by holding that *Chevron* deference applies upon a predicate of formal delegation: "We hold that administrative

---

[158] 467 U.S. 837, at p. 865 (footnotes omitted).

[159] *Id.*, at pp. 865-866.

[160] *See generally* Cass R. Sunstein, "*Chevron* Step Zero," 92 *Va. L. Rev.* 187 (2006).

implementation of a particular statutory provision qualifies for *Chevron* deference when it appears that Congress delegated authority to the agency generally to make rules carrying the force of law, and that the agency interpretation claiming deference was promulgated in the exercise of that authority."[161] But the decision continued just a few pages later to qualify this holding by conceding a certain leeway for exceptions from formality (and thus implicitly subverting the clear rule just announced in the holding): "That said, and as significant as notice-and-comment is in pointing to *Chevron* authority, the want of that procedure here does not decide the case, for we have sometimes found reasons for *Chevron* deference even when no such administrative formality was required and none was afforded."[162]

Even the interpretation of the two steps' requirements as such seems at times enveloped in wooly hermeneutical mystery. In the case of *INS v. Cardoza-Fonseca*, for instance, the majority looked to the legislative history and historical legislative environment of the Immigration Act to ascertain the meaning of the term "well-founded fear" in section 208 (a), authorizing the Attorney General to grant asylum to a refugee unable or unwilling to return to his home country because of persecution or a "well-founded fear" thereof.[163] At issue was whether the same standard of proof would control the application of this provision and that of section 243 (h) of the act, requiring the Attorney General to withhold deportation in cases where an alien could demonstrate that his "life or freedom would be threatened" thereby on account of several factors, by a showing that "it is more likely than not that the alien would be subject to persecution" in the country of return. The court denied deference at step one, showing that the intention of Congress was clear on the matter and expounding the judicial role in applying the test: "The question whether Congress intended the two standards to be identical is a pure question of statutory construction for the courts to decide. Employing traditional tools of statutory construction, we have concluded that Congress did not intend the two standards to be identical."[164] Justice Scalia concurred in the result but wrote an opinion to strenuously object to the interpretive methodology. As he saw it, the incursion into history was barred. If *Chevron* was to be understood as

---

[161] *United States v. Mead Corporation*, 533 U.S. 218, at pp. 226-227 (2001). This appeared in perfect synch with the proposal by Merrill-Hickman 2000-2001 (cited approvingly by the opinion) to reduce Chevron deference to the field of formal actions taken by agencies with the power to take "actions with the force of law" (binding individuals outside the agencies). Informal agency interpretations receive a much weaker, "multiple-factor," pre-*Chevron,* 'presumptive' deference, "depend[ing] upon the thoroughness evident in its consideration, the validity of its reasoning, its consistency with earlier and later pronouncements, and all those factors which give it power to persuade, if lacking power to control," *Skidmore v. Swift & Co.*, 323 U.S. 134, at p. 140 (1944).

[162] 533 U.S. 218, at p. 231.

[163] *INS v. Cardoza-Fonseca*, 480 U.S. 421 (1987). Citing footnote 9 in the Chevron majority opinion to that effect: "If a court, employing traditional tools of statutory construction, ascertains that Congress had an intention on the precise question at issue, that intention is the law and must be given effect." *Chevron*, at p. 843, n. 9.

[164] *Id.*, at 446.

recognizing ambiguity only when no meaning could be attached to the text, then deference was "a doctrine of desperation" and "an evisceration of *Chevron*."[165] The sole legitimate indicator to congressional intentions was, Scalia insisted, the plain meaning of the text itself. To be sure, a doctrine which comes with a specific, mandatory statutory interpretation methodology attached, as a package deal, is a rather strange legal animal. However, since Justice Scalia has been recognized not only as an eminent administrative lawyer but also as the "*Chevron*'s chief judicial champion,"[166] his position deserves respectful attention.

What Scalia pointed out was that "whether Congress has directly spoken" upon an issue is a function of whether and how courts can ascribe meaning to the text. Unless it is associated with a clear hermeneutical benchmark, *Chevron* can provide no objective standard and therefore cannot, by definition, constrain adjudication in any rational way. Through this looking-glass, the relation between *Chevron* and nondelegation becomes much clearer. *Chevron* marks an attempted withdrawal from a nondelegation limitation seemingly unraveled by judicially uncontrollable constitutional normativity into the apparently safer ground of statutory semantics. The text will provide the line of demarcation between law and discretion, adjudication and politics, structurally controlled judicial rationality and the legally arational field of political decision. Justice Scalia's impassionate and repeated profession of faith to interpretative methodologies as the key to law-bound, ideology and politics-free adjudication is well known.[167] This makes it all the stranger that his own methodological position towards the administration of the *Chevron* test has been accused, simultaneously and hence paradoxically, of deferring too much and deferring too little. As the author of a study on the topic, Gregory E. Maggs, observed, it makes little sense to see Scalia equally vilified both for defending a method of interpretation that "poses a threat to the future of the deference doctrine" and being the representative of the "Pontius Pilate school of judging."[168] Logically, it must be either one or the other. Maggs screened all *Chevron* cases in which Scalia voted and defended the latter against the opposite charges, showing that, in fact, the votes cast by the Justice fell uneventfully, most of the time, with the majority of the Court.

Assuming the statistical breakdown to be unassailable, this may have something to do with textualism being embraced by the rest of the Court (as Maggs believes) but that is still no satisfactory response to Scalia critics. An updated, satisfactory statistical response would have to take into account the additional variable of levels

[165] *Ibid.*, at p. 454 (Scalia, J., concurring in the judgment).

[166] Merrill-Hickman 2000-2001, at p. 867.

[167] Namely, constitutional originalism and statutory plain meaning textualism. *See*, respectively, Antonin Scalia (Author) and Amy Gutman (Ed.), *A Matter of Interpretation* (Princeton, NJ: Princeton University Press, 1997) and Scalia 1989.

[168] Gregory E. Maggs, "Reconciling Textualism and the *Chevron* Doctrine: In Defense of Justice Scalia," 28 *Conn. L. Rev.* 393 (1995-1996) (quoting at p. 405 Thomas W. Merrill and at p. 394 William D. Popkin, respectively).

of deference before and after the alleged spread of textualism as prevalent methodology. A normative attempt at an answer is much more interesting. Whether one sees textualism determining too much or too little deference depends on whether one believes that a chosen method of interpretation will determine the meaning of vague statutes or contradictory provisions. Neither the text nor the nominal methodology provides a priori a clear limit to the question of "how clear is clear." Thus, the important but logically subordinate question of whether deferential judges of a textualist persuasion will turn out to be machine-like "paragraph automatons" or covert law-makers, deceitfully decked in the borrowed plumes of judicial objectivity remains also unanswered by either *Chevron* or the interpretive methodology.[169] However, the failure as such of a doctrine based on statutory semantics to replace satisfactorily a doctrine embedded in constitutional normativity as a delegation limit is revealing of a foundational tension. It indicates the complementary aspects of structural erosion of foundational normative limits and the dearth and exiguousness of surrogate solutions.

For the purpose of conclusive and epistemologically representative exemplification of this last remark, a recent comment on *Chevron* deserves mention at the end of our review of American developments. On the one hand, the author, Adrian Vermeule, notes that the *Chevron* doctrine is justifiably "a pillar of American administrative law," since "once the bogus nondelegation principle is cleared away, democratic accountability requires that courts should defer to the democratically superior judgments of administrative agencies, where Congress has not spoken clearly."[170] On the other, Vermeule observes that, indispensable though across-the-board deference may be, the application of *Chevron* poses prohibitive conceptual challenges and thus seems bias- and uncertainty-ridden: "*Chevron* is a poor means for promoting accountability in the world without a nondelegation doctrine...[because it is] vulnerable to a range of problems: conceptual imprecision, cognitive burdens that affect boundedly rational judges, and manipulation on the part of biased judges."[171] This is, the writer argues, because *Chevron* tried to provide a "soft" doctrinal solution to "what is, after all, an institutional problem: the allocation of interpretive authority between agencies and courts when congressional instructions are silent or ambiguous."[172] Vermeule provides therefore a "hard" institutional solution to the institutional problem. This consists in recasting *Chevron* deference as a voting rule by loading the dice "say, by a six-three vote on the Supreme Court, or by a three-zero vote on a court of appeals panel" and changing at

---

[169] Justice Scalia himself opined that his strand of textualism predisposes rather to semantic optimism rather than deference at step one: "One who finds more often (as I do) that the meaning of a statute is apparent from its text and from its relationship with other laws, thereby finds less often that the triggering requirement for *Chevron* deference exists." Scalia 1989, at p. 521.

[170] Adrian Vermeule, *Mechanisms of Democracy: Institutional Design Writ Small* (New York: Oxford University Press, 1997). pp. 175-176.

[171] *Id.*, at p. 144.

[172] *Ibid.*, at p. 146.

the same time the scope of interpretation to *de novo* review.[173] Such rules, differently calibrating judicial votes, already exist, says Vermeule. As evidence, he points to the American example of the so-called "Rule of Four," which allows four justices of the Supreme Court to grant a writ of certiorari. Consequently, the recalibration of *Chevron* as a voting rule would solve systemic deficiencies. The specification of a qualified majority for *Chevron* cases would transform a rule that now needs to be internalized by each individual judge (in a way that cannot apparently be controlled) into an externally controlled "aggregate property of the judicial system."[174] The "loaded" voting rule and the simplification of the doctrinal question would thus predetermine doctrinal consistency. This transition from the two-level interpretive quest of doctrinal *Chevron* to the simplified "correct"/"incorrect" query of *de novo* review reduces the cognitive burden (and the operation of bias), whereas the existing default (deference) is transformed into a procedural-systemic characteristic of the vote aggregation rule (six to one, three to zero, etc.).

Professor Vermeule's argument showcases well the parallel challenges of constitutional modernity: eroded systemic normativity and the impossibility of "external" (non-normative) answers to this erosion. In that, his proposal is also an epiphenomenal manifestation of self-subverting rationality. Veremule's allegedly pragmatic, "no-nonsense, no philosophy" solution promises much more than it can deliver, since it imposes implicitly normative demands on the constitutional structure compared to which those raised by "the bogus nondelegation doctrine" seem diminutive. To begin with, it is true that there are in many jurisdictions judicial screening rules that do not require a majority voting by the court. This is due to the fact that such rules regard administrative, policy decisions, which are rightly premised upon a different kind of rationality, similar to that of legislative decisions. Screening decisions are an excellent epitome thereof. When judges make those decisions, they make them as administrators rather than in the exercise of judicial duties. To wit, grants of certiorari do not need to be motivated precisely due to the fact that, not reaching the merits,[175] they are not exercises of the judicial function proper.[176] Otherwise, majority voting in judicial decisions is an expression of and contingent upon the kind of formalized legal rationality that constitutes the exercise of core judicial functions. This is why one does not tinker with voting rules to affect outcomes. For analogous reasons, describing a deference doctrine as "an allocation of interpretive authority between agencies and courts" is a conceptual

[173] *Ibid.*

[174] *Ibid.*, at p. 167: "One of the key reasons for the apparent failure of Chevron to eliminate if not significantly reduce uncertainty about deference is that the framework makes deference an individual rather than aggregate property of the judicial system, and relies on underspecified norms that are imperfectly internalized by judges."

[175] *Barber v. Tennessee*, 513 U.S. 1184 (1995).

[176] Even though a denial can inflame passions and particular judges may choose to concur or dissent, in order to motivate their positions. But, in so doing, their posture acquires a political character. *See Knight v. Florida*, 528 U.S. 990 (1999).

misnomer. It is no more true (from a *legal* point of view) than describing a tort case as "after all, about whether Tom will collect 100.000 $ for his broken leg" or a criminal case as "essentially about whether Robert goes to jail." Even though the tort case may seem to the proverbial man on the street or indeed to the plaintiff himself to be "about the money," legally speaking the issue is "about" the interpretation and application of tort rules to facts in a rationally accountable way. This is not narrow-minded positivism, since even a marginally sophisticated legal realist position has to take into consideration and account for the professed internal logic of practices. The whole judicial system is organized in a way that gives expression to the position of the judge as a rational seeker of legal truth (need to motivate decisions, standards of proof, careful specification of grounds for appeal, pyramidal structure of courts, indeed judicial independence and impartiality guarantees, etc.).[177] One cannot change a feature of this rational legal structure in a way that does violence to its internal logic (namely, by positing judges as biased/confused policymakers for purposes of changing decisional rules to *explicit* head-counting) without provoking an uncontrollable domino effect that causes the whole constitutional house to topple down. Once one makes politics and political decision-making explicit features of adjudication, none of the rationality-oriented structural characteristics of modern judicial systems (independence and impartiality guarantees spring to mind) are defensible as a matter of principle. Other, less rationally formalized systemic kinds of dispute resolution have existed in history and return is not impossible. But, within the current setting (limited government predicated upon normative constitutionalism), if foundational normative paradoxes and deadlocks cannot be answered and resolved normatively, then perhaps no solution at all is available.

4.3 Continental Distinctions

4.3.1 The Constitutional Normalization of Delegations

> Cinquante années de pratique constitutionnelle ont permis d'observer, d'une part, que la procédure d'adoption des décrets-lois s'est banalisée au point d'être, aujourd'hui, d'un usage si quotidien que l'exceptionnel s'est mué en durable sans acquérir pour autant la stabilité de la règle de droit.[178]
>
> Maryse Baudrez, "Décrets-lois réitérés en Italie : l'exaspération mesurée de la Cour constitutionnelle en 1996" 32 *Revue française de Droit constitutionnel* 745 (1997).

---

[177] *See generally*, Fuller 1978.

[178] Fifteen years of constitutional practice have allowed us to observe that the procedure of adopting decree-laws has been 'banalized' to the point where, today, its use is so casual that the exceptional was transformed into norm without however acquiring the presumptive stability of a rule of law.

European constitutions have adopted, after WWII, provisions that allow the limited delegation to the executive of the power to make rules of legislative force and effect. The adoption of subordinate legislation is commonly reined in at the level of fundamental law both with a number of procedural safeguards and with normative limitations. As previously indicated, although the procedural-institutional aspects (e.g., an obligation to lay the subordinate legislative rules before parliament within a certain deadline) are important and instrumental for disciplining the practice,[179] this aspect is tangential to the current argument. We will therefore be interested only in the comparative impact of normative constitutional limits on the practice of delegation, as indicated by the relative capacity of constitutional adjudication to produce workable tests for enforcing these limitations against a trespassing legislature.

Another aspect of the constitutionally-regulated delegation practices, namely the so-called "quasi-emergency delegations," albeit normatively relevant, warrants only brief mention. Provisions regarding delegation can have detrimental effects on a constitutional system to the extent that the unfortunate choice is made to grant the executive an autonomous and exceptional ordinance-making power based directly on the constitution (without, that is, the need of a prior enabling act). Such is the case, for instance, under the current Italian and the Romanian constitutions. Given that a legislative delegation is already postulated constitutionally as an exception to the norm of parliamentary legislation, the possibility of by-passing the parliament by a delegation based directly on the fundamental law itself constitutes—so to speak—an "exception to the exception."[180] In Italy, for example, as a derogation from the ordinary delegation procedure provided by Art. 76,[181] the executive can, by adopting an Art. 77 decree-law, take "provisional measures of legislative force" ("provvedimenti provvisori con forza di legge"). This includes the authority to legislate in unregulated domains and abrogate or amend existing legislative provisions. A safeguard is provided by the second paragraph of the article, which requires that decrees be laid before Parliament for ratification. If left unconfirmed (i.e., it is not transposed into law) within 60 days from the date of its publication, the decree-law becomes void, yet the Parliament can sanction by law rights and obligations arising out of decrees left unconfirmed.

---

[179] For an up-to-date comparative study of the procedural and institutional aspects respecting the control of delegations to the executive, *see* Pünder 2009 and sources referenced therein.

[180] Marius N. Balan, unpublished constitutional law course notes manuscript on file with the author.

[181] "The exercise of the legislative function may not be delegated to the Government unless principles and criteria have been established and then only for a limited time and for specified purposes." Official English translation available at www.senato.it/documenti/repository/istituzione/costituzione_inglese.pdf (last visited August 26, 2011).

In practice, in cases of decrees left by the Houses of Parliament un-ratified over the 60-day ratification deadline, the executive developed the habit of routinely re-issuing the lapsed norms in a new decree, sometimes over the span of several years. This allowed, in the words of a commentator, "the provisional norm to perpetually subsist provisionally."[182] Even though the Constitutional Court would finally, in 1996, declare unconstitutional the practice of reiterating lapsed decrees, the main and most important problem raised by quasi-emergency decrees still remained. By virtue of the constitutional decision of granting the executive this benefit of spontaneous and autonomous law-making by substitution under a (of necessity often false) plea of necessity, the legislative and the judiciary are placed ex ante in a perpetual default position of inferiority. Given the needs of predictability and stability of a modern legal system and the functional nature of the other two branches, the situation makes it very difficult to change or react to this continuous situation of *fait accompli*. This separation of powers problem is an addition to the representation, publicity,[183] parliamentary minority rights, and rule of law problems caused by the phenomenon of habitual executive legislation. In order to discipline the practice, the constitutional judge would have to define the exception through a test amenable to consistent application. This requirement is in itself a textbook antinomy, since one need not be a "Schmittian" to understand that an exception is by definition a circumstance that cannot be normatively controlled by means of a rule.[184]

---

[182] "la norme provisoire à perdurer, toujours provisoirement," Maryse Baudrez, "Décrets-lois réitérés en Italie : l'exaspération mesurée de la Cour constitutionnelle en 1996," 32 *Revue française de Droit constitutionnel* 745 (1997), at p. 747.

[183] "In principle the democratic and open process of legislation is itself a safeguard of rights." Norman Dorsen, András Sajó, Michel Rosenfeld, and Susanne Baer, *Comparative Constitutionalism-Cases and Materials* (St. Paul, Minn.: West Publ., 2003), at p. 247.

[184] The same pattern can be observed in Romania, where the Constitution gives the Government power to issue "emergency ordinances" without prior parliamentary authorization by an enabling act (Art. 115). Emergency ordinances have as a result become the routine regulatory instrument and their number dwarfs both parliamentary legislation and ordinary delegations. For instance, according to the date on the Chamber of Deputies website, in 2011 as of August 26, 68 emergency ordinances were adopted (http://www.cdep.ro/pls/legis/legis_pck.lista_anuala?an=2011&emi=3&tip=18&rep=0), compared to 12 ordinary ordinances, adopted not on the basis of the constitution but on that of a regular enabling law, hence following the nominally "standard" procedure (http://www.cdep.ro/pls/legis/legis_pck.lista_anuala?an=2011&emi=3&tip =13&rep=0) (both websites last visited August 26, 2011). These general and relative constitutional mechanics are comparable, even though in other respects the normative needs and the general constitutional environment of a transitional post-communist country are distinct from those of the relatively stable Western liberal-constitutional democracies (such as Italy). The epistemological difficulties entailed by the need (and impossibility) to provide a constitutional definition of emergency, for the purposes of judicial review of the predicate for adopting such ordinances are also comparable. *See*, thus, the revealingly tautological definition of emergency given by the Romania Constitutional Court, as "the necessity and urgency of regulating a situation which, due to its exceptional circumstances, requires the adoption of an immediate solution, in view of avoiding a grave detriment to public interest" (Who could, indeed, disagree?) DCC nr. 67/3 februarie 2005, în M.Of. nr. 146/18 februarie 2005.

If procedural limitations are of no direct interest to the book's argument and "quasi-emergency delegations" are unfortunate but idiosyncratic constitutional choices, of limited relevance knowledge-wise, the attempts to limit legislation by way of normative distinctions bears directly on this volume's thesis. As already mentioned, these post-war constitutional rules were adopted in order to counter a broader crisis in pre-war constitutionalism. The crisis manifested itself also through the phenomenon of 'blank cheque' delegations; such delegations had dramatically marked, in both Germany and France, the end of parliamentary democracy and the rise of totalitarianism. By the same token, the failure of European constitutional judges (in France and Germany) to come up with tests for enforcing these limits is the product of and reveals an erosion of contemporary constitutional normativity. In the case of France, delegation is allowed as an exception to parliamentary legislation. Delegation is constitutionally permitted within the legislative domain, which is itself constitutionally posited by the 1958 Constitution as a normative exception to original executive decree-making power. In the case of Germany, the Basic Law allows the delegation of the power to make rules with legislative force and effect (*Rechtsverordnungen*) to specific executive delegates, under restrictive constitutional conditions with respect to the permissible degree of statutory clarity and preciseness. The delegation-related case law of the Federal Constitutional Court is therefore analytically comparable with the US developments under the "intelligible principle" nondelegation test.[185]

4.3.2 France: The Inconsequential Upheaval

> Tout partage a priori résultant d'un système combinant une énumération avec une clause résiduelle—que la première de ces techniques soit appliquée au domaine législatif ou qu'elle le soit au domaine réglementaire, comme l'orientation s'en était précédemment dessinée sans atteindre à une véritable systématisation—est en contradiction avec le caractère continu du processus normatif et le type de cohérence qu'il implique.[186]
>
> Jean Boulouis, "L'influence des articles 34 et 37 sur l'équilibre politique entre les pouvoirs," in Jean Boulouis and Louis Favoreu, *Le domaine de la loi et du règlement* (Paris: Presses Universitaires d'Aix-Marseille, 1981).

[185] Functionally, the reach of the German constitutional provision is more limited than that of the US nodelegation doctrine; Art. 80 (1) of the Basic Law does not apply to delegations to private parties, for instance, and is restricted to delegated legislation proper, i.e., administrative rulemaking (the authorization to make ordinances with legislative force and effect).

[186] "Any a priori division resulting from a system combining enumerated powers with a residual clause—irrespective of whether the first technique applies to the law-making or the regulatory function (the latter case was previously tried, without any systemic effects)—goes against the grain of the continuous character of the normative process and the kind of coherence implicit therein."

After the Fourth Republic, in order to remedy the effects of the "legislative imperialism of a Parliament thought to have been at the same time abusive and powerless,"[187] which had been the norm under the previous two Republics, the founders of the 1958 Constitution chose to allow the delegation of legislation to the executive. The Government was granted the power to legislate within a specified time limit and domain of authorization, by means of ordinances (*ordonnances*).[188]

According to Article 38: "In order to implement its programme, the Government may ask Parliament for authorization, for a limited period, to take measures by Ordinance that are normally the preserve of statute law."[189] The only mandatory constitutional condition, on sanction of automatic voidance (*caducité*), is that an *ordonnance* must be laid before parliament within the time limit set forth by the enabling act. After being laid before Parliament, an ordinance can only be modified by a *loi* (in respect of the provisions which are within the constitutional domain of legislation, according to Art. 34). The enabling law can be challenged to review its conformity with the Constitution, before the Constitutional Council, whereas the ordinance itself can be controlled by the Council of State in judicial review of administrative action for excess of power, primarily with respect to its conformity with the legislative authorization.

This provision has to be perceived in its constitutional context. The drafters of the Fifth Republic Constitution (the document bore in effect the stamp of General de Gaulle and his Minister of Justice, Michel Debré), sought to rationalize parliamentarism. The primary constitutional tool to this effect was the reversal of the traditional distinction between the *loi* and the *règlement* which had been, ever since 1791, the defining mark of orthodoxy in French constitutionalism. Thus, the Constitution of 1958 specified and enumerated the legislative powers of Parliament in Art. 34. Conversely, the Constitution reserved (Art. 37) residual legislative powers to the executive, who can regulate all areas outside the specified competence of Parliament on the basis of original decree-making power (*règlements autonomes*).[190] This division stood the entire logic of classical French constitutionalism, for which legislation had been the axiomatic first-order value

---

[187] Jean Boulouis, "L'influence des articles 34 et 37 sur l'équilibre politique entre les pouvoirs," in *Le Domaine de la loi et du règlement* (Paris : Presses Universitaires d'Aix-Marseille, 1981), at p. 195.

[188] An unsuccessful attempt was made early on to challenge the constitutionality of an enabling act by assimilating the notion of "program" in Art. 38 to the "declaration of program" in Art. 49. *See* 72 DC du 12 janvier 1977 (in Louis Favoreu, Loïc Philip, *Les grandes décisions du Conseil constitutionnel* (Paris: Dalloz, c1997)).

[189] Authorized English translation, found on the website of the French National Assembly, at http://www.assemblee-nationale.fr/english/8ab.asp (last visited August 21, 2011).

[190] Art. 37 Matters other than those coming under the scope of statute law shall be matters for regulation.

Provisions of statutory origin enacted in such matters may be amended by decree issued after consultation with the *Conseil d'État*. Any such provisions passed after the coming into force of the

("the expression of general will"), right on its head. In fact, the abstract a priori control of constitutionality through the Constitutional Council and constitutional review as such were introduced precisely in order to maintain Parliament within its limited and defined constitutional competence.[191]

Nonetheless, in subsequent practice, the intricate set of procedures and delineations of competence set up by the Founding Fathers of the Fifth Republic were by-passed by a relative return to the pre-1958 practice of initial legislative authorizations and implementing executive decree. In 1982, in its *Blocage des prix et des revenus* decision, the Constitutional Council gave official constitutional validation to the practical observation made 1 year earlier by a number of prominent French constitutionalists. By expressly confirming that a *loi* could regulate matters outside the scope of Art. 34, the Constitutional Council declared implicitly that the complicated rearrangement of legislative competencies in the 1958 Constitution had made no essential difference with regards to practices.[192] Line-drawing between competences was essentially left by the constitutional judge to political practice.[193]

In the first elaborate decision on the constitutional aspects of delegation as such, the *Economic Authorization Case* of 1986, the Constitutional Council decided that enabling acts based on Art. 38 would need to be specific enough so that the scope of the authorization would be discernable from the text of the enabling law submitted to the Parliament (not stating simply a goal) and that the enabling act would need to be consistent with the Constitution. The Council insisted on the respect of "rules and

Constitution shall be amended by decree only if the Constitutional Council has found that they are matters for regulation as defined in the foregoing paragraph.

The Constitution gives Government the possibility of modifying legislative norms, enacted prior to the Constitution, falling outside the enumerated legislative competence specified in Art. 34, subsequent to a positive reference by the State Council. The Government can defend its legislative competence against legislative incursions by invoking Art. 37 (2) to de-legalize (and replace by decree regulation) post-1958 parliamentary provisions which encroach upon its Art. 34 residual competence (after a reference by the Constitutional Council that the parliamentary provisions do have in effect a *caractère réglementaire*).

[191] Proposals to introduce American-style judicial review of constitutionality had been rejected during the Third Republic. The prevalent opinion of the times was best represented by a study authored by the influential comparatist Edouard Lambert, arguing against the American-style, reactionary "government of judges," *Le gouvernement des juges et la lutte contre la législation sociale aux États-Unis* (Paris: Giard, 1921).

[192] 82-143 DC, Rec. 57 (30 juillet 1982), reproduced and commented in Favoreu and Philip, *supra*, at pp. 539-554: « Un dernier point mérite d'être souligné: la décision du 30 juillet a pour effet de ruiner définitivement la thèse de la définition matérielle de la loi. Car si une loi peut comporter des dispositions réglementaires sans être inconstitutionnelle, c'est que la loi se définit simplement comme l'acte voté par le parlement selon certaines formes, sans prendre en considération la matière sur laquelle porte cet acte. « (at pp. 547-548).

[193] *See* (in addition to the sources and statistics in support of this claim provided in *Le Domaine de la loi et du règlement),* Louis Favoreu, 'Les règlements autonomes existent-ils ?' *Mélanges Burdeau*, Paris, 1977, pp. 405-420 and 'Les règlements autonomes n'existent pas,' *R.F.D.A.* 1987, pp. 872-884, statistical table at p. 884 : between 1982 and 1986, decrees under Art. 37 totaled a meager 76, compared to 6255 other decrees.

principles of constitutional value" and the strict interpretation of the authorizing enactment with a number of constitutional provisions.[194]

In practice, the procedure of adopting an ordinance is more complex than that which applies when the executive simply concretizes by decrees of public administration (implementing decrees) an "ordinary law."[195] As a result, Art. 38 has acquired a minimal practical value with respect to the actual legislative process. Most revealingly, until 1996, the year up to which the elaborate statistical study of Catherine Boyer-Mérentier provides us with sufficient data, the number of enabling laws (*lois d'habilitation*) adopted by Parliament totaled 26 (under which 160 ordinances were adopted and enforced), representing 0.61% of the number of legislative acts passed (3902).[196] In effect, the substantive legislative reservation is thus rendered coextensive with the constitutional guarantees of rights and freedoms,[197] which can be restricted only on the basis of a *loi,* and with the personal liberty guarantee deriving from the constitutional requirement of Art. 34 (3) that the law determine the essential elements of a crime (*crimes* et *délits*). The Constitutional Council gave this latter requirement an interpretation similar to that obtaining in U.S. Supreme Court void-for-vagueness constitutional adjudication.[198]

[194] DC 86-207 du 25-26 juin 1986 ("Privatisations"), Favoreu-Philip *supra*, pp. 658-682. The strict enumeration of the constitutional limitations on both the enabling act and the ordinance itself is due to the fact that judicial review of administrative action by the Council of State operates traditionally only by strict reference to the law authorizing the decree. The specification was meant to give the Council of State 'supplementary ammunition' by specifying secondary norms of reference by virtue of which the ordinances could be reviewed. In practice, the Council of State only annulled 2 out of 160 ordinances adopted under Art. 38, at the very beginning (from 1959 to 1997, *cf.* Favoreu-Philip, *supra* at 674). The decision is translated and commented in Dorsen et al. 2003, pp. 243-248.

[195] Attempts to by-pass by ordinances, during periods of *cohabitation,* the necessity of presidential signature for the promulgation of *lois*, have failed. Ordinances adopted 'in Council of Ministers' have to be signed by the President as well, *cf.* Arts. 13 and 38. The issue was left open by the Constitutional Council whether the formal condition of presidential signature is a discretionary prerogative (*pouvoir discrétionnaire*) or a constitutional duty of the President (*compétence liée*).

[196] *See* Catherine Boyer-Mérentier, *Les ordonnances de l'article 38 de la Constitution du 4 octobre 1958* (Paris: Presses Universitaires d'Aix-Marseilles, 1996). The figures are provided at pp. 329-330, n. 26.

[197] The express protections provided by the specifications in Art. 34 were extended by the famous 1971 *Associations Law Decision*, 71-41 DC du 16 juillet 1971 (*see* translation and comments in Dorsen et al. 2003, pp. 122-124).

[198] Problems arose, nonetheless, with respect to custodial administrative detentions. *See* Dorsen et al. 2003, at pp. 247-248.

4.3.3 Content, Purpose, and Scope: *Why Simple, When It Can Be So Complicated?*

> Warum einfach, wenn's auch schwierig geht? Nur eine rein formalistische Auslegung des Art. 80 des Grundgesetzes zwinge uns zu einem umständlichen Weg, zu einer Aufzählung aller Einzelheiten, die überhaupt je einmal Gegenstand einer DurchführungsVO sein können.[199]
>
> Address of 03.07.1951 of the Federal Finance Minister Fritz Schäffer in Bundestag (Verhandlungen des Deutschen Bundestages, I. Wahlperiode 1949, Stenographische Berichte, Bd. 6, S. 4711).

> Zur Klärung des dogmatischen Verhältnisses zwischen Parlamentsvorbehalt und Art. 80 Abs. 1 S. 2 hat das Bundesverfassungsgericht bis heute keinen befriedigenden Beitrag geleistet. Festzuhalten bleibt, daß das Bundesverfassungsgericht sich von der seiner frühen Rechtsprechung zugrundeliegenden Auffassung gelöst hat, wonach an Verordnungsermächtigungen lediglich formale, von der Wesentlichkeit/Eigenart der Regelungsmaterie unabhängige Bestimmtheitsanforderungen zu stellen sind.[200]
>
> Wolfram Cremer, "Art. 80, Abs. 1 S. 2 GG und Parlamentsvorbehalt-Dogmatische Unstimmigkeiten in der Rechtsprechung des Bundesverfassungsgerichts", *AöR*, Bd. 122, 248 ff. (1997).

Art. 80, Par. 1 provides that the Federal Government, a Federal Minister or a Land Government may be authorized by a federal statute to adopt ordinances (*Rechtsverordnungen*),[201] i.e., delegated legislation, provisions of general character

[199] Why make it simple, when it can be so complicated? Only the formalistic interpretation of Art. 80 in the Basic Law forces us down this cumbersome road, to enumerate in the text of the law of all possible details which could imaginably, at some indefinite point in time, be the object of an implementing decree.

[200] The Constitutional Court has contributed nothing to a satisfactory clarification of the doctrinal relationship between the parliamentary reservation requirement (*Parlamentsvorbehalt*) and the requirements of Art. 80 Par. 1 Cl. 2. It can be only concluded that the Court has departed from its earlier jurisprudence, according to which enabling laws [according to Art. 80 Par. 1 Cl.2] had to correspond only to formal criteria of determinateness (*Bestimmtheitsanforderungen*), substantively unrelated to the specificity and importance of the normative subject-matter.

[201] Sometimes translated as "statutory instruments." For purposes of terminological consistency, I am using "ordinance." The court subjects statutory enabling provisions to a substantial review, in order to determine if the requirements of Art. 80 (1) are applicable. *See* BVerfGE 10, 20 (*Preußischer Kulturbesitz*), holding that the legislative basis of the Charter (*Satzung*) of the Prussian Cultural Heritage Foundation was subject to the requirements of Art. 80 (1). Insofar as the charter was adopted by the Federal Government with the agreement of the Federal Council and comprised provisions with binding force outside the administration proper, it was in effect a substantive "ordinance" (*Rechtsverordnung*). A different interpretation "would have obscured the clear differentiation between the respective normative provinces of the Legislative and the Executive and thus opened a not unobjectionable road to circumvent Art. 80 (1)." (BVerfGE 10, 20 (51).

with legislative force.[202] The "content, purpose, and scope" (*Inhalt, Zweck und Ausmaß,* Cl. 2) of the authorization must be specified by the enabling law.[203] Like many other features of the constitutional rearrangement in the Bonn Republic, this provision represented a direct reaction to a perceived structural deficiency of the Weimar democracy. Most notably, the already mentioned Enabling Act of March 1933 had symbolized the end of parliamentarism, giving the Reich Government power "*to adopt laws,* outside the ordinary constitutional procedures" (*Reichsgesetze können außer in dem in der Reichsverfassung vorgesehenen Verfahren auch durch die Reichsregierung beschlossen werden*), including legislation infringing on fundamental rights. It is easy to notice that the text of the enabling law did not even deign to pay lip service to the formal, nominal constitutional niceties. The "Reich Government"—in fact, the new Chancellor, Adolf Hitler—was explicitly authorized to adopt "federal legislation" proper (*Reichsgesetze*), not just ordinances (*Rechtsverordnungen*) with legislative effect. However, the law-making formalities were duly preserved afterwards, as a grimly ironic gloss on totalitarian legality; the validity of the enabling law was last extended by a personal decree of Hitler in 1943.[204]

In 1947, the Office of the Military Governor of the US (OMGUS) gave partial impetus to the future constitutional regulation of enabling acts, by issuing a directive regarding the authority of state governments in the American Zone of Occupation to adopt regulations on the basis of former Reich legislation ("Authority of Land Governments to Issue executive Ordinances under former Reichs Law" (sic!)). The directive distinguished between "Supplementing or Amending Ordinances" and "Implementing Ordinances" thus:

> Implementing Ordinances (*Aus- und Durchführungsverordnungen*) are involved, where the policy and the legal principles which are to control in given cases are laid down by the basic law with such definiteness as to provide reasonable standards for the executive to fill in details and to carry out the purposes of the law. Such implementing ordinances, if enacted

---

[202] Delegated legislation adopted on a legislative basis prior to the entry into force of the Basic Law was subjected to the more restrictive requirements of Art. 129.

[203] Durch Gesetz können die Bundesregierung, ein Bundesminister oder die Landesregierungen ermächtigt werden, Rechtsverordnungen zu erlassen. Dabei müssen Inhalt, Zweck und Ausmaß der erteilten Ermächtigung im Gesetze bestimmt werden. Die Rechtsgrundlage ist in der Verordnung anzugeben. Ist durch Gesetz vorgesehen, daß eine Ermächtigung weiter übertragen werden kann, so bedarf es zur Übertragung der Ermächtigung einer Rechtsverordnung. ("The Federal Government, a Federal Minister or the Land Governments may be authorized by a law to issue ordinances having the force of law. The content, purpose and scope of the powers conferred must be set forth in the law. The legal basis must be stated in the ordinance. If a law provides that a power may be further delegated, an ordinance having the force of law is necessary in order to delegate the power." (Translation available at http://www.constitution.org/cons/germany.txt, last visited August 26, 2011.)) Note: The other sections of article 80, which deal with the division of power between states and the federation with respect to delegated law-making, touch on federalism issues that need not further detain us here.

[204] RGBl. 295. In Wilhelm Mößle, *Inhalt, Zweck und Ausmaß. Zur Verfassungsgeschichte der Verordnungsermächtigung* (Berlin: Duncker & Humblot, 1990), at p. 22 n. 58.

under and in pursuance of the law, are not contrary to the constitutional prohibition against excessive delegation of legislative power. . ..[205]

But the American influence was only tangential and formal. The limitation provided by Art. 80 Par. 1 Cl. 2 expressed a deeper constitutional aversion to open-ended enabling laws, which in itself was neither imposed nor influenced by the Office of the Military Governor. Indeed, the notion of constitutionally controlled delegation was initially perceived as too compromising. For instance, the draft of the Bavarian Justice Ministry following the directions of OMGUS and setting forth, accordingly, a restriction of delegations based on the specificity of the enabling law, was received coldly in the constitutional committee of the provincial Bavarian parliament (*Landtag*).[206] The rapporteur of the committee, Dr. Thomas Dehler considered this an open invitation to preserve "Nazi-laws": "the delegation practices of former Nazi-laws (*Nazigesetze*) ought not to be borrowed into our new rule of law-based state practices." Accordingly, he made the proposal to reserve *all law-making* (including implementing norms) to the parliament itself. Dehler's uncompromisingly unrealistic proposal was only rejected in the ensuing debates following a sarcastic counter by the state chancellery representative "whether in pursuance of this notion the parliament would like to regulate the pricing of parquet blocks itself."[207] A compromise draft, which included the obligation to define "content, purpose, and scope of the thus delegated ordinance-making power," in the enabling statute and provided that only implementing, but not supplementing ordinances could be authorized, was eventually adopted in the provincial parliament.[208] Thereafter, the formula was included in the draft constitution proposal submitted for consideration by the Bavarian State Chancellery to the federal constitutional convention at Herrenchiemsee.

The initial Bavarian draft read: "The right of adopting legislation (*das Recht der Gesetzgebung*) can not be delegated, including to committees of the Federal Parliament (*Bundestag*) or the Federal Council (*Bundesrat*). As an exception from this prohibition, the Federal Government can be authorized to adopt Ordinances (*Rechtsverordnungen*) on the basis of a statute; the content, purpose,

[205] *Id.*, at p. 44, n. 152 (Bayr. Staatskanzlei G 67/47-Office of the Military Governor, Berlin, 31st of July 1947).

[206] Bavaria and Hesse formed the biggest part of the US-administered zone.

[207] Mößle 1990, at p. 53.

[208] Gesetz Nr. 122 vom 8. Mai 1948 über den Erlaß von Rechtsverordnungen auf Grund vormaligen Reichsrechts (GVBl. S. 82). *See* Bernhard Wolff, "Die Ermächtigung zum Erlaß von Rechtsverordnungen nach dem Grundgesetz" *AöR* Bd. 78 (1952/1953), p. 194 ff., at p. 205 (observing that the provision is almost identical although superior in its formulation to that of the Federal Constitution, in that it provides that the specification of the purpose bears with precision on the *purpose to be pursued by the delegate*—whereas in the case of the Basic Law, one could very well interpret "purpose" as the *legislature's purpose for delegating*). Interestingly, the content-purpose-scope restriction was not explicitly provided for in the text of the Bavarian Constitution (although the state constitutional court extrapolated the limitation, by way of interpretation, from the general rule of law guarantee (*Rechtsstaatlichkeit*)).

and scope of the authorization have to be however determined and limited in a sufficiently precise manner by the enabling law." This formulation would find its way in the text of the Basic Law, after the elision of the first sentence and the qualification: "sufficiently precise manner." The two specifications were considered redundant, especially as faith was placed by the convention members and the Parliamentary Council in the future Constitutional Court. The Court in Karlsruhe, as they hoped, would itself clarify in time what a "sufficiently precise" determination of "content purpose, and scope" meant.[209] The provision was now, or at least so wrote a commentator in 1950 in categorical terms, very shortly after the adoption of the Basic Law, "simply as complete in itself...as any formulation possibly could be."[210]

This degree of optimism was, as it would later turn out, premature. And yet, the author had at the time good historical excuses for his sanguine anticipations. During the constitutional monarchy, the theory and practice of constitutionalism were primarily concerned with securing the "liberty and property" sphere against the encroachments of the monarchic state, not with the imposition of constitutional restrictions against the legislature itself.[211] The parliament could be relied upon to jealously defend its "property and liberty" legislative reservation. The classical-liberal "liberty and property" legislative reservation was not fully inherited by the Weimar Republic, whose constitution comprised fundamental rights and whose political system was based on universal franchise. However, the environment of almost uninterrupted emergency in which Weimar democracy unraveled and eventually died and the ensuing ominousness of the practice of delegation as such, had made it much easier to believe that the problem of delegation was a discrete evil, related to avoidable past excesses. Delegation was, that is to say, a matter of parliamentary duty and consequent degree of statutory precision that could be severed from the general problematic of the intervening constitutional transformations and indeed even from structural substantive distinctions. It was a question of degree and could therefore be confronted with relatively formalized means. Parliament would now be authorized to delegate to the executive all necessary powers to address the social

[209] Mößle 1990, at pp. 55-56.

[210] "schlechthin so vollkommen...wie eine Formel nur eben vollkommen sein kann", H. J. Müller, *Die Stellung der Rechtsverordnung im deutschen Staatsleben der Gegenwart* (Diss. Köln, 1950, S. 57) quoted after Horst Hasskarl, "Die Rechtsprechung des Bundesverfassungsgerichts zu Art. 80 Abs. 1 Satz 2 GG", *AöR* Bd. 94 (1969), 85 ff, at p. 86.

[211] "The primary task of constitutionalism was the deflection of encroachments from the side of the monarchic administration against the industrial and exchange bourgeois society. Protecting basic rights against the law-maker was, although imaginable, unimportant, since the bourgeoisie was represented in the process of law-making. The right to intervene had to be reserved to the legislature and thus withheld from the administration. No encroachment in the liberty and property sphere without a statute-under this battle flag was carried the fight for legislative reservation, this major legal achievement of the bourgeoisie in its conflict with the crown and its administrative machinery." Bodo Pieroth and Bernhard Schlink, *Grundrechte. Staatsrecht II*, 24.Auflage (Heidelberg: C.F. Müller Verlag, 2008), at p. 10.

and economic needs of a modern bureaucratic-administrative society, provided that the legislature heeded a measure of precision and clarity, providing the "content, purpose, and scope" of the authorization.

Retrospectively, the level of contemporaneous doctrinal confidence in the "content, purpose, scope" provision is surprising. Nonetheless, lack of experience with such constitutional limitations, as well as with constitutional adjudication more generally, and the understandable tendency to relate statutory vagueness to emergency "blanket authorizations" during Weimar and infamous *Nazigesetze*, warranted at the time a measure of hopefulness. For instance, Bernhard Wolff, in his 1952 doctrinal study of Art. 80 and its place in the general Basic Law framework, although proceeding soberly to identify practical and legal caveats, concluded that, all in all, the court could be trusted to administer 'nondelegation' rationally: "it can be conceded that this article does not provide a yardstick, according to which one could measure precisely the permissibility of enabling provisions. But then the use of general concepts is not foreign to the law; one could think of [the "performance according to good faith" provision of] § 242 BGB.[212] Such use, very common in public law (*Staatsrecht*), is in itself not even undesirable."[213]

This is true enough whenever such indeterminate legal concepts and general clauses provide a controllable measure of interpretive flexibility, permitting at the same time consistent interpretation and thus a default rule of predictability. However, as soon as the Constitutional Court started to enforce the "content, purpose, and scope" provision, the interpretation variations immediately started to multiply exponentially and uncontrollably, over a surprisingly short time-span. Horst Hasskarl's 1969 attempt at a synthesis of the first two decades of Art. 80 constitutional enforcement identified five general tests or formulas for applying the provision. Those tests, as the writer noted, were being used by the Constitutional Court by way of an even greater array of variations and permutations. Hasskarl observed at the same time and relatedly, that many of the "formulas" were contradictory, overlapping or constituted reciprocally relational concepts (that is, one could define them circularly through each other's intermediary):

(i) "Foreseeability" (The restriction provided for by Art. 80 (1) could only be interpreted from case to case. However, as a rule, the limitation should be precise enough, so that the "cases of future application and the future general tendency of its use, as well as the content of the adopted ordinance" are already foreseeable on the basis of the enabling provision.)[214];

[212] Paragraph 242 in the Civil Code concerns "performance according to good faith" and reads: "The debtor is bound to perform according to the requirements of good faith, ordinary usage being taken into consideration." (Der Schuldner ist verpflichtet, die Leistung so zu bewirken, wie Treu und Glauben mit Rücksicht auf die Verkehrssitte es erfordern. English translation found in Reinhard Zimmermann and Simmon Whittaker, *Good Faith in European Contract Law* (Cambridge: Cambridge University Press, 2000), p. 18, n. 59).

[213] Wolff 1952/1953, at p. 198.

[214] Hasskarl 1969, at p. 87.

(ii) "Autonomous Decision-making" (*Selbstentscheidung*) ("[T]he law-maker should decide itself which specific questions should be handled, it must draw the boundaries of the subordinate regulation and specify what is the goal (*Ziel*) to be pursued.")[215];
(iii) "Clarity I" (*Deutlichkeitsformel*): The degree of concreteness constitutionally expected of an enabling provision requires "in principle explicitness, but at any rate should be determined with unobjectionable clarity (*mit einwandfreier Deutlichkeit*)."[216];
(iv) "Program-Formula" (The "purpose specificity" requirement is fulfilled, when the statute "explicitly provides or one can deduce from the law the 'general program' to be attained by the ordinances.")[217];
(v) "Clarity II" (It is not necessary that content, purpose, and scope, should be provided for explicitly in the text of the enabling provision, as long as one can extrapolate these statutory requirements by means of a holistic interpretation, following general principles of statutory interpretation. The determinant factor in the analysis is the possibility of extracting from the entire body of the enabling act "the ensuing objective will of the law-maker." To this effect, even research into the legislative history can be used, albeit only to confirm interpretive results arrived at through other methodologies.)[218]

The author concluded that the "unequal, fluctuating, partially contradictory character of the case-law could hardly escape even the inattentive observer."[219] This certainly appears so to the reader of his survey. At the beginning, the Constitutional Court had announced a "case by case" application. Thereafter, when it switched to rules, those rules were sometimes restricted to the enabling provision, sometimes extended to the body of the entire law. Sometimes the Court required "unobjectionable clarity," but sometimes demanded only that the general contours of the delegation needed to be drawn. Sometimes Karlsruhe regarded the three components of Art. 80 (1) as three separate yardsticks: *content; purpose; scope,* from which three sets of separate requirements derived. But the court could just as well make an unexpected doctrinal about-face and sometimes conflated them into one single general constitutional principle, with a view to across-the-board *content-purpose-scope* specificity. The most one could discern, if wanting to bring some order into the random mass of decisions, according to Hasskarl, were general tendencies or phases of the Court's jurisprudence. Enforcement had ranged from a very demanding application, bearing on the black letter of the enabling provision as such, towards a second, more generous hermeneutical mood emphasizing "constitutionally conformant interpretation" (*verfassungskonforme Auslegung*) and a

[215] *Id.*, at p. 88.
[216] *Ibid.*
[217] *Ibid.*, at p. 89.
[218] *Ibid.*, at p. 91.
[219] *Ibid.*, at p. 103.

"mollification" of the requirements, leading finally to a third, then-dominant teleological stage which subordinated "scope and content" to the "purpose" requirement and then subsumed the "purpose" requirement to an even more vague umbrella concept or formula of "general program."[220]

Hasskarl tried to establish a taxonomy and divided the formulas into "rules of interpretation" (the two "clarity" formulations) and "determinateness requirements" (the foreseeability, autonomous decision-making, and "program"-related tests). He further observed that there was a precise logic in the "determinateness" formulations, insofar as these regarded the rule from the benchmark of specificity needs related to the three relevant viewpoints, i.e., that of the citizen (who must foresee executive implementation already from the legislative delegation), legislator (who has the duty to decide), and implementer (who must know what program it must implement).[221] This observation is certainly correct. Indeed, as it was repeatedly observed by the German Constitutional Court itself, a requirement of legislative specificity serves a number of important constitutional purposes, among which are (1) representative democracy-related concerns of legitimacy, accountability and publicity; (2) separation of powers and legality of administration purposes, demanding that executive and administrative action be legislatively predetermined, and; (3) rule of law requirements related to the protection of the individual against adverse state action, reflecting "fair notice" demands as well as the more general liberal-constitutional principle that "official action [will] be comprehensible and to a certain extent predictable by the individual."[222]

But, taxonomy notwithstanding (it is surely the professed purpose of legal doctrine to try and seek to bring analytical order into the often-haphazard chaos of the practice), the general sense conveyed by Hasskarl's early survey is one of steep decline and rapid failure. It is striking how the German Constitutional Court ended, in less than 20 years, precisely at the same doctrinal point where the nondelegation doctrine had already been half-abandoned by the US Supreme Court after two centuries. As of 1969, the only thing that was required of the lawmaker was the specification of a "general program" (which is just another way of saying "intelligible principle"). This metamorphosis is all the more intriguing if we consider strictly the positive legal context (all other idiosyncratic things being equal) in which these developments had originated. The German court had initially started on a vigorous disciplinary rampage, striking down rafts of delegating enactments, on the basis of a severe reading of the "content, purpose, and scope" provision. It ended up rather sheepishly reading down broad provisions on occasion, on the basis of a cautious teleological approach.[223]

---

[220] *Ibid.*, at pp. 103-105.

[221] *Ibid.*, at p 111.

[222] "Emergency Price Control Case," BVerfGE 8, 274, English translation in Donald P. Kommers, *The Constitutional Jurisprudence of the Federal Republic of Germany* (Durham, N.C.: Duke University Press, 1997), at p. 138.

[223] Hasskarl 1969, at p. 107.

At the time, Hasskarl thought, primarily on the basis of a then recent Art. 80-related decision, that he could discern a "slight counter-tendency" towards a fourth phase and partial revival.[224] The object of the decision was a constitutional complaint raised by a number of companies against the fee-setting procedure of the Competition Office (*Bundeskartellamt*) in Berlin. The companies had to pay administrative fees for the processing of price-fixing and price-clearance filing procedures before the *Bundeskartellamt*. One of the main objections stated in the complaint regarded the legal basis of the fee-setting administrative acts, namely, an alleged infringement of the delegation restrictions in Art. 80. The Competition Office had been authorized by ordinance to set fees in order to cover its administrative costs. The legal basis of the ordinance, section 80 of the Law against Competition Infringements, read as follows: "In procedures before the Anti-Cartel Authority fees will be levied to cover administrative costs. Further details (*das Nähere*) regarding such fees . . ..will be set forth by an ordinance of the Federal Government, adopted with the consent of the Federal Council." According to the Finance Ministry, the provision was unobjectionable, since all the requirements had been fulfilled by the enabling provision. It had established the content (the ordinance would set "fees"); purpose (in order to cover administrative costs); and scope (the scope was restricted by the general principles applying to levies, equivalence and costs-covering, as well as the general equality and nondiscrimination provision in Art. 3 of the Basic Law).[225] The Court disagreed and struck down the provision as delegating unconstrained law-making power. According to the holding, only the content and purpose had been specified. The scope of the delegation, which could not be deduced from the other elements, was underspecified and could not be narrowed down solely by recourse to general principles. "Tendency and scope" (*Tendenz und Ausmaß*) needed to transpire from the text, whereas the precise words relating to scope—"further details"—were unconstitutionally vague: "The delegated law-maker can decide by ordinance which administrative acts are subject to fee-setting and which are exempted, who is the fee-debtor, when the fees are due, what is the ceiling, who sets the fees and who collects them, what is the discretionary leeway of the public authority, how are fees to be collected, when and if the duty lapses, when and if the amounts can be reduced or the fees waived. . ..Even when the principles of equivalence and cost-covering are taken into consideration, one can still foresee fully distinct regulations, which would burden the citizen to very distinct degrees."[226] This principle was evident in the case of levies. Given their importance for the citizen, the regulation of essential elements was the duty of parliament: "A legislative delegation has to contain a minimum of material normativity, which must and can serve as 'program' and 'framework' to the ordinance-maker. The enabling act must also set clear boundaries to the exercise

224 BVerfGE 20, 257 (*Bundesrecht in Berlin*, 1966).

225 BVerfGE 20, 257 (264).

226 BVerfGE 20, 257 (270).

of derived authority."[227] This decision proved to be an exception and future developments did not validate Hasskarl's prediction. If anything, the downslope tendencies he noticed at that very early stage, towards invalidation-avoidance and purpose-oriented restrictive interpretation as a substitute, became more entrenched.[228] The general level of clarity and consistency in the doctrine did not increase either.[229] Hasskarl thought the return to a more vigorous enforcement of the nondelegation was also evidenced by the usage, in another contemporaneous decision, of a tamer form of the Clarity I ("with *unobjectionable* clarity" (*mit einwandfreier Deutlichkeit*) test: "content, purpose, and scope have to result *with clarity* (*mit Deutlichkeit*)...from the law itself."[230] For an otherwise perceptive observer, this faith in the power of word permutations, i.e., tautological nondelegation boilerplate, to control adjudication is surprising. These formulations, as the reader already intuits, restate in various forms the question (how clear and precise is clear and precise enough?) rather than provide the answer. But before deriving our own conclusions on the margin of the general transformation, a related aspect of delegation evolutions in Germany must be highlighted, on the basis of another synthesis of the constitutional jurisprudence, three decades forth.

In 1997, looking back over almost half a century of constitutional jurisprudence, another commentator, Wolfram Cremer, observed a disturbing structural anomaly in the case-law. The Constitutional Court seemed to sometimes conflate the logically and dogmatically distinct constitutional problems of legislative reservation (the constitutional need for a formal statute as legal basis/predicate for public action); parliamentary reservation (the constitutional obligation of the parliament to take the essential decisions in a given normative field); and the Art. 80 (1) delegation problem proper (the obligation of the parliament to delegate, when it had the right to do so, with a degree of "content, purpose, and scope specificity"). This latter obligation could very well be regarded, as Cremer observed with a discerning analytical eye, as in essence a formal matter, doctrinally unrelated to the substantive criteria. The inquiry into "content, purpose, and scope" regarded an issue of "how" (if parliament can delegate, how should it do this), not "whether" (whether parliament has an obligation to take the decision itself or the right to delegate). According to the logic of this position, as synthesized by Cremer, the question should always be a tiered two-step analysis of substance and then form: "First with the help of the essentialness criterion (*Wesentlichkeitskriterium*) it is probed whether the

---

[227] *Ibid.*

[228] *Cf.* the comparative study by Uwe Kischel, "Delegation of Legislative Power to Agencies: A Comparison of the United Sates and German Law," 46 *Admin. L. Rev. 213* (Spring, 1994).

[229] *Cf.* David P. Currie who, otherwise enthusiastically praising the German Constitutional Court's attempt to grapple with nondelegation (which he thought contrasted favorably with the lack of stamina in the US jurisprudence), was in the end forced to admit that: "The decisions are numerous and not all easy to reconcile. They document the difficulty and uncertainty of administering a requirement that is necessarily a matter of degree." (Currie 1994, at p. 133).

[230] BVerfGE 20, 283 (291), quoted after Hasskarl 1969, at p. 107.

law-maker has (no) constitutional authority to delegate the decision over a specific subject-matter, in other words whether a delegation threshold exists. For the enabling ordinances, which have survived this threshold, and crossed over the "hurdle" of parliamentary reservation, another scrutiny ensues under Art. 80 (1), with respect to delegation proper, in other words an inquiry into 'how essential these unessential matters are.'"[231] But, Cremer asked, if the issues were analytically and doctrinally distinct, why did the Court waver between various applications of the delegation restriction? The enforcement of Art. 80 (1) had sometimes proceeded as a formal and separate scrutiny. Conversely, sometimes the Court had treated the essentialness and delegation inquiries as if they were substantively fused at the hip. Although noting that the decisions as such were contradictory beyond reconciliation in their respective methodological approaches, the author concluded that a vague, general, and unrationalized tendency to swerve from form to substance in the enforcement of the delegation provision (and therefore a conflation delegation-essentialness) could be discerned.

To exemplify the essentialness/delegation nexus, in the so-called "Mutzenbacher Decision,"[232] the constitutionality of a federal statute (the "Act Concerning the Dissemination of Publications that Endanger the Youth") was challenged, among other grounds, with the argument that it encroached upon the guarantee of artistic freedom in Art. 5 (3) of the Basic Law. The law had established a Federal Reviewing Authority, charged with administering the substantive provisions by, among other attributions, determining the placement of "writings that are capable of morally endangering children and youths" on a restricted list. Placement triggered an advertising ban and a restriction of dissemination and access (especially to children and youth). A writing could however not be listed according to the law if, inter alia, it "served art" (*wenn sie der Kunst dient*). The act provided that the Federal Minister for Youth, Family, Women, and Health would appoint the chairman and a part of the Federal Reviewing Authority's members (federal states had the right to directly nominate their own respective representatives). The federal minister was mandated to select members from among eight broadly identified categories of professional groups and civil society circles ("art, literature, booksellers, publishers, youth associations, youth services, teachers, the churches, the Jewish Culture Communities, and other religious communities organized as bodies regulated by public law").[233] According to the law, residual competence with respect to listings was vested in a twelve-member body, composed of the chairman, three state representatives, and eight representatives of the above-mentioned collective groups. Decisions could only be made with a quorum of eight

[231] Cremer 1997, at p. 255.

[232] BVerfGE 83, 130 (27 November 1990), The references provided are to the German decision, respecting its pagination. For citation, I am using the English translation by Nomos Verlagsgesellschaft (available online at http://www.utexas.edu/law/academics/centers/transnational/work_new/german/case.php?id=628, last visited September 2, 2011).

[233] BVerfGE 83, 130 (132).

members; for listing decisions a two-third majority vote and a minimum of seven votes were necessary.

The publisher of a pornographic novel (*Josephine Mutzenbacher-The Story of a Viennese Whore, as Told by Herself*) placed on the list eventually lodged an administrative complaint. Criminal court decisions had in 1968 banned the volume as criminally obscene. According to the publisher, in view of the "evolving socio-ethical standards," the work needed to be considered art. The authority refused to take the volume off the list, considering that it appealed solely to prurient interests. The lower administrative court reviewed the decision as unobjectionable. On appeal, the Superior Administrative Court admitted that the work constituted art but pointed out that artistic freedom found its limitation in the constitutional value of youth protection, according to Arts. 6 (2) and 1 (1) of the Basic Law. Subsequently, on appeal to the Federal Administrative Court, it was further decided that the rule of law principle did not forbid the use of imprecise legal concepts (*unbestimmte Rechtsbegriffe*), thus the relatively unspecified procedure directing the federal minister to appoint the administrative authority from among broadly defined groups was unobjectionable. The ensuing constitutional complaint did not raise an Art. 80 delegation objection but emphasized specificity needs deriving from the parliamentary reservation. According to the complainant, the law was overall and substantively in breach of the parliament's obligation to make the essential decisions in areas affecting constitutional rights. It was relatedly argued that the vagueness of the appointment procedure represented a dereliction of parliament's constitutional duty to regulate "the essentials" and thus not leave the door open to executive arbitrariness.[234]

On this latter point, the Constitutional Court decided that, given the necessity of balancing and reconciling conflicting constitutional values (right to artistic freedom and protection of the youth) with a view to their optimization, the legislative regulation of the administrative procedure for implementing the act was insufficient with respect to the Art. 80 (1) requirements. The enabling act had not set forth explicitly the precise procedure for the selection of the respective members and the Court held that this vagueness ran counter to the specificity demands made by Art. 80 (1).

In the economy of the argument, the delegation inquiry seems hard to separate from the general problem of essentialness.[235] The substantive essentialness requirements were interpreted to extend to the "details of the law's administrative and judicial application," since the optimization of the competing values had repercussions with respect to the enforcement: "The mandate to realize basic rights

---

[234] BVerfGE 83, 130 (136, 137).

[235] Defined at BVerfGE 83, 130 (142): "The principle of the rule of law and the precept of democracy place upon the legislature the duty of formulating essentially by itself those regulations that are decisive for realization of basic rights-and of not leaving this to [the] activity and decisionmaking authority of the executive. . ..As the intensity of potential infringements in areas protected by basic rights increases, the demands on determinacy also increase."

through appropriate procedural provisions is addressed first to the legislature. If the administrative procedure directly affects positions that are protected by basic rights, then the procedural provisions must, in the interest of those positions, be set in legally binding terms (*rechtssatzförmig*). That has not sufficiently occurred here."[236] Constitutionally conformant enforcement was held to depend in turn on the extent to which the procedure genuinely reflected the relevant viewpoints: "The procedure to be set in legal norms (*rechtssatzförmig*) must take account of the interest in obtaining the most comprehensive investigation of all the viewpoints that the FRA must consider when making its decision regarding a listing.. . .[The legislature] further must regulate how individual members are to be chosen. In doing so, it must attempt to completely comprise, at least in their general tendencies, all the views represented in the participating circles."[237] In the argument, the formulation of Art. 80 is not expressly mentioned and the court does not spell out a delegation test, much less one broken down into "content, purpose, and scope" specifics. What the parliament should not have delegated results implicitly from the observations of the court regarding the essentialness-related duty of parliament to regulate substantively in legally binding terms (*Rechtssätze*).

The subject matter of the inquiry, namely, the "optimization" of a clash between fundamental rights and values provides relative normative focus and mooring to the specificity inquiry invited by the delegation-related provision. How far that duty of legislative specificity extends is still obscured by this flight into procedural specificity, itself inevitable due to the normative imprecision of balancing constitutional rights and values without a common normative scale.[238] Consequently, the discussion still evinces a measure of open-endedness, an exercise so-to-speak in "constitutional interest-balancing."[239] By the same token, this observation provides the answer to the conjoined dilemmas raised by Hasskarl and Cremer. Content, purpose, and scope are conceptually distinct problems. Likewise, the problem of substance (what can be delegated) raised by the "essentialness" inquiry into the

[236] BVerfGE 83, 130 (152).

[237] BVerfGE 83, 130 (153).

[238] *See* Pieroth and Schlink 2008, at pp. 60-63, observing parallel transitions from legislative reservation to parliamentary reservation and from legislative reservation to the "reservation of proportional legislation" (*Vorbehalt des verhältnismäßigen Gesetzes*). *But cf.* the acute skepticism expressed by one of the authors with respect to the possibility of the proportionality inquiry to provide a manageable normative criterion for rational adjudication and jurisprudence, Bernhard Schlink, "Die Entthronung der Staatsrechtswissenschaft durch die Verfassungsgerichtsbarkeit", *Der Staat*, Bd. 28 (1989) S. 161 ff.

[239] It can be asked almost endlessly why specific groups or viewpoints were included in the procedure and why different interests and groups were not taken into consideration. As the ministry also observed in its position on the complaint, "[i]t would be impossible to include all imaginable organizations; a measure of dispositive discretion of the federal minister was constitutionally acceptable" BVerfGE 83, 130 (137, 138): Es sei unmöglich, alle nur denkbaren Organisationen zu beteiligen; gewisse Dispositionsmöglichkeiten des Bundesministers seien von Verfassungswegen hinzunehmen (at 138).

substantive parliamentary reservation is logically distinct. Analytically, that is, it represents a different doctrinal inquiry from the question relating to the precision/clarity degree raised by the delegation scrutiny (how should the parliament instruct its delegates). But, as it is also revealed by the German developments, degrees of legislative clarity and precision cannot be enforced by constitutional adjudication without a stable, structural normative criterion that would help define constitutionally-ideal legislation. The words of the delegation-related constitutional provisions cannot in themselves provide this criterion. And, as the fruitless German search for delegation tests shows, without foundational normative distinctions, neither formal rationality, namely the analytical rigor of doctrinal categories, nor positive fundamental law, namely the conceptual categories provided by the text of the constitution, can help constitutional adjudication to operate in a coherent way.

4.4 Conclusion: The Unity of What?

> And notwithstanding the said words of the said Commission give authority to the Commissioners to do according to their discretions, yet their proceedings ought to be limited and bound with the rule of reason and Law. For discretion is a science or understanding to discern between falsity and truth, between right and wrong, and between shadows and substance, between equity and colorable glosses and pretenses, and not to doe according to their wills and private affections; for as one saith, *Talis discretio discretionem confundit.*
>
> Coke, C.J., *Rooke's Case* 5 Co. Rep. 99b (1598)

This dictum, found in a very early English administrative law case (an action brought by a certain Rooke against the Commissioners of Sewers), is a good introduction to the conclusion of this argument. Looked at through the prism of judicial limitations, the delegation inquiry concerns the constitutionally proper level of statutory specificity and thus the judicially-administered border between discretionary and law-bound action. This reflects, looked at through the other end of the telescope, the difference between the formalized, structurally and institutionally constrained rationality of law and the distinct worlds of political or ideological rationality. If the judge cannot draw the normative lines and thus rationally contain and limit his own decision-making, substantive decisions will simply move as exercises of "will and private affections" from the political branches to the bench. As it was argued here, line-drawing has proven ever more difficult the more constitutionalism has departed from its initial presuppositions. The futile nondelegation quests of contemporary constitutional law in the jurisdictions we have reviewed evidence this Janus-faced systemic uneasiness: the difficulty of confronting with positive constitutional law means an erosion of foundational normative presuppositions and a converse necessity for foundational normative borders.

Occasional denials of this need are, albeit discursively possible, ultimately disingenuous and obfuscating of the real stakes. For instance, in a recent administrative law decision reviewing the denial of a deportation waiver request for "humanitarian and compassionate reasons," *Baker v. Canada (Minister of Citizenship and Immigration)*,[240] the Supreme Court of Canada sought to end a long battle with categorically distinct standards of review. It held thus that legal errors (decisions involving interpretations of rules of law) and discretionary decisions proper could be reviewed in terms of substance using the middle range between correctness and the patent unreasonableness standard, namely reasonableness. Justifying its resort to a single standard, the opinion extemporized in the language of legal philosophical scholarship: "It is...inaccurate to speak of a rigid dichotomy of 'discretionary' or 'non-discretionary' decisions.... there is no easy distinction to be made between interpretation and the exercise of discretion; interpreting legal rules involves considerable discretion to clarify, fill in legal gaps, and make choices among various options."[241] The Court also held, procedure-wise, that the common law imposed on all public decision-makers a duty to give reasons.[242] But as the court hastened to add, "given the difficulty in making rigid classifications between discretionary and non-discretionary decisions" a multi-factor "pragmatic and functional test" would be used to cut the supposedly unitary spectrum of reasonableness.[243] The denial of distinctions between discretion and law has a distinctive touch of normative hyperbole.[244] It makes, namely, the beautiful promise of complete, gapless lawfulness, of public law triumphant: from hither forth, no more "black holes," no more "Schmittian administrative law."[245] A fine volume, to which many prominent Canadian administrative law scholars contributed, was dedicated to the case, to hail the transition to "The Unity of Public Law."[246] But there is something eerily contrasting in this unity, the lofty normative promise of no

---

240 [1999] 2 S.C.R. 817.

241 Par. 54.

242 On this issue, more generally, *see* Dyzenhaus and Fox-Decent 2001.

243 Par. 56: "The pragmatic and functional approach takes into account considerations such as the expertise of the tribunal, the nature of the decision being made, and the language of the provision and the surrounding legislation. It includes factors such as whether a decision is "polycentric" and the intention revealed by the statutory language. The amount of choice left by Parliament to the administrative decision-maker and the nature of the decision being made are also important considerations in the analysis. The spectrum of standards of review can incorporate the principle that, in certain cases, the legislature has demonstrated its intention to leave greater choices to decision-makers than in others, but that a court must intervene where such a decision is outside the scope of the power accorded by Parliament."

244 The entire case is pervaded with a general sense of nobility and elation against the grain of trifling legal technicalities. Much of the decisional outcome in the case was, for example, controlled by the "interpretative incorporation" into the factors controlling the administrative process of the Convention of the Rights of the Child, ratified but un-incorporated into domestic law by Canada (and thus technically of no domestic legal effect). The court glossed in Kantian tenor on how it would be hypocritical to allow the executive to ratify treaties but then allow the state to fully escape its international obligations due to the failure of parliament to incorporate them.

245 *See* Adrian Vermeule, "Our Schmittian Administrative Law,"122 *Harv. L. Rev.* 1095 (2009).

246 Dyzenhaus 2004.

more law-free spaces, no internal systemic dichotomies, coupled clumsily with the elusive instrumentalism of a multi-factor balancing test. The poetics of normative unity written with the pragmatic language of accounting, a Kantian string concerto played on a broken Benthamite harmonica. This conceptual/methodological chasm seems to have escaped the eulogists, as the technical inconsistencies faded far behind the generous promises of rule of law absolutism. Some of the scholars who had hailed *Baker* as revolutionary, would later be nonplussed by the post September 9/11 deportation review in *Suresh v. Canada (*Minister *of Citizenship and Immigration*),[247] where the exact same test as that applied in Baker, the "pragmatic and functional approach" resulted in a very deferential decision. In terms of what has been said so far, it is clear that, to some extent, both the early reveling and the succeeding dissatisfaction were triggered by the results as such, within a of morally-instrumental rather than legal-rational framework of reference. But the professed appeal to an alleged "unity of public law," coupled with the inevitable failure to deliver on the promise (the diversity-oriented "pragmatic and functional approach") makes instrumentalization inescapable. In their enthusiastic attempt to do away with the tragedy of law- and thus rationality-free spaces of public action (there are questions which admit of no legal, thus rational answer), the Canadian justices made a melodramatic promise (everything has a rational explanation in judicial form, in the end law conquers all).

This book purported to offer no practical solutions to such conundrums, save perhaps by serving as a cautionary warning with respect to the possibility of using non- or limited delegation provisions at the level of fundamental law, in order to promote constitutional values by controlling statutory vagueness. This warning is not fully gratuitous or moot. The Treaty of Lisbon, for instance, introduced the "constitutional" limitation of legislative delegation for the first time in EU law, using a mixed formula strikingly reliant on German constitutionalism: "A legislative act may delegate to the Commission the power to adopt non-legislative acts to supplement or amend certain *non-essential elements of the legislative act*. The *objectives, content, scope* and duration of the delegation of power shall be explicitly defined in the legislative acts. The *essential elements of an area* shall be reserved for the legislative act and accordingly shall not be the subject of a delegation of power."[248] [emphases supplied] It is too early to review the jurisprudence of the ECJ but one can suspect that a task that proved impossible in national constitutional law will be all the more difficult to achieve at the level of European Union law. In national systems, constitutional adjudication can to a degree fall back on shared meanings, historical understandings, and tradition in the quest for rational jurisprudence. Contrariwise, the fundamental law of the EU system seems

[247] [2002] 1 S.C.R. 3. Note that in Suresh there was risk of torture attending deportation, so that important Charter values were also implicated in the decision.

[248] Art. 290 (1) TFEU ("Delegated Acts"). The other paragraphs provide procedural controls (possibility of revocation by Parliament and Council or entry into force if no objection has been expressed by these institutions within a deadline set by the enabling act) and the (also German-inspired) formal obligation to expressly state the legal basis in the text of the delegated act.

fully predicated on "the transcendental-theoretical kernel of self-referentiality evinced by the reflexive reason (*die sich selbst beurteilende Vernunft*)".[249]

The argument here was that the rise and fall of nondelegation evidences a larger problem: the simultaneous need of contemporary constitutionalism for foundational normativity and the impossibility of the positive constitutional law to secure the limits and consistency of its practices. A deeper corollary of this erosion of normativity regards the difficulty of foundational legal rationality to operate in the absence of meta-constitutional systemic reason. As it was argued, the general phenomenon for which delegation stands as epiphenomenal proxy is that of a relative incapacity of fundamental juridical practices, severed from their foundational presuppositions, to provide a manageable structure for securing and reconciling coherently collective action and individual autonomy.

[249] Luhmann 1990, at p. 187.

Bibliography

Aleinikoff T A (1987) Constitutional Law in the Age of Balancing. Yale L.J. 96 (5): 943–1005
Alexander, L, Prakash S (Fall 2003) Reports of the Nondelegation Doctrine's Death Are Greatly Exaggerated. U. Chi. L. Rev. 70: 1297–1330
Allen, C K (1931) Bureaucracy Triumphant. Oxford University Press, London: Humphrey Milford.
Aman, A C (1992) Administrative law in a Global Era. Ithaca, N.Y., Cornell University Press.
Aranson, P H, Gellhorn, E, Robinson G O (1982–1983) A Theory of Legislative Delegation. Cornell L. Rev. 68 (1): 1–67
Arendt, Hannah (1958), The Human Condition. University of Chicago Press, Chicago.
Arendt, Hannah (1965), On Revolution. Viking Press, New York
Aristotle (1994) Nicomachean Ethics. H. Rackham translation, Harvard University Press, Cambridge, Mass., and London, England
Aristotle (1948) Politics, translated with notes by Ernest Barker. Clarendon Press, Oxford (I also used the Jowett translation.)
Arthurs H W (April 1979) Rethinking Administrative Law: A Slightly Dicey Business. Osgoode Hall Law Journal 17 (1): 1–45
Atiyah, P S (1979) The Rise and Fall of Freedom of Contract. Clarendon Press, Oxford
Badura P (1967) Das Verwaltungsrecht des liberalen Rechtsstaates. Otto Schwartz & Co., Göttingen
Bagehot, W (1892) The English Constitution, revised American edition. D. Appleton & Company, New York
Baer S. (2004) Verfassungsvergleichung und reflexive Methode: Interkulturelle und intersubjektive Kompetenz. ZaöRV 64: 735–758
Barber, S (1978) The Constitution and the Delegation of Congressional Power. The University of Chicago Press, Chicago and London
Barker, E, Sir (1959) The Political Thought of Plato and Aristotle. Russell & Russell, New York
Barthélemy, J, Duez P (1933), Traité de droit constitutionnel. Librairie Dalloz, Paris
Baudrez, M (1997) Décrets-lois réitérés en Italie : l'exaspération mesurée de la Cour constitutionnelle en 1996. Revue française de droit constitutionnel 32: 745–762
Beard C A. (1935 (First Published 1913)) The Economic Interpretation of the Constitution of the United States. Macmillan, New York
Bentham J (1970) Limits of Jurisprudence Defined-Of Laws in General. Edited by H.L.A. Hart. University College of London, Athlone Press, London
Berle, A. A., Means G (1933) The Modern Corporation and Private Property. Macmillan, New York
Berman H J (1988) Toward an Integrative Jurisprudence: Politics, Morality, History. Cal. L. Rev. 76: 779–802

DOI 10.1007/978-3-642-22330-3,

Berman H J (1983) Law and Revolution: The Formation of the Western Legal Tradition. Harvard University Press, Cambridge, Mass. etc.

Bernstein M H. (1955) Regulating Business by Independent Commission. Princeton University Press, Princeton, N.J.

Bestor A (1973–1974) Separation of Powers in the Domain of Foreign Affairs: The Intent of the Constitution Historically Examined. Seton Hall L. Rev 5: 527–666

Bignami F (1999) Accountability and Interest Group Participation in Comitology: Lessons from American Rulemaking, European University Institute Working Paper, Robert Schuman Centre No. 99/3.

Böckenförde E-W (1981 (1958)) Gesetz und gesetzgebende Gewalt – Von den Anfängen der deutschen Staatsrechtslehre bis zur Höhe des staatsrechtlichen Positivismus. Zweite Auflage. Duncker & Humbolt, Berlin

Böckenförde E-W (1982) Mittelbare/repräsentative Demokratie als eigentliche Form der Demokratie-Bemerkungen zu Begriff und Verwirklichungsproblemen der Demokratie als Staats- und Regierungsform. In Müller G et al. (eds), Staatsorganisation und Staatsfunktionen im Wandel-Festschrift für Kurt Eichenberger zum 60. Geburtstag. Helbing & Lichtenhahn, Basel/Frankfurt am Main, pp. 301–328

Böckenförde E-W (1967) Die Entstehung des Staates als Vorgang der Säkularisation. In Säkularisation und Utopie: Ebracher Studien. Ernst Forsthoff zum 65. Geburtstag, Kohlhammer, Stuttgart u.a., pp. 75–94

Bork R (1993 (1978)) The Antitrust Paradox: A Policy at War with Itself. The Free Press, New York

Boyer-Mérentier C (1996) Les ordonnances de l'article 38 de la Constitution du 4 octobre 1958. Presses Universitaires dAix-Marseilles, Paris

Blackstone W (1845 (1765)) Commentaries on the Laws of England. W. E. Dean Printer & Publisher, New York

Bourdeau F (1995) Histoire du droit administratif (de la Révolution au début des années 1970). Presses Universitaires de France, Paris

Bressman L S (2001–2002) Disciplining Delegation after *Whitman V. American Trucking Ass'ns* Cornell L. Rev. 87: 452–485

Breyer S (1993) Breaking the Vicious Circle: Toward Effective Risk Regulation Harvard University Press, Cambridge, Mass.

Brown W. J. (1921–1922) The Separation of Powers in British Jurisdictions. Yale L. J. 31 (1): 24–51

Brunner O (1959 (vierte, veränderte Auflage)) Land und Herrschaft: Grundfragen der territorialen Verfassungsgeschichte Österreichs im Mittelalter. Rudolf M. Rohrer Verlag, Wien, Wiesbaden

Brunt P.A. (1977) Lex de Imperio Vespasiani. The Journal of Roman Studies 67: 95–116

Calabresi, S G, Rhodes K H (1992) The Structural Constitution: Unitary Executive, Plural Judiciary. Harv. L. Rev. 105: 1153

Calabresi, S G, Prakash S (December, 1994) The President's Power to Execute the Laws. Yale L. J. 104: 541–666

Canning J (1987) The Political Thought of Baldus de Ubaldis. Cambridge University Press, Cambridge

Casper G (Winter, 1989) An Essay in Separation of Powers: Some Early Versions and Practices. Wm. and Mary L. Rev. 30: 211–262

Cassirer E (2007) Die Philosophie der Aufklärung. Felix Meiner, Hamburg

Cassirer E (1951) The Philosophy of the Enlightenment, Fritz C. A. Koellin and James P. Petergrove transl. Princeton University Press, Princeton, N.J.

Caust-Ellenbogen S N (July 1991) Blank Checks: Restoring the Balance of Powers in the Post-Chevron Era. B.C.L. Rev. 32: 757–834

Chroust A-H (Mar., 1944) The Philosophy of Law of Saint Augustine. The Philosophical Review 53 (2): 195–202

Conrad H (1958) Die geistigen Grundlagen des Allgemeinen Landrechts für die preußischen Staaten. Westdeutscher Verlag, Köln und Opladen
Constant B (1993 (c1988)) Political Writings, translated and edited by Biancamaria Fontana. Cambridge University Press, Cambridge
Cooley T M (1868) A Treatise on the Constitutional Limitations Which Rest Upon the Legislative Power of the States of the American Union. Little, Brown and Co., Boston
Corwin E S (1946) The Constitution and What It Means Today. Princeton University Press, Princeton, N.J.
Corwin E S (1957) The President-Office and Powers 1787–1957 – History and Analysis of Practice and Opinion. New York University Press, New York
Cousens T W (February 1935) The Delegation of Federal Legislative Power to Executive Officials. Michigan Law Review 33: 512–544
Currie D P (Summer, 1986) Positive and Negative Constitutional Rights. U. Chi. L. Rev. 53: 864–890
Currie D P (1994) The Constitution of the Federal Republic of Germany. Chicago University Press, Chicago
Cushman R E (1972 (c1941)) The Independent Regulatory Commissions. Pentagon Books, New York
Dahrendorf R (1965) Gesellschaft und Demokratie in Deutschland. Piper & Co., München
Davis K C (1969) Discretionary Justice – A Preliminary Inquiry. Louisiana University Press, Baton Rouge
Davis K C (1978–1984) Administrative Law Treatise. K. C. Davis Pub. Co., San Diego
DeShazo, J R, Freeman J (May 2003) The Congressional Competition to Control Delegated Power. Tex. L. Rev. 81 (6): 1443–1520
Dicey A V (1965) Introduction to the Study of the Law of the Constitution. Macmillan & Co., London, N.Y.
Dicey A V (1915) The Development of Administrative Law in England. Law Quarterly Review 31 (2) 148–153
Diver C S (Nov. 1983) The Optimal Precision of Administrative Rules. Yale L. J. 93: 65–110
Dorsen, N, Sajó, A, Rosenfeld, M, Baer S (c2003) Comparative Constitutionalism – Cases and Materials. West, St. Paul, Minn.
Duff, P W, Whiteside H E (1928–1929) *Delegata Potestas Non Potest Delegari*: A Maxim of American Constitutional Law. *Cornell L. Q.* 14: 168–196
Duguit L (1893) La séparation des pouvoirs et l'Assemblée nationale de 1789. in three parts, Revue d'Économie Politique, Vol. 7
Duguit, Léon (1928) Traité de droit constitutionnel. 3e éd., 5 vol. Fontemoing, Paris
Dunning, W A (Jun., 1886) The Constitution of the United States in Civil War, Political Science Quarterly 1 (2): 163
Dunning, W A (1900) The Politics of Aristotle in Political Science Quarterly 15 (2): 273
Duverger M (1990) Le système politique français. Presses Universitaires de France, Paris
Dyzenhaus, D, Fox-Decent E (Summer, 2001) Rethinking the Process/Substance Distinction: *Baker v. Canada,* U. Toronto L. J. 51: 193–242
Dyzenhaus, D (ed.) (2004) The Unity of Public Law. Hart Publishing, Oxford and Portland, Oregon
Easterbrook F (1988) The Role of Original Intent in Statutory Construction. Harv. J. L. & Pub. Pol'y 11: 59–66
Ebel W (1958) Geschichte der Gesetzgebung in Deutschland, 2, erweiterte Auflage. Otto Schwartz & Co., Göttingen
Ely J H (1980) Democracy and Distrust: A Theory of Judicial Review. Harvard University Press, Cambridge
Epstein, D, O'Halloran S (1999) Delegating Power – A Transaction Cost Politics Approach to Policy Making Under Separate Powers. Cambridge University Press, Cambridge

Esmein A (1894) De la délégation du pouvoir législatif – A l'occasion du projet dit 'des pleins pouvoirs' presente par M. Crispi au Parlement italien. Revue politique et parlementaire
Esmein A (1921) Éléments du droit constitutionnel français et comparé. Sirey, Paris
Farina C (April, 1989) Statutory Interpretation and the Balance of Power in the Administrative State. Colum. L. Rev. 89: 452–528
Farrand M (1974 (c1966)) The Records of the Federal Convention of 1787. Yale University Press, New Haven, Ct. and London, England
Favoreu, L (ed) (1981) Le Domaine de la loi et du règlement. Presses Universitaires d'Aix-Marseille, Paris
Favoreu, L (1977) Les règlements autonomes existent-ils ? *Mélanges Burdeau*, Paris, pp. 405–420
Favoreu, L (1987) Les règlements autonomes n'existent pas. R.F.D.A. 1987: 872–884
Favoreu, L, Philip L (9e éd., 1997) Les grandes décisions du Conseil constitutionnel, Dalloz, Paris
Figgis J N (1970) The Divine Right of Kings. Peter Smith Pub. Inc., Gloucester, Mass.
Fiorina M (1986) Legislator Uncertainty, Legislative Control, and the Delegation of Legislative Power. J. L. Econ. & Org. 2 (1): 33–52
Forsthoff E (1973) Lehrbuch des Verwaltungsrechts, 10. Auflage. C.H. Beck, München
Forsthoff E (1971) Der Staat der Industriegesellschaft. Dargestellt am Beispiel der Bundesrepublik Deutschland. C.H. Beck, München
Forsthoff E (1968) Begriff und Wesen des sozialen Rechtsstaates. In Forsthoff E (ed) Rechtsstaatlichkeit und Sozialstaatlichkeit-Aufsätze und Essays. Wissenschaftliche Buchgesellschaft, Darmstadt, pp. 165–200
Forsthoff E (1961) Deutsche Verfassungsgeschichte der Neuzeit. Ein Abriss. Kohlhammer, Stuttgart
Forsthoff E (1938) Die Verwaltung als Leistungsträger. Kohlhammer, Stuttgart.
Freeman J (2000) The Private Role in Public Governance. N.Y.U. L. Rev. 75 (3): 543–675
Freund E (1928) Administrative Powers over Persons and Property. Chicago University Press, Chicago
Freund E (November, 1915) The Substitution of Rule for Discretion in Public Law. American Political Science Review 9 (4): 666–676
Freund E (September 1894) The Law of the Administration in America. Political Science Quarterly 9 (3): 403–425
Friedrich C J (1968a) Constitutional Government and Democracy: Theory and Practice in Europe and America. Blaisdell Publ., Waltham, Mass.
Friedrich C J (1968b) The Philosophy of Law in Historical Perspective, 2nd ed., The University of Chicago Press, Chicago and London
von Fritz K (1954) The Theory of the Mixed Constitution in Antiquity: A Critical Analysis of Polybius' Political Ideas. Columbia University Press, New York
Frug G (1984) The Ideology of Bureaucracy in American Law. Harv. L. Rev. 97 (6): 1276–1388
Fuller L (December, 1978) The Forms and Limits of Adjudication. Harv. L. Rev. 92 (2): 353–409
Fuller L (1976) Anatomy of the Law. Greenwood Press, Westport, CT
Garrett E (2002–2003) Legislating *Chevron*. Mich. L. Rev. 101: 2637–2676
Garry P M (2006) Accommodating the Administrative State: The Interrelationship between the Nondelegation and *Chevron* Doctrines. Ariz. St. L. J. 38 (4): 921–960
von Gierke O (1902 (1880)) Johannes Althusius und die Entwicklung der naturrechtlichen Staatstheorien, Marcus, Breslau
von Gierke O (1987 (1900)) Political Theories of the Middle Ages, translated by Frederic William Maitland. Cambridge University Press, Cambridge
von Gierke O (1883) Labands Staatsrecht und die deutsche Rechtswissenschaft. Schmollers Jahrbuch für Gesetzgebung, Verwaltung und Volkswirtschaft im Deutschen Reich NF 7: 1097–1195
Goodnow F J (1905) The Principles of the Administrative Law of the United States. Putnam, New York, London

Goodnow F J (1893) Comparative Administrative Law: An analysis of the Administrative Systems National and Local, of the United States, England, France and Germany. Putnam, New York, London

Grimm D (2009a) Souveränität-Herkunft und Zukunft eines Schlüsselbegriffs. Berlin University Press, Berlin

Grimm D (2009b) Gesellschaftlicher Konstitutionalismus – Eine Kompensation für den Bedeutungsschwund der Staatsverfassung? In Festschrift für Roman Herzog zum 75. Geburtstag. C.H. Beck, München, pp. 68–81.

Grimm D (2005) The Constitution in the Process of Denationalization. Constellations 12: 447–463

Grimm D (1988) Deutsche Verfassungsgeschichte 1776–1866: Vom Beginn des modernen Verfassungsstaats bis zur Auflösung des Deutschen Bundes Suhrkamp, Frankfurt a.M.

Grimm D (1987) Recht und Staat der bürgerlichen Gesellschaft. Suhrkamp, Frankfurt a. M.

Grimm D (1970) Europäisches Naturrecht und Amerikanische Revolution - Die Verwandlung politischer Philosophie in politischer Techne. Ius Commune III: 120–151

Grundstein N D (April, 1950) Presidential Power, Administration, and Administrative Law. Geo. Wash. L. Rev. 18 (3): 285–326

Gneist R (1886) The History of the English Constitution. Philip A. Ashworth translation. G. P. Putnam's Sons, New York

Gwyn W G (1965) The Meaning of the Separation of Powers. Tulane University Press, New Orleans

Gueniffey P (1993) Le nombre et la raison – La Révolution française et les élections. Éditions de l'École des Hautes Études en Sciences Sociales, Paris

Guizot F P G (1852) History of the Origin of Representative Government in Europe. Andrew R. Scoble translation. Henry G. Bohn, London

Hale R L (September, 1923) Coercion and Distribution in a Supposedly Non-Coercive State. Political Science Quarterly 38 (3): 470–494

Hansen M H (1991) The Athenian Democracy in the Age of Demosthenes, J. A. Cook transl. Blackwell, Oxford, UK & Cambridge, Mass., USA

Hart J (May, 1942) Limits of Legislative Delegation. Annals of the American Academy of Political and Social Science 221: 87–100

Hart J (1925) The Ordinance Making Powers of the President of the United States. The Johns Hopkins Press, Baltimore

Hart J (1923) The Emergency Ordinance: A Note on Executive Power. Colum. L. Rev. 23: 528–535

Hasskarl H (1969) Die Rechtsprechung des Bundesverfassungsgerichts zu Art. 80 Abs. 1 Satz 2 GG. AöR Bd. 94: 85–115

Hawley E W (1966) The New Deal and the Problem of Monopoly-A Study in Economic Ambivalence. Princeton University Press, Princeton, N.J.

von Hayek F A (1993 (c1982)) Law, Legislation, and Liberty-A New Statement of the Liberal Principles of Justice and Political Economy. Routledge, London

von Hayek F A (1978 (c1960)) The Constitution of Liberty. University of Chicago Press, Chicago

von Hayek F A (1991, c1944) The Road to Serfdom. Routledge, London

Henderson G (1968 (c1924)) The History of the Federal Trade Commission-A Study in Administrative Law and Procedure. Agathon Press, New York

Herring E P (1936) Public Administration and the Public Interest. McGraw-Hill, New York

Herring E P (Dec., 1934) and (Feb., 1935) Politics Personalities, and the Federal Trade Commission, I and II. American Political Science Review 28 (6): 1016–1029 and 29: (1) 21–35

Hewart, Rt. Hon. Lord of Bury (1929) The New Despotism. Ernest Benn, London

Hobbes T (1950) Leviathan. E. P. Dutton and Company, Inc, New York; J. M. Dent and Sons, Limited, London

Hoeflich M H (Apr., 1986) Law & Geometry: Legal Science from Leibniz to Langdell. Am. J. Legal Hist. 30 (2) 95–121

Hogg P W (2003) Constitutional law of Canada. Carswell, Scarborough, Ont.

Holmes, S, Sunstein C R (1999) The Cost of Rights: Why Liberty Depends on Taxes. Norton, New York

Holmes S (1995) Passions and Constraint-On the Theory of Liberal Democracy. The University of Chicago Press, Chicago

Holmes S (1984) Benjamin Constant and the Making of Modern Liberalism. Yale University Press, New Haven and London

Horwitz M J (c1992) The Transformation of American Law 1870–1960 -The Crisis of Legal Orthodoxy. Oxford University Press, New York, London

Hovenkamp H (1995) The Mind and Heart of Progressive Legal Thought. (Presidential Lecture given at the University of Iowa), available at http://sdrc.lib.uiowa.edu/preslectures/hovenkamp95/, accessed October 31, 2010).

Hovenkamp H (1991) Enterprise and American Law 1836–1937. Harvard University Press, Cambridge, Mass.

Hovenkamp H (December, 1985) Evolutionary Models in Jurisprudence. Tex. L. Rev. 64: 645–686

Hurst J W (1967) Law and the Conditions of Freedom in the Nineteenth-Century United States. The University of Wisconsin Press, Madison, etc.

Iancu B (ed.) (2009) The Law/Politics Distinction in Contemporary Public Law Adjudication. Eleven International Publishing, Utrecht & Portland, OR

Jaffe L (May, 1973) The Illusion of Ideal Administration. Harv. L. Rev. 86: 1183–1199

Jaffe L (1965) Judicial Control of Administrative Action. Little, Brown, and Company, Boston, Toronto

Jaffe L (1951) Judicial Review: "Substantial Evidence on the Whole Record". Harv. L. Rev. 64 (8): 1233–1261

Jaffe L (April and May 1947) An Essay on the Delegation of the Legislative Power, I-II, Colum. L. Rev. 47 (3) 359–376 & 47 (4) 561–593

Jaffe L (December, 1937) Law Making by Private Groups. Harv. L. Rev. 51 (2) 201–253

Jesch D (1961) Gesetz und Verwaltung: Eine Problemstudie zum Wandel des Gesetzmäßigkeitsprinzipes. J.C.B. Mohr (Siebeck), Tübingen

Jellinek G (1887) Gesetz und Verordnung: staatsrechtliche Untersuchungen auf rechtsgeschichtlicher und rechtsvergleichender Grundlage. Mohr, Freiburg I.B.

Kagan E (2001) Presidential Administration. Harv. L. Rev. 114: 2245–2385

Kahan D M (Jan., 1999) Democracy Schmemocracy. Cardozo L. Rev. 20 (3): 795–806

Kaminsky H (2002) The Noble Feud in the Later Middle Ages. Past and Present 177 (1) 55–83

Kant I (1797 (1990)) Die Metaphysik der Sitten, Reclam, Stuttgart

Kant I Immanuel Kant, Beantwortung der Frage: Was ist Aufklärung? Berlinische Monatsschrift, Dezember-Heft 1784: 481–494.

Katz S (1976) Thomas Jefferson and the Right to Property in Revolutionary America. J. L. & Econ. 19 (3): 467–488

Kelly J M (1992) A Short History of Western Legal Theory Clarendon Press, Oxford

Kirchheimer O (Dec., 1940) Decree Powers and Constitutional Law in France under the Third Republic. American Political Science Review 34 (6) 1104–1123

Kischel U (Spring, 1994) Delegation of Legislative Power to Agencies: A Comparison of the United Sates and German Law. Admin. L. Rev. 46 (2): 213–256

Kmiec D W (1988) Judicial Deference to Executive Agencies and the Decline of the Nondelegation Doctrine. Admin. L. J. 2 (2): 269–290

Knemeyer F-L (1967) Polizeibegriffe in Gesetzen des 15. Bis 18. Jahrhunderts – Kritische Bemerkungen zur Literatur über die Entwicklung des Polizebegriffs. AöR 92 (2): 153–180

Kommers D P (1997) The Constitutional Jurisprudence of the Federal Republic of Germany. Duke University Press, Durham, N.C.

Krent H J (Fall, 1990) Fragmenting the Unitary Executive: Congressional Delegations of Administrative Authority Outside the federal Government. Nw. U. L. Rev. 85: 62–112

Kunkel W (1996) Roman Legal and Constitutional History. J. M. Kelly transl. Oxford University Press, Oxford

Lambert E (1921) Le gouvernement des juges et la lutte contre la législation sociale aux États-Unis. Giard, Paris

Landis J M (1966 edition with a Foreword by Louis L. Jaffe (c1938)) The Administrative Process. Yale University Press, New Haven and London

Lawrence, David M., "Private Exercise of Governmental Power," 61 *Ind. L. J.* 647 (1985–1986)

Lawson G (January 2005) Discretion as Delegation: The Proper Understanding of the Nondelegation Doctrine. Geo. Wash. L. Rev. 73: 235–268

Lawson G (April 2002) Delegation and Original Meaning. Va. L. Rev. 88 (2): 327–404

Lehmberg S E (Jan., 1970) Early Tudor Parliamentary Procedure: Provisos in the Legislation of the Reformation Parliament. The English Historical Review Vol. 85 (No. 334): 1–11

Lessig, L, Sunstein C R (January, 1994) The President and the Administration. Colum. L. Rev. 94: 1–123

Lewis E (April, 1964) King Above Law? "Quod Principi Placuit" in Bracton. Speculum 39 (2): 240–269

Lieberman D (1989) The Province of Legislation Determined-Legal Theory in Eighteenth Century Britain. Cambridge University Press, Cambridge

Linde H A (1999) Structures and Terms of Consent: Delegation, Discretion, Separation of Powers, Representation, Participation, Accountability. Cardozo L. Rev. 20: 823–852

Lindseth, P L (May, 2004) The Paradox of Parliamentary Supremacy: Delegation, Democracy, and Dictatorship in Germany and France 1920s-1950s. Yale L. J. 113: 1341–1416

Lindseth, P L (2002) The Contradictions of Supranationalism: European Integration and the Constitutional Settlement of Administrative Governance, 1920s-1980s (Ph.D. dissertation, Columbia University, Department of History)

Linz J J (1998) Democracy's Time Constraints. *International Political Science Review* 19 (1): 19–37

Locke J (1980) Second Treatise of Government. C.B. Macpherson (ed). Hackett, Indianapolis, Ind.

Loetscher F W. (Mar., 1935) Saint Augustine's Conception of the State. Church History 4 (1): 16–42

De Lolme J L (MDCCLXXXIV) The Constitution of England or An Account of the English Government In which it is compared, both with the REPUBLICAN form of GOVERNMENT, and the other Monarchies in EUROPE, The Fourth Edition, Corrected and Enlarged. G. Robinson and J. Murray, London

Long, M, Devolvé, P, Braibant, G, Weil, P, Genevois B (10th edition, 1993) Les grands arrêts de la jurisprudence administrative. Dalloz, Paris

Lowi T (Winter, 1987) Two Roads to Serfdom: Liberalism, Conservatism, and Administrative Power. Am. U. L. Rev. 36 (2): 295–302

Lowi T (1979) The End of Liberalism-The Second Republic of the United States, 2nd edition. Norton, New York and London

Luhmann N (1990) Verfassung als evolutionäre Errungenschaft. Rechtshistorisches Journal 9: 176–220

Luebke D M (1999) Frederick the Great and the Celebrated Case of the Millers Arnold (1770–1779)-A Reappraisal. Central European History 32 (4): 379–408

Maggs G E (1995–1996) Reconciling Textualism and the *Chevron* Doctrine: In Defense of Justice Scalia. Conn. L. Rev. 28: 393–424

Magill, Elizabeth (September 2000) The Real Separation in Separation of Powers Law. Va. L. Rev. 86 (2) 1127–1198

Maier H (1966) Die ältere deutsche Staats- und Verwaltungslehre (Polizeiwissenschaft) – Ein Beitrag zur Geschichte der politischen Wissenschaft in Deutschland. Luchterhand, Neuwied am Rhein und Berlin

Majone G (1996) Regulating Europe. Routledge, New York and London

Martin R (Apr.-Jun. 1972) The Two Cities in Augustine's Political Philosophy. Journal of the History of Ideas 33 (2): 195–216

de Malberg R C (1931) La loi, expression de la volonté générale. Sirey, Paris

de Malberg R C (1922) Contributions à la Théorie générale de l'État. Sirey, Paris

Maine H S (2004) Lectures on the Early History of Institutions. Kessinger, Whitefish, Mont.

Maitland F W (1963) The Constitutional History of England. Cambridge University Press, Cambridge

Manin B (1997) The Principles of Representative Government. Cambridge University Press, Cambridge

Manning J F (2000) The Nondelegation Doctrine as a Canon of Avoidance. Supreme Court Review 2000: 223–278

Manning J F (1997) Textualism as a Nondelegation Doctrine. Colum. L. Rev. 97: 673–739

Mashaw, J L, Merril, R A, Shane P M (2003) Administrative Law-The American Public Law System: Cases and Materials. West, St. Paul, Minn.

Mashaw J L (2005) Structuring a 'Dense Complexity': Accountability and the Project of Administrative Law," *Issues in Legal Scholarship*, The Reformation of American Administrative Law, Article 4. http://www.bepress.com/ils/iss6/art4

Mashaw J L (1997) Greed, Chaos, and Governance – Using Public Choice to Improve Public Law. Yale University Press, New Haven, CT

Mashaw J L (1985a) Due Process in the Administrative State. Yale University Press, New Haven, CT

Mashaw J L (1985b) Prodelegation: Why Administrators Should Make Political Decisions. J. L. Econ. & Org. 1 (1): 81–105

Otto Mayer ((1924) 2004) Deutsches Verwaltungsrecht, dritte Auflage, unveränderter Nachdruck. Duncker & Humblot, Berlin

McCraw T K (1984) Prophets of Regulation. Belknap-Harvard University Press, Cambridge, Mass, and London, England

McIlwain C H (1940) Constitutionalism, Ancient and Modern. Cornell University Press, Ithaca, NY

McIlwain C H (1918) (ed) The Political Works of James I: Reprinted from the Edition of 1616. Cambridge University Press, Cambridge

McIlwain C H (1910) The High Court of Parliament and Its Supremacy – An Historical Essay of the Boundaries between Legislation and Adjudication in England Yale University Press, New Haven, CT

Meinecke F (1957) Machiavellism-The Doctrine of Raison d'Etat and Its Place in Modern History. Douglas Scott transl. Yale University Press, New Haven, CT

Meisner H O (1951/1952) Staats- und Regierungsformen in Deutschland seit dem 16. Jahrhundert. AöR 77 (2/3): 225–265

Mendle M (1985) Dangerous Positions – Mixed Government, the Estates of the Realm, and the Answer to the xix propositions. University of Alabama Press, Alabama

Merrill, T W, Hickman K (2000–2001) *Chevron*'s Domain. Geo. L. J. 89: 833–922

Metzger G E (Winter, 2003) Privatization as Delegation. Colum. L. Rev. 103: 1367–1502

Mohnhaupt H (1972) Potestas legislatoria und Gesetzesbegriff im Ancien Régime. *Ius Commune* IV: 188–239

Möllers C (2008) Die drei Gewalten: Legitimation der Gewaltengliederung in Verfassungsstaat, Europäischer Integration und Internationalisierung. Velbrück Wissenschaft, Weilerswist

Möllers C (2005) Gewaltengliederung; Legitimation und Dogmatik im nationalen und internationalen Rechtsvergleich. Mohr Siebeck, Tübingen

Mößle W (1990) Inhalt, Zweck und Ausmaß. Zur Verfassungsgeschichte der Verordnungsermächtigung. Duncker & Humblot, Berlin

Mommsen T (1984 (reprint of the 1892 edition)) Le Droit public romain. trad. P. F. Girard, Coll. Manuel des Antiquités Romaines. Diffusion De Boccard, Paris

Mommsen T (1958) The History of Rome, An Account of Events and Persons from Carthage to the End of the Republic, Dero Saunders and John A. Collins eds. Meridian Books, Inc., Clinton, Mass.
Monaghan H P (January, 1993) The Protective Power of the Presidency. Colum. L. Rev. 93: 1–74
Monaghan H P (January, 1983) *Marbury* and the Administrative State. Colum. L. Rev. 83: 1–34
Montesquieu C L (1849) De L'Esprit des Lois (Esprit des Lois par Montesquieu Avec Les Notes de l'Auteur et un Choix des Observations par De Dupin, Crevier, Voltaire, Mably, La Harpe, Servan, etc.). Librairie de Paris, Firmin-Didot et Cie, Imprimeurs-Éditeurs, Paris
Morrow G R (Mar., 1941) Plato and the Rule of Law. The Philosophical Review 50 (2): 105–126
Mill J S (1991) Considerations on Representative Government. Prometheus Books, Buffalo, NY
Mullan, D J, Evans, J M, Janisch, H N, Risk R C B (2003) Administrative Law-Cases, Texts, and Materials, Fifth Edition. Emond Montgomery, Toronto
Nelson C (April 2007) Adjudication in the Political Branches. Colum. L. Rev. 107 (3) 559–627
Page W H (2009) The Gary Dinners and the Meaning of Concerted Action. SMU L. Rev. 62: 597–620
Pieroth, B, Schlink B (2008) Grundrechte. Staatsrecht II, 24.Auflage. C.F. Müller Verlag, Heidelberg
Pierce R (1996–1997) Reconciling *Chevron* and Stare Decisis. Geo. L. J. 85: 2225-2264
Pierce R (1985–1986) The Role of Constitutional and Political Theory in Administrative Law. Tex. L. Rev. 64: 469–526
Pitkin H F (1967) The Concept of Representation. University of California Press, Berkeley, Los Angeles, London
Plato (2005) The Laws. Trevor Saunders transl. Penguin Books, London
Posner, E A, Vermeule A (Fall 2003) Nondelegation: A Post-Mortem. U. Chi. L. Rev. 70: 1331–1344
Posner, E A, Vermeule A (2002) Interring the Nondelegation Doctrine. U. Chi. L. Rev. 69: 1721–1762
Post G (1964) Studies in Medieval Legal Thought-Public Law and the State, 1100–1322. Princeton University Press, Princeton, NJ
Post G (1950) A Roman Legal Theory of Consent, *Quod Omnes Tangit*, In Medieval Representation. Wis. L. Rev. 1950: 66–78
Postema G J (October 2001) Law as Command: The Model of Command in Modern Jurisprudence. *Noûs* 35: 470–501
Postema G J (1986) Bentham and the Common Law Tradition. Clarendon Press, Oxford
Pound R (April, 1908) Common Law and Legislation. Harv. L. Rev. 21 (6): 383–407
Prakash, S, Ramsey M D (November, 2001) The Executive Power over Foreign Affairs. Yale L. J. 111: 231–356
Pünder H (2009) Democratic Legitimation of Delegated Legislation—A Comparative View on the American, British and German Law. ICLQ 58: 353–378
Rabin R (May, 1986) Federal Regulation in Historical Perspective. Stan. L. Rev. 38: 1189–1326
Reich C A (1963–1964) The New Property. Yale L. J. 73: 733–787
Robbins I P (1988) The Impact of the Delegation Doctrine on Prison Privatization. UCLA L. Rev. 35: 911–952
Rodgers D T (Dec., 1982) In Search of Progressivism. Reviews in American History 10 (4): 113–132
Rogoff M A (1997) A Comparison of Constitutionalism in France and the United States. Me. L. Rev. 49: 21–84
Rohr J A (March 2002) Dicey's Ghost and Administrative Law. Administration and Society 34 (1): 8–31
Rose-Ackerman S (1993–1994) American Administrative Law under Siege: Is Germany a Model? Harv. L. Rev. 107 (6): 1279–1302
Ross A (1958) Delegation of Power-Meaning and Validity of the maxim *delegata potestas non potests delegari*. Am. J. Comp. L. 7: 1–22

Rossiter C (ed) (1961) The Federalist Papers. Mentor Books, NY
Rossiter C (1951) The Supreme Court and the Commander in Chief. Cornell University Press, Ithaca, NY
Rossiter C (1948) Constitutional Dictatorship – Crisis Government in the Modern Democracies. Princeton University Press, Princeton, NJ
Rousseau, J-J (1962) Oeuvres Choisies. Éditions Garnier Frères, Paris
Rubin E L (April, 1989) Law and Legislation in the Administrative State. Colum. L. Rev. 89: 369–426
Sajó A (2006) From Militant Democracy to the Preventive State? Cardozo L. Rev. 27: 2255–2294
Sajó A (1999) Limiting Government-An Introduction to Constitutionalism. Central European University Press, Budapest
Scalia A (1997) (Author) & Amy Gutman (ed) A Matter of Interpretation. Princeton University Press, Princeton, NJ:
Scalia A (1989a) Judicial Deference to Administrative Interpretations of the Law. Duke L. J. 1989: 511–521
Scalia A (1989b) Scalia, Antonin, The Rule of Law as a Law of Rules. U. Chi. L. Rev. 56: 1175–1188
Scalia A (1983) The Doctrine of Standing as an Essential Element of the Separation of Powers. Suffolk U. L. Rev. 17: 881–900
Schlink B (1989) Die Entthronung der Staatsrechtswissenschaft durch die Verfassungsgerichtsbarkeit. Der Staat, Bd. 28: 161–172
Schoenbrod D (2003) Politics and the Principle that Elected Legislators Should Make the Laws. Harv. J. L. & Pub. Pol'y 26: 239–280
Schoenbrod D (1982–1983) Goals Statutes or Rules Statutes: The Case of the Clean Air Act. UCLA L. Rev. 30: 740–828
Schoenbrod D (1993) Power Without Responsibility: How Congress Abuses the People through Delegation. Yale University Press, New Haven
Schmitt C (2000) La Dictature, transl. Mira Köller & Dominique Séglard. Éditions du Seuil, Paris
Schmitt C (1993) Théorie de la Constitution, Lilyane Deroche transl., with an introduction by Olivier Beaud. Presses Universitaires de France
Schmitt C (Spring 1990) The Plight of European Jurisprudence, G. L. Ulmen transl., Telos 83: 35–70
Schmitt C (1988) The Crisis of Parliamentary Democracy, Ellen Kennedy transl. The MIT Press, Cambridge, Mass. and London, England
Schmitt C (1985) Political Theology-Four Chapters on the Concept of Sovereignty, George Schwab transl. The MIT Press, Cambridge, Mass. and London, England
Schmitt C (1938) L'évolution récente du problème des délégations législatives in Introduction à l'etude du droit comparé-Recueil d'Études en l'honneur d'Édouard Lambert. Sirey, Paris
Schmitt C (1936) Vergleichender Überblick über die neueste Entwicklung des Problems der gesetzgeberischen Ermächtigungen (Legislative Delegationen). *ZaöRV* 6: 252–268
Schwartz, B, Wade H W (1972) Legal Control of Government: Administrative Law in Britain and the United States. Clarendon Press, Oxford
Schwartz B (1987) Lions Over the Throne – The Judicial Review of English Administrative Law. New York University Press, New York and London
Shapiro M (1996) The Frontiers of Science Doctrine: American Experiences with the Judicial Control of Science-Based Decision-Making. EUI Working Papers, European University Institute, RSC No. 96/11
Shapiro M (1988) Who Guards the Guardians-Judicial Control of Administration Georgia University Press, Athens and London
Shapiro M (1982–1983) Administrative Discretion: The Next Stage. Yale L. J. 92: 1487–1522
Sharp M (1934–1935) The Classical American Doctrine of "The Separation of Powers" U. Chi. L. Rev. 2: 385–436

Skinner Q (1978) The Foundations of Modern Political Thought. Cambridge University Press, Cambridge

Starr K W (1985–1986) Judicial Review in the Post-*Chevron* Era. Yale J. on Reg. 3: 283–312

Stewart, R B, Sunstein C R (April, 1982) Public Programs and Private Rights. Harv. L. Rev. 95: 1193–1322

Stewart R B (1991) Regulatory Jurisprudence: Canons Redux? (Book Review of Cass R. Sunstein, *After the Rights Revolution*, Cambridge, Mass., Harvard University Press, 1990) Cal. L. Rev. 79: 807–822

Stewart R B (1974–1975) The Reformation of American Administrative Law. Harv. L. Rev. 88: 1667

Stollberg-Rillinger B (2000) Europa im Jahrhundert der Aufklärung. Reclam, Stuttgart

Story J (1891(1833)) Commentaries on the Constitution of the United States. Little, Brown, and Company, Boston

Story J (1839) Commentaries on the Law of Agency as a Branch of Commercial and Maritime Jurisprudence, with Occasional Illustrations from the Civil and Foreign Law. Little, Brown, and Company, Boston

Strayer J R (1970) On the Medieval Origins of the Modern State. Princeton University Press, Princeton

Strayer J R (January1940) The Laicization of French and English Society in the Thirteenth Century. Speculum 15 (1): 76–86

Strauss L (1963) The Political Philosophy of Hobbes-Its Basis and Genesis. transl. by Elsa M. Sinclair. The University of Chicago Press, Chicago and London

Strauss P (April, 1989) Legislative Theory and the Rule of Law: Some Comments on Rubin. Colum. L. Rev. 89: 427–451

Strauss P (1984) The Place of Agencies in Government: Separation of Powers and the Fourth Branch. Colum. L. Rev. 84: 573–669

Sunstein, C R, Ullmann-Margalit E (October, 1999) Second-Order Decisions. Ethics 110 (1): 5–31

Sunstein C R (2006a) Nondelegation Principles. In Bauman, R W, Kahana T (eds.), The Least Examined Branch-The Role of Legislatures in the Constitutional State Cambridge University Press, New York, pp. 139–154

Sunstein C R (2006b) *Chevron* Step Zero. Va. L. Rev. 92: 187–250

Sunstein C R (2001) Designing Democracy-What Constitutions Do. Oxford University Press, Oxford, NY

Sunstein C R (1995) Problems with Rules. Cal. L. Rev. 86: 953

Sunstein C R (1990a) Law and Administration after *Chevron*. Colum. L. Rev. 90: 2071–2120

Sunstein C R (1990b) Reconceiving the Regulatory State: After the Rights Revolution Harvard University Press, Cambridge, Mass.

Sunstein C R (1987a) Constitutionalism after the New Deal. Harv. L. Rev. 101: 421–510

Sunstein C R (1987b) Lochner's Legacy. Colum. L. Rev. 87: 873–919

Sunstein C R (1987c) Changing Conceptions of Administration. BYU L. Rev. 1987 (3): 927–948

Suzman A (January 1933) Administrative Law in England: A Study of the Report of the Committee on Ministers' Powers. Iowa L. Rev. 18 (2) 160–186.

Taggart M (ed) (1997) The Province of Administrative Law. Hart Publishing, Oxford, England

Tiedeman C G (1886) A Treatise on the Limitations of Police Power in the United States. The F. H. Thomas Law Book Co., St. Louis

Tierney B (1982) Religion, Law, and the Growth of Constitutional Thought Cambridge University Press, Cambridge

Tingstén H (1934) Les pleins pouvoirs – L'Expansion des pouvoirs gouvernamentaux pendant et après la grande guerre, traduit du Suédois par E. Söderlindh. Librairie Stock, Delamain et Boutelleau, Publications du Fonds Descartes, Paris

de Tocqueville A (1952) Oeuvres complètes. Librairie Gallimard, Paris

Trémeau J (1997) La réserve de loi-compétence législative et Constitution. Presses Universitaires d'Aix-Marseilles, Aix-en-Provence

Tribe L (2000) American Constitutional Law. 3rd ed. The Foundation Press, New York, NY
Tribe L (1988) 2nd ed. The Foundation Press, Mineola, NY
Troper M (1973) La séparation des pouvoirs et l'histoire constitutionnelle française LGDJ, Paris
Tushnet M (1999) The Possibilities of Comparative Constitutional Law. Yale L. J. 108: 1225–1310
Ullmann W (1966) Principles of Government and Politics in the Middle Ages. 2nd ed. Butler & Tanner Ltd., Frome and London
Verkuil P R (2002–2003), An Outcomes Analysis of Scope of Review Standards. Wm. & Mary L. Rev. 44: 679–736
Verkuil P R (Winter, 1989) The American Constitutional Tradition of Shared and Separated Powers: Separation of Powers, the Rule of Law and the Idea of Independence. Wm. & Mary L. Rev. 30: 301–342
Verkuil P R (1986) Crosscurrents in Anglo-American Administrative Law. Wm. & Mary L. Rev. 27: 685–714
Vermeule A (2009) Our Schmittian Administrative Law. Harv. L. Rev. 122: 1095–1150
Vermeule A (1997) Mechanisms of Democracy: Institutional Design Writ Small Oxford University Press, New York
Vibert F (2007) The Rise of the Unelected: Democracy and the New Separation of Powers Cambridge UP, Cambridge
Vile M J C (1967) Constitutionalism and the Separation of Powers. Clarendon Press, Oxford
Waldron J (Fall, 2000) Legislation by Assembly. Loy. L. Rev. 46: 507–534
Waldron J (1999) Law and Disagreement. Oxford University Press, Oxford
Weber M (1978) Economy and Society: An Outline of Interpretive Sociology, Guenther Roth and Claus Wittich (eds). University of California Press, Berkeley and Los Angeles
White G E (September, 2010) The Lost Origins of American Judicial Review. Geo. Wash. L. Rev. 78 (6): 1145–1161
White G E (2000) The Constitution and the New Deal. Harvard University Press, Cambridge, Mass. and London, England
Wiebe R (1967) The Search for Order, 1877–1920 Hill and Wang, New York, NY
Williams S F (1983). Liberty and Property: The Problem of Government Benefits. J. Leg. Stud. (12) 3–40
Willis J (January 1933) The Delegation of Legislative and Judicial Powers to Administrative Bodies-A Study of the Report of the Committee on Ministers' Powers. Iowa L. Rev. 18 (2): 150–159
Wilson W (June, 1887) The Study of Administration Pol. Sci. Q. 2 (2): 197–222
Wilson W (1956 (1885)), Woodrow Wilson, Congressional Government: A Study in American Politics. Meridian Books, Cleveland, OH
Wolff B (1952/1953) Die Ermächtigung zum Erlaß von Rechtsverordnungen nach dem Grundgesetz. AöR Bd. 78: 194–227
Wood G S (1969) The Creation of the American Republic-1776-1787. The University of North Carolina Press, Chapel Hill
Ziamou T (2001) Rulemaking, Participation and the Limits of Public Law in the USA and Europe. Ashgate, Aldershot, England
Zellmer S B (Fall 2000) The Devil, the Details, and the Dawn of the 21st Century Administrative State: Beyond the New Deal. Ariz. St. L. J. 32: 941–1050

Index

DOI 10.1007/978-3-642-22330-3,

MIX
Papier aus verantwortungsvollen Quellen
Paper from responsible sources
FSC® C105338
FSC
www.fsc.org

If you have any concerns about our products,
you can contact us on
ProductSafety@springernature.com

In case Publisher is established outside the EU,
the EU authorized representative is:
Springer Nature Customer Service Center GmbH
Europaplatz 3, 69115 Heidelberg, Germany

Printed by Libri Plureos GmbH
in Hamburg, Germany